8th Edition

by Bradley L. Jones

PREVIOUS EDITION by Stephen R. Davis

C++ For Dummies®, 8th Edition

Published by: **John Wiley & Sons, Inc.,** 111 River Street, Hoboken, NJ 07030-5774, www.wiley.com

For general information on our other products and services, please contact our Customer Care Department within the U.S. at 877-762-2974, outside the U.S. at 317-572-3993, or fax 317-572-4002. For technical support, please visit https://hub.wiley.com/community/support/dummies.

Wiley publishes in a variety of print and electronic formats and by print-on-demand. Some material included with standard print versions of this book may not be included in e-books or in print-on-demand. If this book refers to media that is not included in the version you purchased, you may download this material at http://booksupport.wiley.com. For more information about Wiley products, visit www.wiley.com.

Library of Congress Control Number is available from the publisher.

ISBN 978-1-394-38044-2 (pbk); ISBN 978-1-394-38048-0 (epdf); ISBN 978-1-394-38046-6 (epub)

SKY10150505_032426

Contents at a Glance

Table of Contents

Introduction

Welcome to C++ *For Dummies*, 8th Edition. Think of this book as *C++, TL;DR Edition* (or the *Reader's Digest* edition), bringing you everything you need to know to start programming without all the boring stuff.

What is C++? C++ is a versatile object-oriented, low-level standardized programming language. As a low-level language similar to and compatible with its predecessor, C, C++ can generate programs that are efficient and *fast*. It's often used to write games, graphics software, hardware control software, and other applications where performance counts.

As an object-oriented language, C++ has the power and extensibility to be used to write large-scale programs. C++ is one of the most popular programming languages for all types of programs. Most of the programs you use on your PC every day are written in C++ (or the subset, which is the C language).

C++ has been certified as a 99.9 percent pure standard, which makes it a portable language. A standard C++ compiler exists for every major operating system. Some versions support extensions to the basic language; however, it is better to learn the standard C++ first. Learning the extensions is easy after you master the basics demonstrated here.

About This Book

C++ For Dummies is an introduction to the C++ language. I start from the beginning (where else?) and work my way from early concepts through more sophisticated techniques. I assume that you have no prior knowledge (at least, not of programming).

The book is full of examples. Every concept is documented in numerous snippets and a vast number of complete programs.

C++ For Dummies considers the Why just as important as the How. The features of C++ are like pieces of a jigsaw puzzle: Rather than just present the features, I believe it's important that you understand how they fit together. You can also use this book as a reference: If you want to understand what's going on with all the multiple inheritance info, for example, just flip to Chapter 26. Each chapter contains necessary references to other, earlier chapters in case you don't read the chapters in sequence.

One superpower of C++ is that it can be used on a variety of platforms. *C++ For Dummies* isn't specific to a single operating system. It's just as useful if you're programming on a system for Macintosh, Linux, or Windows. This book doesn't cover Windows or .NET programming; rather, it focuses on the standard C++ programming language.

What you learn will work on any of the platforms! They key is that you need to first master a powerful programming language, like C++, even if your plan is to become an accomplished Windows application, .NET, mobile, or other type of programmer. Once you've finished *C++ For Dummies*, you will be in position to continue in your area of specialization, whatever it might be.

Conventions Used in this Book

As you work your way through this book, I use conventions to make it as easy for you as possible. For example, the code listings within this book appear this way:

```
// some program
int main()
{
    ...
}
```

When I describe a message that you see onscreen, it appears like this:

```
Hi mom!
```

If you're entering these programs by hand, you must enter the text exactly as shown, with one exception: The amount of *white space* (spaces, tabs, and newlines) is not critical. You can't put a space in the middle of a keyword, but you don't have to worry about entering one too many or too few spaces.

WARNING

Case is *critical.* If you see `int`, it does not mean `Int` or `INT`. In C++, the words Same, same, SAME, and SaMe are four different words because the case of the letters is different. You can say that when it comes to C++, they are all not the same!

C++ words are usually based on English words with similar meanings. This can make reading a sentence containing both English and C++ difficult without a little assistance. To help, C++ commands, function names, and program names appear in a different font, like `this`. In addition, function names are always followed by open and closed parentheses, such as `myFavoriteFunction()`. The arguments to the function are left off except when there's a specific need to make them easier to read.

If you're unsure what things such as functions and arguments are, don't worry: You learn about these within this book. In this introduction, the goal is for you to learn about the conventions you come across as you read the rest of the book.

Sometimes, you're told to use menu commands, such as File ⇨ Open. This notation means to use the keyboard or mouse to open the File menu and then choose the Open option.

As you work through this book, new features are introduced with the following three questions in mind:

- *What* is this new feature?
- *Why* was it introduced into the language?
- *How* does it work?

Small pieces of code are sprinkled liberally throughout the chapters. Each demonstrates some newly introduced feature or highlights some brilliant point I'm making. These snippets may not be complete and certainly don't do anything meaningful. However, every concept is demonstrated in at least one functional program you can execute and play with on your own computer.

A real-world program can take up lots of pages. However, seeing such a program is an important didactic (instructive) tool for any reader. As such, throughout this book, a series of programs has been included along with an explanation of how they work. Although these programs require longer listings, I highly recommend that you enter them in their entirety and run the code. When you do this, you'll likely type something wrong; however, that's a big part of the learning process. In this new edition, more complete listings have been included to give you more opportunities to play with code that can be entered and run.

Be Aware: This Is a Modern C++ Book

C++ has been around for many decades. Over that time, C++ has evolved into a much more modern and safer language.

C++26 NEW

To be clear, this edition of *C++ For Dummies* is about the current version of C++. This book teaches you about the modern application of C++, including the use of features that have been added in C++23 and C++26. Some of the changes in the newest iterations of C++ include basic topics such as how information is displayed to the screen, how you access your computer's file system, or even how you can make your programs less likely to crash.

Some older ways of coding C++ should no longer be used. I mention many of the older strategies so that you can work with older C++ programs as well. Just know, however, that the features of C++26 make it easier to write C++ programs as well as make for cleaner, more modern code that helps reduce the chances of adding errors to your code.

Icons Used in This Book

TIP

Tips highlight points that can save you lots of time and effort.

REMEMBER

Remember this. It's important.

WARNING

Remember this, too. Issues can sneak up on you when you least expect them and generate one of those truly hard-to-find bugs. These warnings will help you be prepared so you don't get surprised!

TECHNICAL STUFF

The Technical Stuff icon highlights discussions of advanced concepts and considerations. While you could skip the technical stuff entirely, it really is good stuff to know as you get more experienced with C++.

C++23 NEW

This icon flags some 2023 additions to the language compared to previous versions of the C++ standard. If you already have some familiarity with C++ and something seems completely new, or if something doesn't work with your existing C++ tools, it may be because it's a newer addition.

C++26 NEW

This icon flags proposed additions to the C++ 2026 standard. These features are the newest, so they might not be implemented in all compilers available as of this writing.

As you work on the concepts presented in this guide, this icon serves as an occasional reminder that there is additional content posted online at www.dummies.com/go/cplusplus8e to take you even further on your programming journey. I'd tell you more, but that's the subject of the very next section.

Beyond the Book

C++ For Dummies, 8th Edition, includes the following goodies online for easy download:

- The **Cheat Sheet,** available online, provides an overview of C++ grammar in one (fairly) easy-to-read page. Just make your way to www.dummies.com and enter **C++ For Dummies** in the handy search box. If you're a beginner, you can print the Cheat Sheet and keep it handy as you work through later chapters. Eventually, C++ syntax becomes second nature and you'll no longer need the Cheat Sheet.
- The **source code** for the examples in this book can be downloaded from www.dummies.com/go/cplusplus8e. The programs are organized by chapter number.
- **Bonus chapters** can also be found online that take you even deeper into C++. Three bonus chapters there provide even deeper insight into intermediate and advanced topics including working with files, programming templates, and using some of the core Standard Template Library code. These can also be downloaded from www.dummies.com/go/cplusplus8e. You won't want to tackle these chapters now. Rather, I mention them within the book when the topics are relevant to extend what you already have learned.
- This book uses the free, open source **Code::Blocks environment** and **GCC C++ compiler.** The version of Code::Blocks used in writing this book is Version 25.03. You can find newer versions of Code::Blocks and releases for various versions of Linux at www.codeblocks.org/downloads/binaries. (Chapter 1 includes basic instructions for how to download and install Code::Blocks.) You can also use other free tools to compile and run the code within this book including Microsoft Visual Studio Code (available at https://code.visualstudio.com/Download). You should consult the tool's documentation for installation of not only the tool but also the latest versions of C++.

I used the GCC compiler with the code in this book because it tends to be the most up-to-date with new standard features. If you already have a C++ compiler installed on your computer that you prefer to use, feel free to do so as long as it's compatible with the C++ standard (most are). Not all compilers have implemented the 2026 standard yet, so newer items have been flagged in this book. In addition, if you use a different compiler, your screen may not look exactly like the figures in the book.

Where to Go from Here

Finding out about a programming language is not a spectator sport. I try to make it as painless as possible, but you need to power up the ol' PC and get down to some serious programming. Limber up the fingers, break the spine on the book so that it lies flat next to the keyboard (and so that you can't return it to the bookstore), and dive in.

1 Getting Started with C++ Programming

IN THIS PART . . .

Explaining the building blocks

Declaring variables

Defining mathematical operators

Using logical operators

Displaying things to the console

Controlling the flow of your programs

IN THIS CHAPTER

» Finding out about C++

» Installing the Code::Blocks environment

» Building your first C++ program

» Executing the program

» Exploring a C++ program

» Creating an expression

Chapter 1
Writing Your First C++ Program

Okay, here we are: No one here but you and me. Nothing left to do but get started. Might as well lay out a few fundamental concepts.

A computer is an amazingly fast but incredibly stupid machine. A computer can do anything you tell it (within reason), but it does *exactly* what it's told — nothing more and nothing less.

Perhaps unfortunately for us, computers don't understand any reasonable human language — they don't speak English, either. I know what you're going to say: "I've seen computers that could understand English." What you really saw was a computer executing a *program* that could meaningfully understand English.

Computers understand a language variously known as *computer language* or *machine language*. It's possible but extremely difficult for humans to speak machine language. Therefore, computers and humans have agreed to sort of meet in the middle, using intermediate languages such as C++. Humans can speak C++ (sort of), and C++ can be converted into machine language for the computer to understand.

Grasping C++ Concepts

A C++ *program* is a text file containing a sequence of C++ commands put together according to the laws of C++ grammar. This text file is known as the *source file* (probably because it's the source of all frustration). A C++ source file normally carries the extension cpp, just as an Adobe Acrobat file ends in pdf or an MS-DOS (remember that?) batch file ends in bat.

The point of programming in C++ is to write a sequence of commands that can be converted into a machine-language program that actually *does* what we want done. This conversion, called *compiling,* is the job of the compiler. The machine code you wrote must be combined with some setup and teardown instructions and some standard library routines in a process known as *linking.* Together, compiling and linking are known as *building.* The resulting *machine-executable* files carry the extension exe in Windows. (They don't carry any particular extension in Linux or Macintosh, although a Macintosh might give the files the app extension.)

That sounds easy enough — what's the big deal? Keep going.

To write a program, you need two specialized computer programs. One (an editor) is what you use to write your code as you build your cpp source file. The other (a compiler) converts your source file into a machine-executable file that carries out your real-world commands (Open Spreadsheet, Make Rude Noises, Deflect Incoming Asteroids — whatever).

Nowadays, tool developers generally combine compiler and editor into a single package — a development *environment.* After you finish entering the commands that make up your program, you need only click a button to build the executable file.

Fortunately, there are public-domain C++ environments. I use one of them in this book — the Code::Blocks environment. This editor works with lots of different compilers, but the version of Code::Blocks combined with the gcc compiler used when writing this book is available for download for Windows. You can also find versions for various versions of Linux and an older version for the Macintosh.

The gcc compiler is maintained by the GNU Project. The compiler is part of a bigger suite of tools that work with a variety of programming languages including python, C, C++, Fortran, Ada, Go, and many more. You can find more on the GNU Project on the official GNU website at https://www.gnu.org. You can find more on the GNU Compiler Collection (GCC) and the gcc compiler at https://gcc.gnu.org. I cover more on the gcc compiler later in this chapter.

REMEMBER

Although Code::Blocks is public domain and listed at no cost, you're encouraged to pay a small fee to support its further development. You don't *have* to pay to use Code::Blocks, but you can contribute to the cause, if you like. See the Code::Blocks website (`www.codeblocks.org`) for details.

I have tested the programs in this book with Code::Blocks 25.03, which comes bundled with gcc version 14.2.0. This version of gcc implements most of the C++2026 standard.

C++26 NEW

You can use different versions of gcc or even different compilers, if you prefer, but they may not implement the complete C++ 26 standard. For that reason, 2026 extensions are marked with the C++ 26 icon shown in the margin.

Okay, I admit it: This book is somewhat Windows-centric. I have tested all the programs in the book on Windows 11. Many have also been tested on Ubuntu Linux as well as on Macintosh OS X. C++ is a cross-platform language, so regardless of which platform you use, if your compiler supports C++26, the code from this book should work.

WARNING

The Code::Blocks/gcc package generates 64-bit programs, but it doesn't easily support creating windowed programs. The programs in this book run from a command-line prompt and write out to the command line. As boring as that may sound, I strongly recommend that you work through the examples in this book first to learn C++ *before* you tackle windowed development. C++ and windowed programming are two separate concepts, and (for the sake of your sanity) should remain so in your mind.

Follow the steps in the next section to install Code::Blocks and build your first C++ program. This particular program's task is to convert a temperature value entered by the user from degrees Celsius to degrees Fahrenheit. (If you're using a different operating system such as macOS or Linux, tips for installing an IDE and C++ are also provided to help get you started.)

Installing Code::Blocks

You can download the most recent version of Code::Blocks from its website at `www.codeblocks.org/downloads/binaries`. There you can find the most recent version of the Code::Blocks environment for Windows, Ubuntu Linux, and Mac OS X. The following section describes installing Code::Blocks on Windows.

Microsoft Windows

The Code::Blocks environment comes in an easy-to-install, compressed executable file that's compatible with all versions of Microsoft Windows after Windows XP. (Though the site might not list Windows 11, it's supported.) Here's the rundown on installing the environment:

1. **Download the executable `codeblocks-25.03.mingw-setup.exe` from `www.codeblocks.org/downloads/binaries` and save the file to your desktop or another place where you can easily find it.**

   TIP

   Note that 25.03 might be a different number. As long as it's larger than 25.03, you're good to go!

   This setup file includes a version of the gcc compiler.

2. **Double-click the program after it has completed downloading.**

   This step starts the installation process.

3. **If (depending on which version of Windows you're using) you get the ubiquitous pop-up warning "An unidentified program wants access to your computer," click Allow to get the installation ball rolling.**
4. **Click Next after closing all extraneous applications, as you're warned in the Welcome dialog box to the Code::Blocks Setup Wizard.**
5. **Read the end user license agreement (EULA) and then click I Agree if you can live with its provisions.**

   It's not like you have much choice — the package won't install itself if you don't accept. Assuming that you *do* click OK, Code::Blocks opens a dialog box showing the installation options. The default options are fine.

6. **Click the Next button.**

   The installation program allows you to install only a subset of the features. You must select at least Default Install and the MinGW Compiler Suite. The default is to install everything — that's the best choice.

   WARNING

   If the MinGW Compiler Suite isn't an option, you must have downloaded a version of Code::Blocks that doesn't include gcc. This version won't work correctly.

7. **Click Install and accept the default destination folder.**

   Code::Blocks begins copying a whole passel of files to your hard drive. Code::Blocks then asks, "Do you want to run Code::Blocks now?"

8. **Click Yes to start Code::Blocks.**

   Code::Blocks now asks which compiler you intend to use. The default is the GNU GCC Compiler, which is the proper selection.

9. **From within Code::Blocks, choose Settings ⇨ Compiler.**

   Doing so opens the Global Compiler Settings dialog box.

10. **Select the Compiler Flags tab.**

    A *compiler flag* is a special option that gets passed to the compiler to enable or disable features such as warnings, language standards, or debugging information. When you select the tab you'll see a long list of flag options with selection boxes on the right, as shown in Figure 1-1.

11. **Scroll to better see the options and make sure the following two flags are selected:**

    - Enable all common compiler warnings.
    - Have g++ follow the C++26 ISO C++ language standard.

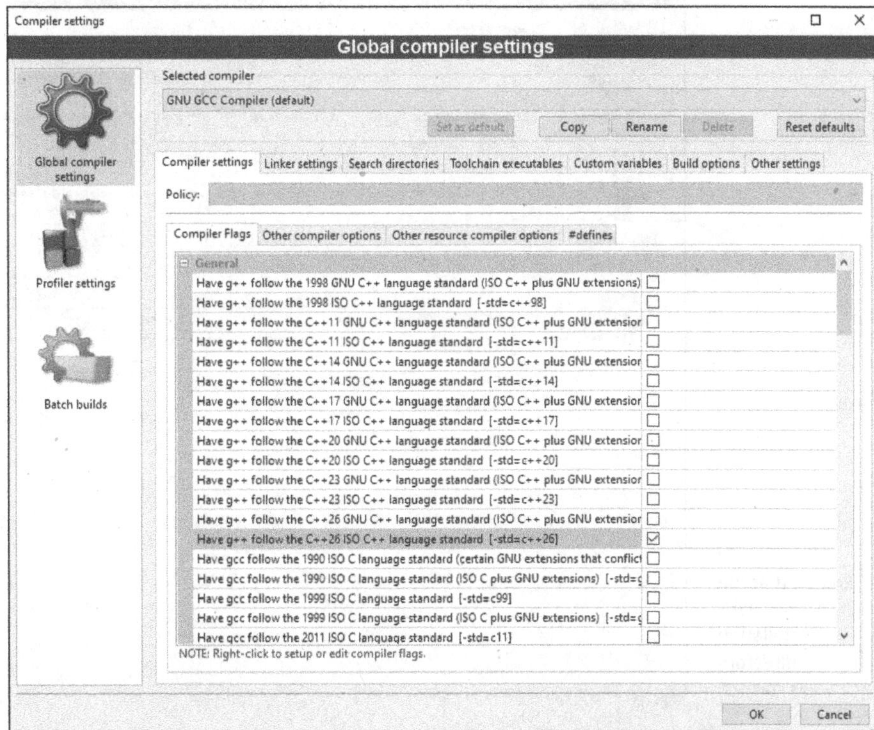

FIGURE 1-1: Ensure that the Enable All Compiler Warnings and the C++ 2026 flags are also set.

12. **In the same Global Compiler Settings dialog box, select the Toolchain Executables tab and make sure it looks like Figure 1-2.**

    The default location for the gcc compiler is the `MinGW\bin` folder within the `Code::Blocks` folder.

WARNING

If the default location is empty, Code::Blocks doesn't know where the gcc compiler is and cannot build your programs. Make sure you've downloaded a version of Code::Blocks that includes gcc and specified MinGW during the installation. If you're using an existing gcc compiler that you've already installed, you need to point Code::Blocks to wherever it's located on your hard drive.

13. **Close the Global Compiler Settings dialog box.**
14. **Click Next in the Code::Blocks Setup dialog box and then click Finish to complete the setup program.**

    The setup program takes the hint and exits.

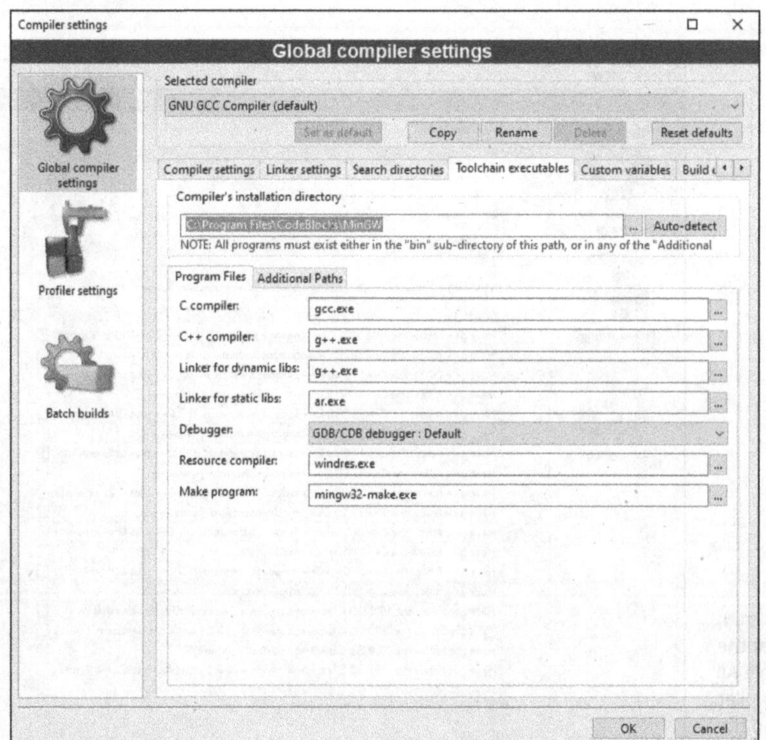

FIGURE 1-2: Ensure that the compiler's installation directory is correct.

Ubuntu Linux

Code::Blocks doesn't include gcc on Linux, so installation is a two-step process. First, you need to install gcc. Then you can install Code::Blocks.

WARNING

Depending on your system, when you install gcc or Code::Blocks, an older version might be installed. You need gcc 14.0 or later and Code::Blocks 25.03 or later in order to compile C++26 code.

The following section lists the default steps for installing these tools. If older versions are installed, you need to update the installation to the newer versions manually.

Installing gcc

The gcc compiler is readily available for Linux. Follow these steps to install it:

1. **Enter the following commands from a command prompt:**

```
sudo apt-get update
sudo apt-get upgrade
sudo apt-get install g++
```

   The standard Ubuntu Linux distribution includes a GNU C compiler but not the C++ extensions and, in particular, not the C++26 standard extensions. The first two commands update and upgrade the tools you already have. The third command installs C++.

2. **Enter the following command from a command prompt:**

```
gcc --version
```

   If your GNU C++ version is 14.0 or later, you're set. If you have an earlier version, some of the C++ 2026 features may not work properly.

TIP

If you're using Debian Linux, the commands are the same. If you're using Red Hat Linux, replace the command `apt-get` with `yum` so that you end up with

```
sudo yum install g++
```

Installing Code::Blocks

If you cannot find Code::Blocks in the Software Center or another app store on your system, you should be able to follow these terminal steps to install Code::Blocks:

1. **If the Universe Repository option on your system isn't already enabled, enable it by entering the following lines:**

```
sudo add-apt-repository universe
sudo apt update
```

2. **Install Code::Blocks by entering the following command:**

```
sudo apt install codeblocks
```

   This step starts the installation process.

   Code::Blocks searches your hard drive for your C++ compiler. It should be able to find it without a problem, but if it doesn't, complete the following steps.

3. **Start Code::Blocks.**
4. **Choose Settings ⇨ Compiler.**

   Doing so opens the Global Compiler Settings dialog box.

5. **Select the Compiler Flags tab.**
6. **Make sure the following two flags are selected:**
   - Enable all common compiler warnings
   - Have g++ follow the C++26 ISO C++ language standard
7. **In the same Global Compiler Settings dialog box, select the Toolchain Executables tab.**
8. **Click the Ellipsis (. . .) button at the right end of the field.**
9. **Navigate to `/usr`, unless you installed the gcc compiler somewhere other than the default location of `/user/bin`.**
10. **The C Compiler option should be gcc, the C++ Compiler option should be g++, and the Linker for Dynamic Libs option should be g++.**
11. **Click OK to close the dialog box.**

REMEMBER

When you start Code::Blocks, you should see version 25.03 or later or a date of 2025-03-29 or later. If an earlier version is shown, you need to consult either the Code::Blocks support site or your operating system's support site for information on updating your system to the latest version.

Macintosh

At the time this book was being written, Code::Blocks didn't have a Macintosh version that supported C++26. Fear not, however: It turns out that C++ is supported on macOS via Xcode, a free development package offered by Apple. To run the Xcode distribution from Apple for its compiler, you need to be running macOS Sequoia 15.6 or later.

Installing Xcode

Look for Xcode 16.3 or later in the Mac App Store or on the Apple Developer site at `https://developer.apple.com`. Note that the download and installation take quite some time because Xcode is several gigabytes in size.

After you've installed Xcode, you need to take one more step to ensure that all the C++ tools you need are installed. This extra step installs the command-line tools. To do this, open a terminal window and run the following command:

```
xcode-select --install
```

This should install all the standalone tools you need as well as some of the C++ support files. To confirm your C++ version, enter the following in the terminal:

```
clang++ --version
```

This command displays the version of C++ you're running. For C++26, you need to be running Xcode 16.3 or later.

Installing a development tool to use C++

Because the Macintosh version of Code::Blocks didn't support C++26 at the time of this writing, you need to use a different tool on your Mac. Suggested tools are JetBrains CLion (found at `www.jetbrains.com/clion`) or Microsoft's Visual Studio Code (found at `https://code.visualstudio.com/download`).

Creating Your First C++ Program

With all the necessary tools installed, it's time to create your first C++ program! That program will be all about converting Celsius temperatures into Fahrenheit, so I'll have you enter your C++ code into a file appropriately called `Conversion.cpp` and then have you convert the C++ code into an executable program.

Creating a project

The first step in creating any C++ program is to create what's known as a project. A *project* tells Code::Blocks the names of the cpp source files to include and what type of program to create. Most of the programs in this book consist of a single source file and use a command-line style:

1. **Start up the Code::Blocks tool.**
2. **From within Code::Blocks, choose File ⇨ New ⇨ Project. . . from the main menu.**
3. **Select the Console Application icon and then click the Go button on the right side of the dialog.**

   The first time you carry out Step 3, you might be presented with a dialog box that welcomes you to the Console Application Wizard. Code::Blocks is simply being friendly! You can just click the Next button. Before clicking Next, you have the option to select the check box to prevent the dialog box from showing up again.
4. **From the next dialog box that appears, select C++ as the language you want to use and then click Next.**

   REMEMBER

   Code::Blocks and gcc also support plain ol' C programs.
5. **In the Folder to Create Project In field, select the Ellipsis (. . .) button.**

   This step takes you to the file system dialog box, where you can specify where you want to create and save the project.
6. **Select Drive C on Windows — Windows (C:).**

   On Linux and Macintosh, you can select the desktop.
7. **Click the New Folder button.**

   It's likely near the top of the dialog box being displayed.
8. **Name the new folder** CPP_Programs_from_Book.

   The result should look like Figure 1-3. This is the folder where you save your programs. You can simply select it for any future programs you create from this book.
9. **Click the Select Folder button to continue.**

   This step returns you to the Console Application Wizard.
10. **In the Project Title field, type the name of the project.**

    In this case, type **Conversion**.

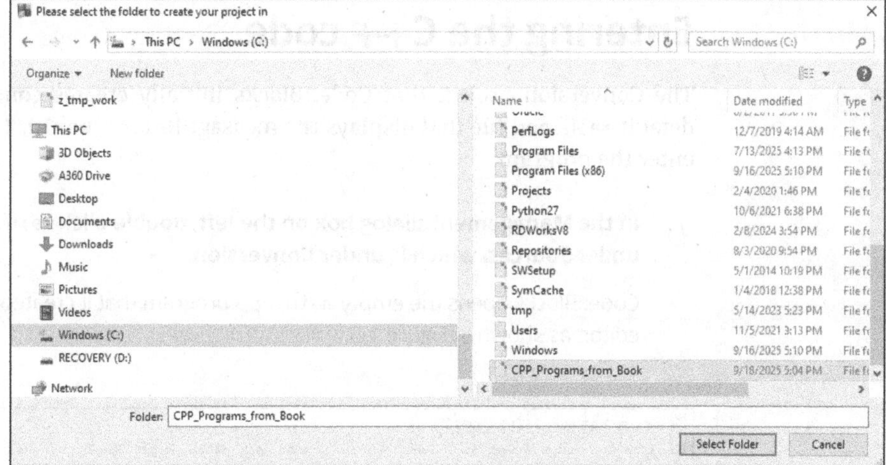

FIGURE 1-3: Put your project in the C:\CPP_Programs_from_Book folder on Windows.

The resulting screen is shown in Figure 1-4 on Windows. (The Linux and Macintosh versions should look the same, except for the path.)

11. **Click the Next button.**

    The next dialog box gives you the option of creating an application for testing or the final version. The default values shown on this dialog are fine.

12. **Click Finish to create the Conversion project.**

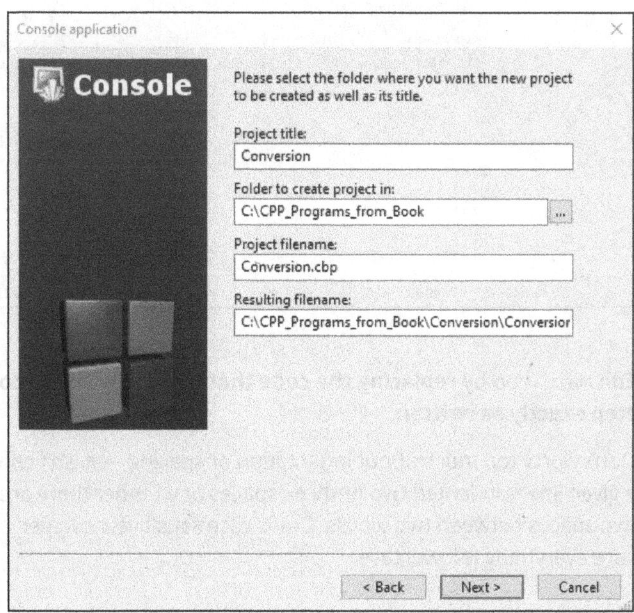

FIGURE 1-4: Creating the Conversion project for your first program.

Entering the C++ code

The Conversion project that Code::Blocks initially creates consists of a single, default `main.cpp` file that displays the message `Hello, world`. The next step is to enter the program:

1. **In the Management dialog box on the left, double-click `main.cpp`, which is under Sources, which is under Conversion.**

   Code::Blocks opens the empty `main.cpp` program that it created in the code editor, as shown in Figure 1-5.

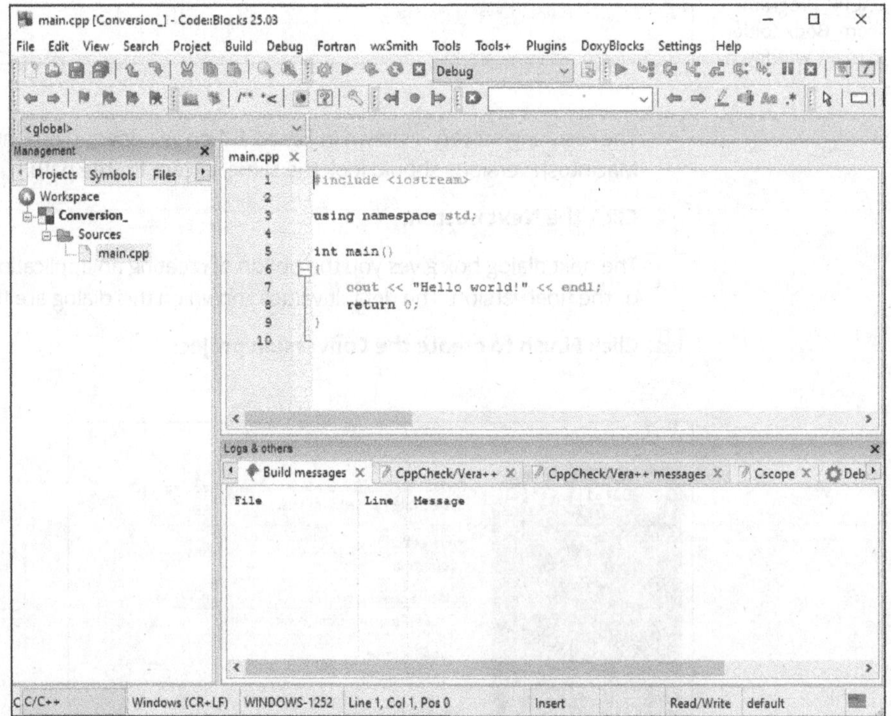

FIGURE 1-5: The Management dialog box displays a directory structure for all available programs.

2. **Edit `main.cpp` by replacing the code that is there with the code in this step exactly as written.**

   Don't worry too much about indentation or spacing — it isn't critical whether a given line is indented two or three spaces or whether there are one or two spaces between two words. C++ is case sensitive, however, so make sure everything is lowercase.

TIP

You can cheat by using the files at `www.dummies.com/go/cplusplus8e`, as described in the next section:

```
// Conversion - Program to convert temperature from
//             Celsius degrees into Fahrenheit:
//             Fahrenheit = Celsius * (212 - 32)/100 + 32
//
#include <iostream>
#include <print>
using namespace std;

int main(int nNumberofArgs, char* pszArgs[])
{
    // enter the temperature in Celsius
    int celsius;
    print("Enter the temperature in Celsius: ");
    cin >> celsius;

    // calculate conversion factor for Celsius
    // to Fahrenheit
    int factor;
    factor = 212 - 32;

    // use conversion factor to convert Celsius
    // into Fahrenheit values
    int fahrenheit;
    fahrenheit = factor * celsius/100 + 32;

    // output the results (followed by a NewLine)
    print("Fahrenheit value is: ");
      println("{}", fahrenheit);

    return 0;
}
```

TECHNICAL STUFF

The lines in the code include comments to help you understand what the code is doing. These are the lines that start with double forward slashes (//). If you are typing the code in, you could technically skip including those lines and the program will still work just fine. Comments, however, make it clearer what the code is doing, so I strongly suggest you enter them as well.

3. **Choose File ⇨ Save file from the main menu to save the source file.**

I know that it may not seem all that exciting, but you've just created your first C++ program!

Cheating

You will find a downloadable file containing the programs in the book at `www.dummies.com/go/cplusplus8e`. Once you've downloaded the file, open it and do one of two things with the CPP_Programs_from_Book folder:

- » Drag the files in it to the same CPP_Programs_from_Book folder that you created a few pages back in the "Creating a project" section; or
- » If you haven't been through that section, copy the CPP_Programs_from_Book folder to the base folder of your computer's C: drive. All of the sources used in the book will then be found at `C:\CPP_Programs_from_Book`.

WARNING

You can put the CPP_Programs_from_Book folder at another location, but don't put your source files in a directory that includes a space in its name. On Windows, that means don't put any of your Code::Blocks folders in My Documents or on the desktop, because they both include a space in their paths.

You can use these files in two ways: One way is to complete the steps I describe in this book to create the program by hand first but then copy and paste from the provided files into your program if you run into trouble (or your fingers start cramping). This is the preferred technique.

A second approach is to use the sources provided and simply copy them into a new project each time:

1. **Double-click `AllPrograms.workspace` in `C:\CPP_Programs_from_Book`.**

   A *workspace* is a single file that references one or more projects. The `AllPrograms.workspace` file contains references to all projects defined in the book.

2. **Right-click the Conversion project in the Management dialog box on the left, and then choose Activate Project from the menu that appears.**

   Code::Blocks turns the Conversion label bold to verify that this is the program you're working on right now. When you subsequently select Build, Code::Blocks always builds the active project.

3. **Double-click the `main. cpp` file under the Conversion project to open the file in the editor.**

As you navigate through his book and work on other listings, you'll often need to repeat Step 2, but each time you should select the appropriate project. The problem with this approach is that you tend to learn little about C++ if you don't enter the code yourself.

Building your program

After you've saved your C++ source file to your hard drive, it's time to generate the executable machine instructions.

To build your `Conversion` program, you choose Build ⇨ Build from the main menu or press Ctrl-F9. Almost immediately, Code::Blocks takes off, compiling your program with gusto. If all goes well, the happy result of `0 Errors, 0 Warnings` appears near the bottom of the Logs & Others section, as shown in Figure 1-6.

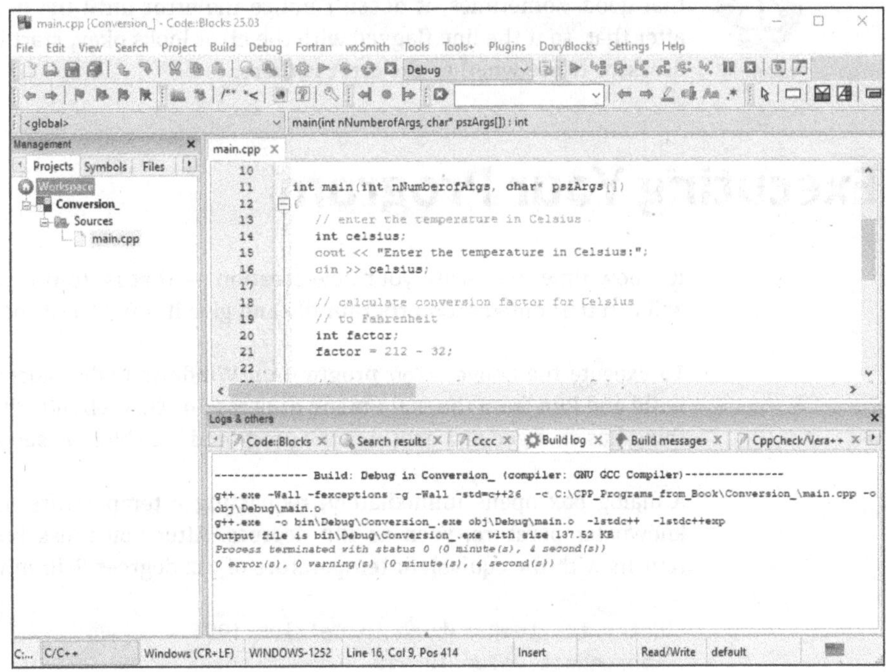

FIGURE 1-6: Code::Blocks builds the Conversion program quickly.

Code::Blocks generates a message if it finds any type of error in your C++ program — and coding errors are about as common as ice cubes in Alaska. You'll undoubtedly encounter numerous warnings and error messages, probably even when entering the simple `Conversion.cpp`.

To demonstrate the error reporting process, try introducing an error into your program — more specifically, change Line 16 from `cin >> celsius;` to `cin >>> celsius;`. You might think such a small change wouldn't be a big deal. It seems an innocent enough offense — forgivable to you and me perhaps, but not to C++. When you go on to choose Build ⇨ Build to start the compile-and-build process. Code::Blocks almost immediately places a red square next to the erroneous line.

The message on the Build Message tab is a rather cryptic `error: expected primary-expression before ' >' token`. To get rid of the message, remove that extra > before `celsius` and recompile.

TIP

You probably consider the error message generated by the example a little mysterious, but give it time — you've been programming for only about 30 minutes now. Over time, you'll come to understand much better the error messages generated by Code::Blocks and gcc.

WARNING

Code::Blocks was able to point directly at the error this time, but it isn't always that good. Sometimes, it doesn't notice the error until the next line or the one after that, so if the line flagged with the error looks okay, start looking at its predecessor to see whether the error is there.

Executing Your Program

It's now time to execute your new creation — that is, to run your program. You will run the `Conversion` program file and give it input to see how well it works.

To execute the `Conversion` program on Windows Code::Blocks, choose Build ⇨ Build and Run from the main menu or press F9. This rebuilds the program if anything has changed and executes the program if the build is successful.

A dialog box opens immediately, requesting a temperature in Celsius. Enter a known temperature, such as 100 degrees. After you press Enter, the program returns with the equivalent temperature of 212 degrees Fahrenheit:

```
Enter the temperature in Celsius:100
Fahrenheit value is:212
```

If you're using Code::Blocks, you also see a message to press any key to continue. The message gives you the opportunity to read what you've entered before it goes away. Press Enter (or any other key), and the dialog box (along with its contents) disappears. Congratulations! You just entered, built, and executed your first C++ program.

REMEMBER

Code::Blocks isn't truly intended for developing windowed programs like those used in Windows. In theory, you can write a Windows application by using Code::Blocks, but it isn't easy. (Building windowed applications is *so* much easier in Visual Studio.)

Windows programs show the user visually oriented output, all nicely arranged in onscreen windows. The 64-bit program `Conversion.exe` executes *under* Windows, but it's not a Windows program in the visual sense.

If you don't know what *64-bit program* means, don't worry about it. As I said, this book isn't about writing Windows programs. The C++ programs you write in this book have a command-line interface executing within an Command Prompt box.

Budding Windows programmers shouldn't despair — you didn't waste your money. Learning C++ is a prerequisite to writing Windows programs. I think they should be mastered separately: C++ first, Windows second.

If you didn't see the Press Any Key message when you ran the `Conversion` program, but rather saw the output flash and then disappear, you need to add a few lines of code to pause the program at the end. Hold tight and I'll show you the code to add later in this chapter!

Reviewing the Annotated Program

Entering data in someone else's program is about as exciting as watching someone else drive a car — you really need to get behind the wheel yourself. Programs are a bit like cars as well. All cars are basically the same with small differences and additions — okay, French cars are much different from other cars, but the point is still valid. Cars follow the same basic pattern: steering wheel in front of you, seat below you, roof above you, and stuff like that.

Similarly, all C++ programs follow a common pattern. This pattern is already present in this first program. We can review the `Conversion` program by looking for the elements that are common to all programs.

Examining the framework for all C++ programs

Every C++ program you write for this book uses the same basic framework — one where, more often than not, you start with one or more statements that say *Include* followed by a main section. The code looks much like this:

```
//
// Template - Provides a template to be used as the
//            starting point.
//
```

```
// The following include files define the majority of
// functions that any given program will need.
#include <iostream>
#include <print>
using namespace std;

int main(int nNumberofArgs, char* argv[])
{
   // Your C++ code starts here.

   return 0;
}
```

Without going into all the boring details, execution begins with the code contained in the open and closed braces immediately following the line beginning with `main()`.

REMEMBER

I've copied this code into a file called `Template.cpp` located in the main `CPP_Programs_from_Book` folder.

If you're using a tool such as Code::Blocks, when you execute code using this structure, Code::Blocks follows the output with a prompt that tells you to press any key to continue. If it didn't do this, when your code runs, a window is opened, the output is displayed, the program ends, and the window then closes. This would happen so fast that you likely wouldn't see the output! Tools like Code::Blocks or Visual Studio Code step in to take care of you by stopping the window from closing.

If you're running code from a tool that doesn't do this or running your compiled program from a tool such as Windows Explorer that closes the output window immediately, you can add a few lines of code to each of your listings to stop this from happening. I've added such code (the bolded stuff) to the following template:

```
// TemplatePause - Provides a template to be used
//               as the starting point. Includes a prompt
//               to pause after running the program.
//
// The following include files define the majority of
// functions that any given program will need.
#include <iostream>
#include <print>
using namespace std;
```

```
int main(int nNumberofArgs, char* argv[])
{
    // your C++ code starts here

    // Wait until user is ready before ending program
    // to allow the user to see the program results.
    println("Press Enter to continue...");
    cin.ignore(10, '\n');
    cin.get();

    return 0;
}
```

This code waits for the user to press a key before terminating the program. It displays a simple message, clears any previous key presses, and then waits for you to press any key before continuing. You can add these lines to the end of the main section of any listings within this book to pause the program.

I've copied this code as well into a file called `TemplatePause.cpp` located in the main `CPP_ Programs_from_Book` folder.

TIP

If the tools you use don't pause so that you can see the output, you should adjust the listings in this book to include the same three lines of code I had you add earlier to the `TemplatePause.cpp` file. As was the case with `TemplatePause.cpp`, these three lines are placed immediately in front of the `return` statement. If a particular listing doesn't have a `return` statement, the code is placed just before the closing bracket (`}`).

Clarifying source code with comments

The first few lines in the `Conversion` program appear to be freeform text. Either this code was meant for human eyes or C++ is much smarter than I give it credit for. These first few lines, along with the first six lines in the `Template.cpp` program listing, are known as *comments:* These are the programmer's explanation of what they're doing or thinking when writing a particular code segment. The compiler ignores comments. Programmers (*good* programmers, anyway) don't.

A C++ comment begins with a double slash (`//`) and ends with a *newline* character, which is the character that terminates a command line. You can put any character you want in a comment. A comment can be as long as you want, but it's customary to limit comment lines to no more than 80 characters. Back in the old days ("old" is relative here), the code length for computer programs was limited to 80 characters. These days, limiting a single line to fewer than 80 characters is just a good practical idea (easier to read and less likely to cause eyestrain — the usual).

A newline was known as a *carriage return* back in the days of typewriters — when the act of entering characters into a machine was called *typing* and not *keyboarding*.

WARNING

C++ allows a second form of comment in which everything appearing after the /* characters and before the */ characters is ignored; however, this form of comment is normally no longer used in C++.

REMEMBER

It may seem odd to have a command in C++ (or any other programming language) that's specifically ignored by the computer. However, all computer languages have some version of the comment. It's critical for the programmer to explain their thinking when they wrote the code. A programmer's thoughts may not be obvious to the next colleague who tries to use or modify the program. In fact, the programmer may forget the program's purpose if they look at it months after writing the original code and the program left no clue.

Basing programs on C++ statements

All C++ programs are based on what are known as C++ statements. This section reviews the statements that make up the program framework used by the `Conversion` program.

A statement is a single set of commands. Almost all C++ statements (other than comments) end in a semicolon. (You see one other exception in Chapter 11 when you learn about the preprocessor.) Program execution begins with the first C++ statement after the open brace that appears after the line containing `main()`. Execution then continues through the listing, one statement at a time.

As you look through the program, you can see that spaces, tabs, and newlines appear in the program. These characters are collectively known as *whitespace* because you can't see them on the monitor.

TIP

You can add whitespace anywhere you like in your program to enhance readability — except in the middle of a word:

```
See wha

t I mean?
```

Although C++ may ignore whitespace, it doesn't ignore case. In fact, C++ is case sensitive to the point of obsession. The variable `fullspeed` and the variable `FullSpeed` have nothing to do with each other. The command `int` is completely understandable, but C++ has no idea what `INT` means. See what I mean about fast-but-stupid compilers?

Writing declarations

The line `int celsius;` is a declaration statement. A *declaration* is a statement that defines a variable. A *variable* is sort of a holding tank for a value of some type. A variable contains a *value*, such as a number or a character.

The term *variable* stems from algebra formulas of the following type:

```
x = 10
y = 3 * x
```

In the second expression, *y* is set equal to 3 times *x*, but what is *x*? The variable *x* acts as a holding tank for a value. In this case, the value of *x* is 10, but I could have just as well set the value of *x* to 20 or 30 or −1. The second formula makes sense no matter what the value of *x* is.

In algebra, you're allowed (but not required) to begin with a statement such as *x* = 10. In C++, the programmer *must* define the variable *x* before it can be used.

In C++, a variable has a type and a name. The variable defined on line 11 is called `celsius` and declared to hold an integer. (Why they couldn't have just said *integer* instead of *int*, I'll never know. It's just one of those things you learn to live with.)

The name of a variable has no particular significance to C++. A variable must begin with the letters *A* through *Z*, the letters *a* through *z*, or an underscore (_). All subsequent characters must be a letter, a digit 0 through 9, or an underscore. Variable names can be as long as you want to make them.

TIP

It's convention that variable names begin with a lowercase letter. Each new word *within* a variable begins with a capital letter, as in `myVariable`.

TIP

Try to make variable names short but descriptive. Avoid names such as *x* because *x* has no particular meaning. A variable name such as `lengthOfLineSegment` is much more descriptive.

Generating output

The lines beginning with `print`, `println`, `cout`, and `cin` are known as input/output statements, often contracted to *I/O statements*. (Like all engineers, programmers love contractions and acronyms.)

It's not hard to figure out the basic function of the `print` and `println` statements. Exactly — they print information to the standard output device. In this case, the standard C++ output device is your monitor (also referred to as the *console* or "your screen"). The difference between `print` and `println` is that `println` adds a carriage return after printing so that the next time you print to the screen, the output starts on a new line.

I listed `cout`, but didn't actually use `cout` in the listing. I could have used the following code as an alternative way to print:

```
cout << "Enter the temperature in Celsius: ";
cin >> celsius;
   ...
cout << "Fahrenheit value is: ";
cout << Fahrenheit << endl;
```

C++23 NEW

The first I/O statement says, "Output the phrase *Enter the temperature in Celsius* to *cout*" (pronounced "see-out"), where *cout* is the name of the standard C++ output device. This does roughly the same thing as the print statements, but in a manner that's older and less safe. Starting with C++23, `print` and `println` were introduced as better ways to display output. As such, they're used throughout this book. (In Chapter 4, I dig deeper into explaining the printing functions and how to do more with them.)

The line that begins with `cin` is exactly the opposite of `cout` and of the printing lines. It says, in effect, "Extract a value from the C++ input device and store it in the integer variable `celsius`." The C++ input device is normally the keyboard. What you have here is the C++ analog to the algebra formula $x = 10$ just mentioned. For the remainder of the program, the value of `celsius` is whatever the user enters there.

Calculating Expressions

All but the most basic programs perform calculations of one type or another. In C++, an *expression* is a piece of code that performs a calculation. Stated another way, an expression is a piece of code that can be evaluated to a value. An *operator* is a symbol that tells you how to combine or compare values within an expression to generate a value.

For example, in the `Conversion` program example — specifically, in the two lines marked as a `calculation expression` — the program declares a variable `factor` and then assigns it the value resulting from a calculation. This particular command calculates the difference of 212 and 32; the operator is the minus sign (−), and the expression is *212−32*.

Unless you're taking a coding class, you likely will never have to explain the difference between a statement, an expression, and an operator. If you do ever need to explain the difference, a simple analogy is to think of a statement as a sentence, an expression as a phrase within that sentence, and an operator as a symbol within the expression.

Storing the results of an expression

The spoken language can be quite ambiguous. The term *equals* is one of those ambiguities. The word *equals* can indicate that two items have the same value, as in "A dollar equals 100 cents." The term *equals* can also imply assignment, as in math when you say that "*y* equals 3 times *x*."

To avoid ambiguity, C++ programmers call the equal sign (=) the *assignment operator*, which says (in effect), "Store the results of the expression to the right of the assignment sign in the variable to the left." When confronted with the first expression, `factor = 212 - 32`, programmers say that "`factor` is assigned the value 212 minus 32." For a shortcut, you can say that "`factor` gets 212 minus 32."

Never say "`factor` is *equal to* 212 minus 32." You'll hear this from some lazy types, but you (and I) know better.

Examining the remainder of Conversion

The second expression in the `Conversion` program presents a slightly more complicated expression than the first:

```
fahrenheit = factor * celsius/100 + 32;
```

This expression uses the same mathematical symbols: the asterisk (*) for multiplication, the slash mark (/) for division, and the plus sign (+) for addition. In this case, however, the calculation is performed on variables and not simply on constants.

The value contained in the variable called `factor` (which was calculated as the results of the expression 212 – 32, by the way) is multiplied by the value contained in `celsius` (which was input from the keyboard). The result is divided by 100 and summed with 32. The result of the total expression is assigned to the integer variable `fahrenheit`.

The next two commands output the string `Fahrenheit value is:` to the display, followed by the value of `fahrenheit` — and all so fast that the user scarcely knows it's going on.

The next three statements prompt the user to press Enter, and then they wait until Enter has been pressed. This is because on some systems the program can display the results and then close the console dialog box so rapidly that you don't even see that anything has happened.

As mentioned previously, on many systems, you can skip these three lines — Code::Blocks keeps the dialog box open until you press Enter anyway — but they don't hurt anything.

The final statement is `return 0`. This statement simply returns a value of `0`, as well as control, to your operating system. The `0` indicates that the program ran successfully and all is good in the world as far as this application is concerned.

And Now, a Few Comments on C++26

You can see that the main program presented in this book uses the `print` statements, which are from C++23 and refined in C++26. The book you're holding in your hands is about the current version of C++: C++26. As a major programming language, C++ has evolved over the years, and with recent updates, has become an even more modern language.

Because the focus of this book is on C++26, some older coding approaches are not used, although I'll talk about them throughout this book. This includes elements such as raw streams, `cout`, and raw pointers. C++ has gotten safer, but that means coding is a little different from what was done a decade ago. If you plan to use only an older C++ compiler or only the older stuff, the best solution is to buy the previous edition of this book. Again, because you'll see the older (less safe) ways of coding in existing C++ programs, I point it out throughout this book, just as I mention cout in this chapter.

If you were able to run the `Conversion` program with the print statements, you should be set with C++26.

IN THIS CHAPTER

- **Declaring variables of various types**
- **Handling wide loads on the char highway**
- **Using variables for doing calculations**
- **Making mixed-mode expressions**
- **Setting a variable's type automatically**

Chapter 2
Storing Stuff in Variables

The most fundamental of all concepts in C++ is the variable. A variable is like a small box: You can store things in the box for later use, particularly numbers. The concept of a variable is borrowed from mathematics. A statement such as

```
x = 1
```

stores the value `1` in the variable `x`. From that point forward, the mathematician can use the variable `x` in place of the constant `1` — until they change the value of `x` to something else.

Variables work the same way in C++. You can make this assignment:

```
x = 1;
```

From that point forward in the execution of the program, the value of `x` is `1` until the program changes the value stored in `x`. References to `x` are replaced by the value `1`. In this chapter, you will find out how to declare and initialize variables in C++ programs. You will also see the different types of variables that C++ defines and when to use each.

Declaring Variables

A mathematician might write some code like the following:

```
(x + 2) = y / 2
x + 4 = y
solve for x and y
```

If you've ever attended an algebra class, you'll realize immediately that the mathematician has introduced the variables *x* and *y*. But C++ isn't that smart. (Computers may be fast, but on their own, they're stupid.)

You need to announce each variable to C++ before you can use it. You must let C++ know that you're using a variable. You have to say something soothing, like this:

```
int x;
x = 10;

int y;
y = 5;
```

These lines of code *declare* that a variable x exists, it's of type `int`. This code also *initializes* the variable x that was just declared by assigning a value to it. In this case the code initializes x by assigning the value `10`. The code also declares that a variable *y* of type `int` exists and then initializes it by assigning the value `5`. (The next section discusses variable types.) You can declare variables (almost) anywhere you want in your program — as long as you *declare the variable before you use it.*

Declaring Different Types of Variables

If you're on friendly terms with math (and who isn't?), you probably think of a variable in mathematics as an amorphous box capable of holding whatever you might choose to store in it. (Again, the box metaphor.) You might easily write something like the following:

```
x = 1
x = 2.3
x = "this is a sentence"
```

Alas, C++ isn't that flexible. (On the other hand, C++ can do things that people can't do, such as add a billion numbers or so in a second, so let's not get too judgmental.) To C++, there are different types of variables just as there are different types of storage bins. Some storage bins are so small that they can handle only a single number. It takes a larger bin to handle a sentence.

TIP

Some computer languages try harder to accommodate the programmer by allowing different types of data to be placed into the same variable. These languages are called *weakly typed* languages. C++ is a *strongly typed* language: It requires variables to not only be declared but also have their exact types determined. While you generally will declare the specific type, I show you later in this chapter that C++ can also help you set the type automatically.

Not all numbers are the same

The variable type *int* is the C++ equivalent of an *integer* — a number that has no fractional part. (Integers are also known as *counting numbers* or *whole numbers.*) Integers are useful for most calculations. I made it through most of elementary school with integers. Not until I turned 11 or so did my teachers start mucking up the waters with fractions. The same is true in C++: It's estimated that around half of all variables in C++ are declared to be of type `int`.

Unfortunately, `int` variables aren't adapted to every problem. For example, if you work through the temperature conversion program in Chapter 1, you might notice that the program has a potential problem: It can calculate temperatures only to the nearest degree. No fractions of a degree are allowed. This integer limitation wouldn't affect daily use because it's unlikely that someone (other than a meteorologist) would get all excited about being off a fraction of a degree. In plenty of cases, however, this isn't the case — for example, you wouldn't want to come up a half-mile short of the runway on your next airplane trip because of a navigational roundoff.

Reviewing the limitations of integers in C++

The `int` variable type is the C++ version of an integer. The `int` variable type suffers the same limitations as the counting-number integer equivalents in math do.

Integer round-off

Lopping off the fractional part of a number is called *truncation.* Consider the problem of calculating the average of three numbers. Given three `int` variables — `nValue1`, `nValue2`, and `nValue3` — here's an equation for calculating the average:

```
int nValue1; int nValue2; int nValue3;
int nAverage;
nAverage = (nValue1 + nValue2 + nValue3) / 3;
```

Because all three values are integers, the sum is assumed to be an integer. Given the values 1, 2, and 2, the sum is 5. Divide that by 3, and you get 1⅔, or 1.666. C++ uses slightly different rules: Given that all three variables nValue1, nValue2, and nValue3 are integers, the sum is also assumed to be an integer. The result of the division of one integer by another integer is also an integer. Thus, the resulting value of nAverage is the unreasonable but logical value of 1.

The problem is much worse in the following mathematically equivalent formulation. This time, I've included a complete listing you can enter:

```
#include <print>

int main() {
    // Declare and initialize integer values
    int nValue1 = 1;
    int nValue2 = 2;
    int nValue3 = 2;

    int nAverage = nValue1/3 + nValue2/3 + nValue3/3;

    std::println("The average is: {}", nAverage);
    return 0;
}
```

You can see that the code assigns the same values 1, 2, and 2. This time, the resulting value of nAverage is 0 (talk about unreasonable). To see how this can occur, consider that ⅓ truncates to 0, ⅔ truncates to 0, and ⅔ truncates to 0. The sum of 0, 0, and 0 is 0. You can see that integer truncation can be completely unacceptable.

TIP

Enter the listing, compile it, and run it. Play around with it by changing the values assigned to nValue1, nValue2, and nValue3.

Limited range

A second problem with the *int* variable type is its limited range. A normal int variable can store a maximum value of 2,147,483,647 and a minimum value of -2,147,483,648 — roughly from positive 2 billion to negative 2 billion, for a total range of about 4 billion.

Two billion is quite a large number — plenty big enough for most uses. But it's not large enough for some applications. That might seem like a lot of numbers, but it isn't even enough to count all the people on the planet!

Solving the truncation problem

The limitations of `int` variables can be unacceptable in some applications. Fortunately, C++ understands decimal numbers that have a fractional part. (Mathematicians also call those *real numbers.*) Decimal numbers avoid many of the limitations of `int` type integers. To C++, all decimal numbers have a fractional part, even if that fractional part is 0. In C++, the number 1.0 is just as much a decimal number as 1.5 or 1.5932. The equivalent integer is written simply as 1. Decimal numbers can also be negative, such as −2.3.

When you declare variables in C++ that will be used to hold decimal numbers, you identify them as floating-point or simply `float` variables. The term *floating-point* means that the decimal point is allowed to float back and forth, identifying as many decimal places as necessary to express the value. Floating-point variables are declared in the same way as `int` variables:

```
float fValue1;
```

REMEMBER

After you declare the type of a variable, you cannot change it — `fValue1` is now a `float` and will be a `float` for the remainder of the program. To see how floating-point numbers fix the truncation problem inherent with integers, consider the averaging problem from earlier. This time, convert all the `int` variables to `float`. Here's what you get:

```
float fValue;
fValue = 1.0/3.0 + 2.0/3.0 + 2.0/3.0;
```

is equivalent to

```
fValue = 0.333...+ 0.666...+ 0.666...;
```

which results in the value

```
fValue = 1.666...;
```

WARNING

I have written the value `1.6666 . . .` as though the number of trailing sixes goes on forever. This isn't necessarily the case. A `float` variable has a limit to the number of digits of accuracy, which I discuss in the next section.

REMEMBER

A constant that has no floating-point value is assumed to be an *int*. A constant that has a decimal point is assumed to be a floating-point value. However, the default type for a floating-point constant is known as *double precision,* which in C++ is called simply `double`, as you can see in the next section.

To demonstrate the round-off error inherent in integer variables, the programs `IntAverage` and `FloatAverage` are available from `www.dummies.com/go/cplusplus83`, in the `CPP_Programs_from_Book\Chap02` folder.

Looking at the limits of floating-point numbers

You might be thinking, "Hey, why risk having round-off errors? I'll simply use floating-point variables to store everything!" That might sound good; however, though floating-point variables can solve many calculation problems, such as truncation, they have some limitations themselves — the reverse of those associated with integer variables. Floating-point variables can't be used to count things, they're more difficult for the computer to handle, and they suffer from round-off errors (though not nearly to the same degree as *int* variables).

Counting

You cannot use floating-point variables in applications where counting is important. This includes C++ constructs that count. C++ can't verify which whole number value is meant by a given floating-point number.

For example, it's clear to you and to me that 1.0 is 1 but not so clear to C++. What about 0.9 or 1.1? Should these also be considered as 1? What about 1.50? Should it be 1 or 2? C++ simply avoids the problem by insisting on using integer values such as *int* when counting is involved.

Calculation speed

Historically, a computer processor can process integer arithmetic more quickly than it can process floating-point arithmetic. Thus, while a processor can add 1 million integer numbers in a given amount of time, the same processor may be able to perform only 350,000 floating-point calculations during the same period.

Calculation speed is becoming less of a problem as microprocessors get faster. In addition, today's general-purpose microprocessors include special floating-point circuitry on board to increase the performance of these operations. However, arithmetic on integer values is just a heck of a lot easier and faster than performing the same operation on floating-point values.

Loss of accuracy

Floating-point `float` variables have a precision of about 6 digits, and an extra economy-size, double-strength version of `float` known as a `double` can handle about 15 significant digits. This can cause round-off problems as well.

Consider that ⅓ is expressed as 0.333 . . . in a continuing sequence. The concept of an infinite series makes sense in math, but not to a computer, because it has a finite accuracy. The FloatAverage program outputs 1.66667 as the average 1, 2, and 2 — that's much better than the 0 output by the IntAverage version, but not even close to an infinite sequence. C++ can correct for round-off errors in many cases. For example, on output, C++ can sometimes determine that the user really meant 1 instead of 0.999999. In other cases, even C++ cannot correct for round-off errors.

Not-so-limited range

Although the float data type has a much larger range than that of an integer, it's still limited. The maximum value for an int is a skosh more than 2 billion. The maximum value of a float variable is roughly 10 to the 38th power. That's 1 followed by 38 zeroes; it eats 2 billion for breakfast. (It's even more than the national debt, at least at the time of this writing.)

WARNING

Only the first 13 digits or so of a float have any meaning; the remaining 25 digits are noise, having succumbed to floating-point round-off error. This is because, technically, values are stored in scientific notation.

Declaring Variable Types

So far in this chapter, I have been trumpeting that variables must be declared and that they must be assigned a type — fortunately. (Ta-da!) I've described two types, int and float, and mentioned a double that is a bigger float. Though these are useful and will work for much of what you do, C++ also provides a number of other variable types. Table 2-1 presents a list of variable types available for you to use, including their advantages and limitations.

TABLE 2-1 Common C++ Variable Types

Variable	Defining a Constant	What It Is
int	1	A simple counting number, either positive or negative.
short int	1	A potentially smaller version of int. It uses less memory but has a smaller range.
long int	10L	A potentially larger version of int; might differ in size depending on your computer's operating system and the compiler you use.

(continued)

TABLE 2-1 *(continued)*

Variable	Defining a Constant	What It Is
`long long int`	`10LL`	A potentially even larger version of int.
`float`	`1.0F`	A single-precision floating-point (real) number. This smaller version uses less memory than a `double` but has less accuracy and a smaller range.
`double`	`1.0`	A standard floating-point variable.
`long double`	`1.0L`	A potentially larger floating-point number. On the PC, `long double` is used for the native size of the 80x86 floating-point processor, which is 80 bits.
`char`	`'c'`	A single `char` variable stores a single alphabetic or digital character. It's generally unsuitable for arithmetic.
`wchar_t`	`L'c'`	A larger character capable of storing symbols with larger character sets, like Chinese.
`char16_t`	`u'c'`	A character type used for UTF-16 encoding.
`char32_t`	`U'c'`	A character type used for UTF-32 encoding.
`char8_t`	`u8'c'`	A large character using UTF-8 encoding, used for better Unicode handling.
`std::string`	`"this is a string"`	A string of characters that can form a sentence or phrase. This isn't technically a fundamental data type, but it is something you'll use often, even as a beginner.
`bool`	`true`	The only other value is `false`. No, I mean, it's *really* false. Logically *false*. Not *false* as in fake or ersatz or — never mind.

The integer types come in both signed and unsigned versions. A signed version allows negative numbers to be stored. An unsigned version will not allow for negative numbers but instead allows for positive numbers that are twice as big to be stored. For example, a signed `char` might store values from -127 to 128 whereas an unsigned `char` could hold values from 0 to 256.

Signed is always the default (for everything except the *char* types). The unsigned version is created by adding the keyword *unsigned* in front of the type in the declaration. The following declares an *unsigned int* variable named *uVariable*:

```
unsigned int uVariable;
```

To assign an unsigned constant to `uVariable`, include a `U` or `u` in the type designation. Thus, the following line assigns the new `uVariable` the value `10`:

```
uVariable = 10U;
```

The following statements declare the two variables lVariable1 and lVariable2 as type long int and sets them equal to the value 1; dVariable is also declared as a double and has its value set to 1.0:

```
// declare two long int variables and set them to 1
long int lVariable1;
long lVariable2;     // int is assumed
lVariable1 = lVariable2 = 1;
// declare a variable of type double and set it to 1.0
double dVariable = 1.0;
```

TIP

Notice in the declaration of lVariable2 that the int is assumed and can be omitted. Also notice that, in the last line, dVariable was declared and initialized in the same statement. The lines in the code that start with the two forward slashes are comments that C++ will ignore. They are added to the code for the programmer's benefit.

In Table 2-1, you can see that a char variable can hold a single character. Note that std::string is listed as well; it can hold a *character string* — one or more characters grouped together, in other words. The following is a complete listing you can enter that lets you create two variables: *cLetter* and *sWord*, both of which hold strings:

```
#include <print>
#include <string>

int main() {
    char cLetter = 'C';         // Holds a single character
    std::string sWord = "C";   // Holds a string

    std::println("Char: {}", cLetter);
    std::println("String: {}", sWord);

    return 0;
}
```

In the code, you can see that 'C' (notice the single quotes) is a char that contains the character C, whereas "C" (notice the double quotes) is a string that contains one character. A rough analogy is that a 'C' corresponds to a letter on a page, whereas "C" corresponds to a word or sentence. (Chapters 8 and 14 describe groups of characters and strings in greater detail.)

WARNING

If an application requires a string, you have to provide one, even if the string contains only a single character. Keep in mind that a character constant is created with single quotes around the character and a string is created with double quotes, regardless of how many letters or characters are included.

Types of constants

A *constant value* is an explicit number or character (such as 1, 0.5, or `'c'`) that doesn't change. As with variables, every constant has a type. In an expression such as *n = 1;*, the constant value `1` is an `int`. To make 1 a `long` integer, write the statement as `n = 1L;`. The analogy is as follows: `1` represents a smaller truck, such as a pickup truck, with one ball in it. The value `1L` represents a bigger truck (say, a dump truck), also with one ball. The number of balls is the same in both cases, but the capacity of one of the containers is much larger. (Column 2 in Table 2-1 shows you how to define a constant for many of the data types.)

Following the `int`-to-`long` comparison, `1.0` represents the value `1`, but in a floating-point container. Notice, however, from Table 2-1 that the default for floating-point constants is `double`. Thus, `1.0` is a `double` number and not a `float`.

REMEMBER

You can use either uppercase or lowercase letters for your special constants. Thus, 10UL and 10ul are both unsigned long integers.

Notice the `bool` data type in Table 2-1. Variables of this type store a value of `true` or `false`. (In keeping with C++'s attention to case, `true` is a constant, but `TRUE` has no meaning.)

Though numbers, letters, and words can be declared as constants, so can a variable. If a variable won't ever change, or if you don't want it to ever change, it can be declared as a constant when it's created, with the help of the keyword `const`:

```
const double PI = 3.14159; // declare a constant variable
```

A `const` variable must be initialized with a value when it's declared, and its value cannot be changed by any future statement.

TIP

Variables declared `const` don't have to be named with all capitals, but by convention, they often are. This is just a hint to the reader that this so-called variable is, in fact, not.

I admit that it may seem odd to declare a variable and then say that it can't change. Why bother? Largely because carefully named `const` variables can make a program much easier to understand. Consider the following two equivalent expressions:

```
double dC = 6.28318 * dR;    // what does this mean?
double dCircumference = TWO_PI * dRadius; // this is a
                                // lot easier to understand
```

It should be much clearer to the reader of this code that the second expression is multiplying the radius of something by 2Π to calculate the circumference.

Range of numeric types

It may seem odd, but the C++ standard doesn't say exactly how big a number each of the data types can accommodate. The standard speaks only to the relative size of each data type. For example, it says that the maximum `long int` is at least as large as the maximum `int`.

The authors of C++ weren't trying to be mysterious. They merely wanted to allow the compiler to implement the absolute fastest code possible for the base machine. The standard was designed to work for all different types of processors running different operating systems.

However, it's useful to know the limits of your particular implementation. Table 2-2 shows the size of each number type on a Windows PC using Visual Studio Code with the GCC compiler on the Windows operating system.

TABLE 2-2 Range of Numeric Types in Visual Studio with GCC on Windows

Variable	Size (in Bytes)	Accuracy	Range
`short`	2	Exact	-32,768 to 32,767
`unsigned short`	2	Exact	0 to 65,645
`int`	4	Exact	-2,147,483,648 to 2,147,483,647
`unsigned int`	4	Exact	0 to 4,294,967,295
`long`	4	Exact	-2,147,483,648 to 2,147,483,647
`unsigned long`	4	Exact	- to 4,294,967,295
`long long int`	8	Exact	-9,223,372,036,854,775,808 to 9,223,372,036,854,775,807
`unsigned long long int`	8	Exact	0 to 18,446,744,073,709,551,615
`float`	4	7 digits	$\pm 3.4028 \times 10^{\pm 38}$

(continued)

TABLE 2-2 *(continued)*

Variable	Size (in Bytes)	Accuracy	Range
`double`	8	16 digits	$\pm1.7977 \times 10^{\pm308}$
`long double*`	12	19 digits	$\pm1.1897 \times 10^{\pm4932}$
`char`	1	Exact	-128 to 127
`unsigned char`	1	Exact	0 to 255
`wchar_t`	2	Exact	0 to 65,535

**Visual Studio Code using MSVC instead of GCC treats a long double as a double.*

Attempting to calculate a number that's beyond the range of its type is known as an *overflow*. The C++ standard generally leaves the results of an overflow as undefined. That's another way the developers who defined C++ kept things flexible.

TIP

On the PC, a floating-point overflow results in an *exception* (a big word meaning "error"), which, if not handled, causes your program to crash. (I discuss exceptions much later, in Chapter 29.) As bad as that sounds, an integer overflow is worse — C++ silently generates an incorrect value without complaint.

Special characters

You can store any printable character you want (such as `'C'` or `'a'` or `'%'`) in a `char` or `string` variable. You can also store a set of nonprintable characters that are used as character constants. See Table 2-3 for a description of these important nonprintable characters.

TABLE 2-3 **Special Characters in C++**

Character Constant	What It Is
`'\n'`	Newline
`'\t'`	Tab
`'\040'`	The character whose value is 40 in octal. (See Chapter 5 for a discussion of number systems.)
`'\x20'`	The character whose value is 20 in hexadecimal. (This is the same as `'\040'`.)
`'\0'`	null (the character whose value is `0`, in other words)
`'\\'`	Backslash

You might have noticed in Table 2-3 that the nonprintable characters actually look like more than one character! For example, the newline character is a backslash followed by the lowercase letter *n*. The newline character breaks a string and puts the parts on separate lines. A newline character may appear anywhere within a string; for example, the line:

```
"This is line 1\nThis is line 2"
```

appears in the output as:

```
This is line 1
This is line 2
```

The backslash is an "escape character" indicating that a special character should be used. As such, though '\n' looks like two characters, it's stored and treated as a single character value. Like the newline character, the \t tab character moves output to the next tab position. (This position can vary, depending on the type of computer you're using to run the program.)

Because the backslash character is used to signify special characters, a character pair for the backslash itself is required. The character pair \\ represents the backslash.

Characters are stored as numeric values. The numerical forms that you can see represented in Table 2-3 allow you to specify any nonprinting character you like, but results may vary if you're using a version of C++ earlier than C++23. The character represented by 0xFB, for example, depends on the font and the character set (and may not even be a legal character).

In C++23, standardized encoding was added to C++. This means that if you assign a character such as 'C' to a char variable, the same numeric value should be stored regardless of which platform and compiler you're using. This coding standard applies to UTF-8 as well.

C++ COLLISION WITH FILENAMES

Windows uses the backslash character to separate folder names in the path to a file. (This is a remnant from MS-DOS that Windows has been unable to shake.) Thus, *Root\FolderA\File* represents *File* within *FolderA*, which is a subfolder of *Root*.

Unfortunately, MS-DOS's use of the backslash conflicts with the use of the backslash to indicate an escape character in C++. The character \\ is a backslash in C++. The MS-DOS path *Root\ FolderA\File* is represented in C++ as the string *"Root\\FolderA\\File"*.

Carrying Wide Loads on the char Highway

The standard `char` variable is a scant 1 byte wide and can handle only 255 different characters. This is plenty for European languages, but not enough to handle symbol-based languages, such as kanji.

Several standards have arisen to extend the character set to handle the demands of these languages. UTF-8 uses a mixture of 8-, 16-, and 32-bit characters to implement almost every kanji or hieroglyph you can think of but still remain compatible with simple 8-bit ASCII. UTF-16 uses a mixture of 16-and 32-bit characters to achieve an expanded character set, whereas UTF-32 uses 32 bits for all characters.

TIP

UTF stands for Unicode Transformation Format, from which it gets the common nickname Unicode.

Table 2-4 describes the various character types supported by C++. At first C++ tried to get by with a vaguely defined wide character type, `wchar_t`. This type was intended to be the wide character type native to the application program's environment. C++11 introduced specific types for UTF-16 and UTF-32 to provide bigger storage areas. Whereas a `char` is generally 8 bits of storage for characters, UTF-16 provides 16 bits and UTF-32 provides 32 bits giving them the ability to store much more complex characters.

TABLE 2-4 The C++ Character Types

Variable	Example	What It Is
`char`	`'c'`	ASCII or UTF-8 characters
`wchar_t`	`L'c'`	Char in wide format
`char_16t`	`u'c'`	UTF-16 character
`char_32t`	`U'c'`	UTF-32 character

TIP

UTF-16 is the standard encoding for Windows applications. The `wchar_t` type refers to UTF-16.

Any of the character types in Table 2-4 can be combined into strings as well:

```
wchar_t* wideString = L"this is a wide string";
```

(Ignore the asterisk for now. I have lots to say about its meaning in Chapter 9.)

C++26 NEW

In C++23, standardized encoding was mandated for UTF-8. This was done to improve cross-platform compatibility. In C++26, Unicode support continues to be improved, including the addition of `'@'`, `'$'`, and ``'`'`` to the basic character set.

C++ allows you to mix variable types in a single expression. That is, you're allowed to add an integer with a `double` precision floating-point value. In the following expression, for example, `nValue1` is allowed to be an `int`:

```
// in the following expression, the value of nValue1
// is converted into a double before performing the
// assignment
int nValue1 = 1;
nValue1 + 1.0;
```

An expression in which the two operands aren't the same type is a mixed-mode expression. *Mixed-mode expressions* generate a value whose type is equal to the more capable of the two operands. In this case, `nValue1` is implicitly converted to a `double` before the calculation proceeds. Similarly, an expression of one type may be assigned to a variable of a different type, as in the following statement:

```
#include <print>  // C++26 simplified printing

int main()
{
    double dVariable = 1.0;     // Floating-point variable
    int nVariable;              // Integer variable

    // The following assigns only the whole number part of
    // dVariable to nVariable (implicit conversion)
    nVariable = dVariable;

    // Print the values
    std::println("Double value: {}", dVariable);
    std::println("Integer value after assignment: {}",
   nVariable);

    return 0;
}
```

REMEMBER

You can lose precision or range if the variable on the left side of the assignment is smaller. In the preceding example, as part of the implicit conversion, C++ truncates the value of `dVariable` before storing it in `nVariable`.

Converting a larger value type into a smaller value type is called *demotion*, whereas converting values in the opposite direction is known as *promotion*. Programmers say that the value of `int` variable `nVariable1` is promoted to a `double` in expressions such as this one:

```
int nVariable1 = 1;
double dVariable = nVariable1;
```

TIP

Mixed-mode expressions aren't a good idea — avoid forcing C++ to do your conversions for you.

NAMING CONVENTIONS

You may have noticed that the name of each of the variables I create begins with a special character that seems to have nothing to do with the name. These special characters aren't special to C++; they're merely meant to jog the reader's memory and indicate the type of the variable. You can see a partial list of these special characters in the following list. Using this convention, I can immediately recognize `dVariable` as a variable of type `double`, for example.

Religious wars worse than the true value of Bitcoin have broken out over whether this naming convention clarifies C++ code. Naming conventions help many developers. Try this convention for a while. If after a few months you don't think it helps, feel free to change your naming convention. Note that many organizations require their programmers to use a naming convention.

Character	Type
n	int
l	long
f	float
d	double
c	char
s	string

Religious wars worse than the true value of Bitcoin have broken out over whether this naming convention clarifies C++ code. It helps us, so I stick with it. Try it for a while. If, after a few months, you don't think it helps, feel free to change your naming convention.

Automatic Declarations

If you're lazy, you can let C++ determine the types of your variables for you using the `auto` keyword. Consider the following declaration:

```
int nVar = 1;
```

You might ask, "Why can't C++ figure out the type of `nVar`?" The answer is that it will, if you ask nicely, like this:

```
auto var1 = 1;
auto var2 = 2.0;
```

This says, "declare `var1` to be a variable of the same type as the constant value `1` (which happens to be an `int`) and declare `var2` to be the same type as `2.0` (which is a `double`)."

Though you might be tempted to try to declare everything as `auto`, you shouldn't. Rather, keep in mind that creating explicit declarations using the specific type makes your code more readable and helps prevent unexpected behavior. Reserve *auto* for those times when it improves the clarity of your code.

WARNING

I consider the term `auto` to be a particularly unfortunate choice for this purpose because, before C++ 11, the keyword `auto` had a completely different meaning. However, `auto` had fallen out of use for at least 20 years, so the people in charge of standards figured that it would be safe to usurp the term. Just be aware that if you see the keyword `auto` in some old code, you need to remove it.

You can also tell C++ that you want a variable to be declared to be of the same type as another variable, whatever that might be, using the keyword `decltype()`:

```
int var1;
decltype(var1) var2; // declare var2 to be of the
                     // same type as var1
```

Note that the format for using `decltype` is a little different from declaring a normal variable; you include the name of the variable within parentheses. For this example, the C++ compiler replaces the `decltype(var1)` with the type of `var1` — which in this case is an `int`.

IN THIS CHAPTER

- » Defining mathematical operators
- » Using the C++ mathematical operators
- » Identifying expressions
- » Increasing clarity with special mathematical operators

Chapter 3 Doing the Math

C++ offers all the common arithmetic operations, which means your C++ programs can multiply, add, divide, and perform other operations with ease. Programs must be able to perform these operations to get anything done. What good is a health insurance program, for example, if it can't calculate how much you're supposed to (over) pay?

C++ operations look like the arithmetic operations you would perform on a piece of paper, except that you need to declare and initialize variables (as detailed in Chapter 2) before you can use them:

```
int var1 = 3;
int var2 = 2;
int sum = var1 + var2;
```

In this code snippet, two variables named `var1` and `var2` are declared. The code initializes `var1` to a value of 3 and `var2` to a value of 2. The values in these two variables are then added together, and the result is stored into the variable called `sum`. To see this in action, you can add the code to a full C++ listing:

```
#include <print>

int main()
{
    int var1 = 3;
```

```
    int var2 = 2;
    int sum = var1 + var2;

    std::println("The value of var1 is {}", var1);
    std::println("The value of var2 is {}", var2);
    std::println("The sum is {}", sum);

    return 0;
}
```

When this code is compiled and run, you should see the following results:

```
The value of var1 is 3
The value of var2 is 2
The sum is 5
```

This chapter describes the complete set of C++ mathematical operators.

Performing Simple Binary Arithmetic

A *binary operator* is one that works with (or has) two arguments. These are generally in the form of:

```
variable1 <operator> variable2
```

The most common binary operators are the simple operations you performed in grade school. The binary operators are listed in Table 3-1. This table also includes a few other things, which I describe a little later in this chapter, including the unary operators and precedence (the order things are evaluated).

TABLE 3-1 Mathematical Operators in Order of Precedence

Precedence	Operator	What It Is or Does
1	+ (unary)	Effectively does nothing
1	- (unary)	Returns the negative of its argument
2	++ (unary)	Increment
2	-- (unary)	Decrement
3	* (binary)	Multiplication

Precedence	Operator	What It Is or Does
3	/ (binary)	Division
3	% (binary)	Modulo
4	+ (binary)	Addition
4	- (binary)	Subtraction
5	=, *=, %=, +=, -= (special)	Assignment types

Multiplication, division, modulo, addition, and subtraction are the operators used to perform arithmetic. In practice, they work just like the familiar arithmetic operations as well. For example, using the binary operator for division with a floating point `double` variable looks like this:

```
double var = 133.0 / 10.0;
```

Each of the binary operators has the conventional meaning you studied in grammar school, with one exception: You may not have encountered modulo in your studies. The *modulo* operator (%) works much like division, except that it produces the remainder *after* division rather than the quotient. For example, 4 "goes into" 14 three times with a remainder of 2. Thus, we say that 14 modulus 4 is 2:

```
int var = 14 % 4; // var is set to 2
```

TECHNICAL STUFF

Note that the modulo operator is often referred to by many C++ programmers as *modulus*.

REMEMBER

Modulo isn't defined for floating-point variables. (I discuss round-off errors in Chapter 2.)

BE CAREFUL WITH DIVISION AND REMAINDERS

Take a look at the expression 133.0 / 10.0, shown earlier. Because these are double values, the result of the division problem will be a double value of 13.3. If the operation was done with integers or variables declared as integers, the result would be an integer value. This means that 133/10 results in the value of 13 because an integer doesn't store a decimal value. The fractional part of the operation would be lost due to truncation.

Decomposing Expressions

The most common type of statement in C++ is the expression. An *expression* is a C++ statement with a value. Every expression also has a type, such as `int`, `double`, or `char`. A statement involving any mathematical operator is an expression because all these operators return a value. For example, 1 + 2 is an expression whose value is 3 and type is `int`. (Remember that a constant without a decimal point is of type `int`.)

Expressions can be complex or extremely simple. In fact, the statement `1` is an expression because it has a value (`1`) and a type (`const int`). The following statement has seven expressions:

```
z = x * y + w;
```

The expressions are:

```
x
y
w
z
x * y
x * y + w
z = x * y + w
```

Determining the Order of Operations

All operators perform a defined function. In addition, every operator has a *precedence* — a specified order in which the expressions are evaluated. Consider, for example, how precedence affects solving the following problem:

```
int var = 1 + 3 * 2;
```

If the addition is performed before the multiplication, the value of the expression is 4 times 2, or 8. If the multiplication is performed first, the value is 6 plus 1, or 7.

The precedence of the operators determines who goes first. Table 3-1 shows that multiplication has higher precedence than addition, so the result is 7. (The concept of precedence is also present in arithmetic. C++ adheres to the common arithmetic precedence.)

So, what happens when two operators of the same precedence appear in the same expression? For example:

```
int var = 8 / 4 / 2;
```

When operators of the same precedence appear in the same expression, they're evaluated from left to right. (The same rule applies in arithmetic.) Thus, in the code snippet example, `var` is equal to 8 divided by 4 (which is 2) divided by 2 (which is 1).

The expression:

```
x / 100 + 32
```

divides x by 100 before adding 32. But what if the programmer wants to divide x by *100 plus 32*? The programmer can change the precedence by bundling expressions in parentheses (shades of algebra!), as follows:

```
x /(100 + 32)
```

This expression has the same effect as dividing x by 132. The original expression:

```
x / 100 + 32
```

is identical to the expression:

```
(x / 100) + 32
```

Performing Unary Operations

Arithmetic *binary* operators — those operators that take two arguments — are familiar to many of us from school days. But consider the *unary* operators, which take a single argument (for example, −*a*). Many unary operations aren't so well known.

The unary mathematical operators are plus, minus, plus-plus, and minus-minus (respectively, +, −, ++, and −−). The minus operator changes the sign of its argument. Positive numbers become negative and vice versa. The plus operator doesn't change the sign of its argument. The plus operator is rarely, if ever, used:

```
int var1 = 10;
int var2 = -var1; // var2 is now -10
```

WHY DEFINE A SEPARATE INCREMENT OPERATOR?

The authors of C++ noted that programmers add 1 more than any other constant. To provide some convenience, a special add 1 instruction was added to the language. In addition, most present-day computer processors have an increment instruction that is faster than the addition instruction. Back when C++ was created — with microprocessors being what they were — saving a few instructions to speed up a program was a big deal. Today, not so much.

The latter expression uses the minus unary operator (-) to calculate the value negative 10.

The ++ and -- operators might be new to you. These operators (respectively) add 1 to their arguments or subtract 1 from their arguments, so they're known (also respectively) as the *increment* and *decrement operators*. Because they're dependent on numbers that can be counted, they're limited to non-floating-point variables. For example, the value of var after executing the following expression is 11:

```
int var = 10;      // initialize var
var++;             // now increment it
                   // value of var is now 11
```

The increment and decrement operators are peculiar in that both come in two flavors: a *prefix* version and a *postfix* version (known as *pre-increment* and *post-increment*, respectively). Consider, for example, the increment operator (the decrement works in the same way).

Suppose that the variable n has the value 5. Both ++n and n++ increment n to the value 6. The difference between the two is that the value of ++n is the value after incrementing (6), whereas the value of n++ is the value before incrementing (5). The following example illustrates this difference:

```
#include <print>

int main()
{
    // declare three integer variables
    int n1, n2, n3;
    n1 = 5;
    n2 = ++n1; // the value of both n1 and n2 is now 6
    std::println("n1 is {} and n2 is {}", n1, n2);
```

```
    n1 = 5;
    n3 = n1++;// the value of n1 is 6 but the value of n3 is 5
    std::println("n1 is {} and n3 is {}", n1, n3);

    return 0;
}
```

Thus, n2 is given the value of n1 after n1 has been incremented (using the pre-increment operator), whereas n3 gets the value of n1 before it is incremented using the post-increment operator. If you compile and run the listing, these are the results you see:

```
n1 is 6 and n2 is 6
n1 is 6 and n3 is 5
```

Using Assignment Operators

An *assignment operator* is a binary operator that changes the value of its left argument. The equal sign (=), a simple assignment operator, is an absolute necessity in any programming language. This operator puts the value of the right-hand argument into the left-hand argument. The other assignment operators are odd enough that they seem to be someone's whim.

So, what about the following?

```
int var1;
int var2 = 2;
var1 = var2 = 1;
```

Using the left-to-right rule, var1 ends up with the value 2 but var2 with the value 1, which is counterintuitive. To avoid this, multiple assignment operators are evaluated from right to left. Thus, the snippet example assigns the value 1 to var2 and then copies the same value into var1.

The creators of C (from which C++ originated) noticed that assignments often follow the form of:

```
variable = variable <op> constant
```

where <op> is a binary operator. Thus, to increment an integer operator by 2, the programmer might write:

```
nVariable = nVariable + 2;
```

This expression says, "Add 2 to the value of nVariable and store the results back into nVariable." Doing so changes the value of nVariable to 2 more than it was.

Because the same variable appears on both sides of the equal sign (=), the same Fathers of the C Revolution decided to create a version of the assignment operator with a binary operator attached. This says, in effect, "Thou shalt perform whatever operation on a variable and store the results right back into the same variable."

Every binary operator has one of these nifty *assignment versions*. Thus, the assignment just given could have been written this way:

```
nVariable = nVariable + 2;
nVariable += 2;
```

Here, the first line says (being quite explicit now), "Take the value of nVariable, add 2, and store the results back into nVariable." The next line says (a bit more abruptly), "Add 2 to the value of nVariable."

REMEMBER

Other than assignment itself, these assignment operators are not used all that often. However, as odd as they might look, sometimes they can actually make the resulting program easier to read.

IN THIS CHAPTER

» Understanding the old way of printing

» Discovering the new and improved printing

» Old versus new: Knowing which is truly better

Chapter 4

Show Me the Good Stuff!

Trying to learn how to program in C++ or any other programming language would be virtually impossible without displaying something onscreen. In fact, the first program used to teach is generally referred to as the "Hello, World" program, one that simply presents the text `Hello, World` to the user. Before continuing with the lessons on the core features of C++, it's worth diving a little deeper into how information simply gets displayed onscreen. You may have already done this in the first three chapters of this book, but in this chapter, I take a step back and look at some of the basic routines C++ provides for you to use to display information and to obtain basic information from the user.

WARNING

Right off the bat, you should know that the C++ standards have changed, but not all C++ programmers have changed — that means it's important to be aware of the old ways while learning the new.

The Old versus the New

People count to ten in different ways. Some use their fingers to count to ten. Others use their toes. A caveman might have used rocks to count. The average C++ developer simply counts to ten in their mind with no need for fingers or toes or rocks.

Who is right and who is wrong in how they count is often a matter of personal opinion. However, the person with experience using their mind to count will likely reach ten quicker and more accurately than the person using their fingers, toes, or rocks. Similarly, people using the new ways made available by the revised C++ standard will likely see better results as well.

C++23 NEW

In this chapter, rather than count, I display information to the screen. As with counting, there are a couple of ways you can accomplish this task. In many of the C++ programs from existing C++ developers, you're likely to see the old way of printing. Having said that, C++23 introduced a new way of printing that provides a much simpler approach — no rocks, fingers, or toes needed!

Printing the Old Way

You should know the old manner of printing because you will come across it in many existing C++ programs. Additionally, sometimes the old method is still easier to use than the new one. You learn when to use the old-versus-new near the end of this chapter.

The older method uses the C++ object called `cout`. You send information to `cout` using the *insertion operator*, a symbol composed of two less-than signs (`<<`) that sends the value on its right to the object that is on its left. So, the following sends `"abc"` to `Alphabet`.

```
Alphabet << "abc"
```

The operator gets its name because this is technically seen as `"abc"` being inserted into `Alphabet`:

The following is a standard "Hello, World" program using `cout`; however, rather than print words, it prints numbers from 1 to 5:

```
#include <iostream>

int main() {
    std::cout << "1 ";
    std::cout << "2 ";
    std::cout << "3 ";
    std::cout << "4 ";
    std::cout << "5";
}
```

If you enter and compile this chunk of code, your results should be:

```
1 2 3 4 5
```

This output is sent to your console (screen). By using the insertion operator, you can send (or *stream*) what you want displayed. Though the preceding characters were within quotes, you can also send variables:

```
#include <iostream>

int main() {
    int nLife = 42;

    std::cout << "The meaning of life is ";
    std::cout << nLife;
}
```

In this case, you can see that this is the output that goes to the console:

```
The meaning of life is 42
```

WARNING

You might be wondering why the number 42 didn't move to a new line because the cout command was on a new line. Simply put, C++ doesn't know to move to a new line unless you explicitly tell it to do so. (More on this in a minute.)

Though cout was called twice in the previous listing, both of the insertion operators could have been included on the same line:

```
std::cout << "The meaning of life is " << nLife;
```

This single line operates exactly like the previous two lines.

This example sent an integer; however, you can send any of the basic data types to the console using cout. You can also perform mathematical and other types of operations, and the results will be displayed:

```
std::cout << "5 + 3 is " << 5+3;
```

The mathematical and other operators have a higher precedence than the insertion operator, so the addition of 5+3 occurs first and then the result is sent to cout. This is the output:

```
5 + 3 is 8
```

Chapter 3 covers operator precedence in detail.

A note about streaming

The cout object is using streaming. Stated differently, *you* are streaming, or *flowing*, the output you want displayed to cout.

REMEMBER

The cout object is also provided as part of iostream. If you had a chance to look at look at the listings in chapters 2 and 3, you might have noticed that iostream is included so that cout is available. In the online Bonus Chapter 1, you see how to use this same process (streaming) to send output to other places, such as files.

You can stream output to cout like a faucet can stream water, so sometimes you need to indicate when the action should stop. You can do this with cout by sending endl:

```
std::cout << "The meaning of life is " << nLife << std::endl;
```

This line would operate like it did in the earlier section "Printing the Old Way," but the results for your program and any future displays to the console should be cleaner because anything that might have been waiting to be output (in the output buffer) will be flushed away. The endl manipulator does one other thing as well: It moves any new text to the next line. In other words, if you use cout again after sending an endl, the output will be on the next line.

While I'm at it: Getting user input

Although I'm talking about printing information to the console, it's worth noting that there's a similar object for receiving information from the keyboard that's also included in the iostream library: cin.

You get information (input) from the user by using cin along with the *extraction operator*, handy little greater-than arrows (>>) that send information from the object on their left to the object on their right. When combined with cin, user information entered on the keyboard goes to the variable on the right when the user hits Enter or Return. The following code shows this in action:

```
#include <iostream>

int main()
{
    int nLucky = 0;
    std::cout << "Enter your luck number: ";
    std::cin >> nLucky;
    std::cout << "You entered " << nLucky << std::endl;
}
```

In this case, you're sending text to the reader and asking for their lucky number. You then use cin to get and place the lucky number into the variable nLucky, which is then printed to the console for the reader to see.

You can capture any of the basic data types by using cin. Note, however, that if you enter the wrong data type, you can get an error. You'll learn more about avoiding such issues as you find out how to do looping and error handling in chapters 6 and 29, respectively. For now, be careful to enter what is expected — in this case, an integer for a lucky number.

REMEMBER

The cin operator uses the insertion operator (<<), and cout uses the extraction operator (>>). If the "arrows" are pointing the wrong way, you'll get an error. You're sending information to (or pointing to, in other words) cout. You're getting information from (pointing away from) cin.

Printing special characters

If you want to print a special character, such as a new line, you can do it in C++. You simply need to use an escape sequence. Similarly, I have used a string of text within double quotes, but what if I want to print double quotes? For example, I might print my name as "Bradley Jones" by doing the following:

```
std::cout << "Bradley Jones" << std::endl;
```

I can also print it as follows:

```
std::cout << "Bradley (\"Brad\") Jones" << std::endl;
```

This line results in the name being displayed this way:

```
Bradley ("Brad") Jones
```

The backslash within a string operates as an escape code telling C++ that a special character is being printed. In this case, it's a double quote. Table 4-1 presents other common escape sequences that can be used — including an escape sequence to print the escape character.

TABLE 4-1 Common Escape Sequences

Escape Code	Meaning	Example
\\	Backslash (\)	`std::cout << "C:\\Projects\\ HelloWorld”;` C:\Projects\HelloWorld
\n	Newline Moves to the beginning of the next line	`std::cout <<"Hello\nWorld");` Hello World
\"	Double quote	`std::cout <<"Hello \”World\”");` Hello "World"
\'	Single quote	`std::cout <<"Hello \'World\'");` Hello 'World'
\t	Tab	`std::cout <<"Hello \tWorld");` Hello World
\r	Return Moves to the beginning of the current line	`std::cout <<"Hello \rWorld");` World
\b	Backspace Deletes the previous character	`std::cout <<"Hello \bWorld");` HelloWorld

Printing the Modern Way

Though you see `cout` often in existing C++ code, it's no longer the modern way to display output. Just as you move from counting to ten on your fingers to simply calculating it in your mind, C++ has modernized to using new functions — `print()` and `println()`, to be precise — for displaying information to the console.

Simple printing

To print basic text with `print()`, you simply enclose the text in double quotes within the parentheses of the print statement. This is similar to `cout`, but you use parentheses around the text rather than use the insertion operator. The following code snippet calls the print command two times. Note that you must add the *#include <print>* statement so that C++ knows to include the print commands for your program to use.

```
#include <print>

int main()
{
   std::print("My name ");
   std::print("is Bradley!");
}
```

This prints `My name is Bradley!` all on one line. If I wanted to print this on two lines, I could add the newline escape character into the string this way:

```
   std::print("My name \n");
```

Or, even better, I could instead use `println()` for the first line and keep `print()` for the second line:

```
#include <print>

int main()
{
   std::println("My name ");
   std::print("is Bradley!");
}
```

As you can see, `print()` and `println()` are quite similar. The key difference is that `println()` simply adds a newline character to what's being displayed, whereas `print()` does not.

Printing variables

Where `print()` and `println()` start to shine over `cout` is when you start printing variables in your output. To print a variable, you use a placeholder in the string of text you include. This placeholder is a set of curly braces: {}. You then list the variables that are placed in these brace locations after the string of text. There is no need for insertion operators. The listing is from the earlier section "Simple printing," but now the string and variable are printed using a clean single line of code:

```
#include <print>

int main() {
    int nLife = 42;
```

```
    std::print("The meaning of life is {}", nLife);
}
```

Similarly, you can print your lucky number by simply calling `println()` instead of needing to use insertion operators and `std::endl`:

```
#include <print>
#include <iostream>

int main()
{
    int nLucky = 0;
    std::print("Enter your luck number: ");
    std::cin >> nLucky;
    std::println("You entered {}", nLucky);
}
```

Adding a little bit of formatting

The `print()` function handles much of the display for you, yet sometimes you want a little more control. For example, when you print currency in the US with floating-point numbers, you don't want to have more than two decimal places. Similarly, sometimes you might want to print a certain number of spaces before or after a variable (or maybe even with the variable's value centered). The `print()` command provides you with a way to indicate this formatting.

Within the curly braces, you can add special syntax to indicate formatting. This starts with a colon and is then followed by the specific formatting you want. For example, if you want only two decimal places displayed, you enclose `:.2f` in braces and add it to your text to indicate two floating-point positions after the decimal. Here's an example of a full listing that shows this in action:

```
#include <print>

int main()
{
   double money = 1234.56789;
   std::println("Money is: ${:.2f}", money);
}
```

This example prints the following:

```
Money is: $1234.56
```

Note that the dollar sign is a part of the text, which is why it's printed. Also note that if the formatting had not been included in the curly braces, the output would have been:

```
Money is: $1234.56789
```

Table 4-2 shows a number of different format options you can use.

TABLE 4-2 Formatting Codes for Printing

Type of Formatting	Syntax	Sample Output
Specify decimal precision	`{:2f}`	123.45
Display a thousands separator	`{:L} (locale-based)`	1,234,567 (US locale)
Left-align	`{:<6}`	"1234 "
Right-align	`{:>6}`	" 1234"
Center-align	`{:^6}`	" 1234 "
Display as Hexadecimal	`{:#x}`	"ox2322"
Display as Octal	`{:#0}`	"0o4D2"
Display as Binary	`{:#b}`	"0b11111111"

WARNING

You can omit the number sign (#) when formatting the hexadecimal, octal, and binary numbers, but you won't get the prefixes. This strategy isn't recommended, because someone might mistake your output for decimal numbers.

TIP

The hard-coded numbers in the syntax can be changed. A number can be included to indicate the precision, which is how many digits should be displayed to the right of a decimal place when using floating point numbers. A number can also be used to set the amount of padding to use. Padding determines how many spaces or slots are used for a number. For example, if you had padding of 6, then the number 42 would have four spaces added as padding: "   42".

For fun, the following longer listing prints a menu using a bit of formatting and your new printing commands. You should enter this listing (or a similar one) and play around with the formatting. Just like learning to count, it gets easier to use printing and formatting with practice!

```
#include <print>
using namespace std;

int main()
{
    float hotdog = 3.99;
    float hamburger = 4.99;
    float fries = 2.99;

    println("{:^40}", "Menu");
    println("========================================");
    println("{:<30}{:>10.2f}", "Hotdog", hotdog );
    println("{:<30}{:>10.2f}", "Hamburger", hamburger );
    println("{:<30}{:>10.2f}", "Fries", fries );
}
```

The output from running this listing is a simple menu with a bit of formatting:

```
                  Menu
========================================
Hotdog                              3.99
Hamburger                           4.99
Fries                               2.99
========================================
```

This listing uses the concepts I explain in this chapter, but I've combined everything in a new way. I also added the `using namespace std` line, which allows me to call `println()` without the `std::` prefix. Namespaces are a topic discussed in Chapter 11.

In the first `println()` call, I simply indicate that I want to center the passed value in an area that's 40 characters wide. No surprise, then, that the text I ask the program to pass (`"Menu"`) ends up centered in a 40-character space. In the three `println()` calls to display the menu items, I'm passing two items, as indicated by the fact that each line has two sets of curly braces. The first item being passed in each line is a simple string of text that's being padded so that it fills exactly 30 spaces. This is followed by the second item, which is using a more complex formatter. In this case, the formatting starts with the greater-than sign, which, from looking at Table 4-2, indicates that the value should be right-justified. Next, the width of the area being formatted is set with the first number, 10. The decimal place (period) then indicates that the number should be displayed to two decimal positions. The result is the well-aligned menu shown in the output.

The Pros and Cons of the Old Ways Versus the New

While you can count to ten using your mind, sometimes it's easier or better to use your fingers or toes. Similarly, when displaying information in C++, sometimes it's better or easier to use `cout` versus `print()` or `println()`. The question is, when are those times?

REMEMBER

Streaming (discussed in greater depth in the online Bonus Chapter 1) is where `cout` is generally the better tool for creating dynamic output; the main area where you will find you need to work with `cout`, however, is with legacy code or if you're using older versions of C++. Pre-C++23 has no `print()` or `println()`, so you have to use `cout`. Finally, sometimes it's easier if you're simply providing a simple prompt to use `cout` before using `cin`.

C++26 NEW

The `print()` and `println()` functions help simplify formatting. They're also more aligned with other languages, such as Python's `print` command, making it easier for those switching from one language to another. Eliminating the need for streaming operations can also make formatting easier and less verbose. It can also end up being more efficient (faster). The use of `println()` also eliminates the need for the clumsy use of the newline escape character (`'\n'`).

Overall, for new C++ projects, the `print()` and `println()` functions are better to use for formatting and presenting simple output.

REMEMBER

Because I want this book to focus on learning the current version of C++, I use `print()` and `println()` — however, you don't need to follow my lead. Just as you're always free to count using your fingers or toes, you can always convert the `print()` statements to `cout` statements.

Make It Stop!

When printing to the console from within an integrated development environment (IDE), sometimes your output gets printed, the program reaches the end, and the output window immediately closes. It all happens so fast that you have no chance to see whether the program displayed your output.

In previous editions of this book, nearly every listing that printed to the console included several lines of code that would make the program stop so that you could see the output before the console window closed. Most modern IDEs now stop the console window from closing without the need for you to add code. As such, this edition no longer includes the code at the end of each listing, thus letting you focus on what's being taught.

Having said that, if you have an IDE that closes before you get a chance to see your program's output, you can add the following code to the end of the listing, just before the `return` statement in `main()`:

```
// wait until user is ready before terminating program
std::cout << "Press Enter to continue..." << endl;
std::cin.ignore(100, '\n');
std::cin.get();
```

This code displays the message `Press Enter to continue ...` It then clears any garbage or extraneous data that was waiting to be read using `std::cin.ignore(10, '\n');`. Finally, it tries to retrieve a single character — any character — using `cin.get()` before continuing to the next line, which is generally a `return` statement to end the program.

I present this code here in case you need it. You can add it to any listing, much like how you might have added it to the `count` program I introduce in the "Printing the Old Way" section, earlier in this chapter:

```
#include <iostream>

int main() {
    std::cout << "1 ";
    std::cout << "2 ";
    std::cout << "3 ";
    std::cout << "4 ";
    std::cout << "5";

    // wait until user is ready before terminating program
    std::cout << "Press Enter to continue..." << std::endl;
    std::cin.ignore(100, '\n');
    std::cin.get();
}
```

IN THIS CHAPTER

- » Recognizing that sometimes you have to make a decision
- » Using sometimes-illogical logical operators
- » Defining logical variables
- » Operating with bits and the bitwise logical operators

Chapter 5 Performing Logical Operations

The most common statement in C++ is the expression. Most expressions involve the arithmetic operators, such as addition (+), subtraction (−) and multiplication (*), as demonstrated in Chapter 3. Just adding things or doing mathematical operations isn't enough on their own. Sometimes you want to evaluate the results and take action. For example, after adding a couple of numbers, you might want to compare the result to other numbers.

In this chapter, I describe two other classes of operators known as the *comparison operators* and the *logical operators*. Both types of operators are used to perform logical operations. I also take a quick peek at a less used set of operators, the bitwise operators.

Why Mess with Logical Operations?

C++ programs make decisions. A program that can't make decisions is of limited use. The temperature conversion program I lay out in Chapter 1 is about as complex as you can get without *some* type of decision-making. Invariably, a computer program gets to the point where it must figure out situations such as "Do *this* if the *a* variable is less than some value; do that *other* thing if it's not."

The ability to make decisions is what makes a computer appear to be intelligent. (By the same token, that same property makes a computer look stupid when the program makes the wrong decision.) Making decisions, right or wrong, requires the use of comparison operators.

Using the Simple Comparison Operators

For a peek at the simple comparison operators, check out Table 5-1. Just as their name implies, each of the comparison operators performs a logical operation that compares two values and returns a result that is either *true* or *false.*

TABLE 5-1 Simple Comparison Operators Representing Daily Logic

Operator	What It Does
==	Equality; true if the leftmost argument has the same value as the right
!=	Inequality; the opposite of equality
>	Greater than; true if the leftmost argument is greater than the rightmost argument
<	Less than; true if the leftmost argument is less than the rightmost argument
>=	Greater than or equal to, less than or equal to; true if either > or == is true, or either < or == is true
<=	Less than or equal to; *true* if either < or == is *true*

The first item in Table 5-1 is the equality operator, which is used to compare two numbers. For example, the following is *true* if the value of *n* is 0, and is *false* otherwise:

```
n == 0;
```

WARNING

Looks can be deceiving. Don't confuse the equality operator (==) with the assignment operator (=). This is not only a common mistake but also one that the C++ compiler generally cannot catch — that makes it more than twice as bad. The following statement doesn't initialize `n` to `0`; it compares the current value of `n` with `0` and then does nothing with the results of that comparison:

```
n == 0;    // programmer meant to say n = 0
```

The greater-than (>) and less-than (<) operators are similarly common in everyday life. The following logical comparison is true:

```
int n1 = 1;
int n2 = 2;
n1 < n2;
```

The greater-than-or-equal-to operator (>=) and the less-than-or-equal-to operator (<=) are similar to the less-than and greater-than operators, with one major exception. They include equality; the other operators don't.

Storing logical values

The result of a logical operation using the comparison operators can be assigned to a variable of type `bool` (the term *bool* refers to Boolean algebra, an algebra of logic invented by the British mathematician George Boole in the 19th century):

```
int n1 = 1;
int n2 = 2;
bool b;
b = (n1 == n2);
```

This expression highlights the difference between the assignment operator = and the comparison operator ==. The expression says, "Compare the variables `n1` and `n2`. Store the results of this comparison in the variable `b`."

The following `BoolTest` program demonstrates the use of a `bool` variable to store the result of a logical operation:

```
// BoolTest - compare variables input from the
//            keyboard and store the result into
//            a logical variable
#include <iostream>
#include <print>

int main()
{
    // input two values
    int nArg1, nArg2;

    std::cout << "Input value 1: ";
    std::cin >> nArg1;
```

```
    std::cout << "Input value 2: ";
    std::cin >> nArg2;

    // compare the two variables and store result in b
    bool b = (nArg1 == nArg2);

    std::println("The statement {} equals {} is {}.",
        nArg1, nArg2, b);

    return 0;
}
```

This program inputs two values from the keyboard and displays the result of the equality comparison. You should run this program multiple times with different values. The following runs the program with the value of 5 entered for both prompts:

```
Input value 1: 5
Input value 2: 5
The statement 5 equals 5 is true
```

As I cover in Chapter 4, `cout` is good to use for simple prompts when also working with `cin`. Using `print()` and `println()` from C++23 and later is better to use when presenting output that needs formatting — in this case, with variable values mixed with text.

Using logical int variables

C++ hasn't always had a `bool` type variable. Back in the old days (when cameras still used film), C++ used `int` variables to store logical values. A value of `0` was considered `false`, and all other values `true`. By the same token, a logical operator generated a `0` for `false` and a `1` for `true`. (Thus, `10 < 5` returned `0`, and `10 > 5` returned `1`.)

C++ retains a high degree of compatibility between `bool` and `int` to support the older programs. Variables of type `int` and `bool` can be mixed in expressions. For example, C++ allows the following bizarre statement without batting an eyelid:

```
int n;
n = (nArg1 == nArg2) * 5;
```

This sets `n` to `5` if `nArg1` and `nArg2` are equal and to `0` otherwise. The specific process is that `nArg1` and `nArge2` are compared and there is a Boolean result of either `true` or `false`. This value is converted to an `int` value of `1` or `0`, respectively, and then multiplied by `5`.

Performing logical operations (carefully!) on floating-point variables

Round-off errors in floating-point computation can create havoc with logical operations. Consider the following example:

```
float f1 = 10.0;
float f2 = f1 / 3;
bool b1 = (f1 == (f2 * 3.0));     // are these two equal?
```

Even though it's obvious to you and to me that `f1` is equal to `f2` times 3, the resulting value of `b1` isn't *necessarily* `true`. A floating-point variable cannot hold an unlimited number of significant digits. Thus, `f2` isn't equal to the number you'd call "three-and-a-third," but rather to `3.3333 . . .`, stopping after some number of decimal places.

REMEMBER

A `float` variable supports about 7 digits of accuracy while a `double` supports a skosh over 16 digits. I say "about" and "skosh" because the computer is likely to generate a number like 3.3333347 because of vagaries in floating-point calculations.

Now, in pure math, the number of 3s after the decimal point is infinite, but no computer built can handle an infinite number of digits. So, after multiplying 3.3333 by 3, you get 9.9999 instead of the 10 you'd get if you multiplied "three-and-a-third" — in effect, a *round-off error*. Such small differences may be unnoticeable to a person, but not to the computer. Equality means exactly that — *exact* equality.

Modern processors are sophisticated in performing such calculations. The processor may, in fact, accommodate the round-off error, but from inside C++, you can't predict exactly what any given processor will do.

The safer comparison is as follows:

```
float f1 = 10.0;
float f2 = f1 / 3;
float f3 = f2 * 3.0;
float delta = f1 - f3;
bool bEqual = -0.0001 < delta && delta < 0.0001;
```

This comparison is `true` if `f1` and `f3` are within some small delta (within one-ten thousandths, to be precise) from each other, which should still be `true` even if you take some small round-off error into account.

Adding Logic with the Logical Operators

Decisions often aren't simple. Often, multiple conditions need to be evaluated to reach a course of action. You might not eat cereal unless the bowl contains cereal AND the bowl has milk in it AND the cereal is coated with sugar (lots of sugar). You might have a Scotch IF it's single-malt AND someone else is paying for it. This is where the simple logical operators in Table 5-2 come to your aid.

TABLE 5-2 Simple Logical Operators

Operator	What It Does
&&	AND; *true* if both the left- and rightmost arguments are *true*
||	OR; *true* if either the left- or rightmost argument is *true*
!	NOT; *true* if its argument is *false*; otherwise, *false*

Logical operators fall into two types: The AND and OR operators are what I call *simple logical operators*. The second type of logical operator consists of the *bitwise* operators. People don't use the bitwise operators in their daily business; they're unique to the computer world. I start out with the simple logical operators and then sneak up on the bitwise later in this chapter.

Making complex decisions

The && (AND) and || (OR) operators work in combination with the other logic operators to build more complex logical expressions. They allow you to combine multiple comparisons to come up with a single answer. Sometimes you want both decisions to be true. In that case, you can use the logical AND operator like this:

```
lowValue < n2 && n2 < highValue;
```

The result of this statement is true if `n2` is greater than `lowValue` AND ALSO less than `highValue`. This is the most common way to determine that `n2` is in the range between the `lowValue` and `highValue`.

Where both values need to be true for the AND operator to result in the statement to return the value of `true`, the OR (||) requires only one of the two sides of the operator to be true. If the expression on either side of the OR (||) is true, the entire statement is true. In the following line, if either `age > 17` OR `withAdult == true` is true, the entire expression results in being `true`:

```
age > 17 || withAdult == true
```

TIP

In Chapter 3, you find out that there's an order of operations when it comes to which arithmetic operators are evaluated first. The same is true for the comparison and logical operators: All comparison operators get evaluated before the logical operators. As such, in the preceding line of code, the > and == are evaluated before the || operation. To make things clear for you and anyone looking at your code, you can use parentheses. Anything placed between parentheses is evaluated before any of the comparison or logical operators. The following line evaluates the code the same as the earlier statement, but is much more obvious in the order of operation:

```
(age > 17) || (withAdult == true)
```

Short circuits and C++

The logical AND (&&) and logical OR (||) operators perform what is called *short-circuit evaluation*. Consider the following:

```
condition1 && condition2
```

If `condition1` is not `true`, the overall result is not `true`, no matter the value of `condition2`. (For example, `condition2` could be `true` or `false` without changing the result.) The same situation occurs in the following line:

```
condition1 || condition2
```

If `condition1` is `true`, the result is `true`, no matter what the value of `condition2` is.

To save time, C++ doesn't evaluate `condition2` if it doesn't need to. For example, in the expression `condition1 && condition2`, C++ doesn't evaluate `condition2` if `condition1` is `false`. Likewise, in the expression `condition1 || condition2`, C++ doesn't evaluate `condition2` if `condition1` is `true`. This is known as *short-circuit evaluation*.

WARNING

Short-circuit evaluation may mean that `condition2` isn't evaluated even if that condition has side effects. Consider the following (admittedly contrived) code snippet:

```
int nArg1 = 1;
int nArg2 = 2;
int nArg3 = 3;
```

```
bool b = (nArg1 > nArg2) && (nArg2++ > nArg3);
```

The variable `nArg2` is never incremented, because the comparison `nArg2++ > nArg3` isn't performed. There's no need because `nArg1 > nArg2` already returned `false`, so the overall expression must be `false`.

Streamlining with the Three-Way Comparison Operator

Starting with C++20, the C++ standard reached for the stars by adding what's known as the *spaceship* operator, or, more officially, the *three-way comparison operator*:

```
<=>
```

Many people think it looks a bit like a flying saucer — thus, the spaceship name.

This is clearly another comparison operator. Like the ones I mention in Table 5-1, this operator allows two variables to be compared:

```
result = value1 <=> value2
```

The difference is that this operation doesn't return `true` or `false`. Rather, it generally returns one of the following:

- A negative value if the variable on the left is less than the variable on the right
- Zero if the variable on the left is equal to the variable on the right
- A positive value if the variable on the left is greater than the variable on the right

In the following listing, the three-way comparison operator is used to compare two numbers. The result of comparing the numbers is assigned to the variable `result`, which is then evaluated using the standard comparison operators to print a message:

```
#include <iostream>

int main() {
    int a = 5, b = 10;
```

```
    auto result = a <=> b;    // Three-way comparison

    if (result < 0) std::cout << "a is smaller\n";
    else if (result > 0) std::cout << "a is greater\n";
    else std::cout << "a is equal to b\n";

    return 0;
}
```

This is a simplified illustration of using the three-way comparison operator. This example might make it seem like the operator is a bit unnecessary when you can simply compare the two numbers as easily as comparing the result. However, when you start working with more complex types of information, such as sorting people by their age or trying to compare points on a grid, this operator becomes much more useful.

Peeking at the Bitwise Logical Operations

C++ is a powerful language, so powerful it can manipulate numbers at the bit level. What's a bit? It is the smallest unit of storage on a computer that can indicate a value of 0 or 1. A bit is like a light switch in that it is either on or off. The switch (or bit) being turned on is the same as being equal to `1` or being `true`. The switch (or bit) being turned off is equivalent to being `0` or `false`.

You might think this description sounds a *bit* technical (pun intended), and you are correct; it is technical. Bit manipulation is used in more advanced situations. Even so, you should be aware that bitwise operators and operations exist. The bitwise operators that C++ uses to manipulate bits are shown in Table 5-3.

TABLE 5-3 Bitwise Operators

Operator	Function
~	NOT: Toggle each bit from 1 to 0 and from 0 to 1.
&	AND each bit of the leftmost argument with that on the right.
|	OR each bit of the leftmost argument with that on the right.
^	XOR (exclusive OR) each bit of the leftmost argument with that on the right.

Using bits can potentially let you store a lot of information in a small amount of memory. Many traits in the world have only two possibilities: either this way or that way. You're either married or you're not. You're either an adult (21) or you're not. (At least that's what a driver's license indicates.) In C++, you can store each of these traits in a single bit — in this way, you can pack 32 separate binary properties into a single 32-bit `int`.

In addition, bit operations can be extremely fast. No performance penalty is paid for the 32-to-1 savings.

The bitwise operators — AND (&), OR (|), and NOT (~) — perform logic operations on single bits. If you consider `0` to be `false` and `1` to be `true` (it doesn't *have* to be this way, but it's a common convention), you can say things like the following for the NOT operator:

```
~1 (true)  is 0 (false)
~0 (false) is 1 (true)
```

The AND operator works with two bits. If they're both `1` (`true`), the result is `true`; otherwise, the result is `0` (`false`). The AND operator is defined as follows:

```
1 (true) & 1 (true)  is 1 (true)
1 (true) & 0 (false) is 0 (false)
```

It's a similar situation for the OR operator; if either side of the operation is `1` (`true`), the result is `1` (`true`):

```
1 (true) | 0 (false) is 1 (true)
0 (false) | 0 (false) is 0 (false)
```

The definition of the AND operator appears in Table 5-4. Read one argument as the column head and the other argument as the row head — the result is the intersection. Thus, `1` AND `1` is `1`; `0` AND `1` is `0`.

TABLE 5-4 Truth Table for the AND Operator

AND	1	0
1	1	0
0	0	0

You read Table 5-4 as the column corresponding to the value of one of the arguments while the row corresponds to the value of the other. Thus, `1 & 0` is `0` (Column 1 and Row 0). The only combination that returns anything other than `0` is `1 & 1`. (This is known as a *truth table*.)

Similarly, the truth table for the OR operator is shown in Table 5-5.

TABLE 5-5

Truth Table for the OR Operator

OR	1	0
1	1	1
0	1	0

One other logical operation that isn't so commonly used in day-to-day living is the OR ELSE (^) operator, commonly contracted to XOR. XOR is `true` if either argument is `true`, but not if both are `true`. The truth table for XOR is shown in Table 5-6.

TABLE 5-6

Truth Table for the XOR Operator

XOR	1	0
1	0	1
0	1	0

Armed with these bit-level operators, you should be in a position to take on the C++ bitwise logical operations.

ON THE WEB

To go deeper into using the bitwise operators would require a larger discussion on number systems and how numbers can be expressed with bits. I have included the document, "Expressing Binary Numbers" as part of the downloads for this book. It provides an overview of number systems and provides examples using the bitwise operators.

IN THIS CHAPTER

» Controlling the flow through the program

» Executing a group of statements repetitively

» Avoiding infinite loops

Chapter 6
Controlling the Flow

The simple programs that appear in chapters 1–5 process a fixed number of inputs, output the result of that calculation, and quit. However, these programs lack any form of flow control. They don't make any sort of tests or decisions. Yet computer programs are *all about* making decisions. When the user presses a key, the program decides what action needs to be taken, and the computer responds accordingly.

For example, if the user presses Ctrl+C on a Windows machine, the computer copies the selected area to the Windows Clipboard. If the user moves the mouse, the pointer moves on the screen. If the user clicks the right mouse button while pressing the Windows key, the computer crashes. (Okay, that last statement might not be true, but logic could be written to make it happen.) Regardless, the list goes on and on. Programs that don't make decisions are generally pretty boring.

Flow-control commands allow the program to decide what action to take based on the results of the C++ logical operations performed (see Chapter 4). C++ basically has three types of flow control statements: the branch, the loop, and the switch.

Controlling Program Flow with the Branch Commands

The simplest form of flow control is the *branch statement* — this instruction allows the program to decide which of two paths to take through C++ instructions, based on the results of a logical expression. (See Chapter 5 for a description of logical expressions.)

In C++, the branch statement is implemented using the `if` statement:

```
if (m > n)
{
    // Path 1
    // ...instructions to be executed if
    // m is greater than n
}
else
{
    // Path 2
    // ...instructions to be executed if not
}
```

First, the logical expression is evaluated. In this case, the logical expression is `m > n`. If the result of the expression is `true`, control passes down the path marked `Path 1` in the previous snippet. If the expression is `false`, control passes to `Path 2`. The `else` clause is optional. If it isn't present, C++ acts as though it's present but empty.

REMEMBER

The braces aren't required if there's only one statement to execute as part of the `if`. Originally, braces were used only if there were two or more statements you wanted to treat as one. However, people quickly realized that it was cleaner and less error-prone to use braces every time, no matter how many statements there are.

The following program demonstrates the `if` statement (note all the lovely braces):

```
// BranchDemo - input two numbers. Go down one path of the
//              program if the first argument is greater
//              than the first or the other path if not
#include <iostream>
#include <print>
using std::print;
using std::println;
```

```
int main()
{
    // input the first argument...
    int nArg1;
    print("Enter arg1: ");
    std::cin >> nArg1;

    // ...and the second
    int nArg2;
    print("Enter arg2: ");
    std::cin >> nArg2;

    // now decide what to do:
    if (nArg1 > nArg2)
    {
        println("Argument 1 is greater than argument 2.");
    }
    else
    {
        println("Argument 1 is not greater than argument 2.");
    }

    return 0;
}
```

Here, the program reads two integers from the keyboard and compares them. If `nArg1` is greater than `nArg2`, control flows to the output statement `println("Argument 1 is greater than argument 2.")`. If `nArg1` is not greater than `nArg2`, control flows to the `else` clause, where the statement `println("Argument 1 is not greater than argument 2.")` is executed. Here's what that operation looks like:

```
Enter arg1: 5
Enter arg2: 6
Argument 1 is not greater than argument 2.
```

TIP

Notice how the instructions within the `if` blocks of this program are indented slightly. This is strictly for human consumption because C++ ignores white space (spaces, tabs, and newline characters). It may seem trivial, but a clear coding style increases the readability of a C++ program. Most modern C++ development tools can add or enforce this style or any one of several other coding styles for you. These are generally in the settings of your editor. For example, in Code::Blocks, you can go to Settings⇨Editor and select Source Formatter from the scrolled list on the left. (I use the ANSI bracket style with four spaces per indent.) In Visual Studio Code, you can configure the setting for aspects such as tab size by going to

File➪Preferences➪Settings. You can then search for options such as tab size to find the correct settings. You can search for the term *Format on Save* to have Visual Studio Code clean up the spacing and formatting each time it saves your file.

Executing Loops in a Program

Branch statements allow you to direct the flow of a program's execution down one path or another. This is a big improvement over simply executing one line of code after the one that came before it.

Consider the problem of updating the computer display. The typical PC must update well over a thousand pixels for each row as it paints an image from left to right. It repeats this process for each of the thousand or so rows on the display, by executing the same small number of instructions, millions of times — once for each pixel.

There must be a better way to work with these pixels than to duplicate the same code millions of times. It is tiring just thinking about how long the code listing would be! The fact is this is perfect excuse to use branching statements. The great thing is, with branching you can skip lines of code or (as with the pixel code) you can even go back and run the same lines of code multiple times (in a loop) — even a million times if you want!

Looping while a condition is true

The simplest form of looping statement is the `while` loop. Here's what the `while` loop looks like:

```
while(condition)
{
    // ...repeatedly executed as long as condition is true
}
```

The *`condition`* is tested. It can be `if var > 10` or `if var1 == var2` or any other expression you might think of, as long as it returns a value of `true` or `false`. If the condition is `true`, the statements within the braces are executed. Upon encountering the closed brace, C++ returns control to the beginning, and the process starts over by checking the condition again. If the condition is `false`, control passes to the first statement after the closed brace. The effect is that the C++ code within the braces is executed repeatedly as long as the condition is `true`. (Kind of like how you get to walk around the yard with your dog until she . . . well, until you're done.)

If the condition were `true` the first time, what would make it `false` in the future? Consider the following sample program:

```
// WhileDemo - input a loop count. Loop while outputting
//             a string equal to the count number.
#include <iostream>
#include <print>
int main()
{
   // input the loop count
   int nLoopCount;
   std::print("Enter loop count: ");
   std::cin >> nLoopCount;

   // now loop that many times
   while (nLoopCount > 0)
   {
      nLoopCount = nLoopCount - 1;
      std::println("Only {} loops to go", nLoopCount);
   }

   return 0;
}
```

The `WhileDemo` program begins by retrieving a loop count from the user, which it stores in the `nLoopCount` variable. The program then executes a `while` loop. The `while` first tests `nLoopCount`. If `nLoopCount` is greater than 0, the program enters the body of the loop (the *body* is the code between the braces), where it decrements `nLoopCount` by 1 and outputs the result to the display. The program then returns to the top of the loop to test whether `nLoopCount` is still positive.

When the `WhileDemo` program is executed, it outputs the results shown in the next snippet. Here, I entered a loop count of 5. The result is that the program loops five times, each time outputting a countdown:

```
Enter loop count: 5
Only 4 loops to go
Only 3 loops to go
Only 2 loops to go
Only 1 loops to go
Only 0 loops to go
Press Enter to continue...
```

If the user enters a negative loop count, the program skips the loop entirely. That's because the specified condition is never `true`, so control never enters the loop. In addition, if the user enters a very large number, the program loops for a long time before completing.

A separate, less frequently used version of the while loop, known as do...while, appears identical except that the condition isn't tested until the bottom of the loop:

```
do
{
   // ...the inside of the loop
} while (condition);
```

Because the condition isn't tested until the end, the body of the do...while is always executed at least once.

WARNING

The condition is checked only at the beginning of the while loop or at the end of the do...while loop. Even if the condition ceases to be true at some point during the execution of the loop, control doesn't exit the loop until the condition is retested.

Using the autoincrement/autodecrement feature

Programmers often use the autoincrement ++ or the autodecrement -- operators with loops that count something. Notice from the following snippet extracted from the WhileDemo example that the program decrements the loop count by using assignment and subtraction statements, like this:

```
// now loop that many times
while (nLoopCount > 0)
{
   nLoopCount = nLoopCount - 1;
   std::println("Only {} loops to go", nLoopCount);
}
```

A more compact version uses the autodecrement feature, which does what you may well imagine:

```
while (nLoopCount > 0)
{
   nLoopCount--;
   std::println("Only {} loops to go", nLoopCount);
}
```

The logic in this version is the same as in the original. The only difference is the way nLoopCount is decremented.

Because the autodecrement decrements its argument *and* returns its value, the decrement operation can be combined with the while loop. In particular, the following version is the smallest loop yet:

```
while (nLoopCount-- > 0)
{
   std::println("Only {} loops to go", nLoopCount);
}
```

Believe it or not, nLoopcount-- > 0 is the version that most C++ programmers would use. It's not that C++ programmers like being cute (although they do). In fact, the more compact version (which embeds the autoincrement or autodecrement feature in the logical comparison) is easier to read, especially as you gain experience.

REMEMBER

Both nLoopCount-- and --nLoopCount expressions decrement nLoopCount. The former expression, however, returns the value of nLoopCount before being decremented; the latter expression does so after being decremented.

How often should the autodecrement version of WhileDemo execute when the user enters a loop count of 1? If you use the pre-decrement version, the value of --*nLoopCount* is 0, and the body of the loop is never entered. With the post-decrement version, the value of nLoopCount is 1, and control enters the loop.

TECHNICAL STUFF

Don't assume that the version of the program with the autodecrement command executes faster than the simple - 1 version (because it contains fewer statements). It probably executes exactly the same. Modern compilers are good at reducing the number of machine-language instructions to a minimum, no matter which of the decrement instructions shown here you use.

Using the for loop

The most common form of loop is the for loop. The for loop is preferred over the more basic while loop because it's generally easier to read (there's really no other advantage).

The for loop has the following format:

```
for (initialization; conditional; increment)
{
   // ...body of the loop
}
```

The for loop is equivalent to the following while loop:

```
{
    initialization;
    while(conditional)
    {
        {
            // ...body of the loop
        }
        increment;
    }
}
```

Execution of the for loop begins with the *initialization clause*, which got its name because it's normally where counting variables are initialized. The initialization clause is executed only once, when the for loop is first encountered.

Execution continues with the *conditional clause*. This clause works just like the while loop: As long as the conditional clause is true, the for loop continues to execute.

After the code in the body of the loop finishes executing, control passes to the increment clause before returning to check the conditional clause — thereby repeating the process. The increment clause normally houses the autoincrement or autodecrement statements used to update the counting variables.

The for loop is best understood by example. The following ForDemo1 program is nothing more than the WhileDemo converted to use the for loop construct:

```
// ForDemo1 - input a loop count. Loop while
//            outputting astring arg number of times.
#include <iostream>
#include <print>

int main()
{
    // input the loop count
    int nLoopCount;
    print("Enter loop count: ");
    std::cin >> nLoopCount;

    // count up to the loop count limit
    for (; nLoopCount > 0;)
    {
        nLoopCount = nLoopCount - 1;
```

```
        println("Only " {} loops to go", nLoopCount);
    }

    return 0;
}
```

The program reads a value from the keyboard into the `nLoopCount` variable. The `for` loop starts out comparing `nLoopCount` to `0`. Control passes into the `for` loop if `nLoopCount` is greater than 0. Once inside the `for` loop, the program decrements `nLoopCount` and displays the result. When that's complete, the program returns to the `for` loop control. Control skips to the next line after the `for` loop as soon as `nLoopCount` has been decremented to `0`.

TIP

All three sections of a `for` loop may be empty. An empty initialization or increment section does nothing. An empty comparison section is treated like a comparison that returns `true`.

This `for` loop has two small problems. First, it's destructive — not in the sense of what a puppy does to a slipper, but in the sense that it changes the value of `nLoopCount`, "destroying" the original value. Second, this `for` loop counts backward from large values down to smaller values. These two problems are addressed by adding a dedicated counting variable to the `for` loop. Here's what it looks like:

```
// ForDemo2 - input a loop count. Loop while
//            outputting astring arg number of times.
#include <iostream>
#include <print>

int main()
{
    // input the loop count
    int nLoopCount;
    print("Enter loop count: ");
    std::cin >> nLoopCount;

    // count up to the loop count limit
    for (int ctr = 1; ctr <= nLoopCount; ctr++)
    {
        println("We've finished {} loops", ctr);
    }

    return 0;
}
```

This modified version of ForDemo loops the same as it did before. Rather than modify the value of nLoopCount, however, this ForDemo2 version uses a new counter variable.

This for loop declares a counter variable ctr and initializes it to 0. It then compares this counter variable to nLoopCount. If ctr is less than nLoopCount, the condition is true and control passes to the output statement within the body of the for loop. Once the body has finished executing, control passes to the increment clause, where ctr is incremented and compared to nLoopCount again, and so it goes.

The following shows sample output from the program:

```
Enter loop count: 5
We've finished 1 loops
We've finished 2 loops
We've finished 3 loops
We've finished 4 loops
We've finished 5 loops
```

WARNING

When a variable such as ctr is declared within the initialization portion of the for loop, it's known or visible only within the for loop itself. Nerdy C++ programmers say that the scope of the variable is limited to the for loop. In the ForDemo2 example just given, the variable ctr isn't accessible from the return statement because that statement isn't within the loop.

Avoiding the dreaded infinite loop

An *infinite loop* is an execution path that continues forever. An infinite loop occurs any time the condition that would otherwise terminate the loop can't occur — usually, the result of a coding error.

Consider the following minor variation of the earlier loop:

```
while (nLoopCount > 0)
{
   println("Only {} loops to go", nLoopCount);
}
```

The programmer forgot to decrement the variable nLoopCount. The result is a loop counter that never changes. The test condition is either always false or always true. If nLoopCount is greater than 0, the program executes in a never-ending (infinite) loop.

I realize that nothing is infinite: Eventually, the power will fail, the computer will shut down, Microsoft will go bankrupt, and dogs will sleep with cats. Either the loop will stop executing or you will no longer care. But an infinite loop continues to execute until something outside the control of the program makes it stop.

You can create an infinite loop in many more ways than shown here, most of which are much more difficult to spot than this one was.

For each his own

An alternative form of the `for` statement, commonly known as the *for each* loop (also known as the *range-based for* loop), is also available in C++. In this `for` loop, the counting variable is followed by a list of values, as shown in the following demo program:

```
// ForEachDemo - The "for each" iterates through each
//               member of a list
#include <iostream>
#include <print>

int main()
{
   std::println("The primes less than 20 are:");
   for(int n : {1, 2, 3, 5, 7, 11, 13, 17, 19})
   {
      std::print("{}, ", n);
   }
   std::println("");

   return 0;
}
```

The values within the curly braces are known as a *list*. The variable `n` is assigned each value in the list: `1` the first time through the loop, and then the value `2`, and then `3`, and then `5`, and so on. The `for` loop terminates when the list is exhausted. The output of this program appears as follows:

```
The primes less than 20 are:
1, 2, 3, 5, 7, 11, 13, 17, 19,
```

I touch on initializer lists again in Chapter 8. I also discuss them in detail in Bonus Chapter 2, "Tempting C++ Templates" available for download at `www.dummies.com/go/cplusplus8e`.

Applying special loop controls

C++ defines two special flow-control commands known as `break` and `continue`. Sometimes, the condition for terminating a loop occurs at neither the beginning nor the end of the loop, but in the middle. Consider a program that accumulates numbers of values entered by the user. The loop terminates when the user enters a negative number.

The challenge with this problem is that the program can't exit the loop until the user has entered a value, but must exit before the value is added to the sum.

For these cases, C++ defines the `break` command. When encountered, `break` causes control to exit the current loop immediately. Control passes from the `break` statement to the statement immediately following the closed curly brace at the end of the loop.

Here's the format of the `break` command:

```
while(condition) // break works equally well in for loop
{
   if (some other condition)
   {
      break; // exit the loop
   }
}           // control passes here when the
            // program encounters the break
```

Armed with this new `break` command, my solution to the accumulator problem appears as the program `BreakDemo`:

```
// BreakDemo - input a series of numbers.
//             Continue to accumulate the sum
//             of these numbers until the user
//             enters a negative number.
#include <iostream>
#include <print>

int main()
{
   // input the loop count
   int accumulator = 0;
   std::println("This program sums values from the user.");
   std::println("Terminate by entering a negative number.");
```

```
    // loop "forever"
    for(;;)
    {
        // fetch another number
        int nValue = 0;
        std::print("Enter next number: ");
        std::cin >> nValue;

        // if it's negative...
        if (nValue < 0)
        {
            // ...then exit
            break;
        }

        // ... otherwise, add the number to the accumulator
        accumulator += nValue;
    }

    // now that we've exited the loop
    // output the accumulated result
    std::println("The total is {}.", accumulator);

    return 0;
}
```

After explaining the rules to the user (entering a negative number to terminate and so on), the program enters what looks like an infinite `for` loop. Once within the loop, `BreakDemo` retrieves a number from the keyboard. Only after the program has read the number can it test to see whether that number matches the exit criteria. If the input number is negative, control passes to the `break`, causing the program to exit the loop. If the input number is *not* negative, control skips over the `break` command to the expression that sums the new value into the accumulator. After the program exits the loop, it outputs the accumulated value and then exits.

TIP

When performing an operation on a variable repeatedly in a loop, make sure the variable is initialized properly before entering the loop. In this case, the program zeroes `accumulator` before entering the loop where `nValue` is added to it.

The result of a sample run appears this way:

```
This program sums values from the user
Terminate by entering a negative number
```

```
Enter next number: 1
Enter next number: 2
Enter next number: 3
Enter next number: -1

The total is 6
```

The `continue` command is similar to `break`, but is used less frequently. When the program encounters the `continue` command, it immediately returns to the top of the loop. The rest of the statements in the loop are ignored for the current iteration.

The following sample snippet ignores negative numbers that the user might input. Only a 0 terminates this version (the complete program appears on the website as `ContinueDemo`):

```
while(true) // this while() has the same effect as for(;;)
{
    // input a value
    std::print("Input a value:");
    std::cin >> nValue;

    // if the value is negative...
    if (nValue < 0)
    {
        // ...output an error message...
        std::println(""Negative numbers are not allowed.");

        // ... and go back to the top of the loop
      continue;
    }

    // ... continue to process input like normal
}
```

TIP

C++20 added a feature to C++ called *concepts*, which allow you to restrict the type of values (such as limiting yourself to only positive numbers). (You can see more about how to use concepts in the online bonus Chapter 2, "Tempting C++ Templates".) Also starting with C++20, the concept of ranges for working with sequences or lists of numbers was made a part of the C++ standard. Ranges and their use with loops are covered in Chapter 8.

Nesting Control Commands

Returning to the PC-screen-repaint problem, surely it must need a loop structure of some type to write each pixel from left to right on a single line. (Do Middle Eastern terminals scan from right to left? I have no idea.) What about repeatedly repainting each scan line from top to bottom? (Do PC screens in Australia scan from bottom to top?) For this particular task, you need to include a left-to-right scan loop within the top-to-bottom scan loop.

A loop command within another loop is known as a *nested loop*. As an example, I have modified the `BreakDemo` program to accumulate any number of sequences. In this `NestedDemo` program, the inner loop sums numbers entered from the keyboard until the user enters a negative number. The outer loop continues accumulating sequences until the sum is 0. Here's what it looks like:

```
// NestedDemo - input a series of numbers.
//              Continue to accumulate the sum of these
//              numbers until the user enters a 0.
//              Repeat the process until the sum is 0.
#include <iostream>
#include <print>

int main()
{
   // the outer loop
   std::println("This program sums multiple series");
   std::println("of numbers. Terminate each sequence");
   std::println("by entering a negative number.");
   std::println("Terminate the series by entering two");
   std::println("negative numbers in a row");

   // continue to accumulate sequences
   int accumulator = 0;
   for(;;)
   {
      // start entering the next sequence
      // of numbers
      accumulator = 0;
      std::println("Start the next sequence");

      // loop forever
      for(;;)
      {
         // fetch another number
```

```
            int nValue = 0;
            std::print("Enter next number: ");
            std::cin >> nValue;

            // if it's negative...
            if (nValue < 0)
            {
                // ...then exit
                break;
            }

            // ...otherwise add the number to the
            // accumulator
            accumulator += nValue;
        }

        // exit the loop if the total accumulated is 0
        if (accumulator == 0)
        {
            break;
        }

        // output the accumulated result and start over
        std::println("The total for this sequence is {}.",
        accumulator );
        std::println(); // print an extra blank line
    }

    return 0;
}
```

Notice that the inner for loop looks like the earlier accumulator example. Immediately after that loop, however, I snuck in an added test. If accumulator is equal to 0, the program executes a break statement that exits the outer loop. Otherwise, the program outputs the accumulated value and starts over.

Switching to a Different Subject?

One last control statement is useful in a limited number of cases. The switch statement resembles a compound if statement by including a number of different possibilities rather than a single test. Each different possibility is identified by using the case keyword:

```
switch(expression)
{
   case value1:
      // go here if the expression == value1
      break;
   case value2:
      // go here if expression == value2
      break;
   default:
      // go here if there is no match
}
```

REMEMBER

The value of *expression* must be an integer (`int`, `long`, or `char`). The values following each use of the `case` keywords (such as `value1` in the sample code) must be constants. Starting with the C++14 standard, a constant expression can also be used (however, I don't describe constant expressions until Chapter 11).

When the `switch` statement is encountered, the expression is evaluated and compared to the various case constants. Control then branches to the case that matches. If none of the cases match, control passes to the `default` clause.

Consider the following example:

```
// SwitchDemo - The switch statement in action!
//
#include <iostream>
#include <print>

int main()
{
int choice = 0;
std::print("Enter a 1, 2 or 3: ");
std::cin >> choice;

switch(choice)
{
   case 1:
     // do "1" processing
     std::println("You entered 1.");
     break;

   case 2:
     // do "2" processing
```

```
      std::println("You entered 2.");
      break;

    case 3:
      // do "3" processing
      std::println("You entered 3.");
      break;

    default:
      std::println("You didn't enter a 1, 2 or 3.");
  }

  return 0;
}
```

REMEMBER

The switch statement *does* have an equivalent; in this case, multiple if statements. However, when there are more than two or three cases, the switch structure is easier to understand.

WARNING

The break statements are necessary to exit the switch command. Without the break statements, control falls through from one case to the next. (Look out below!) Having said that, you'll see that the default case does not include a break statement in my example. This is because it is presented last in the switch statement, so once it reaches the end of its code, you've also reached the end of the switch statement. You could move the default earlier (such as first), in which case you'd need to add a break statement to the end of its code. It's clearer, however, to keep the default last in the switch statement.

When it comes to the values you can include in a switch statement, you'll also see that strings don't work; however, in Chapter 14, I show you to use a special type of string along with a set of if statements to achieve the same kind of functionality you'd get with a switch statement.

2 Becoming a Functional C++ Programmer

IN THIS PART . . .

Writing functions to organize your programs

Grouping similar things using arrays

Understanding the concept of pointers

Defining constants and macros

Organizing your programs with modules

IN THIS CHAPTER

» Writing functions

» Passing data to functions

» Naming functions with different arguments

» Creating function prototypes

» Passing by value versus passing by reference

» Providing default values for arguments

Chapter 7 Creating Functions

The programs developed in earlier chapters have been small enough to be easily read as a single code listing or unit. Larger, real-world programs are often many thousands, if not millions, of lines long. Developers need to break these monster programs into smaller chunks that are easier to conceive, describe, develop, organize, and maintain. Each small part that's broken out can serve to do a specific task.

C++ allows you to divide your code into chunks known as functions. A *function* is a small block of code that can be executed as a single entity. A function is generally focused on doing a single task. Equally important, functions are generally created to be reusable. For example, you've been using the `print()` function to carry out a single task; it prints to the screen. As you may have seen in many of the programs in this book already, the `print()` function is definitely reusable.

Functions can contain other functions as well. These functions can be combined to make up a complete program. This divide-and-conquer approach reduces the complexity of creating a working program of significant size to perform a task that even a mere mortal can achieve.

Writing and Using a Function

Programmers are known for enjoying junk food — especially pizza. Let's assume you've been tasked with ordering pizza to help energize you for an evening of C++ coding. You were about to order your favorite old-world pepperoni pizza from the local pizzeria when you noticed the coupons. The pizzeria is promoting a special where you can buy two small pizzas for the price of a large. You always order the large, but you don't want to miss a good deal. The conundrum is that you don't know whether this is a good deal.

But you're on your way to becoming an excellent C++ programmer, so what better way to determine whether it's a good deal than to write a bit of code to provide an answer? You know that a small pizza measures 11 inches and the large is 16 inches — and the pizzas are round. You need to determine whether the special is "Buy two 11-inch small pizzas for the price of one 16-inch large pizza" is a good deal that will save you money.

You need to compare the sizes and see which option provides more pizza. A good function for this task would be one that calculates the area of a pizza. This can be done with basic math, which in this case would be to find the area of a circle based on its diameter. The formula for finding the area of a circle is $\Pi \times r^2$, which is the same as $\Pi \times r \times r$. You can apply this formula to the pizzas by using half the diameter of the pizza for the radius, and a constant value for Π. The following `PizzaSizer` program provides the answer to the question of whether two small pizzas are a better deal than a large pizza for the same price:

```
// PizzaSizer.cpp - Pizza size comparison program
#include <print>

const double PI = 3.14159;

// Program main function - the starting point!
int main()
{
    std::print("Which is better, two small or one large ");
    std::println("pizza for the same price?");

    int nSmallSize = PI * (11/2) * (11/2);
    int nLargeSize = PI * (16/2) * (16/2);

    std::println("One small is:  {}", nSmallSize);
    std::println("Two small are: {}", (nSmallSize * 2));
    std::println("One large is:  {}", nLargeSize);
```

```
    if (2 * nSmallSize > nLargeSize)
        std::println("Two small pizzas is a better deal.");
    else
        std::println("Better to go with one large pizza.");

    return 0;
}
```

This relatively short program answers the question, but that's all it does. You can see that the code calculates the size of a small pizza, and then the same formula calculates the area of a large pizza. The resulting sizes are then printed to the screen. This is followed by a simple calculation to see which is larger — two small or one large. That result is also printed:

```
Which is better, two small or one large pizza for the
   same price?
One small is:  78
Two small are: 156
One large is:  201
Better to go with one large pizza.
```

As you can see, it's better to buy one large 16-inch pizza than two smaller 11-inch pizzas if the price is the same. This deal from the local pizzeria is clearly a deal for them, not for us.

But what if the small pizza is 12 inches instead of 11? Is it a good deal then? What if the large is only 14 inches instead of 16?

Exploring Functions

As I mention earlier in this chapter, functions allow a programmer to organize their listings. Functions are fundamental to C++ programs. Creating C++ programs requires that you understand how to define, create, and test functions — these are critical. As such, what better way to learn than to add functions to the PizzaSizer program? As the program is expanded to be more useful, functions are used to help organize the code.

REMEMBER

A *function* is a logically separated block of C++ code. A function generally has a specific purpose. For the PizzaSizer program, a function can be added that calculates the area of any pizza. You can tell the function the pizza diameter, and it can tell you (in return) the total area.

A function construct has the following general form:

```
returnType functionName(arguments)
{
    // Function body...
    return expression;
}
```

For the PizzaSizer program, you can create a function called DeterminePizzaArea():

```
int DeterminePizzaArea( int nDiameter )
{
    int nPizzaSize = PI * (nDiameter/2)*( nDiameter/2);
    return nPizzaSize;
}
```

As you can see in the general form, a function has several pieces, including a name. The *functionName* is used to execute the code in the function (said to be *calling* the function). For example, you've used the functions called `print()` and `println()`. For calculating the area of a pizza, you have the function called `DeterminePizzArea()`.

The *arguments* to a function are values that can be passed to the function to be used as input information. For example, to determine a pizza's area, you'd need to provide the diameter (size) of the pizza. This diameter is an argument. In this case, the argument is called `nDiameter`., which is defined to be an integer. (I talk more about arguments later in this chapter.)

The *returnType* indicates the data type of any values the function will return. For example, the `DeterminePizzaArea()` function returns the area that's calculated for a pizza. This area is stored in the variable `nPizzaSize`, which is defined as an integer (`int`), which matches the *returnType*.

WARNING

To clarify, the data type of *expression* being returned must match the *returnType* indicated before *functionName*. The *returnType* is an indicator of what the data type of the return *expression* will be, so if they don't match, you see a compiler error.

Choosing not to respond

A function doesn't have to return a value. It can be created to not respond. Nor do you have to provide arguments. Both the arguments and the return value are optional. If either is absent, the keyword `void` is used instead. That is, if a function has a void argument list, the function doesn't take any arguments when called. The following function doesn't take arguments, nor does it return a value:

```
void displayInstructions(void)
{
   std::println("Let's see if this is a good pizza deal!");
   std::println("Enter the size of the pizzas: ");
   return;
}
```

You can see that this function simply prints messages to the screen. Nothing is returned, and there are no arguments.

TIP

The default argument type to a function is void, meaning that it takes no arguments. That means you can declare a function like `int fn(void)` simply as `int fn()`, if you like. Including void, however, makes it clear that nothing is being provided to the function.

Understanding simple functions

Let's add a function to the PizzaSizer program that calculates the area of a pizza. The `determinePizzaArea()` function presented previously does exactly that:

```
int determinePizzaArea( int nDiameter )
{
   int nPizzaSize = PI * (nDiameter/2)*( nDiameter/2);
   return nPizzaSize;
}
```

This simple function returns an integer value that it has calculated.

REMEMBER

Functions may return any of the intrinsic variable types described in Chapter 2, as well as any of the more complex data types you can learn about later in this book. For example, a function might return a double or a char. If a function returns no value, the return type of the function is labeled void.

TIP

A function may be labeled by its return type — for example, a function that returns an int is often known as an *integer* function. A function that returns no value is known as a *void* function.

When a function is executed, control begins at the open brace and continues through to the return statement. The return statement in a void function isn't followed by a value; in fact, the return statement in a void function is optional.

If it isn't present, execution returns to the calling function when control encounters the close brace.

Writing functions

This chapter started with a nice little program for calculating whether two small pizzas are a better deal than one large; however, it used specific pizza sizes. It would be more useful if the program could answer the question regardless of the size of a pizza. This task requires more code, thus making the listing more complicated. To help make the code more manageable, it can be broken into chunks (those functions I've been talking about) to help organize what is being done. By separating the program into different functions, you can then concentrate on each piece of the program individually.

In the case of the `PizzaSizer` program, a few distinct things can happen to make the program function better: You can

- Give instructions on what the program will do.
- Ask for a pizza size.
- Calculate the area of a pizza based on the given size.
- Show the results of whether two small pizzas are a better deal than one large.

The following listing, `PizzaAnySizer`, shows how the `PizzaSizer` program can be expanded and organized by creating functions for each of the tasks just listed.

TECHNICAL STUFF

You might notice that I sneak into the following listing one item I haven't covered yet: the `const std::string sizeText` code. For now, know that this code is simply designating a word (a *string*) called `sizeText` rather than one of the other data types. (I cover this topic in detail in Chapter 8.) Also, trust that it simply lets a word be shared with a function:

```
// PizzaAnySizer.cpp - Pizza size comparison program
#include <iostream>
#include <string>
#include <print>

const double PI = 3.14159;

// Display instructions for the user
void displayInstructions(void)
```

```
{
   std::println("Let's see if this is a good pizza deal!");
   std::println("Enter the size of the pizzas: ");
}

// Ask user for pizza size (diameter)
int getPizzaSize(const std::string sizeText)
{
   int nSize = 0;
   std::print("Enter size (diameter) of a {} pizza: ",
  sizeText);
   std::cin >> nSize;

   return nSize;
}

// Calculate the area of the pizza based on diameter
int determinePizzaArea( int nDiameter )
{
   int nPizzaSize = PI * (nDiameter/2)*( nDiameter/2);
   return nPizzaSize;
}

void showTheDeal(int nSmall, int nLarge)
{
   displayInstructions();

   std::println("One small is:  {}", nSmall);
   std::println("Two small are: {}", (nSmall * 2));
   std::println("One large is:  {}", nLarge);

   if (2 * nSmall > nLarge)
      std::println("Two small pizzas is a better deal.");
   else
      std::println("Better to go with one large pizza.");
}

// Program main function - The starting point!
int main()
{
   displayInstructions();
```

```
    int nSmallDiameter = getPizzaSize("small");
    int nLargeDiameter = getPizzaSize("large");

    int nSmallSize = determinePizzaArea(nSmallDiameter);
    int nLargeSize = determinePizzaArea(nLargeDiameter);

    showTheDeal(nSmallSize, nLargeSize);

    return 0;
}
```

The listing now has four new functions: `displayInstructions()`, `getPizzaSize()`, `determinePizzaArea()`, and `showTheDetails()`. These functions join the function I previously had called `main()`.

TIP

Function names are normally written as a multiword description with all the words rammed together. I start function names with lowercase letters but capitalize all intermediate words. Function names almost always appear followed by an open-and-close parentheses pair: `()`.

A function doesn't do anything until it's invoked. The program starts executing with the first line in `main()`, just like always. The first noncomment line in `main()` is the call to `displayInstructions ()`:

```
displayInstructions();
```

Because this call specifies one of the four new functions you created (yes, `displayInstructions()`, to state the obvious), program control passes to the first line of that particular function. The computer continues to execute there until it reaches the `return` statement at the end of `displayInstructions()` or until control reaches the close brace at the end of the function. At either point, the program control returns to the code that called the function — in this case, back to `main()`, where it continues evaluating code from where it left off.

TIP

A good function is easy to describe: Limit it to a single sentence, with a minimum of such words as *and, or, unless, until,* and *but.* For example, here's a simple, straightforward definition: "The function `determinePizzaArea()` calculates the area of a pizza based on the pizza's diameter, which is provided." This definition is concise and clear. If you find that you need to add phrases like *and it also* to a description, your function might be doing too much.

Understanding Functions with Arguments

Functions without arguments are of limited use because the communication from such functions is one-way — through the `return` value. For two-way communication to occur, you need function arguments.

Functions with arguments

A *function argument* is a variable whose value is passed to the calling function during the call operation. You saw an argument being passed in the `PizzaSizer` demo earlier in this chapter. For example, the program passed an argument to the `determinePizzaArea()` function. In fact, the function was called twice from within `main()`, passing two different values as arguments:

```
    int nSmallSize = determinePizzaArea(nSmallDiameter);
    int nLargeSize = determinePizzaArea(nLargeDiameter);
```

The value of the arguments (`nSmallDiameter` and `nLargeDiameter`) is passed to the `determinePizzaArea()`'s parameter, `nDiameter`:

```
int determinePizzaArea( int nDiameter )
{
    int nPizzaSize = PI * (nDiameter/2)*( nDiameter/2);
    return nPizzaSize;
}
```

Functions with multiple arguments

Functions may have multiple arguments that are separated by commas. I describe this in the `PizzaSizer` program with the `showTheDeal()` function, which took two integers. As a second example, the following simple function returns the product of its two arguments:

```
int product(int arg1, int arg2)
{
    return arg1 * arg2;
}
```

main() exposed

The keyword `main()` from my standard program template is nothing more than a function. You can see that in the usage of `main()`, it takes no arguments and returns an integer.

REMEMBER

When C++ builds a program from source code, it adds some boilerplate code that executes before your program ever starts. (You can't see this code without digging into the bowels of the C++ library functions.) This code sets up the environment in which your program operates.

After the environment has been established, the C++ boilerplate code calls the function `main()`, thereby beginning execution of your code. When your program finishes, it exits `from main()`. This enables the C++ boilerplate to clean up a few things before turning over control to the operating system that kills the program.

The `int` returned from `main()` is a status indicator. The program returns a 0 (zero) if the program terminates normally. Any other value can be used to indicate an error — the actual value returned indicates the nature of the error that caused the program to quit.

TECHNICAL STUFF

Though `main()` is a regular function, it's irregular in one way: Though it's declared to return an integer, starting with the C++11 standard, `main()` no longer was required to return a value. In many cases — including in this book — you see that there's no `return` statement at the end of `main()`. That's okay — the compiler simply assumes that all is well and returns a 0 (zero) by default.

Overloading Function Names

Just as two people can have the same name, in C++ two functions can also have the same name. Of course, you wouldn't want to name identical twins with the same name, because it would get *confusing*. If the names were the same, you'd need another way to tell them apart.

Similarly, C++ must have a way of telling functions apart. Thus, two functions cannot share the same name and argument list. They must have a different *extended name*, or *signature*. This extended name is simply a combination of the name and its arguments. The following extended function names are all different and can reside in the same program:

```
void someFunction(void)
{
    // ...perform some function
}
void someFunction(int n)
{
    // ...perform some different function
}
void someFunction(double d)
{
    // ...perform some very different function
}
void someFunction(int n1, int n2)
{
    // ...do something different yet
}
```

C++ knows that the functions `someFunction(void)`, `someFunction(int)`, `someFunction(double)`, and `someFunction(int, int)` are not the same.

TIP

This multiple use of names is known as *function overloading.*

Programmers often refer to a function by its shorthand name, which is the name of the function without its arguments, such as `someFunction()`, in the same way that I have the shorthand name Brad. I once had a supervisor whose name was also Brad. To make this situation even more confusing, *that* Brad's boss was also named Brad. So Brad worked for Brad, who also worked for Brad. To be differentiated from the other Brads, we simply included the family ("last") name as well. In the same way, overloaded functions can be differentiated by their argument lists.

Here's a sample snippet from an application that uses overloaded functions with unique extended names:

```
int intVariable1, intVariable2;
double doubleVariable;

// functions are distinguished by the type of
// the argument passed
someFunction();            // calls someFunction(void)
someFunction(intVariable1); // calls  someFunction(int)
someFunction(doubleVariable);// calls someFunction(double)
```

```
someFunction(intVariable1, intVariable2); // calls
                           // someFunction(int, int)

// this works for constants as well
someFunction(1);          // calls  someFunction(int)
someFunction(1.0);        // calls  someFunction(double)
someFunction(1, 2);       // calls  someFunction(int, int)
```

In each case, the type of arguments used matches the extended names of the three functions.

WARNING

The `return` type isn't part of the extended name of the function. The following two functions have the same name, so they can't be part of the same program:

```
int someFunction(int n);    // full name of the function
                            // is someFunction(int)
double someFunction(int n); // same name
long l = someFunction(10);  // call which function?
```

Here, C++ doesn't know whether to convert the value returned from the `double` version of `someFunction()` to a `long` or promote the value returned from the `int` version.

The `PizzaSizer` program assumes that a pizza is round and, thus, when calculating the area, the argument is a diameter. Some pizzerias, however, offer a rectangular pizza. To calculate the area of a rectangular pizza would require a different function. Because this function would need two arguments (a width and a length), you can simply overload the `determinePizzaArea()` function. The following function can be added to the previous listing:

```
int determinePizzaArea( int nWidth, int nLength )
{
   int nPizzaSize = nWidth * nLength;
   return nPizzaSize;
}
```

The program calls the correct function based on how many integers are passed to it: one or two. If the `determinePizzaArea()` function is called with one integer, the pizza is assumed to be round. If it's called with two integers, it's assumed to be rectangular.

Defining Function Prototypes

A function must be declared before it can be used. That's so that C++ can compare the call against the declaration to make sure that any necessary conversions are performed. However, a function doesn't have to be defined when it's first declared. A function may be defined anywhere in the C++ source file.

Consider the following code snippet:

```
int main()
{
    someFunc(1, 2);
}
int someFunc(double dArg1, int nArg2)
{
    // ...do something
}
```

Because `main()` comes first in the listing, it doesn't know the proper argument types of the function `someFunc()` at the time of the call. C++ might surmise from the call that the full function definition is `someFunc(int, int)` and that its return type is `void`; however, the definition of the function that appears immediately after `main()` shows that the programmer wants the first argument converted to a floating-point and that the function does actually return a value.

Yes, I know: C++ could be less lazy and look ahead to determine the extended name of `someFunc()` on its own, but it doesn't. What's needed is some way to inform `main()` of the full name of `someFunc()` before it's used. This is handled by what's called a *function prototype* declaration.

A prototype declaration appears the same as a function with no body. In use, a prototype declaration looks like this:

```
int someFunc(double, int);

int main()
{
    someFunc(1, 2);
}
int someFunc(double dArg1, int nArg2)
{
    // ...do something
}
```

The prototype declaration tells the world (at least that part of the world after the declaration) that the extended name for someFunc() is someFunction(double, int). The call in main() now knows to convert (cast) the 1 to a double before making the call. In addition, main() knows that someFunc() returns an int value to the caller.

It's common practice to include function prototypes for every function in a listing, either at the beginning of the listing or, more often, in a separate file that can be included within other listings at compile-time. That's the function of the #include statements that appear at the beginning of the Official *C++ For Dummies* program template:

```
#include <iostream>
#include <print>
```

These two files, iostream and print, include prototype declarations for the common system functions that I've been using, such as cout << "string". The contents of these files are inserted at the point of the #include statement by the compiler as part of its normal duties. Chapter 11 is dedicated to include files and other preprocessor commands.

Figure 7-1 helps summarize some of the function terminology I use. Don't worry: This is a book, so you don't have to take a pop quiz. Technically speaking, function arguments are the values passed to a function, whereas function parameters are the variables used in a function's signature, although, having said that, many developers use these terms interchangeably. Now if you're hit with a pop quiz on functions, you'll have the answer to at least one question.

```
int function(int, int);

int functionName(int val1, int val2)
{
  // function body
   return val1 + val2;
}
int main()
{
  int retValue = 0;
  retValue = functionName(10, 20);

  return 0;
}
```

Function prototype
Function parameters
Function definition
Passing values
Calling the function
Function arguments

FIGURE 7-1: All about functions.

Defaulting Arguments

You can provide default values for arguments in your function declaration. Consider the following simple example:

```
// isLegal - return true if the age is greater
//           than or equal to the minimum age
//           which defaults to 21
bool isLegal(int age, int minAge = 21)
{
    return age >= minAge;
}
```

This function returns `true` if the first argument passed (`age`) is greater than the second argument, `minAge`, and the second argument defaults to `21` if you don't say otherwise in the function call. Thus, the following calls are both legal:

```
legal = isLegal(age); // same as isLegal(age, 21)
if (inLouisiana())
{
    legal = isLegal(age, 18);
}
```

The call `isLegal(age)` is completely equivalent to `isLegal(age, 21)`. C++ just provides the default argument for you. The call to `isLegal(age, 18)` ignores the default value.

TIP

Normally, the defaults are provided in the prototype declarations.

You can default more than one argument, but defaults must be defined from right to left and filled in from left to right:

```
// the following is legal
bool isWorkingAge(int age, int minAge=18, int maxAge=65);

// check if the worker is between 18 and 65
legal = isWorkingAge(age);

// check if worker is between 21 and 65
legal = isWorkingAge(age, 21);

// check if work is between 21 and 60
legal = isWorkingAge(age, 21, 60);
```

```
// the following does NOT check if the worker is
// between 18 and 60
legal = isWorkingAge(age, 60);
```

The first call uses the default values for both the minimum and maximum age (18 and 65, respectively). The second call uses the default maximum age of 65 but supplies a different minimum age of 21. The third call provides an explicit minimum age as well as a maximum one.

WARNING

The last call doesn't check to see whether the age is between 18 and 60, as you might expect. In this case, the call is made with a minimum age of 60 and a maximum age of 65.

WARNING

Default arguments can sometimes confuse C++ when combined with function overloading. For example, the following snippet isn't legal:

```
bool isLegal(int age);
bool isLegal(int age, int minAge = 21); // not allowed
```

The problem is that if you called `isLegal(10)`, C++ wouldn't know which one of the two functions to call: the first function with just one argument or the second function with the second argument defaulted.

Passing by Value and Passing by Reference

C++ normally passes arguments to functions by value. That is, if you call a function `fn(n)`, it's the value of `n` that gets passed to the function. This allows you to make calls like the following:

```
fn(a + b);     // pass the value of a + b
```

What gets passed in this snippet is the result of the expression `a + b`.

This has perhaps a surprising side effect, demonstrated by the following snippet:

```
#include <print>

void multiplyByTwo(int m)
{
    m *= 2;
}
```

```
int main()
{
    int n = 1;
    multiplyByTwo(n);

    std::print("n = {}", n);
}
```

You may be surprised to find out that this example prints out *n = 1*.

Let's walk through the example one step at a time:

1. The main program declares the variable `n` and initializes it to `1`.
2. The program then passes the value of `n (1)` to the function `multiplyByTwo()` and calls it `m`.
3. The function multiplies the value passed to it by two and stores the result in the local variable, `m`.
4. The `multiplyByTwo()` function discards `m` upon returning.
5. The main program displays the unchanged value of `n (1)`.

TIP

This is called *pass by value* — the alternative is called *pass by reference*.

You can tell C++ that you want to pass not the value of a variable but rather a reference to a variable by adding an ampersand (&) to the type, as in the following snippet:

```
#include <print>
void multiplyByTwo(int&m) // referential argument
{
    m *= 2;
}

int main()
{
    int n = 1;
    multiplyByTwo(n);

    std::print("n = {}", n);
}
```

This example does the following:

1. The main program declares the variable n and initializes it to 1.
2. The program then passes a reference to n to the function multiplyByTwo(), which calls that reference m.
3. The function multiplies by two the variable referenced by m and saves the results back into the variable referenced by m (in other words, the variable n).
4. The main program displays the changed value of n (2).

REMEMBER

Passing by value passes a copy of the value, so the function is changing a copy, not the original. *Passing by reference* passes a reference to the original variable, so the original variable's value is getting changed. I have much more to say about reference arguments in Chapter 9.

Understanding a Variable's Visibility

How visible variables are depends on where and how they're defined in a program or function, as shown in the following example:

```
int globalVariable;
void fn()
{
    int localVariable;
    static int staticVariable = 1;
}
```

Variables declared within a function like localVariable are said to be *local* because they are defined within the current (local) function. The variable localVariable doesn't exist until execution passes through its declaration within the function fn(); localVariable ceases to exist when the function returns. Upon return, whatever value is stored in localVariable is lost. In addition, only fn() has access to localVariable — other functions cannot reach into the function to access it.

By comparison, the variable globalVariable is created when the program begins execution and exists as long as the program is running. All functions have access to globalVariable all the time.

The keyword static can be used to create something between a global and local variable. The static variable staticVariable is created when execution reaches the declaration the first time that function fn() is called, just like a local variable. However, the static variable isn't destroyed when program execution returns from the function. Instead, it retains its value from one call to the next. If fn() assigns a value to staticVariable once, it's still there the next time fn() is called. The initialization portion of the declaration is ignored every subsequent time execution passes through.

REMEMBER

This visibility of variables based on when they're declared is called the variable's *scope*.

Another level of visibility is a more limited version of local. A variable can be declared within a loop, such as in this example:

```
for (int ctr; ctr < 10; ctr++)
{
    // do something
}
```

In this case, the variable ctr is declared when the for loop starts and goes away after the for loop has ended.

Benefiting from Functions

Earlier in this chapter, I spend some time extolling the benefits of functions. One benefit worth mentioning again is that they organize your code and help reduce redundancy. For example, in the PizzaSizer program, the user is asked for the size of a pizza two times. By using a function, the code for this was included only once. You might be thinking, "But wait — that code was only about nine lines long, so it really didn't save much.

Yes, the function was short, but not all functions are that short. More importantly, however, you might find that you need to change the function. In fact, you do need to improve the getPizzaSize() function because, although it works well if the user enters an integer, it goes crazy if you enter a word or a floating-point number.

Another benefit of a function is that you only need to update the function to fix the problem, no matter how many times it was used. In this case, you should update the getPizzaSize() function so that it looks like the following:

```
// Ask user for pizza size (diameter)
int getPizzaSize(const std::string sizeText)
{
```

```
    int nSize = 0;
    do{
        std::println("Enter the size (diameter) of a {} pizza.",
    sizeText);
        std::print  ("Valid sizes are from 2 to 32 inches: ");
        std::cin >> nSize;
        std::cin.clear();                    // Reset any error flags
        std::cin.ignore(1000, '\n');  // Ignore invalid input
                                             // characters
    } while (nSize < 2 || nSize > 32);

    return nSize;
}
```

This update now uses a `do...while` loop to ensure that the pizza size is realistic (between 2 and 32 inches). It also clears any invalid information that's entered. The result of this change is a much better user experience with the program. And because a function was used, you had to change the code in only one place to gain all the added benefits.

IN THIS CHAPTER

» Considering the need for an array

» Introducing the array data type

» Using the most common type of array: the character string

» Figuring out how to avoid overflowing your buffers

Chapter 8
Grouping Similar Things Together Using Arrays

An *array* is a sequence of variables that share the same name and that is referenced using an index. Arrays are useful little critters that allow you to store a large number of values of the same type that are related in some way — for example, the batting averages of all the players on the same team might be a good candidate for storage within an array. Arrays can be multidimensional, too, allowing you, for example, to store an array of batting averages within an array of months, which allows you to work with the batting averages of the team as they occur by month.

In this chapter, you find out how to initialize and use arrays for fun and profit. You also find out about an especially useful form of array called a *char string.*

REMEMBER

So that you aren't surprised later, a few of the concepts I discuss in this chapter have been made easier with library functions provided by the C++ standard over the years. Because those improvements tap into more advanced features of C++, you can learn about those improvements later in this book. It's important, however, to understand how arrays work, so in this chapter, you get a raw look at arrays.

Making the Case for Arrays

Consider the following problem. You need a program that can read a sequence of numbers from the keyboard and display their sum. (You guessed it — the program stops reading in numbers as soon as you enter a negative number.) However, unlike similar programs I talk about in Chapter 6, the program I have in mind keeps track of the entered numbers and outputs all of them before displaying the average.

You can try to store numbers in a set of independent variables, as in:

```
cin >> value1;
if (value1 >= 0)
{
   cin >> value2;
   if (value2 >= 0)
   {
      ...
```

You can see that this approach can't handle sequences involving more than just a few numbers. Besides, it's ugly. What you need is a structure that has a name like a variable but that can store more than one value. May I present to you: the array.

An array solves the problem of sequences nicely.

You can define an array similarly to how you define a variable. Array declarations begin with the type of the array members, followed by the name of the array. The last parts of an array declaration are open and close brackets containing the maximum number of elements the array can hold. The following example shows a standard integer variable being declared as well as an array that can hold 128 integers:

```
int nValue;             // This holds one int
int nValueArray[128];   // This holds 128 ints
```

You access an individual element of an array by providing the name of the array, followed by brackets containing the index. The first integer in the array is `nValuearray[0]`, the second is `nValueArray[1]`, and so on. Let me repeat, and even include a picture (see Figure 8-1), to make this point clear; the index starts with 0 (not 1).

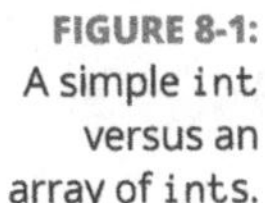

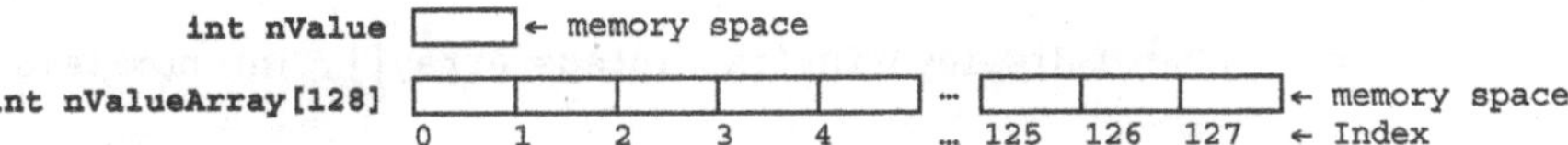

FIGURE 8-1: A simple int versus an array of ints.

So, to access the first item in an array, you'd use an index of 0. The following line assigns a value to the first item in nValueArray:

```
nValueArray[0] = 42;
```

Because I indicated that the array indexes start at 0, the last item in the array will have an index of 1 less than the total number, which in this case would be 127: nValueArray[127].

WARNING

Two common mistakes that beginning C++ programmers make are: thinking that an array starts at 1 rather than 0; and using the number of items in the array as the last index, such as using 128 as the index instead of 128 – 1, which is 127. When you make either of these mistakes, picture me telling you, "I told you so!"

In use, nValueArray[i] represents the ith element in the array. The index variable i must be a counting variable — that is, i must be a char, an int, or a long. If nValueArray is an array of ints, nValueArray[i] is an int.

Using an Array

Of course, the easiest way to understand an array is to show an example. Using a basic array, the following program inputs a sequence of integer values from the keyboard until the user enters a negative number. The program then displays the numbers entered and reports their sum.

REMEMBER

This listing taps into topics covered earlier, including using functions to organize the code.

```
// ArrayDemo - demonstrate the use of arrays
//             by reading a sequence of integers
//             and then displaying them and their sum
#include <iostream>
#include <print>

// prototype declarations
int readArray(int integerArray[], int maxNumElements);
int sumArray(int integerArray[], int numElements);
```

```
void displayArray(int integerArray[], int numElements);

int main()
{
  // input the loop count
  std::println("This program sums values entered by
 the user.");
  std::println("Terminate the loop by entering a negative
 number.");

  // read numbers from the user into a local array
  int inputValues[128];
  int numberOfValues = readArray(inputValues, 128);

  // now output the values and the sum of the values
  displayArray(inputValues, numberOfValues);
  std::println("The sum is {}", sumArray(inputValues,
 numberOfValues));

  return 0;
}

// readArray - read integers from the operator into
//             'integerArray' until operator enters
//             neg. number or the maximum # is reached.
//             Return the number of elements stored.
int readArray(int integerArray[], int maxNumElements)
{
  int numberOfValues = 0;
  while( numberOfValues < maxNumElements )
  {
    // fetch another number
    int integerValue;
    std::print("Enter next number: ");

    std::cin  >> integerValue;
    if (integerValue < 0)  // if it's negative...
    {
      break;               // ...then exit
    }

    // ...otherwise store number in array
    integerArray[numberOfValues] = integerValue;
    numberOfValues++;  // Add 1 to our count of values.
  }
```

```
    // return the number of elements read
    return numberOfValues;
}

// displayArray - display the members of an
//                array of length sizeOfloatArray
void displayArray(int integerArray[], int numElements)
{
    std::println("The values in the array: ");
    for (int i = 0; i < numElements; i++)
    {
        std::println("{}: {}", i, integerArray[i]);
    }
}

// sumArray - return the sum of the members of an
//            integer array
int sumArray(int integerArray[], int numElements)
{
    int accumulator = 0;
    for (int i = 0; i < numElements; i++)
    {
        accumulator += integerArray[i];
    }
    return accumulator;
}
```

The program ArrayDemo begins with prototype declarations of the functions readArray(), sumArray(), and displayArray(), which it will need later. Prototypes provide an idea of the format of a function and are covered in more detail in Chapter 7. The main program starts with a prompt for the user to enter data to be summed.

The program then declares an array inputValues[] to be used to store the values entered by the user. The main program passes this array to readArray(), along with the length of the array.

REMEMBER

You don't want readArray() to read more than 128 values, even if the user doesn't enter a negative number, because that's all the room allocated in the inputValues[] array.

WARNING

The array inputValues is declared as 128 integers long — if you're thinking that this number must be more than enough, don't count on it. No matter how large you make the array, always check to make sure that you don't exceed the limits of the array. Writing more data than an array can hold causes your program to perform erratically and, often, to crash. The main function then calls `displayArray()` to print the contents of the array. Finally, the function calls `sumArray()` to add the elements in the array.

The `readArray()` function takes two arguments: the `integerArray[]` into which to store the values it reads, and `maxNumElements`, the maximum number of integer values for which there's room at the inn. The function begins with a `while` loop that reads integer values. Every non-negative value the function reads is saved into `integerArray[]`. The first element goes into `integerArray[0]`, the second into `integerArray[1]`, and so forth. Each time a value is read, the `numberOfValues` variable is incremented to keep count.

The program reads values until the maximum number of values (`maxNumElements`) has been read or until the user enters a negative number, at which point the program breaks out of the loop. Either way, the function then returns the total `numberOfValues` input.

The `displayArray()` function uses a `for` loop to traverse the elements of the array, starting at 0 and continuing to the last element, which is `numElements - 1`. The final function, `sumArray()`, also iterates through the array but sums the elements stored there into `accumulator`, which it then returns to the caller.

Notice that the index `i` in the `displayArray()` and `sumArray()` functions is initialized to `0` and not to `1`. In addition, notice how the `for` loop terminates as soon as `i` reaches `numElements`. The output from a sample run appears as follows:

```
This program sums values entered by the user
Terminate the loop by entering a negative number
Enter next number: 10
Enter next number: 20
Enter next number: 30
Enter next number: 40
Enter next number: -1
The values in the array:
0: 10
1: 20
2: 30
3: 40
The sum is 100
```

REMEMBER

Just to keep nonprogrammers guessing, the term *iterate* means to traverse through a set of objects, such as an array. Programmers say that the preceding functions iterate through the array.

OH, NO — MY PROGRAM HAS GONE CRAZY!

If you enter values other than numbers into the ArrayDemo listing, you'll likely find that the program will act erratically. It might simply put 0s in all the array elements, or the program might launch into an infinite loop that never stops until you close the output window. I talk more about error handling and other features that help prevent errors from happening in Chapter 27, but for now, you should know that, as a programmer, part of your job is to expect the unexpected. Don't assume that users of your programs will do exactly as you ask them to do — sometimes users do crazy things. You must be prepared so that only the users, and not your programs, are doing crazy things.

If you want to remove some of the craziness from your listing, you can replace the following line in your `readArrays()` function:

```
std::cin  >> integerValue;
```

with the following code:

```
while (!(std::cin >> integerValue)) { // Check if input fails
    std::cin.clear();  // Clear error flag
    std::cin.ignore(1000, '\n'); // Discard bad input
    std::print("Bad input. Please enter an integer: ");
}
```

This code helps ignore any bad (invalid) values entered.

Initializing an array

A local variable doesn't start life with a valid value, not even the value 0. Put another way, a local variable contains garbage until you actually store something in it. Locally declared arrays are the same — each element contains garbage until you assign something to it. Though you should always initialize local variables when you declare them, this rule is even more true for arrays. It's far too easy to overlook initializing the elements of array and then use those elements thinking that they contain valid values (when they don't).

By *local variable*, I mean the normal variables declared within a function. C++ purists call them *automatic variables* to differentiate them from static variables. (For more on this topic, see Chapter 20.)

Fortunately, a small array can be initialized at the time it's declared with an initializer list. The following code snippet demonstrates how to do this:

```
float floatArray[5] = {0.0, 1.0, 2.0, 3.0, 4.0};
```

This line initializes `floatArray[0]` to `0`, `floatArray[1]` to `1.0`, `floatArray[2]` to `2.0`, and so on.

C++ pads the initialization list with 0s if the number of elements in the list is less than the size of the array. In fact, an empty initializer list can be used to initialize an array to 0:

```
int nArray[128] = {}; // initialize array to all 0's
```

The number of initialization constants can determine the size of the array. For example, you (and your C++ compiler) could have determined that `floatArray` has five elements just by counting the values within the braces. C++ can count as well (here's at least one thing C++ can do for itself):

```
float floatArray[] = {0.0, 1.0, 2.0, 3.0, 4.0};
```

Accessing too far into an array

Mathematicians start counting arrays with 1. Most programming languages start with an offset of 1 as well. C++ arrays begin counting at 0. The first member of a C++ array is `valueArray[0]`. That makes the last element of a 128-integer array `integerArray[127]` and not `integerArray[128]`.

Unfortunately for the programmer, C++ doesn't check to see whether the index you're using is within the range of the array. C++ is perfectly happy giving you access to `integerArray[200]`. The `integerArray` yard is only 128 integers long — 200 is 72 integers into someone else's yard. No telling who lives there and what is stored at that location. Reading from `integerArray[200]` returns some unknown and unpredictable value. Writing to that location generates unpredictable results. It may do nothing — the house may be abandoned and the yard unused. On the other hand, it might overwrite some data, thereby confusing the neighbor and making the program act in a seemingly random fashion. Or it might crash the program.

WARNING

The most common wrong way to access an array is to read or write location `integerArray[128]`. Although it's only one element beyond the end of the array, reading or writing this location is just as dangerous as using any other incorrect address.

Arraying range-based for loops

You can iterate through an array using a range-based `for` loop. A range-based `for` loop automatically determines the size of the array (the range), which makes working with the array simpler. The following `for` loop initializes all elements of `nArray` to `0`:

```
int nArray[128];
for(int& n: nArray)
{
    n = 0;
}
```

This loop assigns the variable `n` of type `int` to be a reference to each element of `nArray` in turn. Because `n` is created as a reference (notice the `int&` instead of just `int`), modifying `n` directly modifies the corresponding element within `nArray`; thus, `0` is assigned to each element in `nArray`. (For more on references, see Chapter 7.)

WARNING

Take a look at the following snippet. Do you see what is different? The following range-based `for` loop has no effect:

```
int nArray[128];
for(int n: nArray)
{
    n = 0;
}
```

Without the ampersand (`&`), `n` is assigned a copy of the value of each element of `nArray` in turn. The variable `n` is then overwritten with a `0`, leaving the value of `nArray` unchanged. Compare this to passing arguments to functions by value versus passing by reference. (Again, see Chapter 7 for a more detailed discussion of how passing works.)

REMEMBER

Range-based `for` loops can be used only where C++ knows the size of the array at build time. A range-based `for` loop would not work within the `displayArray()` function, for example. This function is built to handle arrays of any size. You see strange-looking build-time error messages when you use range-based `for` loops on arrays where the size is unknown.

A safer way to use arrays

C++26 NEW

Templates are covered in the online Bonus Chapter 2, but I'll give you a sneak peek here into how they can help with arrays. Starting with C++20 and continuing to be improved with C++26, the C++ standard library includes a template called span. Using span to reference an array is safer than directly referencing the array. Neither does a span require that you know the size of the array at compile time.

The following listing creates a simple array and assigns five values. A std::span called mySpan is then created. The format of the line might look a little weird:

```
std::span<int> mySpan(myArray);
```

The value in the chevrons (angle brackets: <>) is the type of data the array contains — in this case, the data type is int. The mySpan is treated like a function in this case, and the array (myArray) is passed to it. The result is that you can then use mySpan to access the array in a safer manner — with ranges like the ones I show earlier, for example. Here's a complete listing for printing the value from the array using span:

```
//SpanDemo - Using a Span to print the values from
//           An array
#include <print>
#include <span>

int main()
{
    int myArray[5] = {10, 20, 30, 40, 50};

    // Creates a span referencing the array
    std::span<int> mySpan(myArray);

    // Print the span elements directly
    for (int n : mySpan)
    {
        std::print("{} ", n);
    }
    std::println();  // print a new line
}
```

Though this listing simply prints the values in the array, you can also change the values just like you did earlier, by using a reference. The following listing again uses a span, but this time it updates the array by doubling the value of each element in the array. A second range-based `for` loop is used to show that the original array (`myArray`) was also changed with `span`:

```
//SpanDemo2 - Using a Span to change the values in
//            An array
#include <print>
#include <span>

int main()
{
   int myArray[5] = {10, 20, 30, 40, 50};

   // Creates a span referencing the array
   std::span<int> mySpan(myArray);

   // Print the span elements directly
   for (int& n : mySpan)
   {
       n *= 2;  // double the value of n
      std::print("{} ", n);
   }
   std::println();  // print a new line

   // Show that the original array also changed
   for (int n : myArray)
   {
      std::print("{} ", n);
   }
   std::println();  // print a new line
}
```

The output from running this listing confirms the change:

```
20 40 60 80 100
20 40 60 80 100
```

C++26 NEW

In C++26, an additional update was made to make it even easier to initialize a `span`. This was support for an initializer list, as shown in the following listing, which creates a `span` containing a list of constant integers:

```
#include <print>
#include <span>
using namespace std;
```

```
int main()
{
    // The following line is possible with C++ 26
    span<const int> mySpan {{10, 20, 30, 40, 50}};
    for (int n : mySpan)
    {
        print("{} ", n);
    }
}
```

Here's the simple output from this listing:

```
10 20 30 40 50
```

Telling you about span is a bit of a teaser for what you can learn about in later chapters. After you learn about classes and templates, what span is doing makes much more sense! For now, it's a good idea to understand how basic arrays work, too.

Using Arrays of Characters

The elements of an array can be of any type. Arrays of floats, doubles, and longs are all possible; however, arrays of characters have particular significance.

Creating an array of characters

Human words and sentences can be expressed as an array of characters. An array of characters containing the first name of one of the authors would appear as:

```
char sMyName[] = {'B', 'r', 'a', 'd', 'l', 'e', 'y'};
```

The following small program displays this name:

```
// CharDisplay - output a character array to
//               standard output, the MS-DOS window
#include <print>

// prototype declarations
void displayCharArray(char charArray[], int sizeOfArray);
```

```
int main()
{
   char charMyName[]={'B', 'r', 'a', 'd', 'l', 'e', 'y'};
   displayCharArray(charMyName, 7);
   std::println("");

   return 0;
}
// displayCharArray - display an array of characters
//                    by outputting one character at
//                    a time
void displayCharArray(char charArray[], int sizeOfArray)
{
   for(int i = 0; i < sizeOfArray; i++)
{
   std::print("{}", charArray[i]);
   }
}
```

The program declares a fixed array of characters called charMyName that contains — you guessed it — my name. (What better name could I have chosen?) This array is passed to the displayCharArray() function along with its length. The displayCharArray() function is identical to the displayArray() function in the earlier example program except that this version displays chars rather than ints.

TIP

One thing you can do to make this program work even better for you is to change the name from mine to yours. If you do that, make sure you change the number of characters from seven to whatever matches the number of characters in your name. Then you can make the program about you instead of about me.

As a note, this program works fine; however, as you can see, it's inconvenient to pass the length of the array with the array itself. If there was an easy rule for determining the end of the string of characters, then the length wouldn't need to be passed — you'd know that the string was complete when you encountered the special rule that told you so.

Creating a string of characters

In many cases, all values for each element are possible. However, C++ reserves the special "character" 0 as the noncharacter. You can use '\'\o' to mark the end of a character array. (The numeric value of '\0' is 0, but the type of '\0' is char.)

The character '\y' is the character whose octal value is y. The character '\0' is the character with a value of 0, otherwise known as the null character. Using that rule, the previous small program becomes this:

```
// DisplayString - output a character array to
//                 standard output, the MS-DOS window
#include <print>

// prototype declarations
void displayString(char stringArray[]);

int main()
{
   char charMyName[] =
          {'B', 'r', 'a', 'd', 'l', 'e', 'y', '\0'};
   displayString(charMyName);
   std::println("");

   return 0;
}
// displayString - display a character string
//                 one character at a time
void displayString(char stringArray[])
{
   for(int i = 0; stringArray[i] != '\0'; i++)
   {
       std::print("{}",stringArray[i]);
   }
}
```

The declaration of charMyName declares the character array with the extra null character '\0' at the end. The displayString() function iterates through the character array until a null character is encountered.

The function displayString() is simpler to use than its displayCharArray() predecessor because it's no longer necessary to pass along the length of the character array. This "secret handshake" of terminating a character array with a null is so convenient that it's used throughout the C++ language. C++ even gives such an array a special name.

A *string of characters* is a null-terminated character array. It's officially known as a *null-terminated byte string,* or *NTBS.* The simpler terms *C-style string* or *C string* are also used to differentiate from the C++ type string. You can read about the C++ type string in Chapter 14.

The choice of `'\0'` as the terminating character wasn't random. Remember that `0` is the only numeric value that converts to `false`; all other values translate to `true`. This means that the `for` loop can be (and often is) written as:

```
for(int i = 0; stringArray[i]; i++)
```

This whole business of null-terminated character strings is so ingrained in the C++ language psyche that C++ uses a group of characters surrounded by double quotes to be an array of characters automatically terminated with a `'\0'` character. The following are identical declarations:

```
char szMyName[] = "Bradley";
char szAlsoMyName[] =
   {'B', 'r', 'a', 'd', 'l', 'e', 'y', '\0'};
```

The naming convention used here is exactly that: a convention. C++ doesn't care. The prefix `sz` stands for *zero-terminated string*.

REMEMBER

The string `Bradley` is eight characters long and not seven — the null character after the `n` is assumed. The string `""` is one character long, consisting of just the null character.

Manipulating Strings with Character

The following `Concatenate` program inputs two strings from the keyboard and concatenates them into a single string:

```
// Concatenate - concatenate two strings
//               with a " - " in the middle
#include <iostream>
#include <print>
// Reminder: the following lets us drop std:: in the listing
using namespace std;

// prototype declarations
void concatString(char szTarget[], const char szSource[]);

int main()
{
   // read first string...
   char szString1[256];
   print("Enter string #1: ");
```

```
    cin.getline(szString1, 128);

    // ...now the second string...
    char szString2[128];
    print("Enter string #2: ");
    cin.getline(szString2, 128);

    // ...concatenate a " - " onto the first...
   concatString(szString1, " - ");

    // ...now add the second string...
    concatString(szString1, szString2);

    // ...and display the result
    print("{}", szString1);

    return 0;
}
// concatString - concatenate the szSource string
//                onto the end of the szTarget string
void concatString(char szTarget[], const char szSource[])
{
    // find the end of the first string
    int targetIndex = 0;
    while(szTarget[targetIndex])
    {
        targetIndex++;
    }
    // tack the second onto the end of the first
    int sourceIndex = 0;
    while(szSource[sourceIndex])
    {
        szTarget[targetIndex] =
             szSource[sourceIndex];
        targetIndex++;
        sourceIndex++;
    }
    // tack on the terminating null
    szTarget[targetIndex] = '\0';
}
```

The `Concatenate` program reads two separate character strings and appends them together with a " – " in the middle.

The program begins by reading a string from the keyboard. The program doesn't use the normal `cin >> szString1`, for two reasons. First, the `cin >>` operation stops reading when any bit of white space is encountered. Characters up to the first bit of white space are read, the white space character is tossed, and the remaining characters remain in the input hopper for the next `cin >>` statement. Thus, if you were to enter "the Dog", `szString2` would be filled with the word *the*, and the word *Dog* would remain in the input buffer.

The second reason is that `getline()` allows the programmer to specify the size of the buffer. The call to `getline(szString2, 128)` doesn't read more than 128 bytes, no matter how many are input.

Instead, the call to `getline()` inputs an entire line up to (but not including) the newline character at the end. (I review this function in detail with other file I/O functions in Chapter 26.)

After reading the first string into `szString1[]`, the program appends `" - "` to the end by calling `concatString()`. It concatenates the second string by calling `concatString()` with `szString2[]`.

The `concatString()` function accepts a target string, `szTarget`, and a source string, `szSource`. The function begins by scanning `szTarget` for the terminating null character, which it stores in `targetIndex`. The function then enters a second loop in which it copies characters from the `szSource` into `szTarget`, starting at the terminating null. The final statement in `concatString()` slaps a terminating null on the completed string.

An output example from the program appears as follows:

```
Enter string #1:this is a string
Enter string #2:THIS IS A STRING

this is a string - THIS IS A STRING
```

Defining and Using Arrays of Arrays

Arrays are adept at storing sequences of numbers or other value types. Some applications require sequences of sequences. A classic example of this matrix configuration is the spreadsheet. Laid out like a chessboard, each element in the spreadsheet has both an *x* and a *y* offset.

C++ implements the matrix as follows:

```
int intMatrix[10][5];
```

This matrix is 10 elements in one dimension and 5 in another, for a total of 50 elements. In other words, `intMatrix` is a 10-element array, each element of which is a 5- `int` array. As you might expect, one corner of the matrix is in `intMatrix[0][0]`, and the other corner is `intMatrix[9][4]`.

Whether you consider `intMatrix` to be ten elements long in the *x* dimension or in the *y* dimension is a matter of taste. A matrix can be initialized in the same way as an array:

```
int intAnotherMatrix[2][3] = {{1, 2, 3}, {4, 5, 6}};
```

As shown in Figure 8-2, this line of code initializes the 3-element array `intAnotherMatrix[0]` to `1`, `2`, and `3`, and the 3-element array `intAnotherMatrix[1]` to `4`, `5`, and `6`.

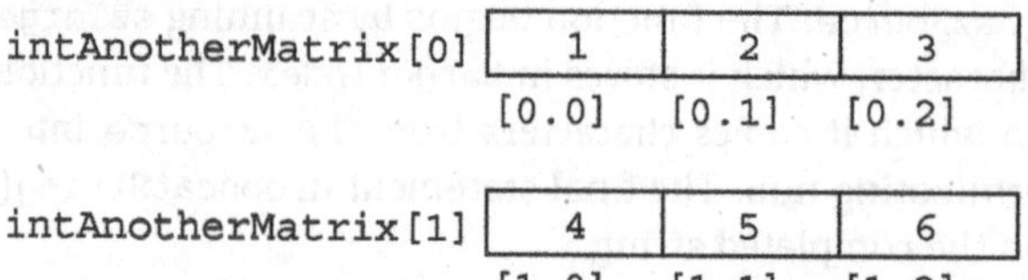

FIGURE 8-2: An array of arrays.

The following simple listing helps illustrate initializing a 2-dimensional array of characters. The program creates a happy little program that uses an array called `smile`. The x-by-8 array is initialized with a bunch of characters, which are then printed:

```
#include <array>
#include <print>
using namespace std;

int main()
{
  char smile[6][8] = {
    {' ', ' ', '-', '-', '-', '-', ' ', ' '},
    {' ', '/', ' ', ' ', ' ', ' ', '\\', ' '},
```

```
    {'|', ' ', '0', ' ', ' ', '0', ' ', '|'},
    {'|', ' ', ' ', ' ', ' ', ' ', ' ', '|'},
    {'|', ' ', '\\', '_', '_', '/', ' ', '|'},
    {' ', '\\', '_', '_', '_', '_', '/', ' '}
  };

  for (const auto& row : smile) {
    for (char ch : row) {
      print("{}", ch);
    }
    println("");
  }
}
```

Note that when this array is printed, you're tapping into C++ to use constants and ranges to do the printing. The first `for` loop pulls each row from the `smile` array and holds it in a variable called `row`. Then a nested loop pulls each character from that row and prints it to the screen. After each row prints, a new line is printed before the outer `for` loop grabs the next row. The resulting output appears to be happy:

```
  ____
 /    \
| 0  0 |
|      |
| \__/ |
 \____/
```

C++23 NEW

You can access arrays using the square brackets after the name, such as `myArray[x][y]`. In C++23, some support was added so that when you create your own types in C++, you can access the multidimensional array using the format of `myArray[x,y]` instead. To do this, you must overload the array operator. (Operator overloading is discussed in Chapter 24.) Starting in C++26, arrays using some standard types also support this comma-separated indexing format.

Using the Array Library Functions

If you have been following along in this chapter, you've seen the special way you can use an array of characters as a string and even write a routine to concatenate two arrays of characters. As part of the learning process, you saw that C++

programmers are often required to manipulate zero-terminated strings. Now for some good news: C++ provides a number of standard string-manipulation functions to make the job easier. A few of these functions are listed in Table 8-1.

TABLE 8-1 String-Handling Functions

Name	Operation
`int strlen(string)`	Returns the number of characters in a string (not including the terminating null)
`char* strcpy(target, source)`	Copies the source string into a target array
`char* strcat(target, source)`	Concatenates the source string onto the end of the target string
`char* strncpy(target, source, n)`	Copies a string up to n characters from the source string into a target array
`char* strncat(target, source, n)`	Concatenates the source string onto the end of the target string or n characters, whichever comes first
`char* strstr(string, pattern)`	Returns the address of the first occurrence of pattern in string; returns a null if pattern isn't found
`int strcmp(source1, source2)`	Compares two strings: returns `-1` if `source1` occurs before `source2` in the dictionary and `1` if later; returns `0` if the two strings match exactly
`int strncmp(source1, source2, n)`	Compares the first n characters in two strings

TIP

You need to add the `#include <cstring>` statement to the beginning of any program that uses a `str...()` function, because this `include` file contains the prototype declarations that C++ requires to check on your work.

WARNING

The arguments to the `str...()` functions appear backward to any reasonable individual. (You might consider this an acid test for what's considered "reasonable.") For example, the function `strcat(target, source)` tacks the second string `source` to the end of the first argument `target`.

The `strncpy()` and `strncat()` functions are similar to their `strcpy()` and `strcat()` counterparts except that they accept the length of the target buffer as one of their arguments. The call `strncpy(szTarget, szSource, 128)` says, "Copy the characters in `szSource` into `szTarget` until you copy a null character or until you've copied 128 characters, whichever comes first." This avoids inadvertently writing beyond the end of the source string array.

And Now the Bad News, Which Is Actually Good News

Learning all about how strings are composed of null-terminated character arrays and how they can be used to work with words might be great fun, but C++ provides a better solution. I can now reveal to you that C++ has a `string` class you can use to work with strings that's safer and more flexible than null-terminated character arrays. Before diving into the C++ `string` and many of its functions, you should learn a bit about classes. As such, Chapter 14 is where you can learn even more about strings.

It's important to understand character array strings — also referred to at times as C-style strings. You find them in lots of legacy C++ code as well as in code that interfaces with C. Additionally, when performance is critical in an application, you might want to use these C-style strings to avoid extra overhead that the C++ string class could add. Finally, if you're writing solutions where memory is critical, such as with embedded systems, then again, the C-style strings mentioned in this chapter will be the most optimized. Having said all of that, most of the time, you'll want to tap into the power, safety, and flexibility of the C++-style strings that I describe in Chapter 14.

Buffer Overflow: Overfilling Your Arrays

Working with character arrays (especially as strings) requires you to be careful. C++ provides great power, but with that power comes great responsibility. Consider the following code:

```
#include <iostream>
#include <print>
using namespace std;

int main()
{
    char name[10];
    print("Enter your name: ");
    cin >> name;

    println("Hello, {}!", name);
    return 0;
}
```

This simple listing sets up an array of characters called name. It is then used to hold a name that the reader enters. When I run the program and enter my name, the output is:

```
Enter your name: Bradley
Hello, Bradley!
```

As you can see, it works well for my name. But what about for someone whose name is longer than 9 characters, such as Christopher, which is 11 characters, and thus needs 12 characters (when you add the null) to store?

Though the program might work, there's a good chance it can cause an error. In fact, it *should* cause an error because you've caused a *buffer overflow* — that is, you've written beyond the end of your array. This error can cause unpredictable results in your program. It also opens your program to hackers who can exploit such an overflow.

REMEMBER

You have to leave one extra byte for the terminating null.

Avoiding buffer overflow

You can avoid buffer overflow risks in a few ways. One is to use the cin.getline() function rather than just cin. With this function, you can pass the maximum size of your buffer to limit how many characters are read in. The updated listing would be:

```
#include <iostream>
#include <print>
using namespace std;

int main()
{
    char name[10];
    print("Enter your name: ");
    cin.getline(name, 10);

    println("Hello, {}!", name);
    return 0;
}
```

You can see that `getline()` gets passed the character array (`name`) to be filled, along with the maximum size (in this case, 10). Of course, to make this even better, you can avoid hard-coding the 10 and instead use the `sizeof()` function to pass the size of your array. The new `getline()` call would be:

```
cin.getline(name, sizeof(name));
```

Now your program is no longer at risk of being hacked by overflowing the buffer!

Checking out a better way to avoid buffer overflow

A better way to avoid buffer overflow is to use the C++ `string` type rather than a character array. The C++ `string` manages memory dynamically for you, so it helps keep your code safer by preventing you from exceeding the buffer size.

I talk more about the `string` type in Chapter 14, but for now, here's a bit of a teaser. You can use `string` in the same way you use other data types. In this case, you'd declare the `name` variable as a string. You will, however, have to change how you get the value as well. Here's another short listing to obtain a person's name:

```
#include <iostream>
#include <print>
using namespace std;

int main()
{
    string name;
    print("Enter your name: ");
    getline(cin, name);

    println("Hello, {}!", name);
    return 0;
}
```

This snippet again avoids a buffer overflow. The call to `getline()` says, "Read from `cin` into the string `name` until either a null or an end-of-line is encountered." The size of the buffer in `name` isn't fixed but expands to hold whatever is thrown at it. The result is that this listing handles Christopher just as easily as Bradley.

Making Room for Wide Strings

In Chapter 2, I talk about how wide characters are used for applications that must support foreign languages, where a measly 255 different characters may not be sufficient. The standard C++ library includes similar functions to handle wide character strings. A few of these functions are listed in Table 8-2.

WARNING

Note that these functions are used in lots of legacy code, so I'm sharing them here. There are better methods for working with wide strings, which I cover later in this book.

TABLE 8-2 Wide String-Handling Functions

Name	Operation
int wcslen(string)	Returns the number of wide characters in a string, not including the terminating null
wchar_t wcscpy(target, source)*	Copies the source wide string into a target array
wchar_t wcscat(target, source)*	Concatenates the source wide string onto the end of the target wide string
wchar_t wcsncpy(target, source, n)*	Copies a wide string up to n characters from the source string into a target array
wchar_t wcsncat(target, source, n)*	Concatenates the source string onto the end of the target string or n characters, whichever comes first
wchar_t wcsstr(string, pattern)*	Finds the address of the first occurrence of `pattern` in `string`. Returns a null if `pattern` isn't found
`int wcscmp(source1, source2)`	Compares two wide strings: Returns -1 if `source1` occurs before `source2` in the dictionary and `1` if later; returns `0` if the two strings match exactly
`int wcsncmp(source1, source2, n)`	Compares the first n wide characters in two wide strings

The following snippet shows a wide-character version of the `Concatenate` program:

```
// ConcatenateWide - concatenate two wide strings
//      with a " - " in the middle using library routines
#include <iostream>
#include <print>
using namespace std;
```

```
// prototype declarations
void concatString(char szTarget[], const char szSource[]);

int main()
{
    // read first string...
    wchar_t wszString1[260];
    print("Enter string #1: ");
    wcin.getline(wszString1, 128);

    // ...now the second string...
    wchar_t wszString2[128];
    print("Enter string #2: ");
    wcin.getline(wszString2, 128);

    // now tack the second onto the end of the first
    // with a dash in between
    wcsncat(wszString1, L" - ", 260);
    wcsncat(wszString1, wszString2, 260);

    println("");
    wcout << wszString1 << endl;

    return 0;
}
```

The wide-character string program looks similar to its single-byte character string cousin, except for the following differences:

- Variables are declared `wchar_t` rather than `char`.
- Constant characters and constant strings appear preceded by an L, as in `L"This is a wide string"`.
- The `wcs...()` functions appear in place of the narrow `str...()` functions.

WARNING

The output from `ConcatenateWide` appears identical to that of the `char`-based `Concatenate` program to those of us who do most of their input/output in European languages. The topic of writing programs capable of handling multiple languages with different alphabets and rules of grammar is known as *localization* and is beyond the scope of a beginner-level book.

TIP

As I tease earlier in this chapter, I show you that ANSI C++ includes a type `string` designed to make it easier to manipulate strings of text, and also a type `wstring` to work with wide strings. However, these types make use of features of the language that you haven't seen yet. I return to the `string` and `wstring` types in Chapter 14.

IN THIS CHAPTER

» Addressing variables in memory

» Declaring and using pointer variables

» Passing pointers to functions

» Allocating objects off the heap (whatever that is)

» Getting smarter with your pointers

Chapter 9

Taking a First Look at C++ Pointers

As a programming language, C++ truly separates itself from the crowd in its use of pointer variables. A *pointer* is a variable that "points at" other variables. (It's a circular argument, but suspend your disbelief at least until you can dig into this chapter.)

This chapter introduces the pointer variable type. It begins with some concept definitions, flows through raw pointer syntax so that you understand how pointers work, and then introduces some of the standard library smart pointers that help keep your use of pointers cleaner and safer.

To be clear, pointers set C++ apart because they give you the power to poke into, and peek into, the mind of your computer. Okay, computers don't have minds, but they do have memory, and pointers help you to directly manipulate that memory.

Before I jump into pointers, you should understand how things are stored. This involves understanding the use of addresses.

REMEMBER

A POINT ABOUT POINTERS

Pointers are one of the hardest concepts for beginning C++ programmers to understand; however, pointers are one of the most powerful features of C++. When writing programs, many issues (or bugs) are a result of pointers being used in the wrong way. As such, you should read this chapter and run the listings to help you understand the concepts.

Most importantly, even though I make the effort to show you how to create and use raw pointers with the `new` and `delete` commands, you should avoid those whenever possible and use smart pointers instead.

What's in an Address?

Like the saying goes, "Everyone has to be somewhere." Every C++ variable is stored somewhere in the computer's memory. Memory is broken into individual bytes, with each byte carrying its own address, numbered 0, 1, 2, and so on.

A variable called `intReader` might be at address 0x100, whereas `floatReader` might be over at location 0x180. (By convention, memory addresses are expressed in hexadecimal.) Of course, `intReader` and `floatReader` might be somewhere else in memory entirely — only the computer knows for sure and only at the time the program is executed.

This is somewhat analogous to a hotel. When you make your reservation, you may be assigned room 0x100. (I know that suite numbers are normally *not* expressed in hexadecimal, but bear with me.) Your buddy may be assigned 80 doors down in room 0x180. Each variable is assigned an address when it's created. (I have more to say on that topic when I start talking about `scope`, later in this chapter.)

Addressing Address Operators

Two pointer-related operators are shown in Table 9-1. The & operator says, "Tell me your address," and * says, "The value at the following address." Note that *unary* means that the operator impacts only one variable.

TABLE 9-1 **Pointer Operators**

Operator	Meaning
& (unary)	(In an expression) The address of
& (unary)	(In a declaration) Reference to
* (unary)	(In an expression) The thing pointed at by
* (unary)	(In a declaration) Pointer to

WARNING

Do not confuse these operators with the binary & and * operators discussed in Chapters 3 and 5. The following `Layout` program demonstrates using the & operator to access the address of a variable:

```
#include <iostream>
using namespace std;

int main()
{
    int myVar = 42;
    cout << "&myVar = " << &myVar << endl;
}
```

The program declares the variable `myVar`. It then uses `cout` to print the address of `myVar` by applying the & operator. The results of one execution of this program on one of our systems appear as follows:

```
&myVar = 0xc6b01ff6bc
```

REMEMBER

The result is a different address. The absolute address of program variables depends on many factors. The C++ standard certainly doesn't specify how variables are to be laid out in memory.

Using Pointer Variables

A *pointer variable* is a variable that contains an address — usually, the address of another variable. Returning to the analogy of hotel room numbers, one of us might tell his kid that his dad will be in room 0x100 on a trip. The kid can act as a pointer variable of sorts. Anyone can ask at any time, "Where's your father staying?" (Include $5 with that question, and the kid will spill their guts without hesitation.)

The following pseudo-C++ code demonstrates how the two address operators shown in Table 9-1 are used:

```
myKid = &DadsRoom;  // tell myKid dad's room address
room = *myKid;      // Gets the value of dad's room
                    // number from myKid
```

The following C++ code snippet shows these operators used correctly:

```
#include <iostream>
using namespace std;

int main()
{
   int nVar;
   int* pnVar;

   pnVar = &nVar;       // pnVar now points to nVar
   *pnVar = 10;         // stores 10 into the int
}                       // location pointed at by pnVar
```

The `main()` function begins with the declaration of `nVar`. The next statement declares the variable `pnVar` to be a variable of type pointer to an `int`.

Pointer variables are declared like normal variables except for the addition of the unary * character. This * character can appear anywhere between the base type and the name — the following two declarations are equivalent:

```
int* pnVar1;
int *pnVar2;
```

Which one you use is a matter of personal preference.

TIP

In an expression, the unary operator & means "the address of." Thus, you would read the assignment `pnVar = &nVar;` as "pnVar gets the address of nVar."

Passing Pointers to Functions

One common use for pointer variables involves passing arguments to functions. To understand why this is important, you need a solid understanding of how arguments are passed to a function. (I touch on this topic in Chapter 7, but, armed with your new understanding of pointers, you're now in a much better place to understand it.)

Passing by value

By default, arguments are passed to functions by value. This means a copy of what is stored in the argument variable is made. This has the (somewhat) surprising result that changing the value of a variable in a function doesn't normally change its value in the calling function. Consider the following sample code segment:

```
//PassingValues.cpp
#include <print>
using namespace std;

void fn(int nArg)
{
    println("nArg value (start of function): {}", nArg);
    nArg = 10;       // value of nArg at this point is 10
    println("nArg value (end of function: {}", nArg);
}
int main()
{
    int n1 = 0;
    println("n1 value (before function): {}", n1);
    fn(n1);
    println("n1 value (after function): {}", n1);
    // value of n1 at this point is still 0}
}
```

Here, the `main()` function initializes the integer variable `n1` to `0`. The value of `n1` is then passed to `fn()`. Upon entering the function, `nArg` is equal to `0` — the value passed. The `fn()` function changes the value of `nArg` to `10` before returning to `main()`. Upon returning to `main()`, the value of `n1` is still `0`. This is the output you see:

```
n1 value (before calling function): 0
nArg value (start of function): 0
nArg value (end of function): 10
n1 value (after function): 0
```

The reason for this behavior is that C++ doesn't pass a variable to a function. Instead, C++ passes a copy of the value contained in the variable at the time of the call. That is, the expression is evaluated, even if it's just a variable name, and the result is passed.

TECHNICAL STUFF

You might think that you can change nArg to be n1 as well. Though you could do that, the n1 in the fn() function would be a completely different variable from the n1 in the main() function. As such, the results would still be the same — a copy of the value would be sent to the function, and the variable in main() would remain unchanged. Try it to see for yourself.

Passing pointer values

Like any other intrinsic type, a pointer may be passed as an argument to a function:

```
//PassingPointers.cpp
#include <print>

void fn(int* pnArg)  // pnArg is a pointer to an int
{
  *pnArg = 10;
}
int main()
{
    int n = 0;
    fn(&n);          // this passes the address of n
                     // now the value of n is 10
    std::println("n after calling function: {}", n );
}
```

In this case, within main(), you can see that the address of n, rather than the value of n, is passed to the fn() function. The significance of this difference is apparent when you consider the assignment within fn().

Suppose that n is located at address 0x100. Rather than the value 10, the call fn(&n) passes the value 0x100. Within fn(), the assignment *pnArg = 10 stores the value 10 in the int variable located at location 0x100, thereby overwriting the value 0. Upon returning to main(), the value of n is 10 because n is just another name for 0x100.

WARNING

Be careful: In fn(), you must remember that you're working with a pointer and that pnArg is an address to a variable. If you try to assign 10 to pnArg without the *, you're trying to change the address rather than the value of n. The compiler helps you avoid this mistake by pointing out (no pun intended) that you're trying to convert from an int to an int *.

Passing by reference

C++ provides a shorthand strategy for passing arguments by address — shorthand that enables you to avoid the hassle that comes with pointers. The following declaration creates a variable `n1` as well as a second reference to the same `n1` but with a new name, `nRef`:

```
int n1;               // declare an int variable
int& nRef = n1;       // declare a second reference to n1

nRef = 1;             // now accessing the reference
                      // has same effect as accessing n1;
                      // n1 is now equal to 1
```

REMEMBER

A reference variable like `nRef` must be initialized when it's declared, because every subsequent time its name is used, C++ assumes that you mean the variable `nRef` refers to.

Reference variables find their primary application in function calls:

```
//PassingReference.cpp
#include <print>

void fn(int& rnArg)// declare reference argument
{
   rnArg = 10;     // change the value of the variable...
}                  //...that rnArg refers to
int main()
{
   int n1 = 0;
   fn(n1);           // pass a reference to n1
                     // here the value of n1 is 10
   std::println("n1 after calling function: {}", n1);
}
```

This is called *passing by reference*. The declaration `int& rnArg` declares `rnArg` to be a reference to an integer argument. The `fn()` function stores the value `10` into the `int` location referenced by `rnArg`.

TIP

Passing by reference is the same as passing the address of a variable. The reference syntax puts the onus on C++ to apply the "address of" operator to the reference instead of requiring the programmer to do so.

WARNING

You cannot overload a pass by value function with its pass by reference equivalent. Thus, you could not define the two functions fn(int) and fn(int&) in the same program. C++ wouldn't know which one to call.

Constant const Irritation

The const keyword means that a variable cannot be changed after it has been declared and initialized:

```
const double PI = 3.1415926535;
```

Arguments to functions can also be declared const, meaning that the argument cannot be changed within the function. C++ also includes a constexpr (see Chapter 11), which also declares variables that can't be changed, but differs in that the variable is evaluated at compile time, which saves processing time when the program is run. For a value like pi (π) — one that is defined and never changes — constexpr would be better, but const also works.

This use of const and constexpr introduces an interesting dichotomy in the case of pointer variables. Consider the following declaration:

```
const int* pInt;
```

Exactly what is the constant here? What can't be changed? Is it the variable pInt or the integer pointed at by pInt?

It turns out that both are possible, but this declaration declares a variable pointer to a constant memory location. Thus, you see the following:

```
const int* pInt;      // declare a pointer to a const int
int nVar;
pInt = &nVar;         // this is allowed
*pInt = 10;           // but this is not
```

You can change the value of pInt, for example, by assigning it the address of nVar. But the final assignment in the snippet example generates a compiler error because you cannot change the value of the const int pointed at by pInt.

What if you had intended to create a pointer variable with a constant value? The following snippet shows this in action:

EVALUATING CONST PLACEMENT

Is it a constant value or a constant pointer? A technique that helps keep them straight is to remember that const (and thus also constexpr) placement is evaluated from right to left:

- const int* pVar: This is a pointer to const data.
- int* const pVar: This is a const pointer to data.
- const int* const pVar: This is a const pointer to const data.

```
int nVar;
int * const cpInt = &nVar;  // declare a constant pointer
                            // to a variable integer
*cpInt = 10;                // now this is legal...
cpInt++;                    // ...but this is not
```

The variable cpInt is a constant pointer to a variable int. The programmer cannot change the value of the pointer (said differently, they can't change what is pointed to), but *can* change the value of the integer pointed at.

The const-ness I'm talking about here can be added via an assignment or initialization, but cannot be (readily) changed. Thus, the following code shows what is legal and what is not:

```
int nVar = 10;
int* pVar = &nVar;
const int* pcVar = pVar;    // this is legal
int* pVar2 = pcVar;         // this is not
```

The assignment pcVar = pVar; is okay — this is adding the const restriction. The final assignment in the snippet isn't allowed, because it attempts to remove the const-ness restriction of pcVar.

A variable can be implicitly recast as part of a function call, as in the following example:

```
void fn(const int& nVar)
{
   // do something
}
```

```
int main()
{
    int n;

    fn(10);    // calls fn(const int&)
    fn(n);     // calls the same function by treating n
}              // as if it were const
```

The declaration `fn(const int&)` says that the `fn()` function doesn't modify the value of its argument. That's important when passing a reference to the constant `10`. It isn't important when passing a reference to the variable `n`, but it doesn't hurt anything, either.

Finally, `const` can be used to discriminate between functions of the same name. It's a valid function overload to have the only difference be the inclusion of `const` on an argument.

Returning a Pointer from a Function

Just as it's possible to pass a pointer to a function, it's possible for a function to return a pointer. A function that returns the address of a `double` is declared as follows:

```
double* fn(void);
```

However, you must be careful when returning a pointer. To understand the dangers, you must know something about variable scope. (No, I don't mean a variable zoom rifle scope.)

Defining limited scope

Besides being a mouthwash, scope is the range over which a variable is defined. Consider the following code snippet:

```
int intGlobal;          // Variable has global scope

void child(void)
{
    int intChild;       // Variable has function scope
}
```

```
void parent(void)
{
    int intParent = 0;  // Variable has function scope
    child();

    int intLater = 0;
    intParent = intLater;
}
int main()
{
    parent();
}
```

This program fragment starts with the declaration of a variable, `intGlobal`. This variable exists from the time the program begins executing until it terminates. I say that `intGlobal` "has program scope." I also say that the variable "goes into scope" even before the `main()` function is called.

The `main()` function immediately invokes `parent()`. The first thing the processor sees in `parent()` is the declaration of `intParent`. At that point, `intParent` goes into scope — that is, `intParent` is defined and available for the remainder of the `parent()` function.

The second statement in `parent()` is the call to `child()`. Once again, the `child()` function declares a local variable — this time, `intChild`. The scope of the `intChild` variable is limited to the `child()` function. Technically, `intParent` isn't defined within the scope of `child()` because `child()` doesn't have access to `intParent`; however, the `intParent` variable continues to exist while `child()` is executing.

When `child()` exits, the `intChild` variable goes out of scope. Not only is `intChild` no longer accessible, it no longer exists. (The memory occupied by `intChild` is returned to the general pool to be used for other operations.)

As `parent()` continues executing, the `intLater` variable goes into scope at the declaration. At the point that `parent()` returns to `main()`, both `intParent` and `intLater` go out of scope.

Because `intGlobal` is declared globally in this example, it's available to all three functions and remains available for the life of the program.

Examining the scope problem

The following code segment compiles without error but doesn't work (don't you just hate that?):

```
double* child(void)
{
   double dLocalVariable = 13;
   return &dLocalVariable;
}
void parent(void)
{
   double* pdLocal;
   pdLocal  = child();
   *pdLocal = 1.0;
}
```

In this particular case, a "good" compiler won't display an error but should give a warning that the address of a local variable is being returned. The problem with this function is that `dLocalVariable` is defined only within the scope of the `child()` function. Thus, by the time the memory address of `dLocalVariable` is returned from `child()`, it refers to a variable that no longer exists. The memory that `dLocalVariable` formerly occupied is probably being used for something else.

WARNING

This error is quite common because it can creep up in many ways. Unfortunately, this error doesn't cause the program to instantly stop. In fact, the program may work fine most of the time — that is, the program continues to work as long as the memory formerly occupied by `dLocalVariable` isn't reused immediately. Such intermittent problems are the most difficult ones to solve.

Using Pointers and Allocating Memory for Variables

Variables, like many things in our world, take up space. With C++, declaring a variable means that space will be set aside for them. (Trust me on that.) What happens, however, when you don't know how many variables you need? For example, you might ask for the grades of students in a class. This would be something to create in an array of integers, but how many student grade variables would you need to have stored in the array of integers? It can be around 30 if you're working with an elementary school class. If, however, you're working with a college class, the number of students might be in the hundreds. An online course can possibly have thousands. You don't want to set up an array to hold thousands of integers if all you need are 30. Sometimes you need to be able to set aside memory dynamically at runtime to adjust to such unknowns.

Enter the heap! The *heap* is an amorphous block of memory that your program can access as necessary. Variables can be created dynamically in the heap, and a pointer can be used to point to where they're located. The caveat, however, is that if your program uses memory from the heap, it must let the computer know when it's done with it.

In the upcoming sections, I walk you through the modern way to allocate memory from the heap using smart pointers. One of the core benefits of smart pointers is that they take care of allocating and freeing memory for you. There's an older way to allocate memory as well — by using what's referred to as *raw* pointers, similar to what I used previously in this chapter. Because you will come across raw pointers in older programs, I cover them after smart pointers, so you are aware of how they operate.

Making Life Safe with Smart Pointers

I mentioned that if you dynamically allocate space for a variable using a pointer, you must remember to return, or free, that space when you're done. If you don't free the space, you risk crashing a computer, because it can eventually run out of free memory to use to run other programs. *Smart* pointers are pointers that not only help you allocate the space but also automatically return the space when you no longer need it. They were designed so that programmers would no longer be forced to remember to free memory.

If you're using a pointer that will be shared, then (starting with C++ 11) `shared_ptr` should be your go-to solution in most cases. To declare a pointer with `shared_ptr`, you use the following syntax:

```
std::shared_ptr<int> pMyPtr;
```

As the code makes quite clear, `shared_ptr` is part of the `std` library. When using `shared_ptr`, you need to indicate the data type that will be used with the pointer. The type is stated between angle brackets (`<>`). In this example, the type is `int`, and it is then followed by the pointer variable name. From this declaration, you see that `pMyPtr` is a shared pointer that will hold the address of an integer. The following declares a pointer called `pMyString` to a `shared` pointer of type `string`:

```
std::shared_ptr<std::string> pMyString;
```

With the shared pointer declared, you'll want to assign it a value. In this case, you use a unique function called make_shared() to assign the value. This function is also a little different from what you might have seen before, because you include the type in angle brackets following the function name to indicate the type of data being created:

```
pMyPtr = std::make_shared<int>( 42 );
orpMyString = std::make_shared<std::string>("123 My Home
  Address");
```

In the first example, pMyPtr points to a location in memory that is holding an int that has the value of 42. In the second example, pMyString is pointing to a location in memory that holds the text string "123 My Home Address", which is a house address. You can say that pMyString holds the address of an address.

Note that shared pointers are a part of the memory header file. This header file needs to be included in your listings on its own or as part of the std library header.

Chapter 11 covers the use of header files.

Stating the obvious, the helpful aspect of a shared pointer is that you can share it. Take a look at this code as an example:

```
//shared.cpp - using a shared pointer
#include <memory>
#include <print>

int main() {
   std::shared_ptr<int> pMyPtr;          // Declare the
                                         //   shared_ptr
   pMyPtr = std::make_shared<int>(42);   // Assign it a
                                         //   value later
   if( *pMyPtr == 42)
   {
      std::shared_ptr<int> pLife = pMyPtr; // Shared ownership
      std::print("Value of pLife: {}\n", *pLife);
   } // pLife goes out of scope
}  // program ends and pMyPtr goes out of scope
```

In this listing, a pointer is declared and assigned the value of 42, just as was shown previously. Once this is done, an if statement checks to see whether the value stored in pMyPtr is 42. You can see that the pointer is used in exactly the same way a pointer was used earlier.

Because the pointer is pointing to a value of 42, the logic in the if statement is executed, which creates a second pointer. This pointer is assigned a copy of the address of the original pointer and then used to print the value pointed to. Once the if statement ends, this new pointer goes out of scope and is automatically deleted for you. The program then ends, and the original pointer is automatically cleaned up as well.

The result is that this listing is cleaner and safer than using raw pointers. You didn't have to think about the questions "If I delete pLife, will it also delete pMyPtr?" or "Do I have other copies of the pointer being used?" You simply use the pointers and let C++ keep track of cleaning things up.

Pointing to an array

When allocating a shared_ptr, you can allocate only a single object. As such, to declare an array, you must create the array at the same time you declare the pointer. This can be done by using the new keyword followed by information on the array you want to create. For example, the following example creates a shared pointer called pScores that holds an array of integers. The size of the array created is determined by the value stored in nbrOfStudents, which would be a simple int:

```
Int nbrOfStudents = 30;
std::shared_ptr<int[]> pScores(new int[nbrOfStudents]);
```

Keeping your pointer to yourself

Keeping track of a shared pointer has some overhead. Sometimes, you simply need or want a pointer for yourself and don't want the overhead. In these cases, you can use unique_ptr to create a unique pointer that won't be shared. This is declared and assigned in the exact same way, but using unique_ptr and make_unique:

```
std::unique_ptr<int> pMyPtr;
pMyPtr = std::make_unique<int>( 42 );
```

This again creates the pointer and assigns it to point to a location in memory that holds the int value of 45. This time, however, only pMyPtr can use this memory. If you try to copy pMyPtr to another pointer, you get an error: The following line of code, taken from the previous listing, gives an error because pMyPtr is unique:

```
std::shared_ptr<int> pLife = pMyPtr; // Attempting to shared
```

WARNING

Even if you change `pLife` to also be a `unique_ptr`, the listing gives an error; `pMyPtr` is unique, so it can't be shared, because you're keeping it to yourself!

Once you've created `pMyPtr`, you can use it like any other pointer of that type. The following declares the `unique` pointer and then changes the value that's being pointed to:

```
//unique.cpp - using a unique pointer
#include <memory>
#include <print>

int main() {
    std::unique_ptr<int> pMyPtr;
    pMyPtr = std::make_unique<int>(42);
    std::print("Value of pLife: {}\n", *pMyPtr);
    *pMyPtr = 99;
    std::print("Value of pLife is now: {}\n", *pMyPtr);
    *pMyPtr = *pMyPtr + 14;
    std::print("Value of pLife changed to: {}\n", *pMyPtr);
}
```

REMEMBER

Unique pointers (`unique_ptr`) should be used unless you know that you'll be sharing an address. That strategy simply keeps your code cleaner. When you need to share, use the `shared` pointers. A third type of smart pointers, `weak_ptr`, can be used along with `shared_ptr`. A `weak_ptr` is a pointer that's used to observe what is at a `shared_ptr` location. It doesn't copy or manipulate the value being pointed to but can simply view it.

Using New Even Though It's Now Old

Let's step back and now look at the old school way of allocating memory from the heap by using raw pointers.

WARNING

These pointers are considered raw because you must allocate the memory yourself (using the `new` keyword), and when you're done using the memory, you must release it back to the heap (using the `delete` keyword). If you don't return it, there's a chance it will be locked up, even after your program ends. If you lock up too much memory, you can crash the computer.

The following line allocates a raw pointer to a double called pdLocalVariable on the heap:

```
double* pdLocalVariable = new double;
```

The space is using the new keyword followed by the type of object you plan to allocate. The new command breaks off the heap a chunk of memory big enough to hold the specified type of object and returns its address. For example, the following code snippet allocates memory that can hold a double variable off the heap:

```
double* child(void)
{
    double* pdLocalVariable = new double;
    return pdLocalVariable;
}
```

Although the pdLocalVariable variable goes out of scope when the child() function returns, the memory to which pdLocalVariable refers does not. A memory location returned by new doesn't go out of scope until it's explicitly returned to the heap using the keyword delete, which is specifically designed for that purpose:

```
void parent(void)
{
    // child() returns the address of a block
    // of heap memory
    double* pdMyDouble = child();

    // store a value there
    *pdMyDouble = 1.1;

    // ...

    // now return the memory to the heap
    delete pdMyDouble;
    // Reassign pdMyDouble to avoid dangling references:
    pdMyDouble = std::nullptr;  // safer than saying = 0

    // ...
}
```

Here, the pointer returned by child() is used to store a double value. After the function is finished with the memory location, it's returned to the heap. The parent() function sets the pointer to the keyword nullptr after the heap memory has been returned. (Setting the pointer to `nullptr` is a way to indicate that a pointer points to nothing. This isn't a requirement but is definitely an excellent idea.) If the programmer mistakenly attempts to store something in `* pdMyDouble` after the `delete`, the program crashes immediately with (I hope) a meaningful error message.

TIP

You can use `new` to allocate arrays from the heap as well, but you must return an array using the `delete[]` keyword.

REMEMBER

While you just learned how to use `new` and `delete` to allocate memory with pointers, you should avoid using them. Be smarter by using smart pointers.

IN THIS CHAPTER

- » Performing arithmetic operations on character pointers
- » Examining the relationship between pointers and arrays
- » Extending pointer operations to various pointer types
- » Using the arguments passed to `main()`

Chapter 10
Taking a Second Look at C++ Pointers

C++ allows programmers to operate on pointer variables much as they would on simple types of variables. (I introduce the concept of pointer variables in Chapter 9.) How and why this is done, along with its implications, are the subjects of this chapter.

Performing Operations on Pointer Variables

Some of the same arithmetic operators I cover in Chapter 3 can be applied to pointer types. This section examines the implications of applying these operators to both pointers and array types. (I discuss arrays in Chapter 8.) Table 10-1 lists the three fundamental operations that are performed on pointers. In Table 10-1, `pointer`, `pointer1`, and `pointer2` are all of some pointer type (say, `char*`), and `offset` is an integer — for example, `long`. C++ also supports the other operators related to addition and subtraction, such as ++ and +=, although they aren't listed in Table 10-1.

TABLE 10-1 **The Three Basic Operations Performed on Pointer Types**

Operation	Result	Meaning
`pointer + offset`	pointer	Calculates the address of the object `offset` entries from `pointer`
`pointer - offset`	pointer	The opposite of addition
`pointer2 - pointer1`	offset	Calculates the number of entries between `pointer2` and `pointer1`

The Neighborhood Memory model is useful to explain how pointer arithmetic works. Consider a city block in which all houses are numbered sequentially, such as the one shown in Figure 10-1. The house at 123 Main Street has 122 Main Street on one side and 124 Main Street on the other.

FIGURE 10-1: Sequential addresses of houses.

Now it's clear that the house four houses down from 123 Main Street must be 127 Main Street; thus, you can say *123 Main + 4 = 127 Main*. Similarly, if you were to ask how many houses there are from 123 Main to 127 Main, the answer would be four: *127 Main − 123 Main = 4*. (Just as an aside, a house is zero houses from itself: *123 Main − 123 Main = 0*.)

But it makes no sense to ask how far away from 123 Main Street is 4 or what the sum of 123 Main and 127 Main is. In a similar fashion, you can't add two addresses. Nor can you multiply an address, divide an address, square an address, or take the square root — you get the idea. You can perform any operation that can be converted to addition or subtraction. For example, if you increment a pointer to 123 Main Street, it now points to the house next door (at 124 Main, of course).

Reexamining arrays in light of pointer variables

Now let us return to the wonderful world of arrays for just a moment. Consider the case of an array of 32 1-byte characters called `charArray`. If the first byte of this array is stored at address 0x100, the array extends over the range 0x100 through 0x11f. So charArray[0] is located at address 0x100, charArray[1] is at 0x101, charArray[2] at 0x102, and so on.

After executing the expression

```
char* ptr = &charArray[0];
```

the ptr pointer contains the address of 0x100. The addition of an integer offset to a pointer is defined such that the relationships shown in Table 10-2 are true. Table 10-2 also demonstrates why adding an offset *n* to ptr calculates the address of the *n*th element in charArray.

TABLE 10-2 **Adding Offsets**

Offset	Result	Is the Address Of
+0	0x100	charArray[0]
+1	0x101	charArray[1]
+2	0x102	charArray[2]
...	...	...
+n	0x100+n	charArray[n]

REMEMBER

The addition of an offset to a pointer is identical to applying an index to an array.

Thus, if

```
char* ptr = &charArray[0];
```

then

*(ptr + n) ← corresponds with → charArray[n]

WARNING

Because * has higher precedence than addition, * ptr + n adds n to the character that ptr points to. The parentheses are needed to force the addition to occur before the indirection. The expression *(ptr + n) retrieves the character pointed at by the pointer ptr plus the offset n. (For more on the concept of precedence, see Chapter 3.)

In fact, the correspondence between the two forms of expression is so strong that C++ considers `array[n]` nothing more than a simplified version of `*(ptr + n)`, where `ptr` points to the first element in `array`:

```
array[n] -- C++ interprets as → *(&array[0] + n)
```

To complete the association, C++ takes a second shortcut. If given,

```
char charArray[20];
```

`charArray` is defined as `&charArray[0];`. That is, the name of an array without a subscript (the "[0]") present is the address of the array itself. Thus, you can further simplify the association to:

```
array[n] -- C++ interprets as → *(array + n)
```

TIP

The type of `charArray` is actually `char const*` — that is, "constant pointer to a character" because its address cannot be changed.

Applying operators to the address of an array

The correspondence between indexing an array and pointer arithmetic is useful. For example, a `displayArray()` function you'd use to display the contents of an array of integers can be written this way:

```
// displayArray - display the members of an
//                array of length nSize
void displayArray(int intArray[], int nSize)
{
   std::println("The value of the array is:");

   for(int n = 0; n < nSize; n++)
   {
       std::println("{}: {}", n, intArray[n] );
   }
   std::print("");
}
```

This version uses the array operations you're likely familiar with by now. A pointer version of the same function appears as follows:

```
// displayArray - display the members of an
//               array of length nSize
void displayArray(int intArray[], int nSize)
{
   std::println("The value of the array is:");

   // initialize the pointer pArray with the
   // the address of the array intArray
   int* pArray = intArray;
   for(int n = 0; n < nSize; n++, pArray++)
   {
      std::println("{}: {}",n, *pArray);
   }
   std::println("");
}
```

The new `displayArray()` begins by creating a pointer to an integer `pArray` that points at the first element of `intArray`.

REMEMBER

The name `intArray` by itself is of type `int*` and refers to the address of the array.

The function then loops through each element of the array. On each loop, `displayArray()` outputs the current integer (that is, the integer pointed at by `pArray`) before incrementing the pointer to the next entry in `intArray`.

You can test `displayArray()` by using the following version of `main()`:

```
#include <print>

int main()
{
   int array[] = {4, 3, 2, 1};
   displayArray(array, 4);
}
```

The output from this program is:

```
The value of the array is:
0: 4
1: 3
2: 2
3: 1
```

REMEMBER

You may think this pointer conversion is silly; however, the pointer version of `displayArray()` is actually more common than the array version among C++ programmers in the know. For some reason, C++ programmers don't seem to like arrays, but they love pointer manipulation.

The use of pointers to access arrays is most common in the accessing of character arrays.

Expanding pointer operations to a string

A *null-terminated string* is simply a constant character array whose last character is a null. C++ uses the null character to indicate the end of the array. This null-terminated array serves as a quasi-variable type of its own. (See Chapter 8 for an explanation of null-terminated string arrays.) Often, C++ programmers use character pointers to manipulate such strings. The following code examples compare this technique to the earlier technique of indexing in the array.

The relationship between a character pointer and a character array is the same as the relationship shared by any other pointer and an array of a corresponding type. However, the fact that strings end in a terminating null makes them especially amenable to pointer-based manipulation, as shown in the following `DisplayString` program:

```
// DisplayString - display an array of characters using
//                 both a pointer and an array index
#include <print>
using namespace std;

int main()
{
   // declare a string
   const char* szString =
       "So long and thanks for all the fish.";
   println("The array is '{}'", szString);

   const size_t length = 36;
   println("Display as an array: ");

   for(size_t i = 0; i < length; i++)
   {
       print("{}", szString[i]);
   }
   println("");
```

```
    println("Display using pointer arithmetic: ");
    const char* pszString = szString;
    while(*pszString)
    {
        print("{}", *pszString);
        pszString++;
    }
    println("");
}
```

The program first makes its way through the array `szString` by indexing into the array of characters. The `for` loop that's chosen stops when the index reaches the length of the string, which in this case was set to 36.

The second loop displays the same string using a pointer. The program sets the variable `pszString` equal to the address of the first character in the array. It then enters a loop that continues until the `char` pointed at by `pszString` is equal to `false` — in other words, until the character is a `null`.

REMEMBER

The integer value `0` is interpreted as `false` — all other values are `true`.

The program outputs the character pointed at by `pszString` and then increments the pointer so that it points to the next character in the string before being returned to the top of the loop.

TIP

Determining the value stored at a pointer (*dereferencing* the pointer) and incrementing the pointer can be (and usually are) combined into a single expression, like this:

```
print("{}", *pszString++);
```

The output of the program appears this way:

```
The array is 'So long and thanks for all the fish.'
Display as an array:
So long and thanks for all the fish.
Display using pointer arithmetic:
So long and thanks for all the fish.
```

TIP

In this listing, you can see that I used a type of `size_t` for the length of the array. You might have expected an `int`, and you could have used an `int` instead. The `size_t` is like an `int` but is more tuned to be used for looping through the size of various objects.

Applying operators to pointer types other than char

It isn't too hard to convince yourself that `szTarget + n` points to `szTarget [n]` when `szTarget` is an array of `char`s. After all, a `char` occupies a single byte. If `szTarget` is stored at 0x100, `szTarget[5]` is located at 0x105.

It isn't so obvious that pointer addition works in exactly the same way for an `int` array because an `int` can take 4 bytes for each `char`'s 1 byte. If the first element in `intArray` were located at 0x100, then `intArray[5]` would be located at 0x120 *(0x100 + (5 * 4) = 0x120)* and not at 0x105.

Fortunately, `array + n` points at `array[n]` no matter how large a single element of `array` might be. C++ takes care of the element size — it's clever that way.

Once again, the old house analogy works here as well. (I mean old analogy, not old house.) The third house down from 123 Main is 126 Main, no matter how large the buildings are and whether they're bungalows or mansions.

Contrasting a pointer with an array

Arrays and pointers have some differences. For one, the array allocates space for the data, whereas the pointer does not. Another difference is that you can use a range-based `for` loop on an array where the size of the array is known, but not on a pointer where the number of elements is not known:

```
char charArray[128];
for(char& c : charArray) { c = '\0';} // initialize array

char* pArray = charArray;
for(char& c : pArray) {c = '\0';} //not legal
```

The first range-based `for` loop can be used to initialize the `charArray` to null characters. The second `for` loop doesn't compile, however. Even though `pArray` is assigned the address of the character array with its 128 characters, C++ doesn't keep that size information with the pointer, so it doesn't know how far to iterate in the range-based `for` loop. (See Chapter 6 for a description of the range-based `for` loop.)

Another difference between a pointer and the address of an array is that `charArray` is a constant, whereas `pArray` is not. Thus, the following `for` loop used to initialize the array `charArray` doesn't work:

```
char charArray[10];
for (int i = 0; i < 10; i++)
{
    *charArray = '\0';        // this makes sense...
    charArray++;             // ...this does not
}
```

The expression charArray++ makes no more sense than 10++. The following version, however, is correct:

```
char charArray[10];
char* pArray = charArray;
for (int i = 0; i < 10; i++)
{
    *pArray = '\0';  // this works great
    pArray++;        // this is okay - not a const pointer
}
```

One more difference is related to initializing pointers versus initializing arrays. The format for initializing a pointer variable is similar to initializing any other simple variable:

```
int i = 1;
const char* pString = "this is a string";
```

Both declarations initialize the variable on the left with the constant value on the right. However, because pString points directly at the immutable string "this is a string," it's important that pString be declared const char* — a pointer to constant characters, in other words.

The equivalent array is more complicated than it first appears:

```
char sChars[] = "this is a string"; // declare an init array
```

This line declares and allocates memory for an array sChars[] and then copies the initialization string into it. Thus, the letter t that is the first character in sChars isn't the same letter t that makes up the immutable initialization string.

In fact, the preceding example is shorthand for the more long-winded but descriptive:

```
char sChars[17];      // declare the array and...
strcpy(sChars, "this is a string"); // ...then initialize it
```

WHEN IS A POINTER NOT?

C++ is completely quiet about what is and isn't a legal address, with one exception. C++ predefines the constant `nullptr` with the following properties:

- It's a constant value.
- It can be assigned to any pointer type.
- It evaluates to *`false`*.
- It's never a legal address.

The constant `nullptr` is used to indicate when a pointer has not been initialized. It's also often used to indicate the last element in an array of pointers in much the same way that a null character is used to terminate a character string. It's a safe practice to initialize pointers to the `nullptr`.

The `strcpy()` function copies the string of characters represented by the second argument into the array pointed at by the first argument. And you should remember to allocate space for the terminating null.

Declaring and Using Arrays of Pointers

If pointers can point to arrays, it seems only fitting that the reverse should be true — you should be able to have an array of pointers. Arrays of pointers are a type of array of particular interest. The following declares an array of pointers to `int`s:

```
int* pInts[10];
```

Given the preceding declaration, `pInts[0]` is a pointer to an `int` value. Thus, the following is `true`:

```
void fn()
{
    int n1;             // an int
    int* pInts[3];      // an array of 3 pointers to ints
    pInts[0] = &n1;     // Address of n1 put in first
                        // element of pInts
```

```
    *pInts[0] = 1;          // value of first element of Pints
                            is set to 1.
}
```

or:

```
void fn()
{
    int n1, n2, n3;
    int* pInts[3] = {&n1, &n2, &n3};
    for (int i = 0; i < 3; i++)
    {
        *pInts[i] = 0;
    }
}
```

or even:

```
#include <memory>

void fn()
{
    std::unique_ptr<int> pInts[3] = {
        std::make_unique<int>(),
        std::make_unique<int>(),
        std::make_unique<int>()
    };
    for (int i = 0; i < 3; i++)
    {
        *pInts[i] = 0;
    }
}
```

Regardless, these types of declaration aren't used often except in the case of an array of pointers to character strings. Yet the following two examples show why arrays of character strings can be quite useful.

Utilizing arrays of character strings

Suppose that you need a function that returns the name of the month corresponding to an integer argument passed to it. For example, if the program is passed a `1`, it returns a pointer to the string `"January"`; if it's passed a `2`, it reports `"February"`, and so on. The month `0` and any numbers greater than 12 are assumed to be invalid.

You might write the function as follows:

```
// int2month() - return the name of the month
const char* int2month(int nMonth)
{
   const char* pszReturnValue;

   switch(nMonth)
   {
      case 1:  pszReturnValue = "January";
               break;
      case 2:  pszReturnValue = "February";
               break;
      case 3:  pszReturnValue = "March";
               break;
      // ...and so forth...
      default: pszReturnValue = "invalid";
   }
   return pszReturnValue;
}
```

REMEMBER

The switch() control command is like a sequence of if statements.

A more elegant solution uses the integer value for the month as an index into an array of pointers to the names of the months. In use, this appears as follows:

```
// define an array containing the names of the months
const char *const pszMonths[] = {"invalid",
                                  "January",
                                  "February",
                                  "March",
                                  "April",
                                  "May",
                                  "June",
                                  "July",
                                  "August",
                                  "September",
                                  "October",
                                  "November",
                                  "December"};

// int2month() - return the name of the month
const char* int2month(int nMonth)
```

```
{
    // first check for a value out of range
    if (nMonth < 1 || nMonth > 12)
    {
        return "invalid";
    }
    // nMonth is valid - return the name of the month
    return pszMonths[nMonth];
}
```

Here, int2month() first checks to make sure that nMonth is a number between 1 and 12, inclusive. (The default clause of the switch statement handled it in the previous example.) If nMonth is valid, the function uses it as an offset into an array containing the names of the months.

TIP

This technique of referring to character strings by index is especially useful when writing your program to work in different languages. For example, a program may declare a ptrMonths of pointers to months in different languages. The program would initialize ptrMonth to the proper names — whether they're in English, French, or German (for example) — at execution time. In that way, ptrMonth[1] points to the correct name of the first month, irrespective of the language.

ON THE WEB

A program that demonstrates int2Month() is included in the extras at www.dummies.com/go/cplusplus8e as DisplayMonths.

Accessing the arguments to main()

In most C++ programs, the main() function is often presented with a couple of arguments as such:

```
int main(int nNumberofArgs, char* pszArgs[])
{
    // do something
    return 0;
}
```

REMEMBER

As I state in Chapter 7, the main() function is special because it's where your C++ programs begin. As I also make clear in Chapter 7, though main() shows a return value of type int, you don't have to actually include it.

The main() function is also special in that it can have two parameters. I named them earlier as nNumberofArgs and pszArgs. Based on what you now know, you should be able to determine that the first argument is simply a number (int).

You can also see that the second parameter to main() is an array of pointers to null-terminated character strings. These strings contain the arguments to the program — the strings that appear with the program name when you launch the program, in other words. The first argument to main() is the number of parameters passed to the program. Suppose that the following command is entered at the command prompt:

```
MyProgram file.txt /w
```

The operating system executes the program contained in the file MyProgram (or MyProgram.exe on a Windows machine), passing it the arguments file.txt and /w. Individual items are determined by white-space breaks (spaces), similar to determining different words in a sentence.

Consider the following simple program:

```
// PrintArgs - write the arguments to the program
//             to the standard output
#include <print>
using namespace std;

int main(int nNumberofArgs, char* pszArgs[])
{
    // print a heading:
    println("The arguments to {} are: ", pszArgs[0]);

    // now write out the remaining arguments
    for (int ctr = 1; ctr < nNumberofArgs; ctr++)
    {
        println("{}:{}", ctr, pszArgs[ctr]);
    }
    println("That's it!");
}
```

As you'd expect, given our previous discussion, the function main() has its two planned parameters. The first parameter is an int that I have called (quite descriptively, as it turns out) nNumberofArgs. This variable is the number of arguments passed to the program. The second parameter is an array of pointers of type char* that I have called pszArgs.

Accessing program arguments, DOS-style

If I were to execute the PrintArgs program from the command prompt window as PrintArgs arg1 arg2 arg3 /w, then nArgs would be 5 (one for each argument).

The first argument, which is the name of the program itself, can be anything from the simple "PrintArgs" to the slightly more complicated "PrintArgs.exe" to the full path — the C++ standard doesn't specify. The environment can even supply a null string ("") if it has no access to the name of the program.

The remaining elements in `pszArgs` point to the program arguments (the arguments passed to the program). For example, the element `pszArgs[1]` points to "arg1" and `pszArgs[2]` to "arg2". Because Windows doesn't place any significance on `"/w"`, this string is also passed as an argument to be processed by the program.

To demonstrate how argument passing works, after building the program, you need to then execute it directly from a command prompt.

REMEMBER

If you're using Code::Blocks, first ensure that Code::Blocks has built an executable by opening the `PrintArgs` projects and choosing Build ⇨ Rebuild.

Next, open a command-prompt window. If you're running Unix or Linux, you're already there. If you're running Windows, choose Program ⇨ Accessories ⇨ Command Prompt to open a window 80 characters wide with a command prompt.

Now you need to use the `CD` command to navigate to the directory where Code::Blocks placed the `PrintArgs` program. If you used the default settings when installing Code::Blocks, that directory is `C:\CPP_Programs_from_ Book\Chap10\PrintArgs\bin\Debug`.

You can now execute the program by typing its name followed by your arguments. Here's what happened when I did it in Windows:

```
C:\>cd \cpp_programs_from_book\Chap10\printargs\bin\debug
C:\CPP_Programs_from_book\Chap10\PrintArgs\bin\Debug>PrintArgs
   arg1 arg2 arg3 /n
The arguments to PrintArgs are:
1:arg1
2:arg2
3:arg3
4:/n
That's it!
```

Now that you know `main()` has parameters that can take command-line arguments, I include the variables in some later listings. It's up to you if you want to include them when you enter the listings.

IN THIS CHAPTER

» Defining constants and macros

» Enumerating alternatives to constants

» Inserting compile-time checks

» Simplifying declarations via `typedef`

» Including source files

» Beyond preprocessing using modules

Chapter 11
Using the C++ Preprocessor

The idea is that you create your C++ programs in a format you can easily read. The source files you create are then converted to bits and bytes that the computer can read and execute. As sometimes happens in life, however, several intermediate steps have to occur for you to get from Point A to Point B, or in this case from code you can easily read to a program that you can execute.

Of course, you may have thought all along that all you had to learn was C++. It turns out that C++ includes a preprocessor that works on your source files before the "real C++ compiler" ever gets to see it. Unfortunately, the syntax of the preprocessor is completely different from that of C++ itself.

Before you despair, however, let me hasten to add that although the preprocessor has been an essential part of creating C++ programs, a number of features have been added to the core C++ language that make the preprocessor almost unnecessary. Nevertheless, if the conversation turns to C++ at your next Coffee Club meeting, you'll be expected to understand the preprocessor, so in this chapter, you can learn about some of the preprocessor directives and then the better, safer, and more modern approaches to accomplishing the same tasks.

What Is a Preprocessor?

Until now, you may have thought of the C++ compiler as munching on your source code and spitting out an executable program in one step, but that isn't quite true.

First, the preprocessor makes a pass through your program to look for preprocessor instructions. The output of this preprocessor step is an intermediate file that has all the preprocessor commands expanded. This intermediate file gets passed to the C++ compiler for processing. The output from the C++ compiler is an object file that contains the machine instruction equivalent to your C++ source code. During the final step, a separate program known as the *linker* combines a set of standard libraries with your object file (or files, as you can see in Chapter 23) to create an executable program.

REMEMBER

Object files normally carry the extension `.o` (although in the past they often had the extension `.obj`). Executable programs always carry the extension `.exe` in Windows and generally have no extension under Linux or Mac OS X. Most modern integrated development environments (IDEs), such as Code::Blocks and Visual Studio, store the object and executable files in their own folders. For example, if you've already built the `IntAverage` program from Chapter 2, you have on your hard drive a folder such as `C:\CPP_Programs_from_book\IntAverage\obj\Debug containing main.o` and a folder such as `C:\CPP_Programs_from_book\IntAverage\bin\Debug` that contains the executable program.

All preprocessor commands start with the hash (also called pound) symbol (`#`) in the first position of the line and end with the newline character.

Like almost all rules in C++, this rule has an exception. You can spread a preprocessor command across multiple lines by ending the line with the backslash character: \. I don't discuss any preprocessor commands that are *that* complicated, however.

TIP

A word to the wise: I highly recommend always putting the starting `#` symbol in first position on a line. If the `#` symbol isn't in the first position, then nothing should precede it on the line. Having said that, you should always put it in the first position.

In this book, I work with these three preprocessor commands:

- `#define` defines a constant or macro.
- `#if` includes a section of code in the intermediary file if the following condition is true.

» #include includes the contents of the specified file in place of the #include statement.

Each of these preprocessor commands is covered in the following sections. After learning about these commands, you learn all about modules, a recent innovation that reduces the need for some preprocessing features and provides better organization for your C++ projects.

#Defining Things

The preprocessor allows the programmer to #define expressions that get expanded during the preprocessor step. For example, you can #define a constant to be used throughout the program.

TIP

In usage, you pronounce the # sign as "pound," so you say "pound-define a constant" to distinguish from defining a constant in some other way:

```
#define TWO_PI 6.2831852
```

This explanation makes the following statement much easier to understand:

```
double diameter = TWO_PI * radius;
```

than the equivalent expression, which is what the C++ compiler actually sees after the preprocessor has replaced TWO_PI with its defined value:

```
double diameter = 6.2831852 * radius;
```

Another advantage is the ability to #define a constant in one place and use it everywhere. For example, you might want to include the following #define in an include file:

```
#define MAX_NAME_LENGTH 512
```

By doing so, you can now truncate the names you read from the keyboard to a common and consistent MAX_NAME_LENGTH throughout the program. This strategy is easier to read and provides a single place in the program to change, in case you want to increase or decrease the maximum name length that you choose to process.

The preprocessor also allows the program to `#define` function-like macros with arguments that are expanded when the definition is used:

```
#define SQUARE(X) X * X
```

In use, such macro definitions look a lot like functions:

```
// calculate the area of a circle
double dArea = PI * SQUARE(dRadius);
```

REMEMBER

The C++ compiler sees the file generated from the expansion of *all* macros, which can lead to some unexpected results. Consider the following code snippets:

```
int nSQ = SQUARE(2);
std::println("SQUARE(2) = {}", nSQ);
```

Reassuringly, this generates the expected output:

```
SQUARE(2) = 4
```

However, the following lines:

```
int nSQ = SQUARE(1 + 2);
std::println("SQUARE(1 + 2) = {}", nSQ);
```

generate this surprising result:

```
SQUARE(1 + 2) = 5
```

The preprocessor simply replaced `X` in the macro definition with what was passed to *SQUARE*. In this case, that's `1 + 2`. What the C++ compiler actually sees is this:

```
int nSQ = 1 + 2 * 1 + 2;
```

Because multiplication has higher precedence than addition, this line is turned into `1 + 2 + 2` — which, of course, is 5. This confusion could be solved by the liberal use of parentheses in the macro definition:

```
#define SQUARE(X) ((X) * (X))
```

This version generates the expected:

```
SQUARE(1 + 2) → ((1 + 2) * (1 + 2)) → 9
```

However, some unexpected results cannot be fixed, no matter how hard you try. Consider the following snippet:

```
int nbr = 3;
std::println("nbr = {}", nbr);

int nSQ = SQUARE(nbr++);
std::println("SQUARE(nbr++) = {}", nSQ);

std::println("Now nbr = {}", nbr);
```

Looking at this code, you would expect the value of nbr to be printed, which is 3. You would then expect nSQ to be assigned the value of nbr squared (3 squared is 9), after which nbr would be incremented to 4 because of the post-increment operator (++). The value of nbr would then be printed as 4.

WARNING

That, however, isn't what is printed. The macro generates the following:

```
nbr = 3;
SQUARE(nbr++) = 12
Now nbr = 5
```

The value generated by SQUARE isn't correct, and the variable nbr has been incremented twice. The reason is obvious when you consider the expanded macro:

```
nSQ = nbr++ * nbr++;
```

Because autoincrement has precedence, the two nbr++ operations are performed first. The first time, *nbr* is used as 3, but then it's incremented to 4. The 4 is then used with the second version of nbr++ before nbr is then incremented to 5. This is the result of the expanded operation after the post-increment operations are complete:

```
nSQ = 3 * 4;
```

These two values are then multiplied together to return the value of 12, which is printed, followed by printing the current value of nbr, which is 5.

REMEMBER

The lesson here is to understand that #define macros do a simple replacement within the code. Though your compiler might warn you that something is off, it's up to you to make sure the logic of expanding the macro is correct.

Okay, how about not defining things?

The sometimes unexpected results from the preprocessor have created heartburn for the fathers (and mothers) of C++ almost from the beginning. C++ has included features over the years to make most uses of `#define` unnecessary.

For example, C++ defines the *inline* function to replace the macro. This looks just like any other function declaration, with the addition of the keyword `inline` tacked to the front:

```
inline int SQUARE(int x) { return x * x; }
```

This inline function definition looks much like the previous macro definition for `SQUARE()`. (I have written this definition on one line to highlight the similarities.) However, an inline function is processed by the C++ compiler rather than by the preprocessor. This definition of `SQUARE()` doesn't suffer from any of the strange effects noted previously.

WARNING

The `inline` keyword is supposed to suggest to the compiler to "expand the function inline" rather than generate a call to some code somewhere to perform the operation. This was to satisfy the speed freaks, who wanted to avoid the overhead of performing a function call compared to a macro definition that generates no such call. The best that can be said is that inline functions may be expanded in place, but then again, they may not. There's no way to be sure without performing a detailed timing analysis or examining the machine code output by the compiler.

A better way to define things

After you learn about `#define`, it's time to learn about a better, more modern way to do the same thing. This time, you use additions to the C++ language that allow you to use a variable declared as `const` to take the place of a `#define` constant, as long as the value of the constant is spelled out at compile time:

```
const int MAX_NAME_LENGTH = 512;
int szName[MAX_NAME_LENGTH];
```

WARNING

A variable declared as `const` can only be read. Once initialized, it cannot be changed. For example, although `MAX_NAME_LENGTH` was declared as an `int` in the previous example, you cannot change the value from 512 to something else later in your code. The following gives an error:

```
const int MAX_NAME_LENGTH = 512;
// Increase name length:
MAX_NAME_LENGTH = 1024;     // ERROR!!!
```

A const variable is often used in function parameters, local variables, global variables, and even with class members. (For more on class members, see Chapter 13.) They're also often used with pointers and references to prevent them from being modified.

Similarly, if you have a function that returns a value that's always used as a constant (like the #define macros I presented previously), you can declare a function that returns a value to be a constexpr:

```
constexpr int square(int n1)
    {return n1 * n1;}
```

You can then use this function anywhere a constant value can be used. For example, declaring the square() function as a constexpr makes a declaration like the following one legal:

```
int matrix[square(5)];
```

REMEMBER

There are restrictions on what can go into a const expression. For example, such a function is pretty much limited to a single line.

TECHNICAL STUFF

In general, a function can be declared a constexpr if all the subexpressions can be calculated at compile time. That's an important point to remember: constexpr tells the compiler to evaluate any code that follows and resolve that code at compile time rather than when the program is run.

Enumerating other options

C++ provides a mechanism for defining constants of a separate, user-defined type. Suppose that you want to write a program that manipulates states of the Union. You can refer to the states by their names, such as "Texas" or "North Dakota." In practice, this strategy isn't convenient because repetitive string comparisons are computationally intensive and subject to error.

You can define a unique value for each state as follows:

```
#define DC_OR_TERRITORY 0
#define ALABAMA 1
#define ALASKA 2
#define ARKANSAS 3
// ...and so on...
```

Or even as:

```
const int DC_OR_TERRITORY 1
const int DC_OR_TERRITORY = 0
const int ALABAMA = 1
const int ALASKA = 2
const int ARKANSAS = 3
// ...and so on...
```

Using these values avoids the clumsiness of comparing strings and (bonus!) allows you to use the names of the states as an index into an array of properties — population, for example. Here's how that would look:

```
// increment the population of ALASKA (they need it)
population[ALASKA]++;
```

A statement such as this one is much easier to understand than the semantically identical `population[2]++`. Using constant values in this manner is such a common thing to do that C++ allows the programmer to define what's known as an *enumeration*:

```
enum STATE {DC_OR_TERRITORY,       // gets 0
            ALABAMA,               // gets 1
            ALASKA,                // gets 2
            ARKANSAS,
          // ...and so on...
```

Using the `enum` keyword, a set of constant values (called *enumerators*) are created and assigned constant values. In this case, the enumerated values are associated as a group called `STATE`.

Each element of this enumeration is assigned a value starting at `0`, so `DC_OR_TERRITORY` is defined as `0`, `ALABAMA` is defined as `1`, and so on. You can override this incremental sequencing by using an assign statement as follows:

```
enum STATE {DC,
            TERRITORIES = 0,
            ALABAMA,
            ALASKA,
            // ...and so on...
```

This version of `STATE` defines an element `DC`, which is given the value `0`. It then defines a new element `TERRITORIES`, which is also assigned the value `0`.

`ALABAMA` picks up with `1`, just as before.

You can also create a user-defined enumerated type as follows (note the addition of the keyword `class` in the snippet; the `class` keyword is discussed in detail in Chapter 13):

```
enum class STATE {DC,
                  TERRITORIES = 0,
                  ALABAMA,
                  ALASKA,
                  // ...and so on...
```

This declaration creates a new type `STATE` and assigns it 52 members (`ALABAMA` through `WYOMING` plus `DC` and `TERRITORIES`). The programmer can now use `STATE` in the same way any other variable type is used. A variable can be declared to be of type `STATE`:

```
STATE s = STATE::ALASKA;
```

As you can see, values can be used from the enumerator by using the type name (`STATE`) followed by two colons and then one of the values that was listed. You see this syntax again when you learn about classes in Chapter 13.

Function calls can be differentiated by this new type:

```
int getPop(STATE s);            // return population
int setPop(STATE s, int pop);   // set the population
```

REMEMBER

The type `STATE` isn't just another word for `int`: For example, the following attempt to use `STATE` as an index into an array isn't legal:

```
int getPop(STATE s)
{
    return population[s]; // not legal
}
```

However, the members of `STATE` can be converted to their integer equivalent (`0` for *DC* and `TERRITORIES`, `1` for `ALABAMA`, `2` for `ALASKA`, and so on). Before C++23, this would have been done with a *cast*, which simply forces a variable to be a different data type. In the following `s` is cast (converted) to become an `int`:

```
int getPop(STATE s)
{
    return population[(int)s]; // is legal
}
```

C++23 NEW

Starting with C++23, you can (and should) use the `to_underlying()` function in the standard library to convert the enumerator to the underlying data type, which in the case of our `STATE` is an `int`:

```
// The following converts to an int
int value = std::to_underlying(STATE:ALASKA);
```

This particular line of code would assign 2 to `value`. An update to the `getPop()` function that avoids using casts is:

```
int getPop(STATE s)
{
    int value = std::to_underlying(s);
    return population[value]; // is legal
}
```

REMEMBER

For you to be able to use `to_underlying()`, you need to either include the standard `std` library or the `utility` library.

Including Things #if I Say So

Another major class of preprocessor statements is the `#if`, which is a preprocessor version of the C++ `if` statement:

```
#if constexpression
// included if constexpression evaluates to other than 0
#else
// included if constexpression evaluates to 0
#endif
```

The use of the `#if` preprocessor statement is known as *conditional compilation* because the set of statements between the `#if` and the `#else` or `#endif` are included in the compilation only if a condition is true. The `constexpression` phrase is limited to simple arithmetic and comparison operators. That's okay because anything more than an equality comparison and the occasional addition is rare.

For example, the following code snippet illustrates a common use for `#if`. You can include the following definition for an inline `logMessage()` function within a file named `LogMessage`:

```
#if DEBUG == 1
inline void logMessage(const char *pMessage)
```

```
        { cout << pMessage << endl; }
#else
#define logMessage(X) (0)
#endif
```

You can now sprinkle informative messages throughout your program wherever you need them. These messages can be placed to let you know when various things are happening so you can confirm your program is operating as you expect. For example, the following calls the `logMessage()` function when the `testFunction()` function is executed:

```
#define DEBUG 1
#include "LogMessage"
void testFunction(char *pArg)
{
    logMessage(pArg);
    // ...function continues...
```

With `DEBUG` set to `1`, the `logMessage()` function is converted into a call to an inline function that outputs the argument to the display. In this code `logMessage()` displays the argument that was passed to the `testFunction()` so you can confirm the function receives the value you expect. Once the program is working properly, you can remove the definition of `DEBUG`. Now the references to `logMessage()` invoke a macro that does nothing.

A second version of the conditional compilation is the `#ifdef` (pronounced "if def"):

```
#ifdef DEBUG
// included if DEBUG has been #defined
#else
// included if DEBUG has not been #defined
#endif
```

There's also an `#ifndef` (pronounced "if not def"), which is the logical reverse of `#ifdef`.

TIP

For more complicated logic that needs to do more than one check, rather than have an `#else` followed by another `#if`, you can use the directive `#elif`. It's cleaner and clearer about what you're doing:

```
#include <print>

#ifdef WINDOWS
```

```
    #define OS_NAME "Windows"
#elifdef LINUX
    #define OS_NAME "Linux"
#elifdef MACOS
    #define OS_NAME "macOS"
#else
    #define OS_NAME "Unknown OS"
#endif

int main() {
    std::println("Running on: {}", OS_NAME);
}
```

C++23 NEW

Starting with C++23, there are also `#elifdef` ("else if defined") and `#elifndef` ("else if not defined") that work with `#ifdef` and `#ifndef`.

Intrinsically Defined Objects

C++ defines a set of intrinsic constants, which are shown in Table 11-1. These are constants that C++ thinks are just too cool to be without — and that you would have trouble defining for yourself, anyway.

TABLE 11-1 Predefined Preprocessor Constant

Constant	Type	Meaning
`__FILE__`	`const char const *`	The name of the source file.
`__LINE__`	`const int`	The current line number.
`__func__`	`const char const *`	The name of the current function (Starting with C++11).
`__DATE__`	`const char const *`	The current date.
`__TIME__`	`const char const *`	The current time.

Constant	Type	Meaning
`__TIMESTAMP__`	`const char const *`	The current date and time.
`__STDC__`	`int`	Contains a value of 1 if the C++ compiler is compliant with the standard.
`__cplusplus`	`int`	Contains a value of 1 if the compiler is a C++ compiler (as opposed to a C compiler), which allows include files to be shared across environments.

These internal macros are particularly useful when generating error messages. You would think that C++ generates plenty of error messages on its own, but sometimes you want to create your own compiler error messages. For you, C++ offers not one, not two, but *three* options: `#error`, `assert()`, and `static_assert()`. Each of these three mechanisms works slightly differently.

The `#error` command is a preprocessor directive (as you can tell by the fact that it starts with the `#` sign). It causes the preprocessor to stop and output a message. Suppose that your program just won't work with anything but standard C++. You can add the following to the beginning of your program:

```
#if !__cplusplus || !__STDC__
#error This is a standard C++ program.
#endif
```

Now, if someone tries to compile your program with anything other than a C++ compiler that strictly adheres to the standards, a single neat-looking error message is presented rather than a raft of potentially meaningless error messages from a confused, nonstandard compiler.

Unlike `#error`, `assert()` performs its test when the resulting program is executed. Suppose that you have written a factorial program that calculates $N * (N - 1) * (N - 2)$ and so on down to 1 for whatever N you pass it. Factorials are defined only for positive integers; passing a negative number to a factorial is always a mistake. To be careful, you should add a test for a nonpositive value at the beginning of the function:

```
int factorial(int N)
{
    assert(N > 0);
    // ...program continues...
```

The program now checks the argument to `factorial()` each time it's called. At the first sign of negativity, `assert()` halts the program with a message to the operator that the assertion failed, along with the file and line number:

```
Assertion failed: N > 0, file yourfile.c, line XX
```

Liberal use of `assert()` throughout your program is a good way to detect problems early during development, but constantly testing for errors that have already been found and removed during testing slows the program needlessly. To keep this from happening, C++ allows the programmer to "remove" the tests when creating the version of the program to be shipped to users: All you have to do is `#define` the constant `NDEBUG` (for "not debug mode"). This causes the preprocessor to convert all calls to `assert()` in your module to "do-nothings" (universally known as NO-OPs).

C++26 NEW

Though `assert()` is helpful for basic error-checking, in C++26 the concept of *contracts* is added, which applies to using an `assert()` in a much more detailed manner. In Chapter 26, you can see how to use `contract_assert()` for assertions, along with how to check for pre and post conditions.

The preprocessor cannot perform certain compile-time tests. Suppose that your program works properly only if the default integer size is 32 bits. The preprocessor is of no help here because it knows nothing about integers or floating points. To address this situation, C++ introduced the keyword `static_assert()`, which is interpreted by the compiler (rather than the preprocessor). It accepts two arguments: a *const* expression and a string, as in the following example:

```
static_assert(sizeof(int) == 4, "int is not 32-bits.");
```

If the `const` expression evaluates to `0` or `false` during compilation, the compiler outputs the string and stops. The `static_assert()` doesn't generate any run-time code.

REMEMBER

The `const` expression here is evaluated at compile time, so it cannot contain function calls or references to objects that are known only when the program executes.

Using Using and Typedef

In the old days of C++, many developers used the `typedef` keyword. This keyword allowed you to create a shorthand name for a declaration. Even now, the careful application of `typedef` can make the resulting program easier to read. (Note that typedef isn't actually a preprocessor command, but it's largely associated with include files and the preprocessor.)

Here's a typedef example:

```
typedef int* IntPtr;
typedef const IntPtr IntConstPtr;

int i;
int *const ptr1 = &i;
IntConstPtr ptr2= ptr1; // ptr1 and ptr2 are the same type
```

The first two declarations in this snippet give a new name to existing types. Thus, the second declaration declares IntConstPtr to be another name for int const*. When this new type is used in the declaration of ptr2, it has the same effect as the more complicated declaration of ptr1.

REMEMBER

Although typedef doesn't introduce any new capability, it can make some complicated declarations much easier to read.

Modern C++ developers, however, lean toward using the using keyword. It works like typedef but is considered by some easier to read (a matter of opinion) as well as more flexible. Most important, however, is that it tends to be more compatible with some of the modern features of C++, as well as working better with templates. (For more on templates, see Bonus Chapter 2.)

This is the format for using using:

```
using IntPtr = int*;
using IntConstPtr = const IntPtr;
```

Other than the different way it has of declaring IntPtr and IntConstPtr, using should work just like the previous typedefs.

#Including Files

The C++ standard library consists of functions that are basic enough that almost everyone needs them. It would be silly to force every programmer to have to write them on their own. For example, the I/O functions, which I have been using to read input from the keyboard and write out to the console, are contained in the standard library. When you use these particular functions, you have the compiler link them into your final program.

C++ generally requires you to have a prototype declaration for any functions you call, whether it's in a library or not. (See Chapter 7 if that statement doesn't make sense to you.) Rather than force you to type all these declarations by hand, the library authors created include files that contain little more than prototype declarations. All you need to do is `#include` or import the source file that contains the prototypes for the library routines you intend to use. Before using modules (which are covered in the next section), you would include this information using the `#include` directive.

Suppose that you have created a library that contains simple math functions, such as `square()`, `cube()`, `power()`, and a whole lot more. You would likely want to create an include file named `mymath` with the following contents to go along with your standard library:

```
// include prototype declarations for my library
int square(int x);
int cube(int x);
// ...more prototype declarations...
```

Any program that wanted to make use of one of these math functions would `#include` that file, enclosing the name of the include file either in brackets or quotes, as in:

```
#include <mymath>
```

or

```
#include "mymath"
```

TECHNICAL STUFF

The difference between the two forms of `#include` is a matter of where the preprocessor goes to look for the `mymath` file. When the file is enclosed in quotes, the preprocessor assumes that the include file is locally grown, so it starts looking for the file in the same directory in which it found the source file for the program using it. If the preprocessor doesn't find the file there, it starts looking in its own include file directories.

The preprocessor assumes that include files in angle brackets are from the C++ library, so it skips looking in the source file directory and goes straight to the standard include file folders. Use quotes for any include file you create and angle brackets for C++ library include files.

Thus, you might write a source file like the following:

```
// MyProgram  -  is very intelligent
#include "mymath.h"
#include <print>

int main()
{
    std::println("The square of 5 is {}.", square(5));
}
```

PLAYING IN YOUR OWN NAME SANDBOX

The authors of the C++ standard worry a lot about name collisions. For example, besides your mathematical function `log(x)` that returns the logarithm of *x*, suppose in another context you had written a function `log(x)` that writes status information to a system log. Clearly, two different functions with the same arguments can't coexist in one program. This is known as a *name collision*.

To avoid this situation, C++ allows the programmer to bundle declarations into a namespace using the keyword of the same name:

```
namespace Mathematics
{
   double log(double x)
   {
       // ...the definition of the function...
   }
}
namespace SystemLog
{
   int log(double x)
   {
       // ...log the value to file...
   }
}
```

(continued)

(continued)

The namespace becomes part of the extended name of the function. Thus, the following code snippet actually logs the logarithm of a value:

```
void myFunc(double x)
{
    // invoke the logarithm function...
    double dl = Mathematics::log(x);

    // ...now log it to disk
    SystemLog::log(dl);
}
```

Fortunately, you don't have to specify the namespace every single time. The keyword `using` allows the programmer to specify a default namespace for a given function:

```
using double Mathematics::log(double);
void myFunc(double x)
{
    // the default is the mathematics version...
    double dl = log(x);

    // ...however, the other version is still accessible by
    // explicitly specifying the namespace
    SystemLog::log(dl);
}
```

You can automatically default every declaration within a namespace:

```
using namespace Mathematics;
void myFunc(double x)
{
    // look in the Mathematics namespace first...
    double dl = log(x);

    // ...however, the other version is still accessible by
    // explicitly specifying the namespace
    SystemLog::log(dl);
}
```

The standard library functions reside in the `std` namespace. The statement `using namespace std`, included at the beginning of each of the programs in this book, gives the programs access to the standard library functions without the need to specify the namespace explicitly.

When it comes to modern programming, the recommended approach is to specify the namespace within your code. This would mean using `std::println()` in your code instead of adding a `using` statement and then using just `println()`. This suggestion is made because it reduces the chance of having a name collision in code that is more complex. Elsewhere in this book, I use a `using` statement to make the code a little easier to see the functions and types being explained. As you write production applications, you should consider including the namespaces within the details of your code.

The C++ compiler sees the following intermediary file after the preprocessor finishes expanding the `#include`:

```
// MyProgram  -  is very intelligent
// include prototype declarations for my library
int square(int x);
int cube(int x);
// ...more prototype declarations...
#include <print>

int main()
{
    std::println("The square of 5 is {}.", squire(5));
}
```

WARNING

Historically, the convention was to end include files with `.h`. C still uses that standard. However, C++ dropped the extension when it revamped the include file structure. Now C++ standard include files have no extension.

Organizing with Modules

I mention in Chapter 7 that functions can be used to help organize your code. Just as functions can make it easier to reuse code logic that performs a single task, using modules can make it easier to share and reuse your code on a larger scale. In simple terms, a *module* is a file that contains related C++ code items such as functions, global variables, and classes. As a bonus, modules can also make compiling your code more efficient.

C++26 NEW

Modules, which were introduced in the C++20 standard, are a modern alternative to the traditional header file used in C++ (and covered earlier in this chapter). In the C++23 and C++26 standards, modules continue to be improved and optimized — adding more to the standard library modules to improve cross-platform compatibility, for example.

Why modules are better

If header files are simply included at the beginning of your code with a simple statement, and if they simply add in code, you might be thinking that they're pretty easy to use — seems a bit crazy to stop using them. The reality is that headers are still relevant and will likely continue to be used. But modules are better!

The following are a few benefits of using modules:

- **Modules compile faster.** You compile them once and then use them.
- **Modules take care of dependencies in their code automatically making them safer to use.** When using header files, you must handle any dependencies yourself.
- **Modules take care of duplication issues**: No need to include the same objects, classes, or other C++ constructs over and over and over again.
- **Modules include built-in controls for importing and exporting**. That adds up to more visibility when it comes to what you can do with them.

Creating a module

Let's look at an example of a module file and dissect how to use it. I keep it simple and create a file that can be reused later. The file has two math functions for squaring and cubing a number and bears the startling unique name `math.cppm`. Here it is, in all its glory:

```
// module: math.cppm
export module math;

export int square(int nbr)
{
   return nbr * nbr;
}

export int cube (int nbr)
{
   Return nbr * nbr * nbr;
}
```

Note that the first line of code (after the comment line) tells you that you're defining a module named `math`. The `export` keyword here and in the following lines of code indicate that this module and the two functions — `square()` and `cube()` — are available for other files to import and use. Other than the use of the word `export`, the rest of the `square()` and `cube()` functions should look much like other functions you've previously created — which they are.

WARNING

If you don't include `export` before the function, you cannot access the function from other files. That, however, might not be a problem. It could be that you have supporting functions within your `module` file that you don't want to share. For example, the following rewrites the `math` module so that `square()` and `cube()` use an internal function called `power()` to do the actual math. The `power()` function would not be available outside the module, but is perfectly fine to use within the `math` module listing:

```
// module: math.cppm -
export module math;

int power( int base, int exp)
{
   int nResult = 1;
   while (exp--)_
   {
      nResult *= base;
   }
}

export int square(int nbr)
{
   return power(x, 2);
}

export int cube (int nbr)
{
   return power(x, 3);
}
```

You should also notice that the math module was named with the `.cppm` extension rather than the `.cpp` extension. This is to help indicate that this is module code, not a standard C++ code listing.

TIP

Note that Microsoft Visual Studio and Visual Studio Code use the `.ixx` extension for modules.

Using a module

To use the module code, you import your module into your primary listing. After they're imported, you can then use the exported functions from your module:

```
// mathDemo.cpp - using our math module
//
import math;
#include <print>

int main()
(
   std::println("The square of 5 is: {}.", square(5));
   std::println("The cube of 5 is: {}.", cube(5));
}
```

REMEMBER

Modules are compiled before they're used. This is a benefit because (unless the code changes within the module) you don't need to spend time recompiling it. Once compiled, the resulting file you end up with will have the extension .0. This object file can then be linked to any C++ programs you create that need to include its functions.

C++23 NEW

MODULES VERSUS HEADERS

Modules are a better, modern approach to working with files in C++. Modules were introduced in C++20 to help improve speed and reduce issues with macros. Converting the entire standard library to modules is a massive project, but starting with C++23, the standard library can be imported into many C++ listings. Theoretically, according to the standards, you could simply add the following to the top of your listings, have access to everything in the standard library, and no longer need to include a bunch of header files:

```
import std;
```

In a perfect world, this would work, but, sadly, the world of C++ isn't always perfect. As such, you will find that some individual modules are not fully converted to modules and thus need to be #included in your listings. In this book, the individual includes have been used; however, if your compiler supports importing the standard library, you should be able to replace all the includes (such as #include <print>) with the single import std; command.

Compiling your app that uses a module

Always consult your compiler's documentation, to not only confirm that it supports the use of modules but also learn how it specifically compiles modules into your programs. At the time this edition of the book was written, Code::Blocks required you to manually configure the build steps for using a module. In addition to including the flag to support C++26 (as shown in Chapter 1), you need to add a flag to the compiler to enable module support:

- `-fmodules-ts` for GCC
- `-fmodules` for Clang

REMEMBER

You might need to compile your module first before moving on to then compile the program using that module.

One More Concept to Cover

C++26 NEW

The preprocessor is all about things happening at compile time. In C++26, another compile-time feature has been added, called *concepts*. This feature adds constraints to your C++ code and, more specifically, adds them to templates. For example, you might want to use integer values only in your template. A concept can help to make sure that happens by flagging whenever a non-integer is used.

You might be wondering what a template is because I just mentioned them. Although you can certainly find out more about templates in Bonus Chapter 2, I do want to mention concepts now because they're like many of the topics you learned in this chapter — to be more specific, they're applied when you're compiling your code rather than when you're running your code. (Again, you get a chance to take a deep dive into concepts in Bonus Chapter 2, where you can also learn all about templates.)

3 Giving Your Program a Bit of Class

IN THIS PART . . .

Reviewing object-oriented programming

Declaring and defining class members

Exploring the difference between groups of letters and strings

Protecting members of your classes

Constructing and destructing objects in your programs

Making copying possible

Defining static member functions

IN THIS CHAPTER

» Making nachos

» Reviewing object-oriented programming

» Introducing abstraction and classification

» Recognizing why object-oriented programming is important

Chapter 12
Examining Object-Oriented Programming

One key feature of C++ — one that sets it apart from the (older) C programming language — is that it can be used to do object-oriented programming. What, exactly, is object-oriented programming? Object-oriented programming, or OOP as those in the know prefer to call it, relies on two principles you learned before you ever got out of diapers: abstraction and classification. To explain, let me tell you a little story.

Abstracting Microwave Ovens

Sometimes when my kids and I are watching football (which happens only when my spouse can't find the remote), we whip up a terribly unhealthy batch of nachos. First we dump some chips on a plate, and then we throw on some beans, cheese, and lots of jalapeños before nuking the whole mess in the microwave. To use our microwave, I open the door, throw the stuff in, and punch a button. After a few minutes, the nachos are done. Simply put, I press the 3 button and 3 minutes later, the nachos are ready to eat, with all their melted gooeyness.

Now think for a minute about all the things I *don't* do to use the microwave:

- I don't rewire or change anything inside the microwave to make it work. The microwave has an interface — the front panel with all the buttons and the little time display — that lets me do everything I need to do.
- I don't have to reprogram the software used to drive the little processor inside the microwave, even if I cooked a different dish the last time I used the microwave.
- I don't look inside the microwave's case.
- Even if I designed microwaves and knew all about the inner workings of a microwave, including its software, I would still use it the same way to heat our nachos without thinking about all that stuff inside.

These are not profound observations. You can deal with only so much stress in your life. To reduce the number of things you deal with, you work at a certain level of detail.

REMEMBER

In object-oriented (OO) computerese, the level of detail at which you're working is called the *level of abstraction*. To introduce another OO term while I have the chance, I *abstract away* the details of the microwave's innards.

When I'm working on nachos, I view my microwave oven as a box. (I can't worry about the innards of the microwave oven and still follow the Indianapolis Colts on the television.) As long as I operate the microwave only by way of its interface (the keypad), there should be nothing I can do to:

- Cause the microwave to enter an inconsistent state and crash
- Turn the nachos into a blackened, flaming mass
- Make the microwave (along with the surrounding house) burst into flames

Preparing functional nachos

Suppose that I asked my kids to write an algorithm for how other dads make nachos. After they understood what I wanted, they would probably write "open a can of beans, grate some cheese, cut the jalapeños," and so on. When it came to the part about microwaving the concoction, they would write something like "cook in the microwave for 3 minutes."

That description is straightforward and complete. But it's not the way a functional programmer would code a program to make nachos. Functional programmers live in a world devoid of objects such as microwave ovens and other appliances. They tend to worry about the detailed process, which can include flowcharts with their myriad functional paths. In a functional solution to the nachos problem, the flow of control would pass through a finger to the front panel and then to the internal workings of the microwave. Pretty soon, flow would be wiggling around through complex logic paths about how long to turn on the microwave tube and whether to sound the "come and get it" tone. Each step is a function within the process of preparing the nachos.

In a world like this one, it's difficult to think in terms of levels of abstraction. This world has no objects, and no abstractions behind which hide inherent complexity.

Preparing object-oriented nachos

In an object-oriented approach to making nachos, I would first identify the types of objects in the problem: chips, beans, cheese, and an oven. Then I would begin the task of modeling these objects in software, without regard to the details of how they'll be used in the final program.

While I am doing this, I'm said to be working (and thinking) at the level of the basic objects. I need to think about making a useful oven, but I don't yet have to think about the logical process of making nachos. After all, the microwave designers didn't think about the specific problem of my making a snack. Rather, they set about the problem of designing and building a useful microwave.

After the objects I need have been successfully coded and tested, I can ratchet up to the next level of abstraction. I can start thinking at the nacho-making level rather than at the microwave-making level. At this point, I can pretty much translate my children's instructions directly into C++ code.

Classifying Microwave Ovens

Critical to the concept of abstraction is that of classification. If I were to ask my kids, "What's a microwave?" they would probably say, "It's an oven that . . ." If I then asked, "What's an oven?" they might reply, "It's a kitchen appliance that . . ." (If I then asked, "What's a kitchen appliance?" they would probably say, "Why are you asking so many stupid questions?")

The answers my kids gave to my questions stem from their understanding of our particular microwave as an example of the type of thing called microwave ovens. In addition, my kids see microwave ovens as just a special type of oven, which itself is just a special type of kitchen appliance.

In object-oriented computerese, the microwave in my kitchen is an *instance* of the *class* microwave. The class microwave is a *subclass* of the class oven, and the class oven is a subclass of the class kitchen appliances. We say that microwaves *inherit* their cooking properties from oven.

Humans classify. Everything about our world is ordered into taxonomies. We do this to reduce the number of things we have to remember. Take, for example, the first time you saw a hybrid car. The advertisement probably called the hybrid "unique, the likes of which have never been seen." But you and I know that that just isn't so. I like hybrids and I will grant you that they have lots of differences under the hood, but, hey — a hybrid is still a car. As such, it shares all of (or at least most of) the properties of other cars. It has a steering wheel, seats, a motor, brakes, and so on. I bet I could even drive one without first reading the owner's manual.

I don't have to clutter my limited storage with all the things a hybrid has in common with other cars. All I need to remember is "a hybrid is a car that . . ." and tack on those few items that are unique to a hybrid (like the price tag). I can go further: Cars are a subclass of wheeled vehicles along with other members, such as trucks and pickups. Maybe wheeled vehicles are a subclass of vehicles, which includes boats and planes. And on and on and on.

Why Classify?

Why do we classify? It sounds like a lot of trouble. Besides, people have been using the functional approach for so long — why change now?

It may seem easier to design and build a microwave oven specifically for this lone problem rather than build a separate, more generic oven object. Suppose that I wanted to build a microwave to cook nachos and only nachos. I wouldn't need to put a front panel on it, other than a Start button. I always cook nachos for the same amount of time, so I could dispense with all that Defrost and Temp Cook nonsense. My nachos-only microwave needs to hold only one flat little plate. Three cubic feet of space would be wasted on nachos.

For that matter, I can dispense with the concept of "microwave oven" altogether. All I really need is the guts of the oven. Then, in the recipe, I add the instructions to make it work: "Put nachos in the box. Connect the red wire to the black wire. Bring the radar tube up to about 3,000 volts. Notice a slight hum. Try not to stand too close if you intend to have children." Stuff like that.

But the functional approach has some problems:

- **Too complex:** I don't want the details of oven building mixed into the details of nacho building. If I can't define the objects and pull them out of the morass of details to deal with separately, I must deal with all the complexities of the problem at the same time.
- **Not flexible:** Someday, I may need to replace the microwave oven with some other type of oven. I should be able to do so as long as its interface is the same. Without being clearly delineated and developed separately, it becomes impossible to cleanly remove an object type and replace it with another. As a second example, if I trade my gas-powered car for an electric car, I should expect to have a similar interface for using it. Accelerating, stopping, turning, or otherwise using the electric vehicle should be pretty much the same as what was used for the gas-powered vehicle.
- **Not reusable:** Ovens are used to make lots of different dishes. I don't want to create a new oven every time I encounter a new recipe. Having solved a problem once, it would be nice to be able to reuse the solution in future programs.

The remaining chapters in this part demonstrate how the object-oriented language features of C++ address these problems.

In real life, object-oriented programming isn't quite as pure as I make it sound here. I can't spend the time to build the software equivalent of a generic microwave oven. After all, teams of engineers spend thousands of developer hours designing microwave ovens (and still the front panel comes out incomprehensible). When you decide to build your classes, you generally build in only the capabilities you need for the particular problem at hand, but still the principle is the same. When I'm building the microwave oven, I need only think about the oven. When I make nachos, I have to think only about using the oven. It's simpler that way.

A Few Other Thoughts on OOP

Before sending you off to the next chapter, I would be remiss not to cover a few common terms used with object-oriented programming. These include encapsulation, inheritance, and polymorphism. These go along with the abstraction already covered. These terms are often used when people describe what OOP is.

Inheritance is also mentioned in describing the oven. Remember that we say that microwaves *inherit* their cooking properties from an oven. This inheritance is a powerful feature for letting you reuse existing code. (You learn how to inherit in C++ in Chapter 21, and then in Chapter 26, inheritance is put on overdrive, in the form of multiple inheritance.)

Another term you should know for any trivia quizzes you encounter asking about OOP is *polymorphism*. This big word simply means "many forms," as in something can take many forms.

If you've already come across the fascinating discussion about overloading functions in Chapter 7, you've already been introduced to polymorphism in C++ — even if I studiously avoided using the term then! There, I talk about how you could call the same function but pass different values — *overloading* the function, as it were. When you declare the different functions with different parameters, you're programming polymorphism into your program! It is such polymorphism that lets you use functions like `print` and `println` to display a bunch of different data types. You simply send the values, and the polymorphic nature of the functions takes care of the rest!

One other term you encounter when talking about OOP is *encapsulation*. In OOP, this term means the exact same thing it means when used for anything else: It's simply the ability to bundle things together. In C++, you can bundle data with functions and create a nice little package. This packaging can also control access to the information as well as the functions.

As an example of encapsulation, you could create a `student` class that keeps track of the name of the student and their grade level, as well as includes functions that let you do things such as view their current GPA. This `student` class might include private information, such as a social security number as well as public information. This can all be done within the class structure. Coincidentally, Chapter 13 teaches you all about adding class to C++.

IN THIS CHAPTER

» Grouping data into classes

» Declaring and defining class members

» Adding active properties to the class

» Accessing class member functions

» Overloading member functions

» Using structs

Chapter 13

Adding Class to C++

Programs often deal with groups of data. For example, a program might deal with a person — one who might have qualities such as name, age, height, birthdate, weight, and other info like that. Any one of these values on their own isn't sufficient to describe a person — only in the aggregate do the values make any sense.

A simple structure such as an array is useful for holding standalone values, but it doesn't work well for data groups. This makes good ol' arrays inadequate for storing complex data. It starts getting complicated quickly. Is the number 62 in a `person` array an age, a height, or (if it's a kid) a weight? You just don't easily know.

In C++, you can group the different attributes together for a person. For reasons that will become clear shortly, I'll call such a grouping of data an *object*. A microwave oven is an object. (See Chapter 12 if that doesn't make sense.) You're an object (no offense). Your savings account information in a database is an object.

Although it's certainly nice that C++ allows us to create objects in C++ that have the relevant properties of the real-world objects we're trying to model, you still need a structure that can hold all the different types of data you need in order to describe a single object. Luckily for us, C++ provides just the ticket. C++ calls the structure that combines multiple pieces of data into a single object a *class*.

Formatting a Class

A class consists of the keyword `class` followed by a name and an open brace and a closed brace. A class that someone would use to describe a savings account (including account number and balance) might appear as follows:

```
class SavingsAccount
{
  public:
     unsigned accountNumber;
     double balance;
};
```

The statement after the open brace is the keyword `public`. (Hold off asking about the meaning of the `public` keyword. I make its meaning public a little later in this chapter.)

Following the `public` keyword are the entries it takes to describe the object. The `SavingsAccount` class contains two elements: an unsigned integer `accountNumber`, which holds a positive number representing the account, and the account `balance`. You can also say that `accountNumber` and `balance` are members or properties of the class `SavingsAccount`.

To create an actual savings account object, you type something like the following:

```
SavingsAccount mySavingsAccount;
```

In this case, `mySavingsAccount` is an *instance* of the class `SavingsAccount`. `mySavingsAccount` is also considered an *object* created based on the class.

TIP

The naming convention I use here is pretty common: Class names are normally capitalized. In a class name with multiple words, such as `SavingsAccount`, each word is capitalized and the words are jammed together without an underscore. Object names follow the same rule of jamming multiple words together, but they normally start with a small letter, as in `mySavingsAccount`. As always, these norms (I hesitate to say *rules*) are to help the human reader — C++ doesn't care one way or the other.

Accessing the Members of a Class

The following syntax is used to access the data members of a particular object:

```
SavingsAccount mySave;
mySave.accountNumber = 1234;
mySave.balance = 6.42;
```

The first line declares the object (`mySave`) using the class `SavingsAccount`. The two lines that follow assign values to the data members of `mySave`. Notice that the format to access the data member is the object name, followed by a period, followed by the data member name. Using this format, the data member is otherwise treated in the same way you treat other variables. The following presents this declaration of an object using a class in a complete listing that you can enter and run:

```
// CreateObjects - Create savings account objects
#include <iostream>
#include <print>
using namespace std;

class SavingsAccount
{
  public:
    unsigned accountNumber;
    double balance;
};

int main(int nNumberofArgs, char* pszArgs[])
{
    // Create a savings account object
    SavingsAccount mySave;
    mySave.accountNumber = 1234;
    mySave.balance = 6.42;

    println("mySave account = {} and balance = {}",
          mySave.accountNumber, mySave.balance);

    // Input a second savings account from the keyboard
    SavingsAccount urSave;
    print("Input your account number: ");
    cin >> urSave.accountNumber;
    print("Input your account balance: ");
    cin >> urSave.balance;
```

```
    println("urSave account = {} and balance = {}",
            urSave.accountNumber, urSave.balance);
}
```

This code declares two objects of class SavingsAccount named mySave and urSave. The snippet initializes mySave by assigning a value to the account number and a 0 to the balance (as per usual for my savings account). It then creates a second object of the same class, urSave. The snippet reads the account number and balance from the keyboard.

An important point to note in this snippet is that mySave and urSave are separate, independent objects. Manipulating the members of one has no effect on the members of the other (luckily for urSave).

WARNING

In addition, the name of the member without an associated object makes no sense. I cannot say either of the following:

```
balance = 0.0;                  // illegal; no object
SavingsAccount.balance = 0.0; // class but still no object
```

Every savings account has its own unique account number variable and maintains a separate balance. (Some properties may be shared by all savings accounts — I get to those in Chapter 20 — but account and balance don't happen to be among them.)

Activating Our Objects

You use classes to simulate real-world objects. The Savings class tries to represent a savings account. This allows you to think in terms of objects rather than simply lines of code. The closer C++ objects are to modeling the real world, the easier it is to deal with them in programs. This sounds simple enough. However, the Savings class doesn't do a good job of simulating a savings account.

Simulating real-world objects

Real-world accounts have data-type properties such as account numbers and balances, the same as the Savings class. This makes Savings a good starting point for describing a real account. But real-world accounts do things. Savings accounts allow you to do things such as deposit funds, accumulate interest, see a balance, or even (if you have any money in the account), withdraw funds!

Programs "do things" through functions. A C++ program might call `strcmp()` to compare two character strings or `max()` to return the maximum of two values. In fact, the online bonus Chapter 1 explains that even stream input and output (`cin >>` and `cout <<`) are a special form of function *call*.

The `Savings` class needs active properties of its own if it's to do a good job of representing a real-world concept. For example, it should allow a deposit to be added to an account:

```
class SavingsAccount
{
  public:
   double deposit(double amount)
    {
        balance += amount;
        return balance;
    }
    unsigned accountNumber;
    double balance;
};
```

In addition to the account number and balance, this version of `SavingsAccount` includes the function `deposit()`. This gives `Savings` the ability to control its own future. The class `SavingsAccount` can also use other functions, such as `accumulateInterest()`, `getBalance()`, or `withdraw()`.

REMEMBER

Functions defined in a class are called *member functions.*

Why bother with member functions?

Why should you bother with member functions? What's wrong with the good ol' days of functional programming where functions simply stood on their own?

TECHNICAL STUFF

I'm using the term *functional programming* synonymously with *procedural programming*, the way programming was done before object-oriented programming came along. With procedural programming, functions are independent in that they are presented by themselves and can be used by any other part of the code, as shown in the following example:

```
class SavingsAccount
{
  public:
    unsigned accountNumber;
```

```
    double balance;
};

double deposit(SavingsAccount& s, double amount)
{
    s.balance += amount;
    return s.balance;
}
```

Here, deposit() implements the "deposit into savings account" function. This functional solution relies on an outside function, deposit(), to implement an activity that savings accounts perform but that SavingsAccount lacks. This gets the job done, but it does so by breaking the object-oriented (OO) rules.

The microwave oven has internal components that it "knows" how to use in order to cook, defrost, and burn to a crisp. Class data members are similar to the parts of a microwave — the member functions of a class perform cook-like functions.

When you make nachos, you don't have to start hooking up the internal components of the oven in a certain way to make it work. Nor do you rely on some external device to reach into a mess of wiring for you. You want your classes to work the same way your microwave does (and, no, I don't mean "not very well"). You want your classes to know how to manipulate their internals without outside intervention.

Adding a Member Function

To demonstrate member functions, start by defining a class, Student. One possible representation of such a class follows (taken from the program CallMemberFunction included in the downloadable files for this book):

```
class Student
{
  public:
    // add a completed course to the record
    double addCourse(int hours, double grade)
    {
        // calculate the sum of all courses times
        // the average grade
        double weightedGPA;
        weightedGPA = semesterHours * gpa;
        // now add in the new course
```

```
        semesterHours += hours;
        weightedGPA += grade * hours;
        gpa = weightedGPA / semesterHours;

        // return the new gpa
        return gpa;
    }
    int semesterHours;
    double gpa;
};
```

The function addCourse(int, double) is called a member function of the class Student. In principle, it's a property of the class, like the data members semesterHours and gpa.

Sometimes, functions that are not members of a class are class "plain ol' functions," but I'll refer to them simply as *nonmembers.*

REMEMBER

In our example, the member functions precede the data members, but there's no hard-and-fast rule that says this must be the case. The members of a class can be listed in any order — I just prefer to put the functions first.

TECHNICAL STUFF

For historical reasons, member functions are also called *methods.* This term originated in one of the original object-oriented languages. The name made sense there, but it makes no sense in C++. Nevertheless, the term has gained popularity in OO circles because it's easier to say than "member function." (The fact that it sounds more impressive probably doesn't hurt, either.) So, if your friends start spouting off at a dinner party about "methods of the class," just replace *methods* with *member functions* and reparse anything they say.

Calling a Member Function

The following CallMemberFunction program shows how to invoke the member function addCourse():

```
// CallMemberFunction - define and invoke a function
//                      that's a member of the class Student
//
#include <print>
#include <iostream>
using namespace std;
```

```
class Student
{
  public:
    // add a completed course to the record
    double addCourse(int hours, double grade)
    {
        // calculate the sum of all courses times
        // the average grade
        double weightedGPA;
        weightedGPA = semesterHours * gpa;

        // now add in the new course
        semesterHours += hours;
        weightedGPA += grade * hours;
        gpa = weightedGPA / semesterHours;

        // return the new gpa
        return gpa;
    }
    int semesterHours;
    double gpa;
};

int main(int nNumberofArgs, char* pszArgs[])
{
    // create a Student object and initialize it
    Student s;
    s.semesterHours = 3;
    s.gpa = 3.0;

    // the values before the call
    println("Before: s = ({}, {})", s.semesterHours, s.gpa);

    // the following subjects the data members of the s
    // object to the member function addCourse()
    println("Adding 3 hours with a grade of 4.0");
    s.addCourse(3, 4.0); // call the member function

    // the values are now changed
    println("After: s = ({}, {})", s.semesterHours, s.gpa);
}
```

The syntax for calling a member function looks like a cross between the syntax for accessing a data member and the syntax used for calling a function. The right side of the dot looks like a conventional function call, but the left side of the dot has an object.

REMEMBER

In the call `s.addCourse()`, we say that "`addCourse()` operates on the object `s`" or, said another way, "`s` is the student to which the course is to be added." You can't fetch the number of semester hours without knowing from which student to fetch those hours, and you can't add a student to a course without knowing which student to add. Calling a member function without an object makes no more sense than referencing a data member without an object.

Accessing Other Members from a Member Function

I can see it clearly: You repeat to yourself, "Accessing a member without an object makes no sense. Accessing a member without an object makes no sense. Accessing . . ." Just about the time you've accepted this, you look at the member function `Student::addCourse()` and — *wham!* — it hits you: `addCourse()` accesses other class members without reference to an object. So, how is that being done?

Okay, which is it — can you or can't you?

Take my word for it — you can't. When you reference a member of `Student` from `addCourse()`, that reference is against the `Student` object with which the call to `addCourse()` was made. Huh? Go back to the `CallMemberFunction` example. A stripped-down version appears here with a second student (`t`) added:

```
int main(int nNumberofArgs, char* pszArgs[])
{
    Student s;
    s.semesterHours = 10;
    s.gpa      = 3.0;
    s.addCourse(3, 4.0); // call the member function

    Student t;
    t.semesterHours = 6;
    t.gpa      = 1.0;      // not doing so good
    t.addCourse(3, 1.5);  // things aren't getting
                          // much better
}
```

When addCourse() is invoked with the object s, all the otherwise unqualified member references in addCourse() refer to s as well. Thus, the reference to semesterHours in addCourse() refers to s.semesterHours, and gpa refers to s.gpa. But when addCourse() is invoked with the Student t object, these same references are to t.semesterHours and t.gpa instead.

REMEMBER

The object with which the member function was invoked is the "current" object, and all unqualified references to class members refer to this object. Put another way, unqualified references to class members made from a member function are always against the current object.

TECHNICAL STUFF

NAMING THE CURRENT OBJECT

How does the member function know what the current object is? It's not magic — the address of the object is passed to the member function as an implicit and hidden first argument. In other words, the following conversion is taking place:

```
s.addCourse(3, 2.5)
```

is like:

```
Student::addCourse(&s, 3, 2.5)
```

(Note that you can't actually use the explicit syntax; this is just the way C++ sees it.)

Inside the function, this implicit pointer to the current object has a name, in case you need to refer to it. It's called this, as in "Which object? *This* object." Get it? The type of this is always a pointer to an object of the appropriate class.

Anytime a member function refers to another member of the same class without providing an object explicitly, C++ assumes that the programmer meant this. You also can refer to this explicitly, if you like. I could have written Student::addCourse() as follows:

```
double Student::addCourse(int hours, double grade)
{
    double weightedGPA;
    weightedGPA = this->semesterHours * this->gpa;

    // now add in the new course
    this->semesterHours += hours;
```

```
        weightedGPA += hours * grade;
        this->gpa = weightedGPA / this->semesterHours;
        return this->gpa;
    }
```

The effect is the same whether you explicitly include `this`, as in the preceding example, or leave it implicit, as you did before.

Scope Resolution (and I Don't Mean How Well Your Telescope Works)

The character combination `::` between a member and its class name is called the *scope resolution operator* because it indicates the class to which a member belongs. The class name before the colons is like the family last name, though the function name after the colons is like the first name — the order is similar to a Chinese name, family name first.

You may have seen the scope resolution operator get used previously whenever you used `std::print` and `std::println`. Now you know that these are member functions of the class `std`!

You also can use the `::` operator to describe a nonmember function by using a null class name. In the following listing, you can see that there's an `addCourse()` function that isn't part of the `Student` class. The nonmember function `addCourse()`, for example, can be referred to as `::addCourse(int, double)`, if you prefer. This is like a function without a home.

Normally, the `::` operator is optional, but on a few occasions, this is not so, as illustrated here:

```
// addCourse - combine the hours and grade into
//             a weighted grade
double addCourse(int hours, double grade)
{
   return hours * grade;
}
class Student
{
  public:
   // add a completed course to the record
```

```
    double addCourse(int hours, double grade)
    {
       // call some external function to calculate
       // the weighted grade
       double weightedGPA=::addCourse(semesterHours,gpa);

       // now add in the new course
       semesterHours += hours;

       // use the same function to calculate the
       // weighted grade of this new course
       weightedGPA += ::addCourse(hours, grade);
       gpa = weightedGPA / semesterHours;

       // return the new gpa
       return gpa;
    }

    int semesterHours;
    double gpa;
};
```

Here, I want the member function `Student::addCourse()` to call the nonmember function `::addCourse()`. Without the `::` operator, however, a call to `addCourse()` from `Student` refers to `Student::addCourse()`. This would result in the function calling itself.

Defining a Member Function in the Class

A member function can be defined either in the class or separately. In the previous examples, I defined the member functions within the classes. When defined in the class definition, the function looks like the following:

```
// Savings - define a class that includes the ability
//           to make a deposit
class Savings
{
  public:
    // define a member function deposit()
    double deposit(double amount)
    {
        balance += amount;
```

```
        return balance;
    }
    unsigned int accountNumber;
    double balance;
};
```

This code can be created in a separate file that the preprocessor (covered in Chapter 11) can then include with your program. This separate file can be an `include` file or a module, as described in Chapter 11. Using the older `include` file approach, the code would be saved in a file named something like `Savings.h`. If you saved this as part of a module (the more modern approach), you'd save it as a file with an extension indicating a module.

Using an `include` file or module is pretty slick. Now a program can include the class definition (along with the definition for the member function). If the previous `Savings` class had been saved in a file called `Savings.h`, then the following shows this being used in the venerable `SavingsClassInline` program:

```
// SavingsClassInline - invoke a member function that's
//                      both declared and defined within
//                      the class Student
//
#include <print>
#include <iostream>

using namespace std;
#include "Savings.h"

int main(int nNumberofArgs, char* pszArgs[])
{
   Savings s;
   s.accountNumber = 123456;
   s.balance = 0.0;

   println("Balance is {}", s.balance);

   // now add something to the account
   println("Depositing 10 to account {}", s.accountNumber);
   s.deposit(10);
   println("Balance is {}", s.balance);
}
```

This is cool because everyone other than the programmer of the `Savings` class can concentrate on the act of performing a deposit rather than on the details of banking. These details are neatly tucked away (some might say *encapsulated*) in their own `include` files.

REMEMBER

The `#include` directive inserts the contents of the file during the compilation process. The C++ compiler actually "sees" your source file with the contents of the `Savings.h` file included. (See Chapter 11 for details on `include` files.)

C++23 NEW

I am showing you how to use a header file included here because that's how most developers now apply classes. Having said that, as newer versions of C++ (such as C++23 and C++26) become more mainstream, modules will become the preferred way to import or include files. For a module, instead of naming the previous listing as `Savings.h`, you'd name it `Savings.cppm` (or `Savings.ixx` for those using Microsoft Visual Studio). See Chapter 11 for a review on how to include this as a module.

TECHNICAL STUFF

INLINING MEMBER FUNCTIONS

Member functions defined in the class default to inline (unless they have been specifically outlined by a compiler switch or for any number of technical reasons). Mostly, this is because a member function defined in the class is usually small, and small functions are prime candidates for inlining.

Remember that an inline function is expanded where it's invoked. (See Chapter 11 for a comparison of inline functions and macros.) An inline function executes faster because the processor doesn't have to jump over to where the function is defined — inline functions usually take up more memory because they are copied into every call instead of being defined just once.

There's another good but more technical reason to inline member functions defined within a class. Remember that C++ structures are normally defined in `include` files, which are then included in the `.CPP` source files that need them. Such `include` files should not contain data or functions, because these files are compiled multiple times. Including an inline function is okay, however, because it (like a macro) expands in place in the source file. The same applies to C++ classes. By defaulting member functions defined in classes inline, you avoid the preceding problem.

Keeping a Member Function after Class

For larger functions, putting the code directly in the class definition can lead to some large, unwieldy class definitions. To prevent this, C++ lets you define member functions outside the class.

TIP

A function that's defined outside the class is said to be an *outline function*. This term is meant to be the opposite of an inline function that has been defined within the class. Your basic functions, such as those that pop up in this book since Chapter 7, are also outline functions.

When written outside the class declaration, the `Savings.h` (or `Savings.cppm` if using modules) file declares the `deposit()` function without defining it, as follows:

```
// Savings - define a class that includes the ability
//           to make a deposit
class Savings
{
  public:
     // declare but don't define member function
     double deposit(double amount);
     unsigned int accountNumber;
     double balance;
};
```

The definition of the `deposit()` function must be included in one of the source files that make up the program. (For simplicity's sake, I defined it within `main.cpp`.)

TIP

You would not normally combine the member function definition with the rest of your program. It's more convenient to collect the outlined member function definitions into a source file with an appropriate name (such as `Savings.cpp`). This source file is combined with other source files as part of building the executable program. (I describe this process in Chapter 23.)

```
// SavingsClassOutline - invoke a member function that's
//                       declared within a class but
//                       defined in a separate file
//
#include <print>

using namespace std;
#include "Savings.h"
```

```
// define the member function Savings::deposit()
// (normally this is contained in a separate file that is
// then combined with a different file that is combined)
double Savings::deposit(double amount)
{
    balance += amount;
    return balance;
}

// the main program
int main(int nNumberofArgs, char* pszArgs[])
{
    Savings s;
    s.accountNumber = 123456;
    s.balance = 0.0;
    // now add something to the account
    println("Depositing 10 to account {}",
        s.accountNumber);
    s.deposit(10);
    println("Balance is {}", s.balance);
}
```

This class definition contains nothing more than a prototype declaration for the function `deposit()`. The function definition appears separately. The member function prototype declaration in the structure is analogous to any other function prototype declaration and, like all prototype declarations, is required. (See Chapter 7 for more on function prototypes.)

Notice how the function nickname `deposit()` was good enough when the function was defined within the class. When defined outside the class, however, the function requires its extended name, `Savings::deposit()`.

Overloading Member Functions

Member functions can be overloaded in the same way that conventional functions are overloaded. (See Chapter 7 if you don't remember what that means.) Remember, however, that the class name is part of the extended name. Thus, the following functions are all legal:

```
class Student
{
  public:
```

```
    // grade -- return the current grade point average
    double grade();
    // grade -- set the grade and return previous value
    double grade(double newGPA);
    // ...data members and other stuff...
};
class Slope
{
  public:
    // grade -- return the percentage grade of the slope
    double grade();
    // ...stuff goes here too...
};

// grade - return the letter equivalent of a number grade
char grade(double value);

int main(int argcs, char* pArgs[])
{
    Student s;
    s.grade(3.5);             // Student::grade(double)
    double v = s.grade();   // Student::grade()

    char c = grade(v);      // ::grade(double)

    Slope o;
    double m = o.grade();   // Slope::grade()
    return 0;
}
```

Each call made from `main()` is noted in the comments with the extended name of the function called.

When calling overloaded functions, not only the arguments of the function but also the type of the object (if any) with which the function is invoked are used to resolve the call. (The term *resolve* is object-oriented talk for "decide at compile time which overloaded function to call." A mere mortal might say *differentiate.*)

Holding a Class in Public: Using Structs

C++ includes another keyword that you're likely to encounter when working with data: `struct`. The `struct` keyword can be used in place of `class`. The two keywords are identical except that the public declaration is assumed in the struct and can be omitted. Otherwise, in C++, anywhere that `class` can be used with public data and functions, `struct` can be used.

Having said that, you should stick with `class` for most programs.

The time when the `struct` keyword is generally used is when you're grouping data without functions and all the data is going to be public. A prime example of a struct is one that would hold a point, which is simply an *x, y* coordinate:

```
struct Point {
    int x;
    int y
}
```

Another good example of a struct is a simple date:

```
struct Date {
    int day;
    int month;
    int year;
}
```

TECHNICAL STUFF

Technically, the difference between a struct and a class is that in a class, members are private by default. In a struct, members are public by default.

TIP

If you're going to include a member function, use `class`. If a member function will never be included and you're simply grouping data variables, you can use `class`, though you might consider `struct`. If you're unsure of which to use, use `class`.

Nesting Structs and Classes

You've seen in this chapter that classes and structs can hold data types such as `int`, `long`, and `double`. A class and struct can contain other classes or structs as well. Keep this in mind as you're designing your classes and structs, to keep things encapsulated and organized.

Going back to the microwave example, the microwave can be a class that defines a microwave. That definition can include classes for objects such as a light, a control panel, and a door. The control handle might be a class that contains buttons and other features.

As a simpler example, consider a class for a line. A `line` class might contain a starting point and an ending point. It might also contain a function for calculating the line length. This sounds like a perfect example to use a class containing two structs:

```
// LineLength - Calculate the length of a line using
//              two points. Shows a struct used within
//              a class.

#include <cmath>    // for std::sqrt and std::pow
#include <print>
using namespace std;

struct Point {
    double x;
    double y;
};

class Line {
  public:
    double length() const
    {
        double diff_x = end.x - start.x;
        double diff_y = end.y - start.y;
        // calculate the length using squareroot function
        // from cmath library
        double linelength = std::sqrt(diff_x * diff_x + diff_y
   * diff_y);
        return(linelength);
    }

    // declare our points in our line class:
    Point start;
    Point end;
};

int main()
{
    // create our points and line
    Point nStart;
    Point nEnd;
    Line myLine;

    // assign some values
    nStart.x = 0.0;
    nStart.y = 0.0;
```

```
    nEnd.x = 3.0;
    nEnd.y = 4.0;
    myLine.start = nStart;
    myLine.end = nEnd;

    println("Length of the line from ({},{}) to ({},{}) is {}.",
            nStart.x, nStart.y, nEnd.x, nEnd.y,
            myLine.length() );

    return 0;
}
```

You can see that a Point struct is declared and then used to define a start point and an end point within the Line class. The use of the structure makes the Line class much more readable.

REMEMBER

When Point nStart is assigned to myLine.start, that myLine.start is simply obtaining a copy of the values and has no other association to nStart. This means that if you change the value to the point nStart.x, it doesn't impact the line. This might seem confusing, but consider the same with two ints:

```
int x = 42;
int y = x;    // y now equals 42
x = 99;       // y still equals 42
```

You can directly change the values of the points within the lines by simply extending your dot notation to include both Line and Point. For the previous listing, you can update the starting point as follows:

```
myLine.start.x = 3;
myLine.start.y = 5;
```

You can use the same notation in order to print as well. In fact, the println() statement from the previous listing would be more accurately presented as follows:

```
    println("Length of the line from ({},{}) to ({},{}) is {}.",
            myLine.start.x, myLine.start.y,
            myLine.end.x, myLine.end.y,
            myLine.length() );
```

REMEMBER

Classes and structs should be used to organize or otherwise group data and functionality. This organization is the core of object-oriented programming because the group of data and function definitions is what you use to create the objects! As you progress through the rest of this book, I expand on the class concept to add more power to what you can do.

IN THIS CHAPTER

» Examining an array of chars versus a string

» Understanding what a string is

» Tapping into the library of string functions

» Viewing, chopping, and otherwise manipulating text strings

» Determining how to format variables into strings

Chapter 14
Separating Letters from Words: Character Arrays versus Strings

We interrupt your regularly scheduled learning of C++ with an important message. In Chapter 13, I talk a lot about classes and objects. Chapter 15 takes another bite of the Classes apple, focusing on how to use them in a variety of ways, including with arrays, functions, and more. For now, however, it's time to do a deep dive into one specific class: the C++ string.

The `string` class, which is a part of the standard C++ library (`std::string`), stores a group of characters and provides many operations that can be performed on those characters through its member functions. The `string` class illustrates the power of C++ and classes. Just as you can use a microwave to heat a plate of nachos, the `string` class can be used to "heat up" what can be done with groups of characters!

Distinguishing Between a String and an Array of Characters

If I tell you that `string` is a class you can use in C++, based on what I describe in earlier chapters, you should be able to determine the following:

- `string` holds a group of characters.
- `string` likely contains member functions to work with those characters.

The second bullet differentiates a string from the array of characters I talk about in Chapter 8. As I spell out there, you declare an array of characters this way:

```
char myText[] = "Hi Mom!";
```

REMEMBER

This line declares a character array variable that holds 8 characters: 'H', 'I', a space, 'M', 'o', 'm', '!', and a null character. Don't forget that null character!

The String Container

The character array is the most common form of array used to display text. Using a character array is relatively easy for doing some basic tasks. For example, printing with a character array, whether a constant or a variable, is simple:

```
std::println("{}", myText); // printing a char array
std::println("Hi Dad!");    // printing a constant
```

But things grow complicated quickly when you try to perform an operation even as simple as concatenating two of these null-terminated strings — as you can see with the `concatCharString()` method in this listing:

```
#include <memory>
#include <cstring>
#include <print>
using namespace std;

unique_ptr<char[]> concatCharString(const char* s1,
  const char* s2)
{
  int length = strlen(s1) + strlen(s2) + 1;
```

```
    auto s = make_unique<char[]>(length);

    strcpy(s.get(), s1);
    strcat(s.get(), s2);

    return s;
}

int main()
{
    char first[] = "Bradley";
    char last[] = "Jones";

    auto full = concatCharString(first, " ");
    full = concatCharString(full.get(), last);
    println("{}", full.get());
}
```

The concatCharString() function is all about splicing together two distinct character arrays. To do this, however, you need to have a new array that's big enough to hold both arrays. Once you have a new array that's big enough, you can then use C-style functions to copy the first string and concatenate the second string to that one. That's a lot of code to do something that seems like it should be simple.

To make life much easier for you and other C++ programmers, the standard C++ library (std) provides a string class to handle strings. The string class provides numerous operations (and overloaded operators) to simplify the manipulation of character strings. The same concatCharString() operation can be performed as follows using string objects:

```
string concatCharString(const string& s1, const string& s2)
{
    return s1 + s2;
}
```

The full listing is simplified as well:

```
#include <string>
#include <print>
using namespace std;

string concatCharString(const string& s1, const string& s2)
{
```

```
    return s1 + s2;
}

int main()
{
    string first = "Bradley";
    string last = "Jones";

    string full = concatCharString(first, " ");
    full = concatCharString(full, last);
    println("{}", full);
}
```

Or, better, you can throw out the new `concatCharString()` function altogether and simplify what is happening in `main()` by using the following:

```
#include <string>
#include <print>
using namespace std;

int main()
{
    string first = "Bradley";
    string last = "Jones";

    println("{}", first);
    println("{}", last);

    string full = first + " " + last;
    println("{}", full);
}
```

Clearly, if you look at this last listing, strings make coding much easier in the C++ world!

Tapping into Your Library of String Functions

The previous section shows you how strings can make concatenating easy when compared to doing the same thing using character arrays. The `string` class has many other functions that you can also tap into, as shown in Table 14-1. For your reference, Table 14-2 is included as well, which lists many of the operators that the `string` class overloads. By overloading the operators (a topic covered in Chapter 24), you can use the operators with a given class. Overloading the addition (+) operator is what makes the concatenation work in the listing in the previous section.

TABLE 14-1 Major Methods of the string Class

Method	What It Does
`string()`	Creates an empty string object
`string(const char*)`	Creates a string object from a null-terminated character array
`string(const string& s)`	Creates a new string object as a copy of an existing string object s
`~string()`	Returns internal memory to the heap and cleans up
`string& append(const string& s)` `string& append(const char* pszS)`	Appends a string to the end of the current string
`char at(size_type index)`	Returns a reference to the `index'`/th character in the current string
`char& back()` `const char& back()`	Accesses the last character of a string
`size_t capacity()`	Returns the number of characters the current string object can accommodate without allocating more space from the heap
`int compare(const string& s)`	Returns `< 0` if the current object is lexicographically less than s, `0` if the current object is equal to s, and `> 0` if the current object is greater than s
`bool contains(const std::string& substr) const;`	Returns `true` or `false` depending on whether `substr` is within a string (new method starting with C++23)
`const char* c_str()` `const char* data()`	Returns a pointer to the null-terminated character array string within the current object
`bool empty()`	Returns `true` if the current object is empty

(continued)

TABLE 14-1 *(continued)*

Method	What It Does

constexpr bool ends_with(std::string_view sv) const noexcept;
constexpr bool ends_with(CharT c) const noexcept;
constexpr bool ends_with(const CharT* s) const;
	Returns `true` or `false` based on whether a string ends with a given sequence of characters

size_t find(const string& s, size_t index = 0);	Searches for the substring s within the current string starting at the `index`'/th character; returns the index of the substring; returns `string::npos` if the substring isn't found
char& front() const char& front()	Accesses the first character of a string
string& insert(size_t index, const string& s) string& insert(size_t index, const char* pszS)	Inserts a string into the current string, starting at offset index
size_t max_size()	Returns the maximum number of objects that a string object can hold, ever
string& replace(size_t index, size_t num, const string& s) string& replace(size_t index, size_t num, const char* pszS)	Replaces num characters in the current string, starting at offset `index` and enlarges the size of the current string if necessary
void resize(size_t size)	Resizes the internal buffer to the specified length
Void shrink_to_fit()	Requests that a string reduce its capacity to match its current size
size_t size() size_t length()	Returns the length of the current string

constexpr bool starts_with(std::string_view sv) const noexcept;
constexpr bool starts_with(CharT c) const noexcept;
constexpr bool starts_with(const CharT* s) const;
	Returns `true` or `false` based on whether a string starts with a given sequence of characters

string substr(size_t index, size_t length)	Returns a string consisting of the current string, starting at offset `index` and continuing for `length` characters

TABLE 14-2 Overloaded Operators in the string Class

Operator	Method	What It Does
=	`string& operator=(const string& s)`	Overwrites the current object with a copy of the string s
>>	`istream& operator>>()`	Extracts a string from the input file and stops when `istream::width()` characters are read, an error occurs, EOF is encountered, or white space is encountered. This method is guaranteed not to overflow the internal buffer
<<	`ostream& operator<<()`	Inserts string to the output file
+	`string operator+(const string& s1, const string& s2) string operator+(const string& s1, const char* pszS2)`	Creates a new string that is the concatenation of two existing strings
+=	`string& operator+=(const string& s); string& Operator+=(const char* pszS)`	Appends a string to the end of the current string
[]	`char& operator[](size_ type index)`	Returns the `index`'th character of the current string
==	`bool operator==(const string& s1, const string& s2)`	Returns `true` if the two strings are lexicographically equivalent
<	`bool operator<(const string& s1, const string& s2)`	Returns `true` if `s1` is lexicographically less than `s2` (if `s1` occurs before `s2` in the dictionary, in other words)
>	`bool operator>(const string& s1, const string& s2)`	Returns `true` if `s1` is lexicographically greater than `s2` (if `s1` occurs after `s2` in the dictionary, in other words)

WARNING

The C++ standard says that string functions such as `max_size()` return a number that is of the type `size_type`. I list the argument types in Table 14-1 as `size_t` because that's the way they're declared in many compilers. Currently, `size_t` is generally defined as `unsigned long`, and `size_type` is defined as a `size_t`. Be forewarned that at some future date, these two types might diverge and the argument types in Table 14-1 might change from `size_t` to `size_type`.

The following `STLString` program demonstrates just a few of the capabilities of the `string` class:

```
// STLString - demonstrates just a few of the features
//             of the string class, which is part of the
//             Standard Template Library
#include <string>
```

```
#include <print>
using namespace std;

// removeSpaces - removes any spaces within a string
string removeSpaces(const string& source)
{
   // make a copy of the source string so that we don't
   // modify it
   string s = source;

   // find the offset of the first space;
   // search the string until no more spaces are found
   size_t offset;
   while((offset = s.find(" ")) != string::npos)
   {
        // remove the space just discovered
        s.erase(offset, 1);
   }
   return s;
}

// insertPhrase - insert a phrase in the position of
//               <ip> for insertion point
string insertPhrase(const string& source)
{
   string s = source;
   size_t offset = s.find("<ip>");
   if (offset != string::npos)
   {
        s.erase(offset, 4);
        s.insert(offset, "L.");
   }
   return s;
}

int main(int argc, char* pArgs[])
{
   // create a string that is the sum of two strings
   println("string1 + string2 = {}",
        (string("string1") + string("string2")));

   // create a test string and then remove all spaces
   // from it using simple string methods
   string s2("This is a test string");
```

```
    println("<{}> minus spaces = <{}>",
        s2, removeSpaces(s2));

    // insert a phrase within the middle of an existing
    // sentence (at the location of "<ip>")
    string s3 = "Bradley <ip> Jones";
    println( "{} -> {}", s3, insertPhrase(s3));
}
```

The `main()` function begins by using `operator+()` to append two strings together; `main()` then calls the `removeSpaces()` method to remove any spaces found in the string provided. It does this by using the `string.find()` operation to return the offset of the first `" "` that it finds. Once a space is found, `removeSpaces()` uses the `erase()` method to remove the space. The function picks up where it left off, searching for spaces and erasing them until `find()` returns `npos`, indicating that it didn't find what it was looking for.

TIP

The constant `npos` is a constant of type `size_t` that is the largest unsigned value possible. It's numerically equal to −1. This is used for the "not found position," just like `'\0'` is the "noncharacter."

The `insertPhrase()` method uses the `find()` method to find the insertion point flagged by the substring `"<ip>"`. The function then calls `erase` to remove the `"<ip>"` flag, and then calls `string.insert()` to insert a new string in the middle of an existing string.

This is the resulting output:

```
string1 + string2 = string1string2
<this is a test string> minus spaces = <thisisateststring>
Bradley <ip> Jones -> Bradley L. Jones
```

WARNING

At its core, a `string` is still an array. The operations provided by the STL make it easier to manipulate `string` objects, but not *that* much faster. For example, inserting something into the middle of a `string` still involves moving around the contents of arrays.

Many of the functions in Table 14-1 let you manipulate (or see a different view of) your strings. The previous listing highlighted `find()`, `removespaces()`, `insert()`, and `erase()`. In the following listing, you get to see a few more string functions in use, including `front()`, `back()`, and `starts_with()`:

```
// moreSTLStringFun.cpp - demonstrates a few more of the
//              string class functions along with a few
```

```
//              character-based functions from the
//              Standard Template Library
#include <string>
#include <print>
#include <cctype>
using namespace std;

int main()
{
   string mySentence = "how now brown cow?";
   string myPath = "http://www.vbjournal.com";
   string myName = "Bradley";

// Make sure first character of a sentence is capitalized
   if ( islower(mySentence.front()) )
   {
       mySentence.front() = toupper((mySentence.front()));
   }
   println("{}", mySentence);

// Statement or question?
   switch( mySentence.back())
   {
       case '.':
          println("Sentence appears to be a statement.");
          break;
       case '?':
          println("Sentence appears to be a question.");
          break;
       case '!':
          println("Sentence appears to be an exclamation.");
          break;
       default:
          println("Not sure what the sentence is");
          break;
   }

// Is the string a URL?
   if( myPath.starts_with("http://") ||
      myPath.starts_with("www." ))
   {
      println("{} appears to be a URL", myPath);
   }
}
```

When you enter and run this code, you should see the following output:

```
How now brown cow?
Sentence appears to be a question.
http://www.vbjournal.com appears to be a URL
```

Most of the code should be easy to follow at this point, based on what I've already discussed about C++. Within this listing, however, a few character-based functions are also included from the cctype library. These allow you to verify whether a letter is lowercase (islower()) as well as to change a character from lowercase to uppercase (toupper()).

TIP

After you enter and run this listing, make changes to the values set to the strings, and then see how the output changes. Hopefully, these examples lead you to consider other ways that string functions can be applied to real-world scenarios.

Gaining a New View of Strings

Sometimes you don't need to own a string, but rather just need to borrow it for a quick view. Starting with C++17, you can save some resources by using a string_view rather than a string. A string_view is considered just a pointer to a string, so it doesn't really contain the string itself. That means if the original string is destroyed or modified or otherwise goes away, the string_view can become invalid. For this reason, you wouldn't want to assign a string_view to a temporary variable or to local variables returned from functions. Rather, you want to use them in cases such as when passing a string to a function, when viewing a string or string literal, or when you need compatibility between strings and C-style strings that include character pointers.

To use a string_view, you need to include the string_view header, which is also a part of the standard template library. Once it's included, you can use the string_view to create a unified interface for accepting strings in a function, as shown in the following code:

```
#include <print>
#include <string_view>
using namespace std;

void sayHello(string_view name)
{
   println("Hello, {}", name);
}
```

```
int main()
{
    string name = "Pinky";
    char name2[] = "Brain";
    const char* name3 = "Dot";

    sayHello(name);
    sayHello(name2);
    sayHello(name3);
    sayHello("Yakko");
    sayHello(string_view("Wakko"));
}
```

This listing declares a simple method to print a greeting. The method isn't planning to do any manipulations of the string being provided, so a `string_view` works. Notice also that the `string_view` is compatible with various storage methods for holding a string. This includes a normal string, C-style strings (character arrays), a literal string, and (obviously) other `string_views`.

Taking a Deeper Dive into Formatting

Now that you're more aware of strings and what you can do with them in C++, it's time to look at another function that was added to C++ in the C++20 standard: the `format()` function. This function makes it easy for you to combine data types into a string.

Let me share a little secret with you, though: What `format()` allows you to do is what you've been doing with print statements already! The difference between using `format()` and using the various printing functions is that the result of the `format()` function is sent to another string rather than to the console. For example, in the listing in the previous section, the following print statement is used:

```
println("Hello, {}", name);
```

The `println()` function is doing the formatting for you by combining the initial string with the variables that follow. You can do the same thing using `format()` and assign the value to another string:

```
string formattedGreeting = format("Hello, {}", name);
```

In this case, the result is that `formattedGreeting` would contain the formatted text. You can confirm this by updating the `sayHello()` function in the previous listing with the following snippet:

```
void sayHello(string_view name)
{
    string formattedGreeting = format("Hello, {}", name);
    println("{}", formattedGreeting);
}
```

Adding modifiers to your formatting

Chapter 5 presents a number of modifiers that you can use when printing. Those same modifiers are included in Table 14-3; they can be used to format numbers and other values when adding them into a formatting string, whether you're using `print()`, `println()`, or `format()`.

TABLE 14-3 **Formatting Codes for format**

Type of Formatting	Syntax	Sample Output
Decimal precision	`{:2f}`	123.45
Add a thousands separator	`{:L}` (locale-based)	1,234,567 (US locale)
Left aligned	`{:<6}`	"1234 "
Right aligned	`{:>6}`	" 1234"
Center aligned	`{:^6}`	" 1234 "
Hexadecimal	`{:#x}`	"ox2322"
Octal	`{:#0}`	"0o4D2"
Binary	`{:#b}`	"0b11111111"

WARNING

Note that you can leave off the `"#"` when formatting the hexadecimal, octal, and binary numbers, but you won't get the prefixes. This isn't recommended, because someone might mistake your output for decimal numbers.

TIP

The hard-coded numbers in the syntax can be changed. Those indicate either precision or the amount of padding to use.

For fun, the following listing is taken from Chapter 4. This time, the listing is using the format() function to format the lines of a menu that are then stored in an array of strings that are then printed. As with Chapter 4's listings, you should enter this listing (or a similar one) and play around with the formatting:

```
#include <string>
#include <print>
using namespace std;

int main()
{
    float hotdog = 3.99;
    float hamburger = 4.99;
    float fries = 2.99;

    string menuLine[5];

    menuLine[0] = format("{:^40}", "Menu");
    menuLine[1] =
   format("========================================");
    menuLine[2] = format("{:<30}{:>10.2f}", "Hotdog", hotdog );
    menuLine[3] = format("{:<30}{:>10.2f}", "Hamburger",
   hamburger );
    menuLine[4] = format("{:<30}{:>10.2f}", "Fries", fries );

    // print the menu
    for( const string& line : menuLine )
    {
        println("{}", line);
    }
}
```

The output from running this listing is a simple menu with a bit of formatting:

```
                  Menu
========================================
Hotdog                              3.99
Hamburger                           4.99
Fries                               2.99
========================================
```

You can see in the code that what is passed to the format() function is similar to what was used in the print statements in Chapter 4. This is no coincidence. The print() and println() functions actually call format() internally.

But wait! Why not just println(line)?

In the listing in the previous section, you might wonder why you can't just print the `line` string:

```
println(line);   // won't work
```

WARNING

You would think this would work, but, alas, it doesn't, because the print functions expect the first argument to be a format string (one that contains modifiers) or they expect a string literal (constant text in double quotes that doesn't change). In the previous listing, the value of `line` can change at runtime, which doesn't align with what is expected for the first parameter of the print functions. For that reason, you need to include the `format` string, even if it's simply holding a single placeholder that will be replaced with a string:

```
println("{}", line);   // works!
```

Changing Numbers to Strings

Before moving on from the topic of character arrays versus strings, one additional topic is worth mentioning: Starting with C++11, the C++ standard library includes the function `STD::to_string()`, which can convert standard number types to a string. Using `to_string()`,you can convert each of the following types to a string:

- `int`
- `long`
- `long long`
- `unsigned`
- `unsigned long`
- `unsigned long long`
- `float`
- `double`
- `long double`

C++26 NEW

Internally, starting with C++26, the to_string() function was updated to be more consistent in formatting, in the same way that the format() function presented numbers. This means that floating numbers are generally presented in a cleaner, shorter format. For example, to_string(0.99) is more likely to return "0.99" rather than "0.990000". Of course, if you want the more verbose "0.990000" instead, you can always use format() to convert the number and use a modifier:

```
std::string myNumberString = std::format("{:.6f}", 0.99);
```

IN THIS CHAPTER

» **Examining the object(ive) behind arrays of objects**

» **Getting a few pointers on object pointers**

» **Strong typing — getting picky about pointers**

» **Navigating through lists of objects**

» **Getting a bit smarter with smart pointers**

Chapter 15
Pointing and Staring at Objects

C++ programmers are forever generating arrays of things — arrays of `int`s, arrays of `double`s — so why not arrays of students? Students stand in line all the time — much more than they care to. The concept of `Student` objects all lined up quietly awaiting their names to be called so that they can jump up to perform some mundane task is just too attractive to pass up.

Declaring Arrays of Objects

Arrays of objects work the same way arrays of simple variables work. (Chapter 8 goes into the care and feeding of arrays of simple — *intrinsic* — variables, and Chapters 9 and 10 describe simple pointers in detail.) Take, for example, the following ArrayOfStudents program, which creates an array of Student objects and then assigns values to one of them:

```
// ArrayOfStudents - define an array of student objects
//                   and access an element in it.
#include <print>
using namespace std;

class Student
{
  public:
   int semesterHours;
   double gpa;
   double addCourse(int hours, double grade)
   {
       double weightedGPA = (semesterHours * gpa) +
  (hours * grade);
       semesterHours += hours;
       gpa = weightedGPA / semesterHours;
       return gpa;
   }
   void printStudent() const
   {
       println("Student GAP:   {:.2f}", gpa);
       println("Student Hours: {}", semesterHours);
   };
};

int main()
{
   Student s[10]; // declare an array of 10 students

   // assign the 5th student a gpa of 4.0 (lucky guy)
   s[4].gpa = 4.0;
   s[4].semesterHours = 32;
   s[4].printStudent();

   // add another course to the 5th student;
   // this time they failed - serves them right
   s[4].addCourse(3, 0.0);
   s[4].printStudent();
}
```

Here, `s` is an array of `Student` objects; `s[4]` refers to the fifth `Student` object in the array. By extension, `s[4].gpa` refers to the GPA of the fifth student. Further, `s[4].addCourse()` calls the `addCourse()` member function to add a course to the fifth `Student` object.

You can see that the data members in the array of `Student` objects are handled by combining what you can see in earlier chapters. You access the specific student in the array by using the array name (`s`, in this case) with the index subscript for the element you want. This is the same as how you access array items made of `int`s, `char`s, or other data types. The other piece is accessing the object's members by using the method I outline in Chapter 13, which is to use the dot operator and the data member name: `s[4].gpa`. It's as easy as heating nachos in a microwave!

Declaring Pointers to Objects

Pointers to objects work like pointers to the simple types I talk about in Chapter 9, as you can see in the sample program `ObjPtr`:

```
// ObjPtr - define and use a pointer to a Student object
#include <print>
using namespace std;

class Student
{
  public:
   int semesterHours;
   double gpa;
   double addCourse(int hours, double grade);
};

int main()
{
   Student s;     // create a Student object
   s.gpa = 3.0;  // assign a value to a member

   // now create a pointer pS to a Student object
   Student* pS;

   // make pS point to our Student object
   pS = &s;
```

```
    // now output the gpa of the object,
    // once via the variable name and a
    // second time via the pointer pS
    println("s.gpa = {}", s.gpa);
    println("pS->gpa = {}", pS->gpa);
}
```

The program declares a variable s of type Student. It then goes on to declare a pointer variable pS of type "pointer to a Student object," also written as Student*. After initializing the value of one of the data members in s, the program then proceeds to assign the address of s to the variable pS. Finally, the program refers to the same Student object, first using the object's name, s, and then using the pointer to the object, pS. (I explain the strange notation pS->gpa; in the "Pointing toward arrow pointers" section, later in this chapter.)

Dereferencing an object pointer

In Chapter 10 you learn that dereferencing a pointer means you determine the value stored at the pointer. In Chapter 10 you learned to do with pointers to basic data types such as int, char, and double by using an asterisk with the pointer's name.

By analogy of pointers to simple variables, you might think that the following refers to the GPA of student s:

```
int main()
{
   Student s;
   Student* pS = &s; // create a pointer to s

   // access the gpa member of the obj pointed at by pS
   // (this doesn't work)
   *pS.gpa = 3.5;
}
```

WARNING

As the comments indicate, this code doesn't work. The problem is that the dot operator (.) is evaluated before the pointer (*). Thus, *ps.gpa is interpreted as if written *(ps.gpa). Parentheses (see the bold in the following snippet) are necessary to force the pointer operator to be evaluated before the dot:

```
int main()
{
   Student s;
```

```
    Student* pS = &s; // create a pointer to s
    // access the gpa member of the obj pointed at by pS
    // (this works as expected)
    (*pS).gpa = 3.5;
}
```

The *pS evaluates to the pointer's Student object pointed at by pS. The .gpa refers to the gpa member of that object.

Pointing toward arrow pointers

Using the asterisk operator together with parentheses works just fine for dereferencing pointers to objects; however, even the most hardened techies would admit that this mixing of asterisks and parentheses is a bit tortured.

C++ offers a more convenient operator for accessing members of an object to avoid clumsy object pointer expressions. The -> operator is defined as follows:

```
ps->gpa is equivalent to (*pS).gpa
```

This leads to the following:

```
int main()
{
    Student s;
    Student* pS = &s; // create a pointer to s

    // access the gpa member of the obj pointed at by pS
    pS->gpa = 3.5;
}
```

REMEMBER

The arrow operator is used almost exclusively because it is easier to read; however, the two forms are completely equivalent.

Passing Objects to Functions

Passing objects to functions is just one of the many ways to entertain yourself. You can accomplish this goal with pointer variables. Because passing objects to functions is a task you'll need to do as you program in C++, you should understand how it works.

Calling a function with an object value

C++ passes arguments to functions by reference when the argument type is flagged with the & property. (Chapter 9 has more on that topic.) However, by default, C++ passes arguments to functions by value. (You can check Chapter 7 on this one, if you insist.)

Complex, user-defined class objects are passed the same as simple `int` values, as shown in the following `PassObjVal` program:

```
// PassObjVal - attempts to change the value of an
//     object in a function fail when the object
//     is passed by value
#include <print>
using namespace std;

class Student
{
   public:
   int semesterHours;
   double gpa;
};

void someFn(Student copyS)
{
   copyS.semesterHours =  10;
   copyS.gpa           =  3.0;
   println("The value of copyS.gpa = {}", copyS.gpa);
}

int main()
{
   Student s;
   s.gpa = 0.0;

   // display the value of s.gpa before calling someFn()
   println("The value of s.gpa = {}", s.gpa);

   // pass the address of the existing object
   println("Calling someFn(Student)");
   someFn(s);
   println("Returned from someFn(Student)");

   // the value of s.gpa remains 0
   println("The value of s.gpa = {}", s.gpa);
}
```

The main() function creates an object s and then passes s to the someFn() function.

REMEMBER

It is not the object s itself that is passed, but rather a copy of s.

The object copyS in someFn() begins life as an exact copy of the variable s in main(). Because it's a copy, any change to copyS made within someFn() has no effect on s back in main(). Executing this program generates the following (understandable but necessarily disappointing) response:

```
The value of s.gpa = 0
Calling someFn(Student)
The value of copyS.gpa = 3
Returned from someFn(Student)
The value of s.gpa = 0
```

Calling a function with an object pointer

Most of the time, a programmer wants any changes made in the function to be reflected in the calling function as well. For this, the C++ programmer must pass either the address of an object or a reference to the object. By passing the address, you can avoid the (understandable but necessarily disappointing) response seen in the previous section with the PassObjVal program.

The following PassObjPtr program uses the address approach:

```
// PassObjPtr - change the contents of an object in
//              a function by passing a pointer
#include <print>
using namespace std;

class Student
{
  public:
   int semesterHours;
   double gpa;
};
void someFn(Student* pS)
{
   pS->semesterHours = 10;
   pS->gpa           = 3.0;
   println("The value of pS->gpa = {}", pS->gpa );
}
```

```
int main()
{
   Student s;
   s.gpa = 0.0;

   // display the value of s.gpa before calling someFn()
   println("The value of s.gpa = {}", s.gpa );

   // pass the address of the existing object
   println("Calling someFn(Student*)");
   someFn(&s);
   println("Returned from someFn(Student*)");

   // the value of s.gpa is now 3.0
   println("The value of s.gpa = {}", s.gpa );
}
```

Here, `Student*`, a pointer to a `Student` object, is the argument that gets passed to `someFn()`. This is reflected in the way the program calls `someFn()`, passing the address of `s` rather than the value of `s`. Giving `someFn()` the address of `s` allows it to modify whatever value is stored there. Conceptually, this is akin to writing down the address of the house `s` on the piece of paper `pS` and then passing that paper to `someFn()`. The function `someFn()` uses the arrow syntax for dereferencing the `pS` pointer.

The output from `PassObjPtr` is much more satisfying (to me, anyway):

```
The value of s.gpa = 0
Calling someFn(Student*)
The value of pS->gpa = 3
Returned from someFn(Student*)
The value of s.gpa = 3
```

Calling a function by using the reference operator

Chapter 7 introduces the concept of passing simple argument types to functions by reference using the `&` operator. The following `PassObjRef` program demonstrates the same for user-defined objects:

```
// PassObjRef - change the contents of an object in
//              a function by using a reference
#include <print>
using namespace std;

class Student
{
  public:
   int semesterHours;
   double gpa;
};

// same as before, but this time using references
void someFn(Student& refS)
{
   refS.semesterHours = 10;
   refS.gpa = 3.0;
   println("The value of copyS.gpa = {}", refS.gpa;
}

int main()
{
   Student s;
   s.gpa = 0.0;

   // display the value of s.gpa before calling someFn()
   println("The value of s.gpa = {}", s.gpa );

   // pass the address of the existing object
   println("Calling someFn(Student*)");
   someFn(s);
   println("Returned from someFn(Student&)");

   // the value of s.gpa is now 3.0
   printn("The value of s.gpa = {}", s.gpa );
}
```

In this example, C++ passes a reference to `s` rather than to a copy. The output from this version is identical to the `PassObjPtr` program — changes made in `someFn()` are retained in `main()`.

Why Bother with Pointers or References?

Okay, so both pointers and references provide relative advantages, but why bother with either one? Why not just always pass the object? I mention one obvious answer earlier in this chapter: You can't modify the object from a function that gets nothing but a copy of the object.

Here's a second reason: Some objects are large — *really* large. An object representing a screen image can be many megabytes long. Passing such an object by value means copying the entire thing into the function's memory.

The object will need to be copied again should that function call another, and so on. After a while, you can end up with dozens of copies of this very large object. That consumes memory, and copying all the objects can make execution of your program slower than booting up Windows.

WARNING

The problem of copying objects gets worse. Chapter 19 fills you in on how making a copy of an object can be even more painful than simply copying some memory around.

REMEMBER

Passing a pointer (or a reference) is *fast*. A pointer is 4 bytes, no matter how big the object being pointed at is.

WHICH TO USE?

Whether you should pass by value, by pointer, or by reference can depend on what you're trying to do and what you need:

Pass by value when:

- The object you're passing is small. For example, basic data types (`int`, `char`, book, `float`) are small, so passing by value works.
- You don't want to change the object, and thus a copy satisfies your needs.

Pass by pointer when:

- You want to change the original object.
- The object you're passing might not contain a value.
- You might need to manage memory dynamically (for example, allocating memory).

Pass by reference when:

- You need to modify the original item.
- You want cleaner and easier-to-read syntax. (No arrow operators needed!)
- You know that the passed object exists (isn't null).

Returning to the Heap

The problems that exist with using simple types of pointers also plague class object pointers. In particular, you must make sure that the pointer you're using actually points to a valid object. For example, don't ever return a reference to an object you've defined as local to the function:

```
MyClass* myFunc()
{
    // the following does not work
    MyClass mc;
    MyClass* pMC = &mc;
    return pMC;
}
```

Upon return from `myFunc()`, the `mc` object goes out of scope. This means that the pointer returned by `myFunc()` is not valid in the calling function, which will lead to unpredictable results for your program.

REMEMBER

I tackle the problem of returning memory that's about to go out of scope in more detail in Chapter 10.

Allocating the object off the heap solves the problem. The *heap* is an area of memory where you can allocate space for your objects to live; however, you must remember to return the space when you are done using it. The following shows this being done using a basic, built-in pointer type:

```
MyClass* myFunc()
{
    MyClass* pMC = new MyClass;
    return pMC;
}
```

Here, the memory allocated off the heap is not returned when the variable pMC goes out of scope. This can also be done using a smart pointer, which is the better, safer solution because the smart pointer will take care of deleting the allocation automatically:

```
#include <memory>

std::shared_ptr<MyClass> myFunc()
{
    auto pMC = std::make_shared<MyClass>();
    return pMC;
}
```

REMEMBER

Programmers allocate memory from the heap if they don't want the memory to be lost when any particular variable goes out of scope. If you use a raw pointer, you're responsible for both allocating and returning heap memory. For modern C++ programming, you should avoid raw pointers and use smart pointers (such as unique_ptr or shared_ptr) because they're safer and less prone to hard-to-find bugs in your programs. (For more on smart pointers, see Chapter 9.)

Allocating heaps of objects

It's also possible to allocate an array of objects off the heap. Again, the following example shows how to carry this out using raw pointers (the old way of doing this), followed by using a smart pointer. The following syntax uses raw pointers:

```
class MyClass
{
  public:
    int nValue;
};
void fn()
{
    MyClass* pMC = new MyClass[5]

    // reference individual members like any array
    for (int i = 0; i < 5; i++)
    {
        pMC[i].nValue = i;
    }
    // uses a different delete keyword to return memory
    // to the heap
    delete[] pMC;
};
```

Notice also that you use the slightly different keyword `delete[]` to return arrays of class objects to the heap. The same code using the more modern approach of smart pointers doesn't require the use of `delete` or `delete[]`; the smart pointer takes care of returning memory for you:

```
#include <memory>

class MyClass
{
  public:
    int nValue;
};
void fn()
{
    std::shared_ptr<MyClass> pMC =
    std::make_shared<MyClass[]>(5);

    // reference individual members like any array
    for  (int i = 0; i < 5; i++)
    {
        pMC[i].nValue = i;
    }
    // no need to delete, because it is done automatically
};
```

In both listings, notice that, once allocated, `pMC` can be used like any other array, with `pMC[i]` referring to the `i`th object of type `MyClass`.

When memory is allocated for you

Many classes (particularly, the `string` class from Chapter 14 and the containers described in the downloadable bonus Chapter 3) manage heap memory for you. For example, the `string` class maintains a character string in memory that it allocates off the heap. The authors of these classes are careful to return heap memory in all the right places so that it's safe to write a function like the following:

```
string myFunc()
{
    string localString;
    localString << cin;
    return localString;
}
```

The object `localString` allocates heap memory when it's created, but carefully returns said memory when it goes out of scope at the end of the function. (I show you how this magic is performed in Chapters 18 and 19.)

Linking Up with Linked Lists

Let's dig into a longer example of using pointers with objects. The second most common structure after the array is called a *list*. Lists come in different sizes and types; however, the most common one is the linked list. In the *linked list*, each object points to the next member in a sort of chain that extends through memory. The program can simply point the last element in the list to a new object to add the new object to the list. This means that the user doesn't have to declare the size of the linked list at the beginning of the program — you can add and remove objects from the list by merely unlinking them. In addition, you can sort the members of a linked list — without actually moving data objects around — by changing the links.

REMEMBER

The cost of such flexibility is speed of access. You can't just reach in and grab the tenth element, for example, like you would in the case of an array. Instead, you have to start at the beginning of the list and link ten times from one object to the next.

As shown in Figure 15-1, a linked list has one other feature besides its run-time expandability (that's good) and its difficulty in accessing an object at random (that's bad): A linked list makes significant use of pointers. This makes linked lists a useful tool for giving you experience in manipulating pointer variables. (That's very good.)

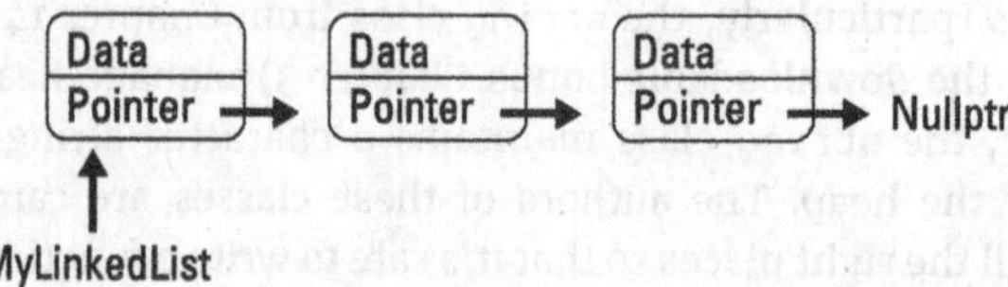

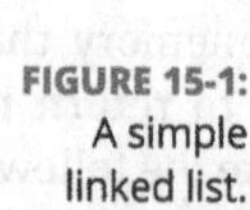

FIGURE 15-1: A simple linked list.

TIP

The C++ standard library offers a number of different types of lists. You can see them in action in the downloadable bonus Chapter 3; however, it's always good to implement your first linked list yourself to get some practice in manipulating pointers.

Not every class can be used to create a linked list. Using a raw pointer, you declare a linkable class as follows:

```
class LinkableClass
{
  public:
    LinkableClass* pNext;
    // other members of the class
};
```

Using a smart pointer is a similar (yet safer) solution:

```
class LinkableClass
{
  public:
    shared_ptr<LinkableClass> pNext;
    // other members of the class
};
```

Either way, the key to a linkable class is the `pNext` pointer. At first blush, this seems odd indeed — a class contains a pointer to itself? Actually, `pNext` is not a pointer to itself but rather to another, different object of the same type.

A linked list is similar to a chain of schoolchildren crossing the street. The `pNext` pointer corresponds to a child's arm reaching out and grabbing the child next to him.

Somewhere outside the linked list is a pointer to the first element of the list, the head pointer. The *head pointer* is simply a pointer of type `LinkableClass*:`, sort of like the teacher holding onto the first kid in the chain.

TIP

Always initialize any pointer to `nullptr`, the pointer that doesn't point to anything, the nonpointer:

```
LinkableClass* pHead = nullptr;
```

or

```
shared_ptr<LinkableClass> pHead = nullptr;
```

To see how linked lists work in practice, consider the following function, which adds the argument passed it to the beginning of a list. Here's the function using a raw pointer:

```
void addHead(LinkableClass* pLC)
{
    pLC->pNext = pHead;
    pHead = pLC;
}
```

And now using a smart pointer:

```
void addHead(smart_ptr<LinkableClass> pLC)
{
    pLC->pNext = pHead;
    pHead = pLC;
}
```

Note that the body of the function is the same. In both cases, the `pNext` pointer of the object is set to point to the first member of the list. This is akin to grabbing the hand of the first kid in the chain. For one instruction, both you and the teacher have hold of this first kid in the list. The second line points the head pointer to the object, sort of like having the teacher let go of the kid you're holding on to and grabbing you instead. That makes you the first kid in the chain.

Performing other operations on a linked list

Adding an object to the head of a list is the simplest operation on a linked list. Moving through the elements in a list gives you a better idea about how a linked list works:

```
// navigate through a linked list
shared_ptr<LinkableClass> pL = pHead;
while(pL != nullptr)
{
    // perform some operation here
    // get the next entry
    pL = pL->pNext;
}
```

The program initializes the `pL` smart pointer to the first object of a list of `LinkableClass` objects through the pointer `pHead`. (Grab the first kid's hand.) The program then enters the `while` loop. If the `pL` pointer is non-null, it points to some LinkableClass object. Within the while loop, the program can perform whatever operation it wants on the object pointed at by pL.

The assignment pL = pL->pNext "moves" the pL pointer over to the next kid in the list of objects. The program checks to see whether pL is null, meaning that I've exhausted the list — I mean, run out of kids, not exhausted all the kids in the list.

Hooking up with a LinkedListData program

The LinkedListData program shown here implements a linked list of objects containing a person's name. The program could easily contain whatever other data you might like, such as Social Security number, grade point average, height, weight, and bank account balance. I've limited the information to just a name to keep the program as simple as possible.

ON THE WEB

Note that I've used a smart pointer in this listing. If you download the code for this book, you'll also find a version of this listing (labeled LinkedListDataRaw.cpp) that uses raw pointers. (It's a little more complex because it includes the cleanup logic for deleting the allocated memory.)

```
// LinkedListDataSharedPtr - store data in a linked list
#include <iostream>
#include <string>
#include <print>
#include <memory>
using namespace std;

// NameDataSet - stores a person's name (these objects
//               could easily store any other information
//               desired).

class NameDataSet
{
  public:
   string sName;
   shared_ptr<NameDataSet> pNext;  // link to next list entry
};

// the pointer to the first entry in the list
shared_ptr<NameDataSet> pHead = nullptr;

// add - add a new member to the linked list
```

```
void add(shared_ptr<NameDataSet> pNDS)
{
   pNDS->pNext = pHead; // point current entry to beginning
                        // of list
   pHead = pNDS;        // point head pointer to current entry
}

// getData - read a name; return nullptr if no more
shared_ptr<NameDataSet> getData()
{
   string name;
   print("Enter name: ");
   cin >> name;              // read the name

   // if the name entered is 'exit'...
   if (name == "exit")
   {
      // ...return a null pointer to terminate input
      return nullptr;
   }

   // get a new entry and fill in values
   auto pNDS = make_shared<NameDataSet>();
   pNDS->sName = name;

   // return the address of the object created
   return pNDS;
}

int main()
{
   println("Read names of students");
   println("Enter 'exit' for first name to exit");
   // create (another) NameDataSet object
   shared_ptr<NameDataSet> pNDS;
   while((pNDS = getData()))
   {
      add(pNDS); // add it to the list of
                       // NameDataSet objects
   }

   // to display the objects, iterate through the
   // list (stop when the next address is NULL)
   println("\nEntries:");
```

```
    for(shared_ptr<NameDataSet> pIter = pHead;
                    pIter; pIter = pIter->pNext)
    {
        // display name of current entry
        println("{}", pIter->sName);
    }
}
```

Although somewhat lengthy, the `LinkedListDataSharedPtr` program is simple if you take it in parts. The `NameDataSet` structure has room for a person's name and a link to the next `NameDataSet` object in a linked list. (I mention earlier in this section that this class would have other members in a real-world application.)

TIP

I have used the `string` class to contain the person's name; as Chapter 14 shows, it's much easier to use the `string` class than zero-terminated character strings.

REMEMBER

You see the `string` class used in preference to character strings in most applications these days. The `string` class has become about as close to an intrinsic type in the C++ language as possible.

The `main()` function starts looping, calling `getData()` on each iteration to fetch another `NameDataSet` entry from the user. The program exits the loop if `getData()` returns a null, the "nonaddress," for an address.

The `getData()` function prompts the user for a name and reads in whatever the user enters. If the string entered is equal to `exit`, the function returns a null to the caller, thereby exiting the `while` loop. If the string entered is not `exit`, the program creates a new `NameDataSet` object, populates the name, and, finally, returns the node's address to `main()`, where it's used in the `add()` function.

REMEMBER

Never leave link pointers uninitialized. Use the old programmer's wives' tale: "When in doubt, zero it out." (I mean "old tale," not "tale of an old wife.")

The `main()` function adds each object returned from `getData()` to the beginning of the linked list pointed at by the global variable `pHead`. Control exits the initial `while` loop when `getData()` returns a null. `main()` then enters a second section that iterates through the completed list, displaying the name from each object. This time, I use a `for` loop because it's functionally equivalent to the earlier `while` loop. The `for` loop initializes the iteration pointer `pIter` to point to the first element in the list through the assignment `pIter = pHead`. It next checks to see whether `pIter` is null, which will be the case when the list is exhausted. It then enters the loop. On each round trip through the `for` loop, the third clause moves `pIter` from one object to the next with the assignment `pIter = pIter->pNext` before repeating the test and the body of the loop. This pattern is commonly followed for all list types.

The output of a sample run of the program appears as follows:

```
Read names of students
Enter 'exit' for first name to exit
Enter name: Randy
Enter name: Johnny
Enter name: Melissa
Enter name: exit

Entries:
Melissa
Johnny
Randy
```

TIP

The program outputs the names in the opposite order in which they were entered. This is because each new object is added to the beginning of the list, so the list head is always pointing to the last node added, as shown in Figure 15-2. Alternatively, to maintain the order items were entered, you can add each object to the end of the list — doing so just takes a little more code. It links newly added objects to the end of the list so that the list comes out in the same order it was entered. The only difference is in the *add()* function. See whether you can create this forward version before you peek at my solution.

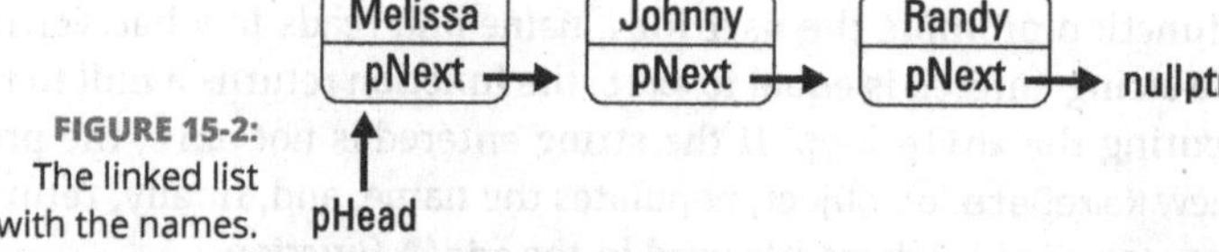

FIGURE 15-2: The linked list with the names.

A difference between unique and shared pointers

In presenting the linked list in earlier sections, I show both the use of raw pointers and the use of a smart pointer. You're likely to see the use of raw pointers in older code, so it's important to understand how they work. The use of smart pointers, however, is the recommended method for coding pointers going forward with C++ because they're safer and cleaner.

I mention two types of smart pointers in this book: `shared_ptr` and `unique_ptr`. In the linked list code, I used a `shared_ptr`. Some might argue that a `unique_ptr` would be a better solution because only a single node is holding the pointer. If you download the files that accompany this book, you'll find a third linked-list listing, `LinkedListDataUniquePtr.cpp`, that replaces the use of `shared_ptr` with `unique_ptr`. The use of `make_shared()` is also replaced by the corresponding `make_unique()` calls.

Two other changes you'll see in the `LinkedListDataUniquePtr.cpp` listing involve the addition of the member functions `move()` and `get()`. These are added because a unique pointer is being used rather than a shared one. The `move()` and `get()` functions are important to be aware of because they are used in more than just linked lists.

REMEMBER

A unique pointer is, well, unique. That means you can't make a copy of it.

In the linked list program, the `pNext` pointer is being copied with the assignment operation from one node to another in the `add()` member function:

```
void add(shared_ptr<NameDataSet> pNDS)
{
    pNDS->pNext = pHead; // point current entry to beginning
                         // of list
    pHead = pNDS;        // point head pointer to current entry
}
```

Using an assignment operation to copy a `unique_ptr` pointer is a no-no. Rather than copy the pointer, you need to move it so that it retains its "uniqueness." Thus, the `move()` function gets added to the mix:

```
void add(unique_ptr<NameDataSet> pNDS)
{
    pNDS->pNext = move(pHead);
    pHead = move(pNDS);
}
```

You can see that `pHead` is now moved to the `pNext` pointer in `pNDS`, and then the pointer to `pNDS` is similarly moved to be the new head of the list, `pHead`.

REMEMBER

These added steps help ensure that only one use of each unique smart pointer is maintained. The shared pointer did not have this issue because, well, because it allows for a pointer to be shared.

You might wonder why you wouldn't just use shared pointers for everything because it is easier to code. The answer is overhead and performance. Though shared pointers allow for multiple copies, that also means the system needs to keep track of usage for all of the pointers so that it knows when to automatically delete the memory usage. The simpler code comes at the cost of performance. Similarly, you might find there are times when you need the most performance possible, which could lead you to using raw pointers.

Here's another scenario where the difference between unique and shared pointers plays a role: Suppose you need to simply borrow the address so that you can do something such as print the values in the nodes. (You aren't changing or manipulating the data being pointed to, but rather just viewing it.) Now, a memory address can have only one unique pointer holding on to it. However, you can have a raw pointer point to that address.

This fact results in the other change required in the linked list listing when using unique pointers. The program contains the addition of `get()`, which can be used when you want to use the raw value contained within a unique pointer. For example, you use the `for` loop in the `main()` function of the linked list to print the lists' names. It uses the `pHead` pointer value to access those names. The loop also uses the `pNext` unique pointer to iterate, so you need to get its value as well. You can see the two accesses of `pNext` in the original `for` loop:

```
for(shared_ptr<NameDataSet> pIter = pHead;
                pIter; pIter = pIter->pNext)
```

To work with a unique pointer, `pIter` can't also be a unique pointer, because it wouldn't be able to point to the same memory location as `pHead`. Thus, you need to change `pIter` to a raw pointer. Similarly, you can't assign (copy) the `pNext` pointer to `pIter`; you need to get a copy, which means you need to assign the value of `pNext` to the raw pointer, `pIter`. The new `for` loop looks like this:

```
for(NameDataSet* pIter = pHead.get();
                pIter; pIter = pIter->pNext.get())
```

If you don't include `get()` in order to access the raw value of a unique pointer, you will get a compiler error.

You will likely use `shared_ptr` for much of what you do, but sometimes `unique_ptr` is the better solution. Table 15-1 summarizes the key differences between shared and unique smart pointers.

TABLE 15-1 **Contrasting Shared and Unique Smart Pointers**

`shared_ptr`	`unique_ptr`
Shared ownership of memory; used when there is a single owner	Unique ownership of memory; used when there are multiple owners
Can be copied	Cannot be copied; must use `move()`
Can use directly because it can be shared	Need to use `get()` for raw access
Adds overhead for keeping track of references	Less overhead because of single ownership; best used when performance is critical

Ray of Hope: A List of Containers Linked to the C++ Library

ON THE WEB

I believe that everyone should walk before they run, figure out how to perform arithmetic in their heads before using a calculator, and write a linked list program before using a list class written by someone else. That being said, in the downloadable bonus Chapter 3 I describe the `list` class provided by the C++ environment. You can find that and other cool stuff at `www.dummies.com/go/cplusplus8e`.

IN THIS CHAPTER

» Declaring members private

» Accessing private members from within the class

» Accessing private members from outside the class

» Restricting access with getters and setters

Chapter 16
Protecting Members: Do Not Disturb

Chapter 13 introduces the concept of the class. That chapter describes the `public` keyword as though it were part of the class declaration — just something you do. When it comes to things being public, lots of popular idioms and phrases come to mind, such as "What happens behind closed doors . . .," "Discretion is the better part of valor," and (a truly good one) "Loose lips sink ships."

A benefit of object-oriented programming is the ability to encapsulate items and then allow the public to interface in a controlled manner. Often, an object will have a public interface and then hide many of the inner workings to protect them. For example, a microwave has its keypad as an interface for you to heat items. You use this public interface to control what you want done. The microwave hides the internal details from you to protect them from being changed. If there weren't a case protecting the internals, you might try moving a wire or poking the magnetron or waveguide. Do you need to know what a magnetron or waveguide is to use the microwave to heat nachos? Nope! That's why they're protected inside the case.

Another value of a user not having access to the internal workings is that the manufacturer can replace the internal parts or systems on a newer model of a microwave, yet the interface you use can remain the same. They simply change the internal components and wiring, which you never see.

Just as a microwave protects its parts to keep users safe and the microwave working, you can also protect things in your classes to keep users safe and protect the inner workings of the objects created with your classes. Though I have you use the `public` keyword in your classes in other chapters in this book, it should be obvious that making everything public might not be the best — or even safest — approach. That's why class members, by default, are not public. Rather, class members are private by default.

The reality is that C++ has three primary access levels:

- Public
- Private
- Protected

Everything you want accessible by your users from outside of your class should be *public*, whereas *private* items are used internally within your class. Then there's also *protected*, which keeps things private except when deriving from your classes — a topic I cover in greater detail when I talk about inheritance in Chapter 21. This chapter focuses on adding privacy to your classes by using *private*.

Making Members Private

The members of a class can be marked private, which makes them inaccessible outside the class. As I mention earlier, an alternative is to make the members public. Public members are accessible to all.

REMEMBER

You should understand the term *inaccessible* in a weak sense. Any programmer can go into the source code, remove the `private` *or* `protected` keyword, and do whatever they want. Further, any hacker worth their salt can code into a protected section of code. The `private` keyword is designed to protect a programmer by preventing inadvertent access — it's to protect you from *yourself*.

Why you need private members

To understand the role of making members private and using the `private` keyword, think about the goals of object-oriented programming:

- **To protect the internals of the class from outside functions:** Suppose that you have a plan to build a software microwave (or whatever), provide it with a simple interface to the outside world, and then place a box around it to prevent others from messing with the insides. In this example, the class creates the box, and the `private` keyword decides which parts are hidden inside of it.

- **To make the class responsible for maintaining its internal state:** It's not fair to ask the class to be responsible if others can reach in and manipulate its internals (any more than it's fair to ask a microwave designer to be responsible for the consequences of our mucking with a microwave's internal wiring).
- **To limit the interface of the class to the outside world:** It's easier to figure out and use a class that has a limited interface (the public members). Private members are hidden from the user and need not be learned. The interface becomes the class; this is called *abstraction* (see Chapter 12 for more on abstraction).
- **To reduce the level of interconnection between the class and other code:** *Interconnection* refers to how much code outside of the class can reach into the internals and thus depend upon those internals. By limiting interconnection by keeping some code private, you can more easily replace one class with another or use the class in other programs.

Now, I know what you might be saying if you're the non-object-oriented type: "You don't need some fancy feature to do all that. Just make a rule that says certain members are publicly accessible and others are not."

Although that's true in theory, it doesn't work in object-oriented programming. People start with all kinds of good intentions, but as long as the language doesn't at least discourage direct access of private members, these good intentions get crushed under the pressure to move the product out the door.

Discovering how private members work

By default, the members of a class are private, which means they are not accessible by nonmembers of the class. Adding the keyword `public` to a class makes subsequent members public, which means nonmember functions can access them. Adding the keyword `private` makes subsequent members of the class private. You can switch between `public` and `private` as often as you like.

Suppose you have a class named `Student`. In this example, the following capabilities are all that a fully functional, upstanding `Student` needs (notice the absence of `spendMoney()` and `drinkBeer()` — this is a highly stylized student):

`addCourse(int hours, double grade)`: Adds a course

`grade()`: Returns the current grade point average

`hours()`: Returns the number of hours earned toward graduation

The remaining members of Student can be declared private to keep other functions' prying expressions out of Student' s business:

```
class Student
{
  public:
    // grade - return the current grade point average
    double grade() { return gpa;}

    // hours - return the number of semester hours
    int hours() {   return semesterHours; }
    // addCourse - add a course to the student's  record
    double addCourse(int hours, double grade);

    // the following members are off-limits to others
  private:
    int semesterHours; // hours earned toward graduation
    double gpa;        // grade point average
};
```

Now the member's semester hours and gpa are accessible only to other members of Student. Thus, the following doesn't work:

```
Student s;
int main()
{
   // raise my grade (don't make it too high; otherwise, no
   // one would believe it)
   s.gpa = 3.5;                // <- generates compiler error
   double gpa = s.grade(); // <- this public function reads
                             // a copy of the value, but you
   return    0;               // can't change it from here
}
```

The application's attempt to change the value of gpa is flagged with a compiler error.

REMEMBER

A class member can also be private by declaring it protected. The difference between private and protected has to do with inheritance, which is presented in Chapter 21.

Making an Argument for Using Private Members

Now that you know (presumably) a little more about how to use private members in an actual class, I can replay the arguments for using private members.

Protecting the internal state of the class

Making the gpa member private in our Student class precludes the application from setting the grade point average to some arbitrary value. The application can add courses, but it can't change the grade point average directly.

If the application has a legitimate need to set the grade point average directly, the class can provide a member function for that purpose, this way:

```
class Student
{
  public:
    // same as before
    double grade() { return gpa; }
    // here we allow the grade to be changed
    double grade(double newGPA)
    {
       double oldGPA = gpa;
      // only if the new value is valid
      if (newGPA > 0 && newGPA <= 4.0)
      {
          gpa = newGPA;
      }
       return oldGPA;
    }
  // ...other stuff is the same including the
  //       data members:
  private:
     int semesterHours; // hours earned toward
                        // graduation
     double gpa;
};
```

The addition of the member function grade(double) allows the application to set the gpa. Notice, however, that the class still hasn't given up control completely. The application can't set gpa to any old value; only a gpa in the legal range of values (from 0 through 4.0) is accepted.

Thus, the Student class has provided access to an internal data member without abdicating its responsibility to make sure that the internal state of the class is valid.

Using a class with a limited interface

A class provides a limited interface. To use a class, you need to know only its public members, what these members do, and their arguments. This can drastically reduce the number of topics you need to master and remember to use the class.

As conditions change or as bugs are found, you want to be able to change the internal workings of a class. Changes to those details are less likely to require changes in the external application code if you can hide the internal workings of the class.

A second, and perhaps more important, reason lies in the limited ability of humans (I can't speak for dogs and cats) to keep a large number of facts in their minds at any given instant. Using a strictly defined class interface allows the programmer to forget the details that happen behind it. Likewise, a programmer building the class need not concentrate to quite the same degree on exactly how each of the functions is being used.

Getting and setting data members

A standard practice when encapsulating data members in a class is to prevent direct access to them and instead control their access through what are called accessor and mutator methods. Accessor methods are also called getters because they get the value of a data member. Mutators are called setters because they set the values of data members.

The grades() function in our earlier example sets a new value for the gpa, so this can be referred to as a setter function. Often, however, getter and setter functions are named using the prefixes of get and set:

```
class Student
{
  public:
    double getGpa() const { return gpa; }
    void   setGpa(double newGpa) { gpa = newGpa; }
```

```
    int  getSemesterHours() const { return semesterHours; }
    void setSemesterHours(int hours) { semesterHours = hours; }

private:
    int semesterHours; // hours earned toward graduation
    double gpa;        // grade point average
};
```

In addition to letting you restrict access to a class's data members, getters and setters allow you to access the data within a class without touching the private members of the class itself. This is similar to a keypad on a microwave that lets you interact with the microwave without touching the wiring inside. For a microwave, the only way to set a cook time is through the buttons on the keypad. Similarly, with a class, the way to access or change data values is with the getters and setters.

REMEMBER

Using getters and setters encapsulates the internals of a class, which gives you the ability to change them in the future without having to change the programs that use the class. With setters, you can include additional code to restrict what the application allows — such as restricting the GPA to be between 0.0 and 4.0. Of course, if you find that a school uses a weighted GPA, you might need to change the range to allow for higher GPAs. This change can happen within the `Student` class without impacting any programs that might already use the class.

The following listing presents the `GetSetStudent` program, which applies getters and setters to the `Student` class:

```
// GetSetStudent - Using getters and setters
#include <print>
using namespace std;

class Student
{
  public:
    double getGpa() const
           { return gpa; }
    void   setGpa(double newGpa)
           { gpa = newGpa; }
    int    getSemesterHours() const
           { return semesterHours; }
    void   setSemesterHours(int hours)
           { semesterHours = hours; }
```

```
    double addCourse(int hours, double grade)
    {
        // calculate the sum of all courses times
        // the average grade
        double weightedGPA;
        weightedGPA = semesterHours * gpa;

        // now add in the new course
        semesterHours += hours;
        weightedGPA += grade * hours;
        gpa = weightedGPA / semesterHours;

        // return the new gpa
        return gpa;
    };

  private:
    int semesterHours; // hours earned toward graduation
    double gpa;        // grade point average
};

int main(int nNumberofArgs, char* pszArgs[])
{
   // create a Student object and initialize it
   Student s;
   s.setSemesterHours(3); // replaces s.semesterHours = 3;
   s.setGpa(3.0);         // replaces s.gpa = 3.0;

   // the values before the call - using getters
   println("Before: s = ({}, {})", s.getSemesterHours(),
  s.getGpa());

   println("Adding 3 hours with a grade of 4.0");
   s.addCourse(3, 4.0);

   // the values are now changed - using getters
   println("After: s = ({}, {})", s.getSemesterHours(),
  s.getGpa());
}
```

Much of this code is taken from Chapter 13. A few things to notice are that the getters and setters are declared in the `Student` class. In the `main()` function, these are then used to set values when initializing the class. They are also used with the `println()` function to get the values instead of calling the variables directly.

As mentioned previously, if you try to access `s.gpa` or `s.semesterHours` directly from `main()`, you will get an error saying these are private.

You should also notice that because `addCourse()` is a part of the `Student` class, it's okay for it to access the private variable directly. It's internally a part of `Student`, so the private members are not hidden from it.

Getting Friendly with Your Private Members

Occasionally, you want a nonmember function to have access to the private or protected members of a class. You do so by declaring the function to be a friend of the class by using the keyword `friend`. (In C++, a *friend* is a special function that provides access to a class's private or protected members.)

The `friend` declaration appears in the class that contains the private or protected member and is similar to a prototype declaration in that it includes the extended name and the return type. (For more on prototype declarations, see Chapter 7.) In the following example, the function `initialize()` can now access anything it wants in `Student`:

```
class Student
{
     friend void initialize(Student*);
   public:
     // same public members as before...
  private:
      int semesterHours; // hours earned toward graduation
      double gpa;
};

// the following function is a friend of Student
// so it can access the private members
void initialize(Student *pS)
{
   pS->gpa = 0;              // this is now legal...
   pS->semesterHours = 0;    // ...when it wasn't before
}
```

A single function can be declared a friend of two classes at the same time. Although this can be convenient, it tends to bind the two classes together. This binding of classes is normally considered bad because it makes one class dependent on the other. If the two classes naturally belong together, however, it's not all bad, as shown here:

```
class Student; // forward declaration
class Teacher
{
    friend void registration(Teacher& t, Student& s);
  public:
    void assignGrades();
  private:
    int noStudents;
    Student *pList[100];
};
class Student
{
    friend void registration(Teacher& t, Student& s);
  public:
    // same public members as before...
  private:
    Teacher *pT;
    int semesterHours; // hours earned toward graduation
    double gpa;
};
void registration(Teacher& t, Student& s)
{
  // initialize the Student object
  s.semesterHours = 0;
  s.gpa = 0;

  // if there's room...
  if (t.noStudents < 100)
  {
    // ...add it onto the end of the list
    t.pList[t.noStudents] = &s;
    t.noStudents++;
  }
}
```

In this example, the `registration()` function can reach into both the `Student` and `Teacher` classes to tie them together at registration time, without being a member function of either one.

REMEMBER

The first line in the example declares the class `Student`, but none of its members. This *forward declaration* just defines the name of the class so that other classes, such as `Teacher`, can define a pointer to it. Forward declarations are necessary when two classes refer to each other.

A member function of one class may be declared a friend of another class, as shown here:

```
class Teacher
{
    // ...other members as well...
  public:
      void assignGrades();
};
class Student
{
      friend void Teacher::assignGrades();
  public:
      // same public members as before...
  private:
      int semesterHours; // hours earned toward graduation
      double gpa;
};
void Teacher::assignGrades()
{
     // can access private members of Teacher from here
}
```

REMEMBER

Unlike in the nonmember example, the member function `assignGrades()` must be declared before the class `Student` can declare it to be a friend.

An entire class can be named a friend of another. This has the effect of making every member function of the class a friend:

```
class Student; // forward declaration
class Teacher
{
  private:
      int noStudents;
      Student *pList[100];
  public:
      void assignGrades();
};
```

```
class Student
{
    friend class Teacher; // make entire class a friend
  public:
    // same public members as before...
  private:
    int semesterHours; // hours earned toward graduation
    double gpa;
};
```

Now, any member function of `Teacher` has access to the private members of `Student`. Declaring one class a friend of the other inseparably binds the two classes together.

IN THIS CHAPTER

» Creating and destroying objects

» Declaring constructors and destructors

» Invoking constructors and destructors

» Mixing smart pointers with destructors

Chapter 17

"Why Do You Build Me Up, Just to Tear Me Down, Baby?"

Objects in programs are built and scrapped just like objects in the real world. If the class is to be responsible for its well-being, it must have some control over this process. As luck would have it (I suppose some planning was involved as well), C++ provides just the right mechanism.

Creating Objects

Let's talk about what it means to create an object. Sadly, some people become somewhat sloppy in using the terms *class* and *object*. That's why I'll cover this topic again. What's the difference? What's the relationship?

I can create a class Dog that describes the relevant properties of man's best friend. My family has two dogs. Thus, my single class *Dog* has two instances, *Mac* and *Buffy*. (Well, I *think* there are two instances — I haven't seen Buffy in a few days.)

REMEMBER

A class describes a type of thing. An object is one of those things. An object is an *instance* of a class. There is only one class Dog, no matter how many dogs I have.

Objects are created and destroyed, but classes simply exist. Pets come and go, but the class Dog (evolution aside) is perpetual.

Different types of objects are created at different times. *Global* objects are generally created when the program first begins execution. *Local* objects are created when the program encounters their declaration.

REMEMBER

A *global* object is one that is declared outside a function. A *local* object is one that is declared within a function and is therefore local to the function. In the following example, the variable me is global, and the variable notMe is local to the function pickOne():

```
int me = 0;
void pickOne()
{
   int notMe;
}
```

WARNING

According to the rules, global objects are initialized to all zeros when the program starts executing. Objects declared local to a function have no particular initial value. Having all data members have a random state may not be a valid condition for all classes. It is good programming practice to always initialize your variables so that you know they have a value and what that value is.

But wait, you say. The classes in earlier chapters of this book have variables included within them. In Chapter 16, for example, the Student class has a couple of variables — semesterHours and gpa:

```
class Student
{
  public:
    // some functions
  private:
    int semesterHours;
    double gpa;
}
```

Though these are not within a function, they are *not* global. Rather, they are simply an internal part of the class. The objects created with the class, however, follow the rules of being local or global based on where they are declared.

This leads us to the important topic of this chapter. C++ allows the class to define a special member function that is invoked automatically when an object of that class is created. This member function, called the *constructor*, initializes the object to a valid initial state. In addition, the class can define a destructor to handle the destruction of the object. These two functions — constructors and destructors — are the stars of this chapter.

Using Constructors

The *constructor* is a member function that is called automatically when an object is created. Its primary job is to initialize the object to a legal initial value for the class. (It's the job of the remaining member functions to ensure that the state of the object stays legal.)

The constructor carries the same name as the class to differentiate it from the other members of the class. The designers of C++ could have made up a different rule, such as: "The constructor must be called `init()`." It wouldn't have made any difference, as long as the compiler can recognize the constructor. In addition, the constructor has no return type (not even `void`), because it is called only automatically — if the constructor did return something, there would be no place to put it.

REMEMBER

A constructor cannot be invoked manually.

Constructing a single object

With a constructor, the class `Student` appears as follows:

```
// Constructor - example that invokes a constructor
//
#include <print>
using namespace std;

class Student
{
  public:
    Student()
```

```
    {
        println("constructing student");
        semesterHours = 0;
        gpa = 0.0;
    }
    // ...other public members...
  private:
    int semesterHours;
    double gpa;
};

int main()
{
    println("Creating a new Student object");
    Student s;

    println("Creating a new object off the heap");
    Student* pS = new Student;

    return 0;
}
```

At the point of the declaration of s, the compiler inserts a call to the constructor `Student::Student()`. Allocating a new `Student` object from the heap has the same effect, as demonstrated by the output from the program:

```
Creating a new Student object
constructing student
Creating a new object off the heap
constructing student
```

I wrote this simple constructor as an inline member function, meaning its definition was included within the definition of the class itself. You can also write a constructor outside of the main class definition (referred to as an outline function), as shown here:

```
class Student
{
  public:
    Student();
    // ...other public members...
  private:
    int semesterHours;
    double gpa;
};
```

```
Student::Student()
{
    println("constructing student");
    semesterHours = 0;
    gpa = 0.0;
}
```

Constructing multiple objects

Each element of an array must be constructed on its own. For example, the following `ConstructArray` program creates five `Student` objects by declaring a single 5-element array:

```
// ConstructArray - example that invokes a constructor
//                  on an array of objects
//
#include <print>
using namespace std;

class Student
{
  public:
    Student()
    {
        println("constructing student");
    }
};

int main(int nNumberofArgs, char* pszArgs[])
{
    println("Creating an array of 5 Student objects");
    Student s[5];
    return 0;
}
```

Executing the program generates the following output:

```
Creating an array of 5 Student objects
constructing student
constructing student
constructing student
constructing student
constructing student
```

Constructing a duplex

In the real world, classes are rarely as simple as those presented in books. In fact, classes can be built out of other classes, which means objects can contain other objects. For example, you could have a class for a course that contains a teacher. This course class would be a *duplex* — a class that is composed of other classes. When a duplex class is used to create an object, that object will contain sub-objects.

If a class contains a data member that is an object of another class, the constructor for that class is called automatically as well. Consider the following `ConstructMembers` sample program. I added output statements so that you can see the order in which the objects are invoked:

```
// ConstructMembers - the member objects of a class
//                    are each constructed before the
//                    container class constructor gets
//                    a shot at it
//
#include <print>
using namespace std;

class Course
{
  public:
    Course(){ println("constructing course");}
};

class Student
{
  public:
    Student()
    {
        println("constructing student");
        semesterHours = 0;
        gpa = 0.0;
    }
  private:
    int semesterHours;
    double gpa;
};
class Teacher
{
  public:
    Teacher(){ println("constructing teacher");}
  private:
```

```
    Course c;
};
class TutorPair
{
  public:
    TutorPair()
    {
        println("constructing tutorpair");
        noMeetings = 0;
    }
  private:
    Student student;
    Teacher teacher;
    int     noMeetings;
};

int main(int nNumberofArgs, char* pszArgs[])
{
    println("Creating TutorPair object");
    TutorPair tp;
    return 0;
}
```

Executing this program generates the following output:

```
Creating TutorPair object
constructing student
constructing course
constructing teacher
constructing tutorpair
```

Creating the object `tp` in `main` automatically invokes the constructor for `TutorPair`. Before control passes into the body of the `TutorPair` constructor, however, the constructors for the 2-member objects, `student` and `teacher`, are invoked. The constructor for `Student` is called first (because it is declared first); the constructor for `Teacher` is called next.

The member `Teacher` of class `Course` is constructed as part of building the `Teacher` object. As shown in Figure 17-1, the `Course` constructor gets the first shot.

Each object within a class must construct itself before the class constructor can be invoked. Otherwise, the main constructor would not know the state of its data members.

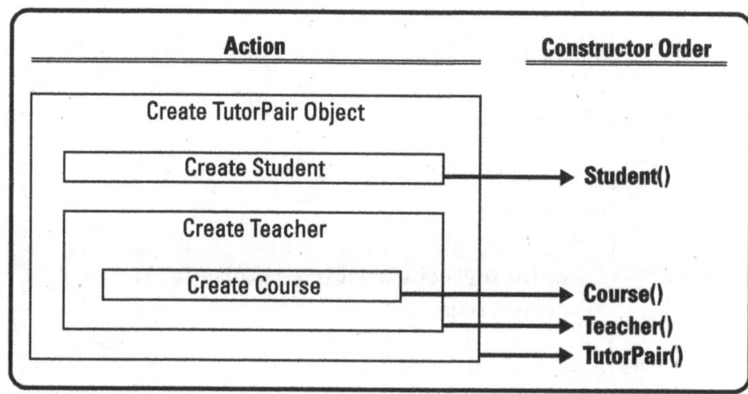

FIGURE 17-1: The order constructors are called.

After all member data objects have been constructed, the program flow returns to beginning of the `TutorPair` constructer (to the open brace), and the constructor for `TutorPair` is allowed to construct the remainder of the object.

Dissecting a Destructor

Just as objects are created, so are they destroyed (ashes to ashes, dust to dust). If a class can have a constructor to set things up, it should also have a special member function to take the object apart. This member is called the *destructor.*

Why you need the destructor

A class may allocate resources in the constructor; these resources need to be deallocated before the object ceases to exist. For example, if the constructor opens a file, the file needs to be closed before leaving that class or the program. Or, if the constructor allocates memory from the heap using raw pointers, this memory must be freed before the object goes away. The destructor allows the class to complete these cleanup tasks automatically, without relying on the application to call the proper member functions.

Working with destructors

The destructor member has the same name as the class but with a tilde (~) added at the front. (C++ is being cute again — the tilde is the symbol for the logical `NOT` operator. Get it? A destructor is a "not constructor." Très clever.) Like a constructor, the destructor has no return type. For example, the class `Student` with a destructor added appears as follows:

```
class Student
{
  public:
    Student()        // The constructor
    {
        semesterHours = 0;
        gpa = 0.0;
    }
    ~Student()       // The destructor
    {
        // ...whatever assets are returned here...
    }
  private:
    int  semesterHours;
    double gpa;
};
```

The destructor is invoked automatically when an object is destroyed, or, in C++ parlance, when an object is *destructed*. That sounds sort of circular ("the destructor is invoked when an object is destructed"), so I've avoided the term until now. For nonheap memory, you can also say, "when the object goes out of scope." A local object goes out of scope when the function returns. A global or static object goes out of scope when the program terminates.

But what about heap memory? An object that has been allocated off the heap is destructed when it's returned to the heap using the `delete` command. This is demonstrated in the following `DestructMembers` program:

```
// DestructMembers - this program both constructs and
//                   destructs a set of data members
//
#include <print>
using namespace std;

class Course
{
  public:
    Course()  { println("constructing course"); }
    ~Course() { println("destructing course");  }
};

class Student
{
  public:
```

```
    Student() { println("constructing student");}
    ~Student() { println("destructing student"); }
};
class Teacher
{
  public:
    Teacher()
    {
        println("constructing teacher");
        pC = new Course;
    }
    ~Teacher()
    {
        println("destructing teacher");
        delete pC;
    }
  private:
  Course* pC;
};
class TutorPair
{
  public:
    TutorPair(){ println("constructing tutorpair"); }
   ~TutorPair(){ println("destructing tutorpair"); }
  private:
    Student student;
    Teacher teacher;
};

TutorPair* fn()
{
   println("Creating TutorPair object in function fn()");
   TutorPair tp;
   println("Allocating TutorPair off the heap");
   TutorPair* pTP = new TutorPair;
   println("Returning from fn()");
   return pTP;
}

int main(int nNumberofArgs, char* pszArgs[])
{
   // call function fn() and then return the
   // TutorPair object to the heap
```

```
    TutorPair* pTPReturned = fn();
    println("Return heap object to the heap");
    delete pTPReturned;
    println("Now end the program");
    return 0;
}
```

The function main() invokes a function fn() that defines the object tp — this is to allow you to watch the variable go out of scope when control exits the function. The fn() function also allocates heap memory that it returns to main() where the memory is returned to the heap.

If you execute this program, it generates the following output:

```
Creating TutorPair object in function fn()
constructing student
constructing teacher
constructing course
constructing tutorpair
Allocating TutorPair off the heap
constructing student
constructing teacher
constructing course
constructing tutorpair
Returning from fn()
destructing tutorpair
destructing teacher
destructing course
destructing student
Return heap object to the heap
destructing tutorpair
destructing teacher
destructing course
destructing student
Now end the program
```

In this listing, each constructor is called in turn as the TutorPair object is built up, starting from the smallest data member and working up to the TutorPair::TutorPair() constructor function.

Two TutorPair objects are created. The first, tp, is defined locally to the function fn(); the second, pTP, is allocated off the heap. The tp object goes out of scope and is destructed when control passes out of the function. The heap memory whose address is returned from fn() is not destructed until main() deletes it.

REMEMBER

When an object is destructed, the sequence of destructors is invoked in the reverse order in which the constructors were called.

C++ provides a separate keyword for deleting arrays, delete[]:

```
Student* pS = new Student[5];    // construct 5 Students

// ...later in the program...
delete[] pS;                 // delete heap memory and invoke
                             // destructor on each object
```

Only the delete[] keyword knows to invoke the destructor for each object allocated.

Smart Pointers, Deleting, and Destruction — Oh, My!

One area that has troubled C++ programs in the past involves cleaning up the allocation of memory. Often, memory is allocated by a class and then needs to be freed when the class goes out of scope. This sad state of affairs was a result of using raw pointers.

Smart pointers in C++ have improved this situation somewhat because they take care of managing the allocation and freeing memory for you. When you create a smart pointer, however, you're creating a pointer to an object and thus that object's constructor will be called. When that pointer goes out of scope, its destructor will be called as well. If no constructor or destructor has been created, then, as with any other class, defaults will be called.

In the following listing, you can see a smart pointer being created and then the program ends:

```
// SmartPointerConstructed.cpp
//
#include <print>
#include <memory>
using namespace std;

class Student
{
  public:
```

```
    Student()  { println("Constructing Student"); }
    ~Student() { println("Deconstructing Student"); }

  private:
    int semesterHours = 0;
    double gpa = 0.0;
};

int main()
{
    println("Program started");
    println("Creating a smart pointer to a student");
    shared_ptr<Student> newStudent = make_shared<Student>();
    println("Exiting program");
}
```

Although this isn't a particularly useful program, you can see by its output that it does indeed call the constructor for the `Student` class when the smart pointer is created. Moreover, just before the program ends and the pointer goes out of scope, you can see that the destructor is called. Here is the output:

```
Program started
Creating a smart pointer to a student
Constructing Student
Exiting program
Deconstructing Student
```

For those classes where you have been using smart pointers, you don't need to deal with making or cleaning up memory allocations. You don't need to call `delete` or `delete[]`. This cleanup is done for you.

As your classes get more complex, there will be other things your constructor and destructor might need to handle. You can be assured that the class constructor and destructor will still be called even if you're using smart pointers.

IN THIS CHAPTER

» Making argumentative constructors

» Overloading the constructor

» Creating objects by using constructors

» Invoking member constructors

» Constructing the order of construction and destruction

» Choosing to simply ignore a value

Chapter 18

Making Constructive Arguments

A class represents a type of object in the real world. For example, elsewhere in this book, I use the class `Student` to represent the properties of a student. Just like students, classes are autonomous. Unlike a student, a class is responsible for its own care and feeding — a class must keep itself in a valid state at all times.

The default constructor I present in Chapter 17 isn't always sufficient. For example, a default constructor can initialize the student ID to `0` so that it doesn't contain a random value; however, a student ID of `0` probably isn't valid. (It would be nice to be able to create a student with a valid ID, wouldn't it?)

C++ programmers often need a constructor that accepts some type of argument to initialize an object to other than a default value — such as a valid student ID when constructing a `Student`. This chapter examines exactly how to do that. (Spoiler alert: It involves constructors with arguments.)

Outfitting Constructors with Arguments

C++ enables programmers to define a constructor with arguments. (Thank goodness.) The following shows a `Student` constructor that takes an argument called `pName`:

```
class Student
{
  public:
    Student(const char *pName);

    // ...class continues...
};
```

Conceptually, the idea of adding an argument is simple. A constructor is a member function, and member functions can have arguments. Therefore, constructors can have arguments. Q.E.D.

The thing is you don't call the constructor like a normal function. Therefore, the only time to pass arguments to the constructor is when the object is created. For example, the following program creates an object `s` of the class `Student` by calling the `Student(const char*)` constructor. The object `s` is destructed when the function `main()` returns:

```
// ConstructorWArg - a class may pass along arguments
//                   to the members' constructors
#include <memory>
#include <print>
using namespace std;

class Student
{
  public:
    Student(const char* pName)
    {
        println("constructing Student {}", pName);
        name = pName;
        semesterHours = 0;
        gpa = 0.0;
    }

  // ...other public members...
  private:
    string  name;
```

```
    int     semesterHours;
    double  gpa;
};

int main(int argcs, char* pArgs[])
{
    // create a student locally
    Student s1("Ross");
    // create a student using a smart pointer
    shared_ptr<Student> pS3 = make_shared<Student>("Joey");
    // create a student directly off the heap
    Student* pS2 = new Student("Chandler");

    // be sure to delete pointer the heap student
    delete pS2;
}
```

The `Student` constructor here looks like the constructors shown in Chapter 17 except for the addition of the `const char*` argument `pName`. The constructor initializes all data members to their empty start-up values *except for* the data member `name`, which gets its initial value from `pName` because a `Student` object without a name is not a valid student.

The object `s1` is created in `main()`. The argument to be passed to the constructor appears in the declaration of `s1`, right next to the name of the object. Thus, the student labeled `s1` is given the name `Ross` in this declaration.

A second student (`pS2`) is allocated off the heap on the very next line using a raw pointer to a `Student`. The arguments to the constructor in this case appear next to the name of the class.

TIP

Because `pS2` is allocated using `new`, you also need to use `delete` to return the newly allocated object to the heap before exiting the program. Though Windows or Unix will close any files you may have open and return all heap memory when a program terminates (even if you forget to do so yourself), you should still make sure to delete any memory you allocate. It's simply good practice to delete your heap memory when you're finished.

A third student (`pS3`) is also allocated off the heap, but this time more appropriately using a smart pointer. As the listing shows, whenever you use a smart pointer, the argument for the constructor is passed in the parentheses of the `make_shared()` function.

REMEMBER

The `const` in the constructor declaration `Student::Student(const char*)` is necessary to allow statements such as this one:

```
Student s1("Ross");
```

The type of `"Ross"` is *const char**. A pointer could not be passed to a constant character string to a constructor simply declared `Student(char*)`. A function, including a constructor, declared this way might attempt to modify the character string, which would not be good. You cannot strip away the *const* part of a declaration.

You can add `const`-ness, however, as in the following:

```
void fn(char* pName)
{
    // the following is allowed even though constructor
    // declared Student(const char*)
    Student s(pName);
    // ...do whatever...
}
```

The function `fn()` passes a `char*` string to a constructor that promises to treat the string as though it were a constant. No harm there!

Placing Too Many Demands on the Carpenter: Overloading the Constructor

I can draw one more parallel between constructors and other, more normal, member functions in this chapter: Constructors can be overloaded.

REMEMBER

Overloading a function means to define two functions with the same name but with different types of arguments. See Chapter 7 for the latest news on function overloading.

C++ chooses the proper constructor based on the arguments in the declaration of the object. For example, the class `Student` can have all three constructors shown in the following snippet at the same time:

```
// OverloadConstructor - provide the class multiple
//                       ways to create objects by
//                       overloading the constructor
```

```
#include <memory>
#include <print>
using namespace std;

class Student
{
  public:
    Student()
    {
          println("constructing student No Name");
          name = "No Name";
          semesterHours = 0;
          gpa = 0.0;
    }
    Student(const char *pName)
    {
         println("constructing student with name {}",
                   pName);
         name = pName;
         semesterHours = 0;
         gpa = 0;
    }
    Student(const char *pName, int xfrHours, float xfrGPA)
    {
         println("constructing student {}", pName);
         name = pName;
         semesterHours = xfrHours;
         gpa = xfrGPA;
    }
  private:
    string    name;
    int       semesterHours;
    float     gpa;
};

int main(int argcs, char* pArgs[])
{
    // the following invokes three different constructors
    Student noName;
    Student freshman("Phil O. Sophy");
    Student xferStudent("Alge Braxton", 80, 2.5);
}
```

Because the object noName appears with no arguments, it's constructed using the constructor Student::Student(). This constructor is called the *default* constructor. The freshman is constructed using the constructor that has only a const char* argument, and the xferStudent uses the constructor with three arguments.

Sometimes, defaulting is good

Notice the similarity in all three constructors. The number of semester hours and the GPA default to 0 if only the name is provided. Otherwise, there's no difference between the first two constructors. You wouldn't need both constructors if you could just specify a default value for the two arguments.

C++ enables you to specify a default value for a function argument in the declaration to be used in the event that the argument is not present. By adding defaults to the last constructor, all three constructors can be combined into one. For example, the following class combines all three constructors into a single, clever constructor:

```
// ConstructorWDefaults - multiple constructors can be
//      combined with the definition of default arguments
#include <print>
using namespace std;

class Student
{
  public:
    Student(const char *pName = "No Name",
            int xfrHours = 0,
            double xfrGPA = 0.0)
    {
        println("constructing student {}", pName);
        name = pName;
        semesterHours = xfrHours;
        gpa = xfrGPA;
    }

  private:
    string   name;
    int      semesterHours;
    double   gpa;
};
```

```
int main(int argcs, char* pArgs[])
{
    // the following invokes the same constructor
    // that is using default values
    Student noName;
    Student freshman("Phil O. Sophy");
    Student xferStudent("Alge Braxton", 80, 2.5);
}
```

Now all three objects are constructed using the same constructor; defaults are provided for nonexistent arguments in noName and freshman.

Sometimes, using someone else's code is okay

A slightly more flexible alternative added in the C++11 standard has you invoke one constructor from another, as shown in ConstructorsCallingEachOther. This is known as *delegating constructors*:

```
// ConstructorsCallingEachOther - one constructor can
//          invoke another constructor in the same class
#include <print>
using namespace std;

class Student
{
  public:
    Student(const char *pName,
            int xfrHours,
            double xfrGPA)
    {
        println("constructing student {}", pName);
        name = pName;
        semesterHours = xfrHours;
        gpa = xfrGPA;
    }
    Student() : Student("No Name", 0, 0.0) {}
    Student(const char *pName): Student(pName, 0, 0.0){}

  private:
    string  name;
```

```
    int     semesterHours;
    double  gpa;
};

int main(int argcs, char* pArgs[])
{
    // the following invokes 3 different constructors
    Student noName;
    Student freshman("Phil O. Sophy");
    Student xferStudent("Alge Braxton", 80, 2.5);
}
```

Here the declaration `Student noName` invokes the no-argument constructor, which turns around and calls the constructor that takes three parameters using default arguments. The `Student freshman` declaration invokes the `Student(const char*)` constructor, which invokes the constructor that takes three parameters as well. This time, however, the `pName` is passed along, and only the last two arguments are defaulted.

This strategy is more flexible because you can default arguments other than the last one. In addition, you have more control over how arguments are defaulted. For example, it makes no sense to construct a student with semester hours but no GPA. This version would not allow such an object to be constructed, because no `Student(const char*, int)` is provided.

TIP

If the syntax seems somewhat bizarre, don't fret! The syntax will seem much more reasonable by the time you reach the end of this chapter.

Defaulting default Constructors

As far as C++ is concerned, every class must have a constructor; otherwise, you can't create objects of that class. If you don't provide a constructor for your class, C++ should probably just generate an error, but it doesn't. To provide compatibility with existing C code, which knows nothing about constructors, C++ automatically provides a default constructor (sort of a default default constructor).

REMEMBER

If you define a constructor for your class, C++ doesn't provide the automatic default constructor on its own. By creating a constructor, the author is, in effect, telling C++ that the default constructor isn't good enough.

The following code listing demonstrates this point. This code is legal:

```
#include <string>
using namespace std;
class Student
{
  public:
     string name;
};

int main(int argcs, char* pArgs[])
{
    Student noName;
}
```

The automatically provided default constructor invokes the default `string` constructor to create an empty `name` object.

Now take a look at the following code — code that doesn't compile properly:

```
#include <string>
using namespace std;
class Student
{
  public:
    Student(const char *pName) {name = pName;}

    string name;
};

int main(int argcs, char* pArgs[])
{
   Student noName;     // doesn't compile
}
```

The seemingly innocuous addition of the `Student(const char*)` constructor precludes C++ from automatically providing a `Student()` constructor with which to build object `noName`. Again, don't fret: C++ allows you to "get the default constructor back" via the keyword `default`:

```
#include <string>
using namespace std;
```

```
class Student
{
  public:
    Student(const char *pName) { name = pName; }
    Student() = default;

    string name;
};

int main(int argcs, char* pArgs[])
{
   Student noName;
}
```

The `default` keyword says, in effect, "I know that I defined a constructor, but I still want my automatic default constructor back."

But what if you don't want a default constructor? C++ allows you to explicitly remove the default constructor by using the keyword `delete`, which can be used in the following manner:

```
class Student
{
  public:
    Student() = delete; // remove the default constructor

    string name;
};
```

Constructing Class Members

In earlier examples in this chapter, all data members are of simple types, such as `int` and `double`. With simple types, all you have to do is assign a value to the variable within the constructor. Problems arise when initializing certain types of data members, such as complex data members or constant data members.

Constructing a complex data member

Members of a class have the same problems as any other variable. It makes no sense for a `Student` object to have a default ID of `0`. This is true even if the object is a member of a class. Consider the following example, which creates a new class,

`StudentId`, to manage the student identification numbers instead of relying on a plain ol' integer variable:

```
// ConstructingMembers - a class may pass along
//      arguments to the members' constructors
#include <string>
#include <print>
using namespace std;

int nextStudentId = 1000; // first legal Student ID
class StudentId
{
  public:
    // default constructor assigns id's sequentially
    StudentId()
    {
        value = nextStudentId++;
        println("Take next student id {}", value);
    }
    // int constructor allows user to assign id
    StudentId(int id)
    {
        value = id;
        println("Assign student id {}", value);
    }
  private:
    int value;
};

class Student
{
  public:
    Student(const char* pName)
    {
        println("Constructing Student ()", pName);
        name = pName;
        semesterHours = 0;
        gpa = 0.0;
    }

  // ...other public members...
  private:
    string  name;
    int     semesterHours;
```

```
    double   gpa;
    StudentId id;
};

int main(int argcs, char* pArgs[])
{
    // create a couple of students
    Student s1("Luffy");
    Student s2("Roronoa");
}
```

A student ID is assigned to each student as the `Student` object is constructed. In this example, the default constructor for `StudentId` assigns IDs sequentially, using the global variable `nextStudentId` to keep track.

The `Student` class invokes the default constructor for the two students `s1` and `s2`. The output from the program shows that this is working properly:

```
Take next student id 1000
Constructing Student Luffy
Take next student id 1001
Constructing Student Roronoa
```

Notice that the message from the `StudentId` constructor appears before the output from the `Student` constructor. This implies that the constructor `StudentId` was invoked even before the `Student` constructor got under way.

If the programmer doesn't provide a constructor, the default constructor provided by C++ automatically invokes the default constructors for data members. The same is true when the time comes to delete everything. The destructor for the class automatically invokes the destructor for data members that have destructors. The destructor provided by C++ does the same.

Calling class data member constructors

Okay, this is all great for the default constructor. But what if you want to invoke a constructor other than the default? Where do you put the object? The `StudentId` class provides a second constructor that allows the student ID to be assigned to any arbitrary value. The question is, how do you invoke it?

ON THE WEB

Let me first show you what doesn't work. Consider the following program segment. Only the relevant parts are included here — the entire program, `ConstructSeparateID`, is with the material that accompanies this book at `www.dummies.com/go/cplusplus8e`:

```
class Student
{
  public:
    Student(const char *pName, int ssId)
    {
        println("constructing student {}", pName);
        name = pName;
        // don't try this at home kids. It doesn't work
        StudentId id(ssId);    // construct a student id
    }
  private:
    string    name;
    StudentId id;
};

int main(int argcs, char* pArgs[])
{
    Student s("Luffy", 1234);
    println("This message is from main");
}
```

Within the constructor for `Student`, *the* programmer (that's me) has (cleverly) attempted to construct a `StudentId` object named `id`. (I also added a destructor to `StudentId` that does nothing but output the ID of the object being destroyed.)

If you look at the output from this program, you can see the problem:

```
take next student id 1000
constructing student Luffy
assign student id 1234
destructing 1234
This message from main
destructing 1000
```

This seems to be constructing two `StudentId` objects: The first one is created with the default constructor as before. After control enters the constructor for `Student`, a second `StudentId` is created with the assigned value of 1234. Mysteriously, this 1234 object is then destroyed as soon as the program exits the `Student` constructor.

The explanation for this rather bizarre behavior is clear. The data member `id` already exists by the time the body of the constructor is entered. Rather than construct the existing data member `id`, the declaration provided in the constructor creates a local object of the same name. This local object is destructed upon returning from the constructor.

What's needed is a different mechanism to indicate "construct the existing member; don't create a new one." This mechanism needs to appear after the function argument list but before the open brace of the class. Wouldn't you know it, C++ provides a construct for this, as shown in the following subset taken from the ConstructDataMembers program (the only change between this program and its predecessor is to the Student class constructor — the entire program is stashed with all the other accompanying material at www.dummies.com/go/cplusplus8e):

```
class Student
{
  public:
    Student(const char *pName, int ssId)
      : name(pName), id(ssId)
    {
        println("constructing student {}", pName);
    }
  private:
    string name;
    StudentId id;
};
```

Notice in particular the first line of the constructor. Here's something I haven't covered: That lonesome colon (:) means that what follows are calls to the constructors of data members of the current class. To the C++ compiler, this line reads, "Construct the members name and id using the arguments pName and ssId, respectively, of the Student constructor. Whatever data members are not called out in this fashion are constructed using their default constructor."

REMEMBER

The string type is actually a conventional class defined in an include file, which is included by string. Programs earlier than this example have been using the default string constructor to create an empty name and then copying the student's name into the object within the body of the constructor. It's more efficient to assign the string object a value when it's created, if possible.

This new program generates the expected result:

```
assign student id 1234
constructing student Luffy
This message from main
destructing 1234
```

Now you can see where the syntax for invoking one constructor from another came from!

Combining this with member initialization

What happens when a constructor competes with a member initializer? Consider the following (contrived) example:

```
// ConstructMembersWithInitializers - this program
//          demonstrates what happens when a data member
//          with an initializer is constructed
#include <string>
#include <print>
using namespace std;

class StudentId
{
  public:
    StudentId(int id) : value(id)
    {
       println("id = {}", value);
    }

  private:
    int value;
};

int nextStudentId = 1000;
class Student
{
  public:
    Student(const char *pName, int ssId)
      : name(pName), id(ssId)
    {
        println("constructing student {}", pName);
    }
    Student(const char *pName): name(pName)
    {
        println("constructing student {}", pName);
    }
  private:
    string name;
    StudentId id = nextStudentId++;
};
```

```
int main(int argcs, char* pArgs[])
{
    Student s1("Luffy", 1234);
    Student s2("Roronoa");
}
```

Here I have provided the StudentID class with a single constructor. It's now up to the Student class to decide which id to use. The output from this program is enlightening:

```
id = 1234
constructing student Luffy
id = 1000
constructing student Roronoa
```

In the first case, the student Luffy is created using the student ID 1234 provided in the constructor. The student Roronoa accepts the default student ID, the next value starting with 1000. But this is curious — if the member initializer had been invoked when Luffy was constructed, Roronoa should have been assigned the ID 1001.

WARNING

The moral to this story is that the member initializer (that's the StudentId id = nextStudentId++) is ignored if the member is constructed in the class constructor.

Constructing a constant data member

Argument construction solves a similar problem with const data members, as shown in the following example:

```
class Mammal
{
  public:
    Mammal(int nof) : numberOfFeet(nof) {}
  private:
    const int numberOfFeet;
};
```

Ostensibly, a given Mammal has a fixed number of feet (barring amputation). The number of feet can, and should, be declared const. This constructor definition assigns a value to the variable numberOfFeet when the object is created. The numberOfFeet cannot be modified after it has been declared and initialized.

Reconstructing the Order of Construction

When there are multiple objects, all with constructors, programmers usually don't care about the order in which things are built. If one or more of the constructors has side effects, the order can make a difference.

These are the rules for the order of construction:

- **Local and static objects are constructed in the order in which their declarations are invoked.**
- **Static objects are constructed only once.**
- **All global objects are constructed before `main()`.**
- **Global objects are constructed in no particular order.**
- **Members are constructed in the order in which they're declared in the class within a given access type.** (In other words, all public members are declared in the order declared, and all the private members in the order *they're* declared.)
- **Objects are destructed in the opposite order in which they were constructed.**

REMEMBER

A *static variable* is a variable that is local to a function but retains its value from one function invocation to the next. A *global variable* is a variable declared outside a function.

Now let's consider each of the preceding rules in turn.

Local objects construct in order

Local objects are constructed in the order in which the program encounters their declaration. Normally, this order is the same as the order in which the objects appear in the function, unless the function jumps around particular declarations. (By the way, jumping around declarations is a bad thing. It confuses the reader and the compiler.)

Static objects construct only once

Static objects are like local variables, except that they're constructed only once. C++ waits until the control passes through the static variable's declaration for the first time before constructing the object. Consider the following trivial `ConstructStatic` program:

```
// ConstructStatic - demonstrate that statics are only
//                   constructed once
#include <print>
using namespace std;

class DoNothing
{
  public:
    DoNothing(int initial) : nValue(initial)
    {
        println("DoNothing constructed with a value of {}",
            initial);
    }
    ~DoNothing()
    {
        println("DoNothing object destructed");
    }
    int nValue;
};
void fn(int i)
{
    println("Function fn passed a value of {}", i);
    static DoNothing dn(i);
}
int main(int argcs, char* pArgs[])
{
   println("Start of main()");
   fn(10);
   fn(20);
   println("End of main()");
}
```

Executing this program generates the following result:

```
Start of main()
Function fn passed a value of 10
DoNothing constructed with a value of 10
Function fn passed a value of 20
End of main()
DoNothing object destructed
```

Notice that the message from the function `fn()` appears twice, but the message from the constructor for `DoNothing` appears only the first time `fn()` is called. This indicates that the object is constructed the first time `fn()` is called, but not thereafter. Also notice that the destructor is not invoked until the program returns from `main()` as part of the program shutdown process.

All global objects construct before main()

All global variables go into scope as soon as the program starts. Thus, all global objects are constructed before control is passed to `main()`.

Initializing global variables can cause real debugging headaches. Some debuggers try to execute up to `main()` as soon as the program is loaded and before they hand over control to the user. This can be a problem because the constructor code for all global objects has already been executed by the time you can wrest control of your program. If one of these constructors has a fatal bug, you never even get a chance to find the problem. In this case, the program appears to die before it even starts!

The best way I've found to detect this type of problem is to use your integrated development environment (IDE) to set a breakpoint in every constructor that you even remotely suspect of being problematic as well as the first statement in `main()`. You will hit a breakpoint for each global object declared as soon as you start the program. Press Continue after each breakpoint until the program crashes — now you know that you pressed Continue once too often.

Restart the program and repeat the process, but stop on the constructor that caused the program to crash. You can now single-step through the constructor until you find the problem. If you make it all the way to the breakpoint in `main()`, the program did not crash while constructing global objects.

Global objects construct in no particular order

Figuring out the order of construction of local objects is easy. An order is implied by the flow of control. With global declarations, no such flow is available to indicate the order. All globals go into scope simultaneously — remember? Okay, you argue, why can't the compiler just start at the top of the file and work its way down the list of global objects?

That would work fine for a single file (and I presume that's what most compilers do). Most programs in the real world consist of several files that are compiled separately and then linked. Because the compiler has no control over the order in which these files are linked, it cannot affect the order in which global objects are constructed from file to file.

Most of the time, the order of global construction is pretty ho-hum stuff. Once in a while, though, global variables generate bugs that are extremely difficult to track down. (It happens just often enough to make it worth mentioning in a book.)

Consider the following example:

```
class Student
{
  public:
    Student (int id) : studentId(id) {}
    const int studentId;
};
class Tutor
{
  public:
    Tutor(Student& s) : tutoredId(s.studentId) {}
    int tutoredId;
};

Student randy(1234);    // set up a student
Tutor janet(randy);     // assign that student a tutor
```

Here the constructor for `Student` assigns a student ID. The constructor for `Tutor` records the ID of the student to help. The program declares a student `randy` and then assigns that student a tutor `janet`.

The problem is that the program makes the implicit assumption that `randy` is constructed before `janet`. Suppose it were the other way around. Then `janet` would be constructed with a block of memory that had not yet been turned into a `Student` object and, therefore, had garbage for a student ID.

TIP

The preceding example isn't too difficult to figure out and is more than a little contrived. Nevertheless, problems deriving from global objects being constructed in no particular order can appear in subtle ways. To avoid this problem, don't allow the constructor for one global object to refer to the contents of another global object.

Members construct in the order in which they are declared

Members of a class are constructed according to the order in which they're declared within the class. This isn't quite as obvious as it may sound. Consider the following example:

```
class Student
{
  public:
    Student (int id, int age) : nAge(age), nId(id){}
    const int    nId;
    const int    nAge;
          double dAverage = 0.0;
};
```

In this example, nId is constructed before nAge, even though nId appears second in the constructor's initialization list because it appears before nAge in the class definition. The data member dAverage is constructed last for the same reason. The only time you might detect a difference in the construction order is when both data members are an instance of a class that has a constructor that has some mutual side effect.

Destructors destruct in the reverse order of the constructors

Finally, no matter in which order the constructors kick off, you can be assured that the destructors are invoked in the reverse order. (It's nice to know that at least one rule in C++ has no ifs, ands, or buts.)

Constructing Arrays

When you declare an array, each element of the array must be constructed. For example, the following declaration calls the default Student constructor five times, once for each member of the array:

```
Student s[5];
```

C++ allows you to invoke a constructor other than the default constructor using an initializer list, as shown in this truncated sample program (the full program is available in the online material at www.dummies.com/go/cplusplus8e):

```
//  ConstructArray - construct an array of objects
//

// ...same Student class with overloaded constructors...
```

```
int main(int argcs, char* pArgs[])
{
    // the following invokes 3 different constructors
    Student s[]{"Marian Haste", "Pikup Andropov"};
    Student t[]{{"Luffy", 0, 0.0}, {"Roronoa", 12, 2.5}};
}
```

The array s is created with two members by calling the `Student(const char*)` constructor twice. The array t is also constructed with two members by calling the `Student(const char*, int, double)` constructor. The output of this program appears as follows:

```
constructing student with name Marian Haste
constructing student with name Pikup Andropov
constructing student Luffy
constructing student Roronoa
```

You can also do the following declaration:

```
Student t[]{{"Luffy", 0, 0.0}, "Roronoa", "Nami"};
```

This declaration would call the `Student(const char*, int, double)` constructor for `Luffy` followed by calling the `Student(const char*)` constructor for `Roronoa` and `Nami`. Of course, your code would be cleaner if you kept the items being used to initialize the array consistent.

REMEMBER

A string of objects contained within braces is known as an *initializer list*.

Constructors as a Form of Conversion

C++ views constructors with a single argument as a way of converting from one type to another. Consider a user-defined type `Complex` designed to represent complex numbers. Without getting too technical (for me, not for you), there's a natural conversion between real numbers and complex numbers just like the conversion from integers to real numbers, as in the following example:

```
double d = 1;      // this is legal
Complex c = d;     // this should be allowed as well
```

In fact, C++ looks for ways to try to make sense of statements like this. If the class `Complex` has a constructor that takes as its argument a `double`, C++ uses that constructor as a form of conversion, as though the preceding statement had been written as follows:

```
double d = 1;
Complex c(d);
```

REMEMBER

Some constructor-introduced conversions make no sense. For example, you may not want C++ to convert an integer into a `Student` object just because a `Student(int)` constructor exists. Unexpected conversions can lead to strange run-time errors when C++ tries to make sense out of simple coding mistakes.

Starting with C++11, you can use the keyword `explicit`, or (starting with C++20) you can use *`explicit(true)`* to avoid creating unexpected and unintended conversion paths. A constructor marked `explicit` cannot be used as an implicit conversion path:

```
class Student
{
  public:
    // the following "No Name" constructor cannot be
    // used as an implicit conversion path from int
    // to Student
    explicit Student(int nStudentID);
};

Student student1 = 1;         // generates compiler error
Student student2(123456);     // this is still allowed
```

The declaration of `student1` doesn't implicitly invoke the `Student(int)` constructor, because it's flagged as "explicitly invokable only." The explicit invoking of the constructor to create the object `student2` is still okay.

Though the preceding snippet uses the keyword `explicit`, you can add conditional logic to determine whether only explicit handling should be allowed. This is done by passing an expression to `explicit` that evaluates to either `true` (in which case explicit constructing is in place) or `false` (in which case implicit can be allowed):

```
explicit(true) Student(int nStudentID);
```

This statement is silly because `explicit(true)` is the same as simply saying `explicit`. However, you can replace `true` with any condition. If that expression evaluates to `true`, it's the equivalent of using `explicit` on its own:

```
explicit(!std::is_integral_v<T>) Student(int nStudentID);
```

The expression !std::isintegral_v<T> makes more sense if you decide to learn all about templates in Bonus Chapter 2. For now, know that the expression evaluates to either a true or false result. If true, the constructor is explicit; otherwise, it allows implicit conversions.

The following is a complete listing using a simplified Student class:

```
// StudentTypeConversion
#include <print>
using namespace std;

class Student
{
  public:
    // the following constructor cannot be used
    // as an implicit conversion path from int
    // to Student
    explicit Student(int nStudentID)
    {
        setID(nStudentID);
    }
    void setID(int nID) { StudentID = nID; }
    int  getID() { return(StudentID); }
  private:
    int StudentID;
};

int main()
{
    Student S1(123456);        // this is still allowed
    println("S1 = {}", S1.getID());
    Student S2 = 1;            // generates compiler error
    println("S2 = {}", S2.getID());
}
```

WARNING

As expected, this listing gives an error as presented due to the use of explicit and the attempt to assign 1 to Student S2. You can either remove the explicit keyword to allow the implicit conversion or change explicit to explicit(false).

ON THE WEB

I came up with the program TypeConversion (included with the online material at www.dummies.com/go/cplusplus8e) to demonstrate explicit. You can check it out there.

Ignore That Value, Please

C++26 NEW

Though you might rarely ever use it or see it, this seems like a good time to mention another element that has been added to C++26: the placeholder element represented by an underscore (_).

Sometimes you have a value that you just don't care about. For instance, a function might return a value that you simply want to ignore. This might happen in a constructor, or it could happen elsewhere. For example, when creating a `Student`, you might want to call a function that has the potential to return an error code. You can capture this error code in a variable as such:

```
int err = LogStudentCreation(name);
```

Having called this function, if you choose to not do anything with the `err` variable, the compiler gives a warning stating that you have an unused variable.

One way to eliminate the warning is to call the function and simply not assign the return value to anything:

```
LogStudentCreation(name);
```

A better coding practice, however, is to capture that return value or at least indicate that you know it's being sent. This would show that you didn't simply forget to capture the return value. By adding the placeholder, you make it clear that you're ignoring any return values. You simply replace with the underscore any variables you're not interested in:

```
int _ = LogStudentCreation(name);
```

Now you'll avoid getting a warning from the compiler about an unused variable, and you'll let others know you're intentionally ignoring the return value. The following is a complete listing showing this in action:

```
#include <print>
using namespace std;

int LogStudentCreation(const string name)
{
    println("Doing some validation...on student {}", name);
    // this could be logic that might generate
    // an error code...
```

```
    return 42; // just for demonstration, we
               // return a value
}

class Student
{
  public:
    Student(string name)
    {
        int _ = LogStudentCreation(name);
        name = name;
    }
  private:
    string name;
};

int main()
{
    Student s{"Monkey D. Luffy"};
}
```

At other times in more advanced C+ coding, the placeholder variable is more useful. This includes working with structured bindings or Lambdas. For now, just know that you now have a way of saying you don't care about something!

IN THIS CHAPTER

» Introducing the copy/move constructor

» Making copies

» Having copies made for you automatically

» Creating shallow copies versus deep copies

» Avoiding all those copies with a move constructor

Chapter 19

Making Copies with the Copy/Move Constructor

The constructor is a special function that C++ invokes automatically when an object is created to allow the object to initialize itself. Chapter 17 introduces the concept of the constructor, whereas Chapter 18 delves deeper into the constructor universe. This chapter takes things one step further by examining two particular variations of the constructor known as the *copy* and *move* constructors.

In the olden days of C++, if someone wanted to transfer a value stored in a class, C++ would create a copy and then get rid of the original. This added lots of unnecessary overhead, so starting way back with C++11, an update was made to allow things to be simply moved. As a result, you now have the option of either copying or moving your class objects.

Copying an Object

A copy constructor is the constructor that C++ uses to make copies of objects. A copy constructer looks like this:

```
class X
{
  public:
     X( const X& anotherX )
     {
         // Copy constructor
     };
};
```

Or like this, if declared outside of the class:

```
X::X( const X& anotherX )
{
   // copy constructor
};
```

As you can see, the copy constructor carries the name `X::X(const X&)`, where `X` is the name of the class. That is, it's the constructor of class `X`, which takes as its argument a reference to an object of class `X` that is `const`. Now, this might sound like a bit much, but just give me a chance to explain why C++ needs such beasties.

The move constructor allows an object to be transferred. This differs from a copy because resources the object might control, such as heap memory or file handles, don't have to be copied, thus making a move more efficient. A move constructor has the following format:

```
class X
{
  public:
     X( const X&& anotherX )
     {
         // Move constructor
     };
};
```

Or, if declared outside of the class:

```
X::X( const X&& anotherX )
{
```

```
    // move constructor
};
```

Most of this chapter concerns the copy constructor. I present the details of the move constructor toward the end of this chapter.

Why you need the copy constructor

Think for a moment about what happens when you call a function like the following:

```
void fn(Student fs)
{
    // ...same scenario; different argument...
}
int main()
{
    Student ms;
    fn(ms);
}
```

In the call to `fn()`, C++ passes a copy of the object `ms` and not the object itself.

Now consider what it means to create a copy of an object. First, it takes a constructor to create an object — even a copy of an existing object. C++ could create a default copy constructor that copies the existing object into the new object one byte at a time. That's what older languages such as C do. But what if the class doesn't want a simple copy of the object? What if something else is required? (Ignore the "why?" for a little while.) The class needs to be able to specify exactly how the copy should be created.

Thus, C++ uses a copy constructor in the preceding example to create a copy of the object `ms` on the stack during the call of function `fn()`. This particular copy constructor would be `Student::Student(Student&)` — say that three times quickly.

Using the copy constructor

The best way to understand how the copy constructor works is to see one in action. Consider the following `CopyConstructor` program:

```
// CopyConstructor - demonstrate a copy constructor
//
#include <print>
```

```
using namespace std;

class Student
{
  public:
    // conventional constructor
    Student(const char *pName = "no name", int ssId = 0)
      : name(pName), id(ssId)
    { println("Constructed {}", name); }

    // copy constructor
    Student(const Student& s)
      : name("Copy of " + s.name), id(s.id)
    { println("Constructed {}", name); }

    ~Student() { println("Destructing {}", name); }

  private:
    string name;
    int id;
};
// fn - receives its argument by value
void fn(Student copy)
{
    println("In function fn()");
}
int main(int nNumberofArgs, char* pszArgs[])
{
    Student Luffy("Luffy", 1234);
    println("Calling fn()");
    fn(Luffy);
    println("Back in main()");
}
```

The output from executing this program appears as follows:

```
Constructed Luffy
Calling fn()
Constructed Copy of Luffy
In function fn()
Destructing Copy of Luffy
Back in main()
Destructing Luffy
```

The normal `Student` constructor starts by generating the first message from the declaration on the first line of `main()` about creating `Luffy`. The function `main()`

then outputs the `Calling...` message before calling `fn()`. As part of the function call process, C++ invokes the copy constructor to make a copy of `Luffy` to pass to `fn()`. The copy constructor adds the string "Copy of" to the student's name before displaying it on the console. The function `fn()` outputs the `In function...` message. The copied `Student` object `copy` is destructed at the return from `fn()`. (You can tell it's the copy because of the string "Copy of" added to the front.) The original object, `Luffy`, is destructed at the end of `main()`.

The Automatic Copy Constructor

Like the default constructor (see Chapter 16), the copy constructor is important — important enough that C++ thinks no class should be without one. If you don't provide your own copy constructor, C++ generates one for you. (This differs from the default constructor that C++ provides unless your class has constructors defined for it.)

The copy constructor provided by C++ performs a member-by-member copy of each data member. You can see this in the following `DefaultCopyConstructor` program. (I left out the definition of the `Student` class to save space — it's identical to the one shown in the `CopyConstructor` program in the previous section. The entire `DefaultCopyConstructor` program is available online at `www.dummies.com/go/cplusplus8e`.)

```
class Tutor
{
  public:
    Tutor(Student& s)
        : student(s), id(0)
    { println("Constructing Tutor object"); }
  private:
    Student student;
    int id;
};

void fn(Tutor tutor)
{
    println("In function fn()");
}

int main(int argcs, char* pArgs[])
{
    Student Luffy("Luffy");
```

```
    Tutor tutor(Luffy);
    println("Calling fn()");
    fn(tutor);
    println("Back in main()");
}
```

Executing this program generates the following output:

```
Constructed Luffy
Constructed Copy of Luffy
Constructing Tutor object
Calling fn()
Constructed Copy of Copy of Luffy
In function fn()
Destructing Copy of Copy of Luffy
Back in main()
Destructing Copy of Luffy
Destructing Luffy
```

Constructing the `Luffy` object generates the first output message from the "plain Jane" constructor. The constructor for the `Tutor` object invokes the `Student` copy constructor to generate its own `Student` data member and then outputs its own message. This accounts for the next two lines of output.

The program then passes a copy of the `Tutor` object to the function `fn()`. Because the `Tutor` class doesn't define a copy constructor, the program invokes the default copy constructor to make a copy to pass to `fn()`.

The default `Tutor` copy constructor invokes the copy constructor for each data member. The copy constructor for `int` does nothing more than copy the value. I've already described how the `Student` copy constructor works. This is what generates the `Constructed Copy of Copy of Luffy` message. The destructor for the copy is invoked as part of the return from function `fn()`. The final destructors are invoked when the program returns from `main()`.

Creating Shallow Copies versus Deep Copies

Performing a member-by-member copy seems the obvious thing to do in a copy constructor. Other than adding the capability to tack on silly things such as `Copy of` to the front of students' names, when would you ever want to do anything but a member-by-member copy?

Consider what happens if the constructor allocates an asset, such as memory off the heap using raw pointers. If the copy constructor simply makes a copy of that asset without allocating its own asset, you end up with a troublesome situation: two objects thinking they have exclusive access to the same asset. This situation becomes nastier when the destructor is invoked for both objects and they both try to put the same asset back. To make this more concrete, consider the following class example:

```
// ShallowCopy - performing a byte-by-byte (shallow) copy
//               is not correct when the class holds assets
//
#include <memory>
#include <print>
using namespace std;

class Person
{
  public:
    Person(const char *pN)
    {
        println("Constructing {}", pN);
        pName = new string(pN);
    }
    ~Person()
    {
        void* addr = pName;
        println("Destructing {:p} ({})", addr, *pName );
        *pName = "already destructed memory";
        // delete pName;
    }
  private:
    string *pName;
};
void fn()
{
    // create a new object
    Person p1("This_is_a_very_long_name");
    // copy the contents of p1 into p2
    Person p2(p1);
}
```

```
int main()
{
    println("Calling fn()");
    fn();
    println("Back in main()");
}
```

This program generates the following output:

```
Calling fn()
Constructing This_is_a_very_long_name
Destructing 0x18952e121f0 (This_is_a_very_long_name)
Destructing 0x18952e121f0 (already destructed memory)
Back in main()
```

The constructor for `Person` allocates memory off the heap to store the person's name. The destructor would normally return this memory to the heap using the `delete` keyword; however, in this case, the call to `delete` has been replaced with a statement that replaces the name with a message. (Note that I've assigned the address of the allocated memory to the variable `addr` so that I can display it to the screen in the `println()` statement.)

The main program calls the function `fn()`, which creates one person, `p1`, and then makes a copy of that person, `p2`. Both objects are destructed automatically when the program returns from the function.

Only one constructor output message appears when this program is executed. That's not too surprising because the copy constructor provided by C++ that's used to build `p2` generates no output. The `Person` destructor is invoked twice, however, as both `p1` and `p2` go out of scope. The first destructor outputs the expected message `This_is_a_very_long_name`. The second destructor indicates that the memory has already been deleted. Notice also that the address of the memory block is the same for both objects (`0x18952e121f0`).

WARNING

If the program really were to delete the name, the program would become unstable after the second deletion and might not even complete properly without crashing.

The problem is shown graphically in Figure 19-1. The object `p1` is copied into the new object `p2`, but the assets are not. Thus, `p1` and `p2` end up pointing to the same assets (in this case, heap memory). This is known as a *shallow* copy because it just "skims the surface," copying the members themselves.

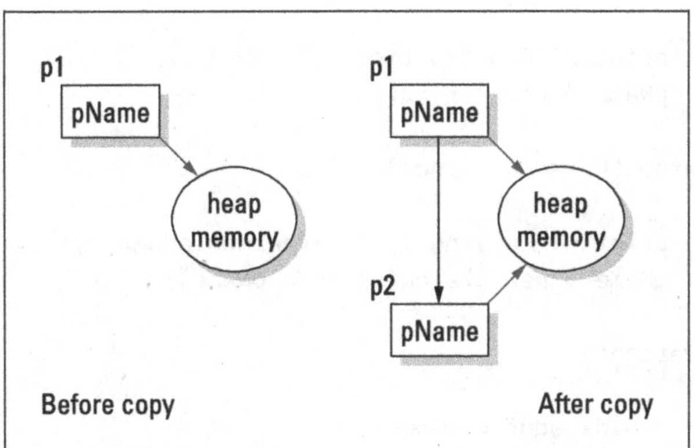

FIGURE 19-1: Shallow copy of p1 to p2.

The solution to this problem is demonstrated visually in Figure 19-2. This figure represents a copy constructor that allocates its own assets to the new object.

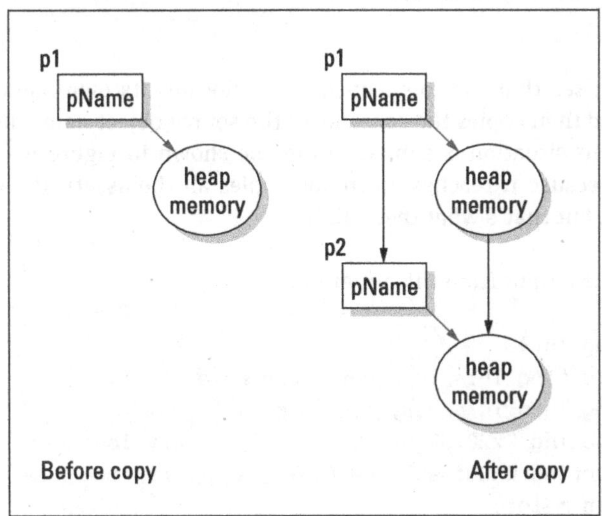

FIGURE 19-2: Deep copy of p1 to p2.

The following example shows an appropriate copy constructor for class `Person`. (This class is embodied in the program `DeepCopy`, which is part of this book's online material at `www.dummies.com/go/cplusplus8e`.)

```
class Person
{
  public:
    Person(const char *pN)
    {
```

```
        println("Constructing {}", pN );
        pName = new string(pN);
    }
    Person(Person& person)
    {
        println("Copying {} ", *(person.pName) );
        pName = new string(*person.pName);
    }
    ~Person()
    {
         void* addr = pName;
         println("Destructing {:p} ({})", addr, *pName );
        *pName = "already destructed memory";
        // delete pName;
    }
    private:
        string *pName;
}
```

Here you see that the copy constructor allocates its own memory block for the name and then copies the contents of the source object name into this new name block. This situation is similar to the one shown in Figure 19-2. *Deep copy* is so named because it reaches down and copies all the assets. (Okay, the analogy is strained, but that's what they call it.)

Here's the output from this program:

```
Calling fn()
Constructing This_is_a_very_long_name
Copying This_is_a_very_long_name
Destructing 0x20f09b02540 (This_is_a_very_long_name)
Destructing 0x20f09b024b0 (This_is_a_very_long_name)
Back in main()
```

The destructor for `Person` now indicates that the string pointers in `p1` and `p2` don't point to the same block of memory — the addresses of the two objects are different — and the name in the version owned by the copy has not been overwritten, indicating that it has been deleted.

REMEMBER

The real `~Person` destructor should delete `pName`.

REMEMBER THOSE SMART POINTERS

The issues that arise with shallow copies can be prevented by avoiding the use of raw pointers. Though the example of copying the Person objects was great for illustrating shallow-versus-deep copies, another lesson to keep in mind is that the issue of double-deleting memory can be avoided by using smart pointers. Remember that a smart pointer keeps track of deleting memory for you. The following is a rewrite of the Person class using a unique smart pointer. The output is the same as the DeepCopy program.

```
class Person
{
  public:
    Person(const char *pN)
    {
       println("Constructing {}", pN );
       pName = make_unique<string>(pN);
    }
    Person(Person& person)
    {
       println("Copying {} ", *(person.pName) );
       pName = make_unique<string>( *(person.pName) );
    }
    ~Person()
    {
        println("Destructing {}", *pName );
       *pName = "already destructed memory";
    }
    private:
       unique_ptr<string> pName;
};
```

If your class is using smart pointers, you should be doing deep copies, not shallow ones.

It's a Long Way to Temporaries

Passing arguments by value to functions is the most obvious (but not the only) example of the use of the copy constructor. C++ creates a copy of an object under other conditions as well.

Consider a function that returns an object by value. In this case, C++ must create a copy using the copy constructor. This situation is demonstrated in the following code snippet:

```
Student fn()       // returns object by value
{
   Student newStudent;
   return newStudent;
}

int main()
{
   Student s;
   s = fn();           // call to fn() creates temporary

   // how long does the temporary returned by fn()last?
}
```

The function `fn()` returns an object by value. Eventually, the returned object is copied to `s`, but where does it reside until then?

C++ creates a temporary object into which it stuffs the returned object. "Okay," you say. "C++ creates the temporary object, but how does it know when to destruct it?" Good question. It really doesn't make much difference because you are done using the temporary object once the copy constructor copies it into `s`. But what if `s` is defined as a reference? It makes a big difference in how long temporary objects live because `refS` exists for the entire function:

```
int main()
{
    Student& refS = fn();
    // ...now what?...
}
```

Temporary objects created by the compiler are valid throughout the extended expression in which they were created and no further. Such objects are generally destructed as soon as the expression is completed.

In the following function, I mark the point at which the temporary object is no longer valid:

```
Student fn1();

int fn2(const Student&);

int main()
{
   int x;
   // create a Student object by calling fn1().
   // Pass that object to the function fn2().
   // fn2() returns an integer that is used in some
   // silly calculation.
   // All this time the temporary returned from fn1()
   // remains valid.
   x = 3 * fn2(fn1()) + 10;

   // the temporary returned from fn1() is now no longer valid
   // ...other stuff...
   return 0;
}
```

This makes the reference example invalid because the object may go away before `refS` does, leaving `refS` referring to a non-object.

C++26 NEW

In versions of C++ before C++26, you could simply pass `Student& to fn2()` and it would accept it. Starting with C++26, the `const` reference to a temporary value is needed to help prevent the temporary object's value from being changed. This helps keep things safer because you aren't changing things that could be going away. The `const` reference helps extend the lifetime of the temporary object for the duration of the call to `fn2()`.

Avoiding temporaries permanently

It may have occurred to you that all this copying of objects hither and yon can be a bit time-consuming. What if you don't want to make copies of everything? The most straightforward solution is to pass objects to functions and return objects from functions by reference. Doing so avoids the majority of temporary objects.

But what if you're still not convinced that C++ isn't out there craftily constructing temporary objects that you know nothing about? Or what if your class allocates unique assets that you don't want copied? What do you do then?

You can add an output statement to your copy constructor. The presence of this message when you execute the program warns you that a copy has just been made.

TIP

A cleverer approach to stopping a copy from happening outside of your class is to declare the copy constructor private:

```
class Student
{
  private:
    Student(Student&s){}
  public:
    // ...everything else normal...
};
```

With the copy constructor being private, only your class can make copies of Students.

Saying goodbye to copying

C++ also allows the programmer to delete the copy constructor using the delete keyword:

```
class Student
{
   Student(Student&s) = delete;
   // ...everything else normal...
};
```

Just as when you declare the copy constructor private or protected, assigning it to delete entirely precludes any external functions from constructing a copy of your class objects. In this code example, no one can invoke the copy constructor, so no copies are being generated. Voilà.

The Move Constructor

Under certain conditions, C++ can create a copy of an object that is used only for the duration of a single statement. Such temporary objects are destructed as soon as the expression is completed. It doesn't make sense to make copies of temporary objects that are about to be destructed anyway.

Sometimes, rather than make copies, you might find it better simply to move control. C++ allows you to create a constructor — yes, a *move* constructor — that moves assets from the source to the destination. This is a perfect solution for when you want to avoid making unnecessary copies. Move constructors have the format `X::X(X&&)`.

Consider the highly contrived example that follows the Tip paragraph.

TIP

C++includes several return optimizations designed to avoid the creation of unnecessary copies of objects. My example has to defeat these optimizations in order to demonstrate the move constructor. (You'll see much less contrived examples in the discussion of overloading operators in Chapter 24.)

```
// Move - demonstrate the principle of moving a
//        temporary rather than creating a copy
//
#include <print>
using namespace std;

class Person
{
  public:
    Person(const char *pN)
    {
       pName = pN;
       println("Constructing {}", pName);
    }
    Person(const Person& p)
    {
       println("Copying {}", p.pName);
       pName = "Copy of " + p.pName;
    }
    Person(Person&& p)
    {
       println("Moving {}", p.pName);
       pName = p.pName;
       p.pName = "";
    }
    ~Person()
    {
      if (pName.empty()) // checks to see if pName == ""
      {
        println("Destructing null object");
      }
```

```
        else
        {
            println("Destructing {}", pName);
        }
    }
  private:
    string pName;
};
Person fn2(Person p)
{
    println("Entering fn2");
    return p;
}
Person fn1(const char* pName)
{
    println("Entering fn1");
//    return fn2(*new Person(pName));
    return fn2(Person(pName));
}

int main()
{
    Person s(fn1("Luffy"));
    println("End of main");
}
```

Notice how the move constructor assigns the pName pointer from the source object p and then zeroes out that pointer so that the destructor doesn't return the memory when the temporary object is destructed. This is much more efficient than allocating yet another string object off the heap and copying the contents of p.pName to this new string.

The output from this program appears as follows:

```
Entering fn1
Constructing Luffy
Entering fn2
Moving Luffy
Destructing null object
End of main
Destructing Luffy
```

In this case, fn1() creates a Person object. It then copies this object in the call to fn2() using the copy constructor. The function fn2() does nothing more than return a copy of this object to `fn1()`; however, this copy is just a temporary object that `fn1()` returns to `main()`. Rather than use the copy constructor to create a "Copy of copy of Luffy," C++11 invokes the move constructor to transfer the contents of the temporary object into the newly created return-value object. When this temporary object is subsequently destructed, it's a "null object" because its `pName` has been taken away and reassigned.

TIP

You don't have to create a move constructor. The program would have worked just fine, albeit a hair slower, with just the copy constructor. Move constructors should be considered an advanced topic.

Just Because It Can Doesn't Mean It Will

TECHNICAL STUFF

Now that you know a bit about copy and move constructors (including how to add them to your programs), you should be aware that there are times when they might not get used.

You can ask a kid to do something, but, sadly, they won't always do it. For example, I said earlier in this chapter that the following code looks like it should call a copy constructor when returning the object:

```
Student addStudent()
{
    Student tempStudent;
    // The following line might skip copy/move constructors
    return tempStudent;
}

Student newStudent = addStudent();
```

Though it looks like a `Student` object should be copied or moved, there's a chance that the C++ compiler may optimize this code by building the `newStudent` object directly without making a copy from the `addStudent()` function. This process is called return value optimization (RVO), a form of *elision* — a term describing when the compiler skips calling a constructor in order to make your code faster and cleaner.

What you do know is that copy and move constructors will be called when you're passing or returning an object by value to or from a function, when you're initializing one object from another, or when you use a function such as `std::move()` to explicitly move an object.

RVO and elision are handled by the compiler. As such, until you start getting into advanced coding, just be aware that they exist and are working to help make your code faster!

On a related note, C++26 added a concept called *trivial relocatability*. This advanced topic is also beyond the scope of this book, but it's worth a mention so that you're aware of it. You're more likely to need to know about it if you're doing something such as creating high-performance systems or highly optimized systems, frameworks, or high-performance solutions.

Trivial relocatability is a feature that checks to see whether a type can be safely copied using a low-level operation (with memory) without needing to call special copy or move constructors. The standard library includes concepts that help with this process, such as `std::is_trivially_copyable`. Again, this is advanced stuff, but at least you're now aware of it, in case you need it in the future!

IN THIS CHAPTER

» Defining and using static member functions

» Declaring static member data

» Using `static` to control visibility

» Understanding how objects can refer to themselves

Chapter 20

Adding Static Members: Can Fabric Softener Help?

Sometimes it's nice to share. By default, data members are allocated on a per-object basis so that each object has its own members. For example, each person has their own name. But classes can also share an item across objects of that class by declaring that member static. The term *static* applies to both data members and member functions, although the meaning is slightly different. This chapter describes both static data members and static member functions, beginning with static data members.

Creating a Function that Remembers

Before looking at how sharing works in classes, let me show you something a tad simpler: creating a function that can remember a data value. A variable can be declared within a function using the `static` keyword as part of the declaration. Such members are called *static variables*. Once declared static, the variable's value will be retained between calls to the function.

As an example, the following simple counter function declares a variable named `count` as a static `int`:

```
int counter()
{
    static int count = 0;
    count++;
    return count;
}
```

In this function, the variable `count` is treated as if it were a global variable after the first time it's called. The first time this function is called, `count` is set to `0`, which is what you would expect for a local variable. When the function ends, however, `count` doesn't get tossed away, like all other local variables.

Stated differently, if `count` were not declared as `static`, then because it is a local variable, when control leaves the `counter()` function, the `count` variable would go out of scope and disappear. Because it's declared as `static`, however, it clings on and persists so that if the function is called again, it remains — just like a global variable. You can test this concept with a simple program:

```
// StaticCling - using static in a function
#include <print>
using namespace std;

int counter()
{
    static int count = 0;
    count++;
    return count;
}

int main()
{
    for( int x = 1; x <= 5; x++)
    {
        println("Counter is now {}", counter());
    }
}
```

When you run this program, you see that the counter retains its value:

```
Counter is now 1
Counter is now 2
Counter is now 3
```

```
Counter is now 4
Counter is now 5
```

If you remove the word `static`, you see that the `count` variable is reset as a local variable each time the function is called:

```
Counter is now 1
Counter is now 1
Counter is now 1
Counter is now 1
Counter is now 1
```

Defining a Static Member

The `static` keyword can also be used with classes. When working with classes, you can make a data member common to all objects of the class by adding `static` to the declaration. Such members are called *static data members.* (It would be odd if they were called something else.)

Why you need static members

Most data members and methods are properties of the object. Using the well-worn (one might say *threadbare*) `Student` example, data members such as name, ID number, and courses are specific to the individual student. However, all students can share some properties — for example, the number of students enrolled, the highest grade of all students, or a pointer to the first student in a linked list.

You can easily store this type of information in a common, ordinary, garden-variety global variable. For example, you can use a lowly `int` variable to keep track of the number of `Student` objects. The problem with this solution is that global variables are outside the class. It's like putting the voltage regulator for a microwave outside the enclosure. Sure, I could do it, and it would probably work — the only problem is that I wouldn't be too happy if my dog got into the wires and I had to peel him off the ceiling. (The dog wouldn't be thrilled about it, either.)

If a class is going to be held responsible for its own state, objects such as global variables must be brought inside the class (*encapsulated in the class,* to use an object-oriented programming term), just as the voltage regulator must be inside the microwave lid, away from prying paws. This is the idea behind static members.

TIP

You may hear static members referred to as *class members*; this is because all objects in the class share them. By comparison, normal members are referred to as *instance members*, or *object members*, because each object receives its own copy of these members.

Using static members

A *static* data member is one that has been declared with the `static` storage class. This storage class is simply added to the declaration as shown here:

```
class Student
{
  public:
    Student(string pName = "no name") : name(pName)
    {
         nbrOfStudents++;
    }
    ~Student(){ nbrOfStudents--; }

    static int nbrOfStudents;
    string name;
};
```

Using this class, you can declare a couple of instances of `Student`:

```
Student s1;
Student s2;
```

The data member `nbrOfStudents` is part of the class `Student` but is not part of either `s1` or `s2`. That is, for each object of class `Student`, there is a separate `name` but only one `nbrOfStudents`, which all `Students` share.

"Well then," you ask, "if the space for `nbrOfStudents` is not allocated in any of the objects of class `Student`, where is it allocated?" The answer is, "It isn't." You must specifically allocate space for it, as follows:

```
int Student::nbrOfStudents = 0;
```

This somewhat peculiar-looking syntax allocates space for the static data member and initializes it to `0`. (You don't have to initialize a static member when you declare it; C++ invokes the default constructor if you don't.) Static data members must be global — a `static` variable cannot be local to a function.

REMEMBER

The name of the class is required for any member when it appears outside its class boundaries.

TIP

This business of allocating space manually is somewhat confusing until you consider that class definitions are designed to be written into files that are included by multiple source code modules. C++ needs to know in which of those .cpp source files it should allocate space for the static variable. This is not a problem with nonstatic variables because space is allocated in every object created.

Referencing static data members

The access rules for static members are the same as the access rules for normal members. From within the class, static members are referenced like any other class member. Public static members can be referenced from outside the class, whereas well-protected static members can't. The following code snippet uses the declaration of Student from the previous section to show the access of a static member from outside the class:

```
void fn(Student& s1, Student& s2)
{
   // reference public static
   println("Number of students {}",
            s1.nbrOfStudents ); // reference from outside
                                // of the class
}
```

In fn(), nbrOfStudents is referenced using the object s1. But s1 and s2 share the same member nbrOfStudents. How did I know to choose s1? Why didn't I use s2 instead? It makes no difference. You can reference a static member using any object of that class. Here's a full listing with fn() function and Student class, but this time using s2:

```
// staticStudents - accessing a static member
//
#include <print>
using namespace std;

class Student
{
  public:
```

```
    Student(string pName = "no name") : name(pName)
    {
        nbrOfStudents++;
    }
    ~Student(){ nbrOfStudents--; }

    static int nbrOfStudents;
    string name;
};
int Student::nbrOfStudents = 0;

void fn(Student& s1, Student& s2)
{
  // reference public static
  println("Number of students {}",
         s2.nbrOfStudents ); // reference from outside
                             // of the class
}

int main(int nNumberofArgs, char* pszArgs[])
{
  Student s1;
  Student s2;
  fn(s1, s2);
}
```

In fact, you don't even need an object — you can use the class name directly instead, if you prefer, as in the following:

```
// ...class defined the same as before...
void fn(Student& s1, Student& s2)
{
  // the following produce identical results
  println("Number of students {}", Student::nbrOfStudents );
}
```

If you do use an object name when accessing a static member, C++ uses only the declared class of the object.

This is a minor technicality, but in the interest of full disclosure: The object used to reference a static member is not evaluated even if it's an expression. For example, consider the following case:

```
class Student
{
  public:
    static int nbrOfStudents;
    Student& nextStudent();
    // ...other stuff the same...
};

void fn(Student& s)
{
   println("{}", s.nextStudent().nbrOfStudents );
}
```

The member function `nextStudent()` is not actually called. All C++ needs to access `nbrOfStudents` is the return type, and it can get that without bothering to evaluate the expression. This is true even if `nextStudent()` should do other things, such as wash windows or shine your shoes. None of those things will be done. Although the example is obscure, it does happen. That's what you get for trying to cram too much stuff into one expression.

Uses for static data members

Static data members have umpteen uses, but let me touch on a few here. First, you can use static members to keep count of the number of objects floating about. In the `Student` class, for example, the count is initialized to `0`, the constructor increments it, and the destructor decrements it. At any given instant, the static member contains the count of the number of existing `Student` objects. Remember, however, that this count reflects the number of `Student` objects (including any temporary objects) and not necessarily the number of students.

A closely related use for a static member is as a flag to indicate whether a particular action has occurred. For example, a class `Radio` may need to initialize hardware before sending the first `tune` command, but not before subsequent `tunes`. A flag indicating that this is the first `tune` is just the ticket. This includes flagging when an error has occurred.

Another common use is to provide space for the pointer to the first member of a list — the head pointer. (See Chapter 15 if this statement doesn't sound familiar.) Static members can allocate bits of common data that all objects in all functions share. (Overuse of this common memory is a bad idea because doing so makes tracking errors difficult.)

Keeping static variables inline

Earlier in this chapter, I mention that you need to allocate space for your static data members. This was done outside of the class using a command such as the following:

```
int Student::nbrOfStudents = 0;
```

You might think this would be nicer to do within the class. The reality is that you can actually allocate the space within the class as well, as long as you're using a basic integral type (such as `int`, `char`, or `bool`).

In the case where the static data member you're creating is a `const` value (one that won't change), you can go ahead and define it directly within your class. The following works because `nbrOfStudents` is a `const` value:

```
class Student
{
  public:
    static const int nbrOfStudents = 30;
};
```

Starting with the C++17 standard, you can go ahead and allocate the space within your function by using the keyword `inline`. This can be used with even non-integral types and doesn't require `const`:

```
class VideoGame
{
  public:
    inline static int highScore = 0;
    inline static string gameName = "Gem Miners";
};
```

If you are curious, you can learn more about the keyword `inline` in Chapter 11.

Declaring Static Member Functions

Member functions can be declared static as well. Static member functions are useful when you want to associate an action with a class, but you don't need to associate that action with a particular object. For example, the member function `Duck::fly()` is associated with a particular duck, whereas the rather more drastic member function `Duck::goExtinct()` is not.

Like static data members, static member functions are associated with a class and not with a particular object of that class. This means that, like a reference to a static data member, a reference to a static member function does not require an object. If an object is present, only its type is used.

Thus, both calls to the static member function `getStudentCount()` in the following example are legal. This brings us to my static program — I mean, my first program using static member functions — `CallStaticMember`:

```
// CallStaticMember - demonstrate two ways to call a
//                    static member function
//
#include <print>
using namespace std;

class Student
{
  public:
     Student(const char* pN = "no name") : sName(pN)
     {
         nbrOfStudents++;
     }
     ~Student()
     {
         nbrOfStudents--;
     }
     const string& getName() { return sName; }
     static int getStudentCount() { return nbrOfStudents; }

  private:
     string sName;
     static int nbrOfStudents;
};
int Student::nbrOfStudents = 0;

int main(int argcs, char* pArgs[])
{
    // create two students and ask the class "how many?"
    Student s1("Chester");
    // Using a raw pointer so we can control the deleting
    Student* pS2 = new Student("Scooter");

    println("Created {} and {}", s1.getName(), pS2->getName());
```

```
    println("Number of students is {}", s1.getStudentCount());

    // now get rid of a student and ask again
    println("Deleting {}", pS2->getName());
    delete pS2;
    println("Number of students is {}",
    Student::getStudentCount());
}
```

This program creates two Student objects, one locally and one off the heap. It then displays their names and the count of the number of students. Next, the program deletes one of the students (or more specifically, one of the Student objects) and asks the class how many students are out there. The output from the program appears as follows:

```
Created Chester and Scooter
Number of students is 2
Deleting Scooter
Number of students is 1
```

This class keeps its data members protected and provides access functions that allow outside (non-Student) code to read but not modify them.

TIP

Declaring the return type of the getName() method to be string& rather than simply string causes the function to return a reference to the object's existing name rather than create a temporary string object. (See Chapter 19 for a brilliant treatise on constructing and avoiding temporary objects.) Adding the *const* to the declaration keeps the caller from modifying the class's name member.

Notice how the static member function getStudentCount() can access the static data member nbrOfStudents. In fact, that's the only member of the class it can access: A static member function is not associated with any object. Were getName() to be declared as static, I could refer to Student::getName(), which would immediately beg the question, "Which name?"

The following snippet is only one case I'm aware of where a static method can refer directly to a nonstatic member:

```
class Student
{
  public:
    static int elementsInName()
    {
        int sizeOfArray = sizeof(name);
```

```
        return sizeOfArray/sizeof(char);
    }
  private:
    char name[MAX_NAME_SIZE];
};
```

Here the static method `elementsInName()` refers to `name` without referencing any object. This was not legal before the 2011 standard. It's allowed now because the `sizeof name` is the same for all objects. Thus, it doesn't matter which object you refer to.

TECHNICAL STUFF

You may wonder why I divided `sizeof(name)` by `sizeof(char)`. The `sizeof(name)` returns the number of bytes in the array name. But what I want is the number of elements in `name`, so I have to divide by the size of each element in `name`. But isn't `sizeof(char)` equal to 1? Well, maybe, but maybe not. Dividing the size of the array by the size of a single element always works for all array types.

Static at a Global Level

When you create larger C++ solutions, you will likely place your code into multiple files. In fact, if you have been working with the information in some of the other chapters in this book, you've already been creating programs that use code in multiple files! The print commands you've been using are included from a separate file, as are many of the other library files you use.

Using the `static` keyword, you can restrict the visibility of an item to the current file. For example, if you declared the following outside of any classes or functions, it would be considered a global variable for your entire program:

```
int internalCounter = 0;
```

If, however, you add the `static` keyword to the declaration, `internalCounter` will be visible only to the code in the current file:

```
static int internalCounter = 0;
```

The value of making the variable static is that it can help prevent naming conflicts in cases where another file might have included the same name for a global variable.

What Is This About Anyway?

How does a nonstatic object method know which object it's referring to? In other words, when I ask the Student object for its name, how does getName() know which sName to return?

The answer is simply that the address of the current object is passed as an implied first argument to every nonstatic method. When it's necessary to refer to this object, C++ gives it the name this — a keyword in every object method meaning "the current object." This particular use of this is illustrated in the following code snippet:

```
class SC
{
  public:
    void dyn(int a);          // like SC::dyn(SC *this, int a)
    static void stat(int a); // like SC::stat(int a)
};

void fn(SC& s)
{
   s.dyn(10);  // -converts to-> SC::dyn(&s, 10);
   s.stat(10); // -converts to-> SC::stat(10);
}
```

That is, the function dyn() is interpreted almost as though it were declared void SC::dyn(SC *this, int a). The call to dyn() is converted by the compiler (as shown in the comments) with the address of s passed as the first argument. (You can't actually write the call this way, but this is what the compiler is doing.)

References to other nonstatic members within SC::dyn() automatically use the this argument as the pointer to the current object. When SC::stat() was called, no object address was passed because the static function is tied to the class, not to any specific object. Thus, it has no this pointer to use when referencing non-static functions, which is why I say that a static member function is not associated with any current object.

You can see this used explicitly in an object-oriented version of the linked list program from Chapter 15, called LinkedListClass. The entire program is available with the online material at www.dummies.com/go/cplusplus8e; the NameDataSet class appears here:

```
// NameDataSet - stores a person's name (these objects
//               could easily store any other information
```

```
//                 desired).
class NameDataSet
{
  public:
     NameDataSet(string& refName)
       : sName(refName), pNext(nullptr) {}
     // add self to beginning of list
     void add()
     {
         this->pNext = pHead;
         pHead = shared_ptr<NamedDataSet>(this);
     }
     // access methods
     static shared_ptr<NameDataSet> first() { return pHead; }
            shared_ptr<NameDataSet> next()  { return pNext; }
            const string& name()  { return sName; }
  private:
    string sName;
    // the link to the first and next member of list
    static shared_ptr<NameDataSet> pHead;
    shared_ptr<NameDataSet> pNext;
// allocate space for the head pointer
shared_ptr<NameDataSet> NameDataSet::pHead = nullptr;
```

Here you can see that the pHead pointer to the beginning of the list has been converted into a static data member because it applies to the entire class. In addition, pNext has been made a data member, and access methods have been provided to give other programs access to the now private members of the class.

The add() method adds the current object to the list by first setting its pNext pointer to the beginning of the list. The next statement causes the head pointer to point to the current object via the assignment of the current name (this) as a smart pointer to pHead.

```
class NameDataSet
{
  public:
    NameDataSet(string& refName)
        : sName(refName), pNext(nullptr) {}

    // add self to beginning of list
    void add()
    {
        pNext = pHead;
        pHead = shared_ptr<NameDataSet>(this);
    }

    // access methods
    static shared_ptr<NameDataSet> first() {return pHead;}
    shared_ptr<NameDataSet> next() {return pNext;}
    const string& name() {return sName;}

  protected:
    string sName;
    // the pointer to the first member of the list
    static shared_ptr<NameDataSet> pHead;
    shared_ptr<NameDataSet> pNext;
};
// allocate space for the head pointer
shared_ptr<NameDataSet> NameDataSet::pHead = nullptr;
```

Here you can see that the static pointer to the beginning of the list has been converted into a static data member because it applies to the entire class. In addition, pNext has been made a data member, and access methods have been provided to give other programs access to the now private members of the class.

The add() method adds the current object to the list by first setting its pNext pointer to the beginning of the list. The next statement causes the head pointer to point to the current object via the assignment of the current name (this) as a smart pointer to pHead.

4 A First Look at Inheritance

IN THIS PART . . .

Inheriting a base class

Exploring relationships

Learning to keep things private

Factoring common properties

Declaring abstract classes

IN THIS CHAPTER

» Defining inheritance

» Inheriting a base class

» Constructing the base class

» Exploring meaningful relationships: The IS_A versus the HAS_A relationship

Chapter 21
Passing the DNA: Sharing Code with Inheritance

This chapter discusses another core part of object-oriented programming: *inheritance*, which is the ability of one class to inherit capabilities or properties from another class.

Inheritance is a common concept. I am a human (except when I first wake up in the morning). I inherit certain properties from the class `Human`, such as my ability to converse (more or less) intelligently and my dependence on air, water, and carbohydrate-based nourishment (a little too dependent on the latter, I'm afraid). These properties are not unique to humans. The class `Human` inherits the dependencies on air, water, and nourishment from the class `Mammal`, which inherited it from the class `Animal`.

The capability of passing down properties is a powerful one. It enables you to describe things in an economical way. For example, if my daughter asks, "What's a duck?" I can say, "It's a bird that goes quack, quack." Despite what you may think, that answer conveys a considerable amount of information. She knows what a bird is, and now she knows all those same things about a duck, plus the duck's additional property of "quackness." (Refer to Chapter 13 for a further discussion of this and other profound observations.)

Object-oriented (OO) languages express this inheritance relationship by allowing one class to inherit from another. OO languages can generate a model that's closer to the real world — remember that real-world stuff! — than the model generated by languages that don't support inheritance.

C++ allows one class to inherit another class as follows:

```
class Student
{
   // Student class stuff
};

class GraduateStudent : public Student
{
   // GraduateStudent stuff
};
```

Here a GraduateStudent inherits all the members of Student. Thus, a GraduateStudent IS_A Student. (The capitalization of IS_A stresses the importance of this relationship.) Of course, GraduateStudent may also contain other members that are unique to a GraduateStudent.

Do I Need My Inheritance?

Inheritance was introduced into C++ for several reasons. Of course, the major reason is the capability of expressing the inheritance relationship. (I return to that topic in a moment.) A minor reason is to reduce the amount of typing. Suppose that you have a class Student, and you're asked to add a new class called GraduateStudent. Inheritance can drastically reduce the number of items you have to put in the class. All you really need in the class GraduateStudent are things that describe the differences between students and graduate students.

Another minor side effect has to do with software modification. Suppose you inherit from some existing class. Later, you find that the base class doesn't do exactly what the subclass needs. Or perhaps the class has a bug. Modifying the base class might break other code that uses that base class. Creating and using a new subclass that overloads the incorrect feature with a corrected version solves your problem without causing someone else further problems.

Because base class and subclass might be new terms for you, Figure 21.1 helps illustrate the relationship using two examples. Note that GraduateStudent IS_A Student just as Duck IS_A Bird.

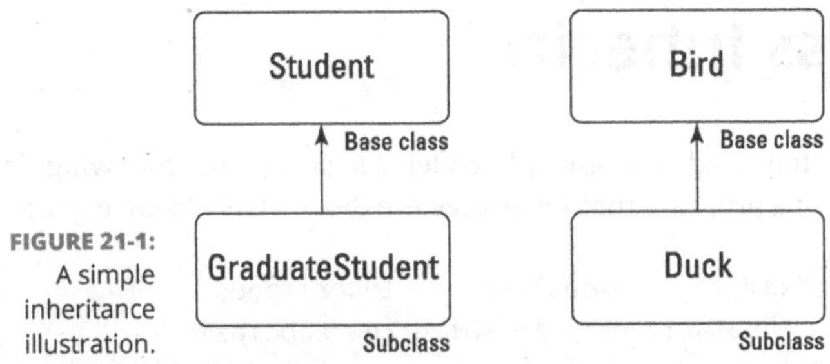

FIGURE 21-1: A simple inheritance illustration.

THIS IS_A-MAZING

To make sense of their surroundings, humans build extensive taxonomies. Fido is a special case of dog, which is a special case of canine, which is a special case of mammal, and so it goes. This concept shapes our understanding of the world.

To use another example, a student is a (special type of) person. Having said this, I already know lots of things about students (American students, anyway). I know that they have Social Security numbers, they spend too much time online, and they tend to eat on a regular basis (some more than others). I know all these things because these are properties of all people.

In C++, you say that the class `Student` inherits from the class `Person`. Also, you say that `Person` is a *base class* of `Student`, and `Student` is a *subclass* of `Person`. One final phrase and then I'll stop: `Student` extends the class `Person`.

Finally, you say that a `Student` IS_A `Person`. (Using all caps is a common way of expressing this unique relationship — I didn't make it up.) C++ shares this terminology with other object-oriented languages.

Notice that although `Student` IS_A `Person`, the reverse is not true. A `Person` IS not a `Student`. (A statement like this one always refers to the general case. It could be that a particular `Person` is, in fact, a `Student`.) Many people who are members of class `Person` are not members of class `Student`. In addition, class `Student` has properties it does not share with class `Person`. For example, `Student` has a grade point average, but `Person` does not.

The inheritance property is transitive. For example, if I define a new class `GraduateStudent` as a subclass of `Student`, `GraduateStudent` must also be `Person`. It must be that way: If a `GraduateStudent` IS_A `Student` and a `Student` IS_A `Person`, a `GraduateStudent` IS_A `Person`.

How Does a Class Inherit?

Okay, too much talk and not enough code! As such, the following is the `InheritanceExample` program that illustrates the `GraduateStudent` example:

```
// InheritanceExample - demonstrate an inheritance
//                  relationship in which the subclass
//                  constructor passes argument information
//                  to the constructor in the base class
//
#include <print>
#include <iostream>
using namespace std;

class Advisor {}; // define an empty class

class Student
{
  public:
     Student(const string pName = "no name")
        : name(pName), average(0.0), semesterHours(0)
     {
        println("Constructing student {}", name);
     }
     void addCourse(int hours, float grade)
     {
        println("Adding grade to {}", name);
        average = semesterHours * average + grade;
        semesterHours += hours;
        average = average / semesterHours;
     }
     int hours() { return semesterHours;}
     float gpa() { return average;}
  protected:
     string name;
     double average;
     int    semesterHours;
};

class GraduateStudent : public Student
{
```

```
public:
    GraduateStudent(const string pName, Advisor adv,
                    double qG = 0.0)
      : Student(pName), advisor(adv), qualifierGrade(qG)
    {
        println("Constructing graduate student {}", pName);
    }

    double qualifier() { return qualifierGrade; }

  protected:
    Advisor advisor;
    double qualifierGrade;
};

int main(int nNumberofArgs, char* pszArgs[])
{
    // create a dummy advisor to give to GraduateStudent
    Advisor adv;
    // create two Student types
    Student stud("Cy N Sense");
    GraduateStudent gs("Matt Madox", adv, 1.5);

    // now add a grade to their grade point average
    stud.addCourse(3, 2.5);
    gs.addCourse(3, 3.0);

    // display the graduate student's qualifier grade
    println("Matt's qualifier grade = {}", gs.qualifier());
}
```

This program demonstrates the creation and use of two objects: one of class `Student` and a second of `GraduateStudent`. Here's the output of this program:

```
Constructing student Cy N Sense
Constructing student Matt Madox
Constructing graduate student Matt Madox
Adding grade to Cy N Sense
Adding grade to Matt Madox
Matt's qualifier grade = 1.5
```

Using a subclass

The class Student has been defined in the conventional fashion. The class GraduateStudent is a bit different, however. It starts with the following line:

```
class GraduateStudent : public Student
```

The colon followed by the phrase public Student at the beginning of the class definition declares GraduateStudent to be a subclass of Student.

TIP

The appearance of the keyword public implies that there is probably private and protected inheritance as well. All right, it's true, but *private* and *protected* inheritance are not used as much, and they are beyond the scope of this book.

Programmers love inventing new terms or giving new meaning to existing terms. Heck, programmers even invent new terms and then give them a second meaning. Here's a set of equivalent expressions that describe the same relationship:

- GraduateStudent is a subclass of Student.
- Student is the base class or is the parent class of GraduateStudent.
- GraduateStudent inherits or is derived from Student.
- GraduateStudent extends Student.

As a subclass of Student, GraduateStudent inherits all its members. For example, a GraduateStudent has a name even though that member is declared in the base class. However, a subclass can add its own members — for example, qualifierGrade. After all, gs quite literally IS_A Student plus a little bit more.

The main() function declares two objects: stud of type Student and gs of type GraduateStudent. It then proceeds to access the addCourse() member function for both types of students. main() then accesses the qualifier() function that is only a member of the subclass.

Let's talk about protecting your privates

You should also notice that the InheritanceExample program uses the keyword protected instead of private when setting up some of the data members. If you recall, private hides data members. That includes hiding them from any classes that might inherit those data members. Though sometimes you might want to keep things private from inheriting classes, that is often not the case. In this case, you might want to let the GraduateStudent class have access to the private data members but still keep the members private otherwise.

The keyword protected allows you to keep members of your class private for everywhere other than those classes that inherit. In this case, because Student has defined access to name, average, and semesterHours as protected, the GraduateStudent class can use them as though they were its own. If these were defined as private, GraduateStudent would not have access.

The way the program is listed, GraduateStudent isn't using any of those variables, but it could. For example, you can update the qualifier() member function to print a line displaying the student's name. Here's the updated function:

```
double qualifier()
{
    println("Current student: {}", name );
    return qualifierGrade;
}
```

If you make this update and run the program, the line Current student: Matt Madox is added to the output that gets displayed. If, however, you were to change the access in Student from protected to private, then when you compile, you get an error saying that the name is private, so GraduateStudent can't access it.

Constructing a subclass

Even though a subclass has access to the protected members of the base class and can initialize them, each subclass is responsible for initializing itself.

Before control passes beyond the open brace of the constructor for GraduateStudent, control passes to the proper constructor of Student. If Student were based on another class, such as Person, the constructor for that class would be invoked before the Student constructor gained control. Like a skyscraper, the object is constructed starting at the "base"-ment class and working its way up the class structure one story at a time.

TIP

If you are not sure what's up with constructors (or destructors, for that matter), see Chapter 18.

As with member objects, you often need to be able to pass arguments to the base class constructor. The sample program declares the subclass constructor as follows:

```
GraduateStudent(const char *pName, Advisor adv,
                double qG = 0.0)
    : Student(pName), advisor(adv), qualifierGrade(qG)
```

```
{
  // whatever else the constructor does
}
```

Here, the constructor for `GraduateStudent` invokes the `Student` constructor, passing it the argument `pName`. C++ then initializes the members `advisor` and `qualifierGrade` before executing the statements within the constructor's open and close braces.

The default constructor for the base class is executed if the subclass makes no explicit reference to a different constructor. Thus, in the following code snippet, the `Pig` base class is constructed before any members of `LittlePig`, even though `LittlePig` makes no explicit reference to that constructor:

```
class House {};
class Pig
{
  public:
    Pig() : pHouse(nullptr) {}
  protected:
    House* pHouse;
};
class LittlePig : public Pig
{
  public:
    LittlePig(double volStraw, int numSticks,
              int numBricks)
        : straw(volStraw), sticks(numSticks),
          bricks(numBricks) { }
  protected:
    double straw;
    int sticks;
    int bricks;
};
```

Similarly, the copy constructor for a base class is invoked automatically.

Destructing a subclass

Following the rule that destructors are invoked in the reverse order of the constructors, the destructor for `GraduateStudent` is given control first. After it's given its last full measure of devotion, control passes to the destructor for `Advisor` and then to the destructor for `Student`. If `Student` were based on a class `Person`, the destructor for `Person` would gain control after `Student`.

This is logical. The blob of memory is first converted to a `Student` object. Only then is it the job of the `GraduateStudent` constructor to transform this simple `Student` into a `GraduateStudent`. The destructor simply reverses the process.

Inheriting constructors

A subclass can inherit the constructor of its base class as well. This is done by applying the `using` keyword within the subclass's constructor, as shown in the following snippet:

```
class Student
{
  public:
    Student(string name);
};
class GraduateStudent : public Student
{
  public:
    using Student::Student; // inherit base constructors
};
```

This creates a `GraduateStudent(string)` constructor exactly as though the following had been entered:

```
class GraduateStudent : public Student
{
  public:
    GraduateStudent(string name) : Student(name) {}
};
```

The advantage of inheriting the constructors of the base class is that the subclass inherits all the base class constructors. This is useful when building a subclass that extends an important base class in some trivial way.

Having a HAS_A Relationship

Notice that the class `GraduateStudent` includes the members of class `Student` and `Advisor`, but in a different way. By defining a data member of class `Advisor`, you know that a `Student` has all the data members of an `Advisor` within it. However, you can't say that a `GraduateStudent` is an `Advisor` — instead, you say that a `GraduateStudent` HAS_A `Advisor`. What's the difference between this and inheritance?

Use a car as an example. You can logically define a car as being a subclass of vehicle, so it inherits the properties of other vehicles. At the same time, a car has a motor. If you buy a car, you can logically assume that you're buying a motor as well (unless you go to a used-car lot and end up with a junk heap).

If friends ask you to show up at a rally on Saturday with your vehicle of choice and you travel in your car, they can't complain (even if someone else shows up on a bicycle) because a car IS_A vehicle. But, if you appear on foot carrying a motor, your friends will have reason to laugh at you because a motor is not a vehicle. A motor is missing certain critical properties that all vehicles share — such as a place to ride.

From a programming standpoint, the HAS_A relationship is just as straightforward. Consider the following:

```
class Vehicle {};
class Motor {};
class Car : public Vehicle
{
  public:
     Motor motor;
};

void VehicleFn(Vehicle& v);
void MotorFn(Motor& m);

int main(int nNumberofArgs, char* pszArgs[])
{
   Car car;
   VehicleFn(car);    // this is allowed
   MotorFn(car);      // this is not allowed
   MotorFn(car.motor);// this is allowed
   return 0;
}
```

The call `VehicleFn(c)` is allowed because `car` IS_A `vehicle`. The call `MotorFn(car)` is not allowed, because `car` is not a `Motor`, even though it contains a `Motor`. If the intention were to pass the `Motor` portion of `c` to the function, this must be expressed explicitly, as in the call `MotorFn(car.motor)`.

IN THIS CHAPTER

» Seeing how polymorphism (also known as *late binding*) works

» Finding out how safe polymorphic nachos are

» Overriding member functions in a subclass

» Checking out special considerations with polymorphism

» Taking a moment to reflect on reflection

Chapter 22

Creating Virtual Member Functions: Are They for Real?

A function has a short name and an extended name. The short name is simply the name of the function without including any of the arguments, such as `someFn()`. The full, or *extended*, name includes the number and type of a function's arguments. The full name enables you to give two functions the same short name as long as the extended name is different:

```
void someFn(int);
void someFn(char*);
void someFn(char*, double);
```

In all three cases, the short name for these functions is `someFn()`. (Hey! This is *some* fun.) The extended names for all three differ: `someFn(int)` versus `someFn(char*)`, and so on. C++ is left to figure out which function is meant by the arguments during the call. This concept of having different extended names for the same short name is called *overloading.*

Member functions can be overloaded. The number of arguments, the type of arguments, and the class name are all part of the extended name.

Inheritance introduces a whole new wrinkle, however. What if a function in a base class has the same name as a function in the subclass? Consider, for example, the following simple code snippet:

```
class Student
{
  public:
    double calcTuition();
};
class GraduateStudent : public Student
{
  public:
    double calcTuition();
};

int main(int argcs, char* pArgs[])
{
    Student s;
    GraduateStudent gs;
    s.calcTuition();    //calls Student::calcTuition()
    gs.calcTuition();  //calls GraduateStudent::calcTuition()
    return 0;
}
```

As with any overloading situation, when the programmer refers to `calcTuition()`, C++ has to decide which `calcTuition()` is intended. Obviously, if the data types of the arguments of the two functions differ, then there's no problem. Even if the arguments were the same, the class name should be sufficient to resolve the call, and this example is no different. The call `s.calcTuition()` refers to `Student::calcTuition()` because s is declared locally as a `Student`, whereas `gs.calcTuition()` refers to `GraduateStudent::calcTuition()`.

But what if the exact class of the object can't be determined at compile-time? To demonstrate how this can occur, change the preceding program in a seemingly trivial way:

```
// OverloadOverride - demonstrate when a function is
//    overloaded at compile time vs. overridden at runtime
```

```
//
#include <print>
using namespace std;

class Student
{
  public:
    // uncomment one or the other of the next
    // two lines; one binds calcTuition() early and
    // the other late

    void calcTuition()
//    virtual void calcTuition()
    {
        println("We're in Student::calcTuition");
    }
};

class GraduateStudent : public Student
{
  public:
    void calcTuition()
    {
        println("We're in GraduateStudent::calcTuition");
    }
};
void fn(Student& x)
{
   x.calcTuition();   // which calcTuition()?
}

int main(int nNumberofArgs, char* pszArgs[])
{
   // pass a base class object to function
   // (to match the declaration)
   Student s;
   fn(s);

   // pass a specialization of the base class instead
   GraduateStudent gs;
   fn(gs);
}
```

Rather than call `calcTuition()` directly, the call is now made through an intermediate function, `fn()`. Depending on how `fn()` is called, `x` can be a `Student` or a `GraduateStudent`. A `GraduateStudent` IS_A `Student`.

REMEMBER

Refer to Chapter 21 if you don't know why a `GraduateStudent` IS_A `Student`.

The argument `x` passed to `fn()` is declared to be a reference to `Student`.

REMEMBER

Passing an object by reference can be much more efficient than passing it by value. See Chapter 19 for a treatise on making copies of objects.

You might want `x.calcTuition()` to call `Student::calcTuition()` when `x` is a `Student`, but you'd probably want it to call `GraduateStudent::calcTuition()` when `x` is in fact a `GraduateStudent`. It would be cool if C++ were that smart.

TIP

The type I've shown you until now is called the *static*, or *compile-time*, type. The compile-time type of `x` is `Student` in both cases because that's what the declaration in `fn()` says. The other kind of type is the *dynamic*, or *runtime*, type. In the case of the sample function `fn()`, the runtime type of `x` is `Student` when `fn()` is called with `s` and `GraduateStudent` when `fn()` is called with `gs`. (Aren't we having fun?)

The capability of deciding at runtime which of several overloaded member functions to call based on the runtime type is called *polymorphism*, or *late binding*. Deciding which overloaded function to call at compile-time is called *early binding* because it sounds like the opposite of late binding.

Overloading a base class function polymorphically is called *overriding the base class function*. This new name is used to differentiate this more complicated case from the normal overload case.

Why You Need Polymorphism

Polymorphism is a key to the power of object-oriented programming. It's so important that languages that don't support polymorphism can't advertise themselves as OO languages. (Conspiracy theorists think it could be a government regulation — you can't label a language *OO* if it doesn't support polymorphism unless you add a disclaimer from the surgeon general, or something like that.)

Without polymorphism, inheritance has little meaning. In an earlier chapter, I talk about making nachos in the oven. I can now reveal that, in this sense, I was acting as the late binder. The recipe read: Heat the nachos in the oven. It didn't read: If the type of oven is microwave, do this; if the type of oven is conventional, do that; if the type of oven is convection, do this other thing. The recipe (the code) relied on me (the late binder) to decide what the action (member function) "heat" means when applied to the oven (the particular instance of class `Oven`) or any of its variations (subclasses), such as a microwave oven (`Microwave`). This is the way people think, and designing a language along the lines of the way people think allows the programming model to more accurately describe the world in which people live.

How Polymorphism Works

Any given language can support either early or late binding based on the whims of its developers. Older languages like C tend to support early binding alone. C++, however, supports both early and late binding.

You may be surprised that the default for C++ is early binding. The output of the `OverloadOverride` program the way it appears is as follows:

```
We're in Student::calcTuition
We're in Student::calcTuition
```

The reason is simple, if a little dated. First, C++ has to act as much like C as possible by default to retain upward compatibility with its predecessor. Second, polymorphism adds a small amount of overhead to every function call in terms of both data storage and code needed to perform the call. The founders of C++ were concerned that any additional overhead would be used as a reason not to adopt C++ as the system's language of choice, so they made the more efficient early binding the default.

To make a member function polymorphic, the programmer must flag the function with the C++ keyword `virtual`, as shown in the following modification to the declaration in the `OverloadOveride` program:

```
class Student
{
  public:
    virtual void calcTuition()
    {
       println("We're in Student::calcTuition");
    }
};
```

The keyword `virtual` tells C++ that `calcTuition()` is a polymorphic member function. That is to say, declaring `calcTuition()` as `virtual` means that calls to it will be bound late if there's any doubt about the runtime type of the object with which `calcTuition()` is called.

Executing the `OverloadOveride` program with `calcTuition()` declared as `virtual` generates the following output:

```
We're in Student::calcTuition
We're in GraduateStudent::calcTuition
```

If you're comfortable with the debugger that comes with your C++ environment, you should single-step through this example. It's so cool to see the program single-step into `Student::calcTuition()` the first time that `fn()` is called but into `GraduateStudent::calcTuition()` on the second call. I don't think you can truly appreciate polymorphism until you've tried it.

You need to declare the function `virtual` only in the base class. The "virtualness" is carried down to the subclass automatically. In this book, however, I follow the coding standard of declaring the function `virtual` everywhere (virtually).

When Is a Virtual Function Not?

Just because you think a particular function call is bound late doesn't mean that it is. If not declared with the same arguments in the subclasses, the member functions are not overridden polymorphically, whether or not they are declared `virtual`.

One exception to the identical declaration rule is that if the member function in the base class returns a pointer or reference to a base class object, an overridden member function in a subclass may return a pointer or reference to an object of the subclass. In other words, the function `makeACopy()` is polymorphic in the following code snippet, even though the return type of the two functions differs:

```
class Base
{
  public:
    // return a copy of the current object
    Base* makeACopy();
};

class SubClass : public Base
{
```

```
  public:
    // return a copy of the current object
    SubClass* makeACopy();
};

void fn(Base& bc)
{
    Base* pCopy = bc.makeACopy();

    // proceed on...
}
```

In practice, this is quite natural. A `makeACopy()` function should return an object of type `SubClass`, even though it might override `BaseClass::makeACopy()`.

This business of silently deciding when a function is overridden and when it's not is often a source of error in C++; so much so that the descriptor `override` was added so that you can indicate the intent to override a base class function. C++ generates a compiler error if a function is declared `override` but does not, in fact, override a base class function for some reason (such as a mismatched argument), as in the following example:

```
class Student
{
  public:
    virtual void addCourseGrade(double grade);
};
class GradStudent : public Student
{
  public:
    virtual void addCourseGrade(float grade) override;
};
```

This snippet generates a compile-time error because the method `GradStudent::addCourseGrade(float)` was declared `override`, but it does not, in fact, override the base class function `Student::addCourseGrade(double)`, because the argument types don't match.

The programmer can also declare a function as not overrideable using the `final` keyword, even if that function itself overrides some earlier base class function, as demonstrated in the following additional `PostDoc` class:

```
class GradStudent : public Student
{
  public:
```

```
    virtual void addCourseGrade(double grade) final;
};
class PostDoc : public GradStudent
{
  public:
    virtual void addCourseGrade(double grade);
};
```

Since Student::addCourseGrade() is marked final, the declaration of PostDoc:: addCourseGrade() generates an error because it attempts to override the Student method.

In addition, an entire class can be declared final:

```
class GradStudent final: public Student
```

This affects more than just the virtual methods of the class. A final class cannot be inherited from.

Considering Virtual Considerations

You need to keep in mind a few things when using virtual functions. First, static member functions cannot be declared virtual. Because static member functions are not called with an object, there is no runtime object on which to base a binding decision.

Second, specifying the class name in the call forces a call to bind early, whether or not the function is virtual. For example, the following call is to Base::fn() because that's what the programmer indicated, even if fn() is declared virtual:

```
void test(Base& b)
{
  b.Base::fn();     // this call is not bound late
}
```

Finally, constructors cannot be virtual because there is no (completed) object to use to determine the type. At the time the constructor is called, the memory the object occupies is just an amorphous mass. It's only after the constructor has finished that the object is a member of the class in good standing.

Virtual Destructors

By comparison, the destructor should almost always be declared `virtual`. If not, you run the risk of improperly destructing the object, as in the following circumstance:

```
class Base
{
  public:
    ~Base();
};

class SubClass : public Base
{
  public:
    ~SubClass();
};

void finishWithObject(Base* pHeapObject)
{
    // ...work with object...
    // now return it to the heap
    delete pHeapObject;  // this calls ~Base() no matter
}                        // the runtime type of
                         // pHeapObject
```

If the pointer passed to `finishWithObject()` points to a `SubClass`, the `SubClass` destructor is not invoked properly; because the destructor has not been declared `virtual`, it's always bound early. Declaring the destructor `virtual` solves the problem.

So, when would you not want to declare the destructor `virtual`? There's only one case: `Virtual` functions introduce a "little" overhead. Let me be more specific: When the programmer defines the first `virtual` function in a class, C++ adds an additional, hidden pointer: not one pointer per `virtual` function — just one pointer if the class has any `virtual` functions. A class that has no `virtual` functions (and does not inherit any `virtual` functions from base classes) does not have this pointer.

Now, one pointer doesn't sound like much, and it isn't, unless the following two conditions are true:

» The class doesn't have many data members (so that one pointer represents a lot compared to what's there already).

» You intend to create lots of objects of this class (otherwise, the overhead makes no difference).

If these two conditions are met and your class doesn't already have `virtual` member functions, you may not want to declare the destructor `virtual`.

WARNING

Except for this one case, always declare destructors to be `virtual`, even if a class is not subclassed (yet) — you never know when someone will come along and use your class as the base class for their own. If you don't declare the destructor `virtual`, declare the class `final` (if your compiler supports this feature) and document it!

Let's Go on a Tangent and Reflect on a New Topic

As you work with classes and they grow more complicated with concepts such as inheritance and polymorphism, it's good to have the tools needed to reflect on the code that you've created or that is being used. In fact, C++ provides *reflection* as part of the programming language.

C++26 NEW

C++26 introduced new features that improve what C++ can do in this regard:

» The ability to inspect class members, types, and base classes at the time your code is being compiled

» The ability to generate code based on a class structure

» The ability to access a type's structural information without manually tagging each member

» The ability to convert type information into strings

» and so much more. . .

WARNING

Reflection occurs at the time you compile your program. Most of these reflection features are beyond the scope of this book, and covering the topic requires pulling in a bit of what is covered in Bonus Chapter 2 — the templates chapter. Even more so, not all compilers were supporting this feature at the time I wrote this chapter.

Even so, let's look at a topic that can save you a bit of coding when it does get fully implemented. Let's look at the ability to generate code based on a class structure.

In this case, I'll use this almost magical ability of reflection to print the contents of a class:

```
// Reflecting - An example of using reflection
#include <print>
#include <string>
#include <format>

using namespace std;

class Student {
public:
    Student(const string pName = "no name", int hours = 0)
        : name(pName), semesterHours(hours) {}

    string name;
    int semesterHours;
};

class GraduateStudent : public Student {
public:
    GraduateStudent(const string pName, int hours = 0,
   double qG = 0.0)
        : Student(pName, hours), qualifierGrade(qG) {}

    double qualifierGrade;
};

// Reflection-enabled formatters
template <>
struct std::formatter<Student> :
          std::formatter<decltype(^Student)> {};

template <>
struct std::formatter<GraduateStudent> :
          std::formatter<decltype(^GraduateStudent)> {};

int main(int nNumberofArgs, char* pszArgs[]) {
    Student s1("Luffy", 1);
    GraduateStudent g1("Nami", 1234, 42);

    println("Printing student:  {}", s1);
    println("Printing graduate: {}", g1);
}
```

As you can see in the code, you didn't need to specify in the call to `println()` the specific details held in your class. Rather, C++ uses reflection to determine the elements and print them for you. The only thing you had to set up was a basic formatter that the call to printing routines can use to do the formatting:

```
struct std::formatter<Student> :
        std::formatter<decltype(^Student)> {};
```

This formatter is using a template and, yes, templates get covered only in Bonus Chapter 2, but the key here is that the only thing you're giving the formatter is the name of your class — in this case, `Student` (or `^Student`). That's all you're passing. C++26 uses reflection to break out the class into a format that can be printed without your doing anything else. The resulting output from running the listing is:

```
Printing student:  Student{.name="Luffy", .semesterHours=1}
Printing graduate: GraduateStudent{.name="Nami",
    .semesterHours=1234, .qualifierGrade=42.0}
```

This is the power of C++, classes, and polymorphism all working together!

WARNING

I mentioned that reflection was an advanced topic. it is also a leading-edge concept being added to C++. As such, not all compilers support it. Additionally, how it is imlemented might change from what I just presented. For now, reflection is great to know about, but might be one to wait on before using.

IN THIS CHAPTER

» Factoring common properties into a base class

» Using abstract classes to hold factored information

» Declaring abstract classes

» Inheriting from an abstract class

» Packing with tuples

Chapter 23 Factoring Classes

The concept of *inheritance* allows one class to inherit the properties of a base class. Inheritance has several purposes, including paying for my kids' college expenses. The main benefit of inheritance is the ability to point out the relationship between classes. This is the IS_A relationship — a *MicrowaveOven IS_A Oven, a GraduateStudent IS_A Student, a Circle IS_A Shape,* and stuff like that.

Identifying the classes inherent in a problem and drawing the correct relationships among these classes is a process known as factoring. Said differently, *factoring* is the process of determining shared attributes and behaviors (functions) from multiple classes and moving those into a common base class.

Factoring does great work if you make the correct correlations. For example, the microwave-versus-conventional-oven relationship seems natural. Claim that a microwave is a special kind of toaster, and you're headed for trouble. True, they both make things hot, they both use electricity, and they're both found in the kitchen, but the similarity ends there — a microwave can't make toast, and a toaster can't make nachos.

Factoring helps reduce redundance in your classes and code, which in turn helps make maintaining your code and classes easier. When working with inheritance and classes, factoring also helps to clarify the relationship between your various classes. (The word *factoring* is related to the arithmetic you were forced to learn about in grade school: factoring out the least common denominators, such as 12 is equal to 2 times 2 times 3.)

Factoring

This section describes how you can use inheritance to simplify your programs using a bank account example. Suppose that you're asked to write a simple bank program that implements the concept of a savings account and a checking account.

I can talk until I'm blue in the face about these classes; however, object-oriented programmers have come up with a concise way to describe the salient points of a class in a drawing. The `Checking` and `Savings` classes are shown in Figure 23-1. (This is only one of several ways to graphically express the same concept.)

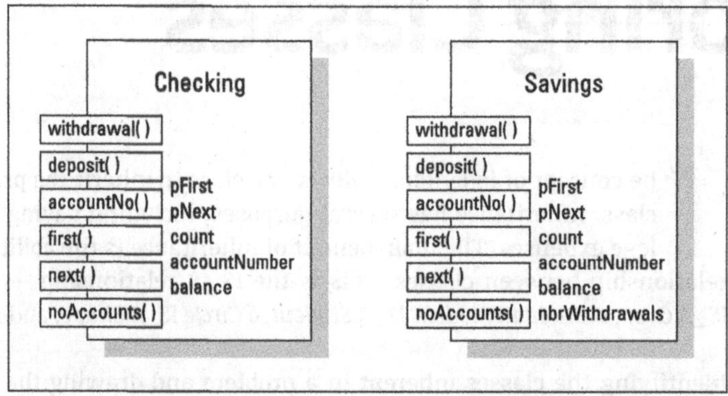

FIGURE 23-1: Independent classes *Checking* and *Savings*.

To read this figure and the other figures, remember the following statement:

- The big box is the class, with the class name at the top, such as `Checking` or `Savings`, in this case.
- The names in little boxes on the left side of each big box are member functions, such as `withdrawal()` or `deposit()`.
- The names not in boxes are data members, such as `pFirst`, `pNext`, or `count`.
- The member function names that extend partway out of the class boxes are publicly accessible members; that is, these members can be accessed by functions that are not part of the class or any of its descendants. Those members that are completely within the box are not accessible from outside

the class. In the case of Figure 23-1, you can see that all member functions are publicly accessible.

- An arrow with a hollow triangle (see Figure 23-2) represents the IS_A relationship.
- An arrow with a hollow diamond represents the HAS_A relationship.

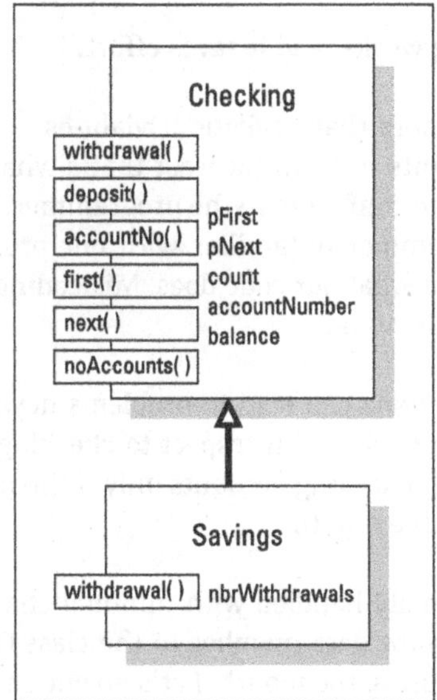

FIGURE 23-2: *Savings,* implemented as a subclass of *Checking.*

REMEMBER

A *Car* IS_A *Vehicle,* but a *Car* HAS_A *Motor.*

You can see in Figure 23-1 that the `Checking` and `Savings` classes have much in common. For example, both classes have a `withdrawal()` and `deposit()` member function. Because the two classes aren't identical, however, they must remain as separate classes. (In a real-life bank application, the two classes would be a good deal more different than in this example.) Still, there should be a way to avoid this repetition.

You could have one of these classes inherit from the other. `Savings` has more members than `Checking`, so you could let `Savings` inherit from `Checking`. This arrangement is shown earlier, in Figure 23-2. The `Savings` class inherits all members from `Checking`. The class is completed with the addition of the data member `nbrWithdrawals` and by overriding the function `withdrawal()`.

REMEMBER

You have to override `withdrawal()` because the rules for withdrawing money from a savings account are different from those for withdrawing money from a checking account.

Although letting `Savings` inherit from `Checking` is labor-saving, it's not completely satisfying. The main problem is that, like the weight listed on my driver's license, it misrepresents the truth. This inheritance relationship implies that a savings account is a special type of checking account, which it is not.

"So what?" you say. "Inheriting works, and it saves effort."

True, but my reservations are more than stylistic trivialities — my reservations are at some of the best restaurants in town (at least that's what all the truckers say). Such misrepresentations are confusing to the programmer, both today's and tomorrow's. Someday, a programmer unfamiliar with our programming tricks will have to read and understand what our code does. Misleading representations are difficult to reconcile and understand.

In addition, such misrepresentations can lead to problems down the road. Suppose that the bank changes its policies with respect to checking accounts. Say it decides to charge a service fee on checking accounts only if the minimum balance dips below a given value during the month.

A change like this one can be easily handled with minimal changes to the class `Checking`. You'll have to add a new data member to the class `Checking` to keep track of the minimum balance during the month. Let's go out on a limb and call it `minimumBalance`.

But now you have a problem. Because `Savings` inherits from `Checking`, this new data member is a part of `Savings` as well. `Savings` has no use for this member because the minimum balance doesn't affect savings accounts, so it just sits there. (Remember that every checking account object has this extra `minimumBalance` member.) One extra data member may not be a big deal, but it adds further confusion.

Changes like these accumulate. Today it's an extra data member — tomorrow it's a changed member function. Eventually, the savings account class is carrying lots of extra baggage that is applicable only to checking accounts.

Now the bank comes back and decides to change its savings account policy. This requires you to modify some of the functionality within `Checking`. Changes in the `Checking` base class automatically propagate down to the subclass unless the function is already overridden in the subclass `Savings`. Suppose that the bank decides to give away toasters for every deposit into the checking account.

(Hey — it could happen!) Without the bank (or its programmers) knowing it, deposits to checking accounts would automatically result in toaster donations. Unless you're very careful, changes to Checking may unexpectedly appear in Savings.

How can you avoid these problems? Claiming that Checking is a special case of Savings changes but doesn't solve our problem. What you need is a third class (call it Account, just for grins) that embodies the things that are common between Checking and Savings, as shown in Figure 23-3.

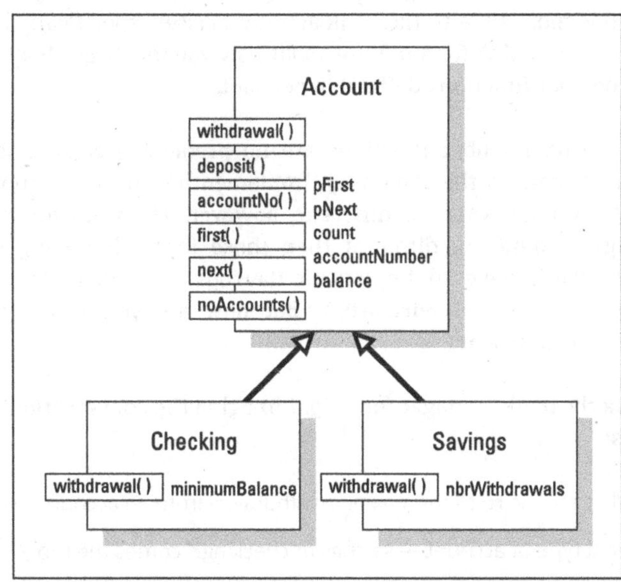

FIGURE 23-3: Basing Checking and Savings on a common Account class.

How does building a new account solve the problems? First, creating a new Account class is a more accurate description of the real world (whatever that is). In our concept of things (or at least in mine), there really is something known as an account. Savings accounts and checking accounts are special cases of this more fundamental concept.

In addition, the class Savings is insulated from changes to the class Checking (and vice versa). If the bank institutes a fundamental change to all accounts, you can modify Account, and all subclasses will automatically inherit the change. But if the bank changes its policy only for checking accounts, you can modify just the Checking account class without affecting Savings.

This process of culling common properties from similar classes is the essence of class factoring.

WARNING

Factoring is legitimate only if the inheritance relationship corresponds to reality. Factoring together a class `Mouse` and `Joystick` because they're both hardware pointing devices is legitimate. Factoring together a class `Mouse` and `Display` because they both make low-level operating system calls is not.

Implementing Abstract Classes

As intellectually satisfying as factoring is, it introduces a problem of its own. Return one more time to the bank account classes, specifically the common base class `Account`. Think for a minute about how you might go about defining the different member functions defined in `Account`.

Most `Account` member functions are no problem because both account types implement them in the same way. Implementing those common functions with `Account::withdrawal()` is different, however. The rules for withdrawing from a savings account are different than those for withdrawing from a checking account. You'll have to implement `Savings::withdrawal()` differently than you do `Checking::withdrawal()`. But how are you supposed to implement `Account::withdrawal()`?

Let's ask the bank manager for help. I imagine the conversation going something like this:

> "What are the rules for making a withdrawal from an account?" you ask.
>
> "What type of account — savings or checking?" comes the reply.
>
> "From an account," you say. "Just an account."
>
> Blank look. (One might say a "blank bank look." And then again, maybe not.)

The problem is that the question doesn't make sense. There's no such thing as "just an account." All accounts (in this example) are either checking accounts or savings accounts. The concept of an account is an abstract one that factors out properties common to the two concrete classes. It's incomplete because it lacks the critical property `withdrawal()`. (After you dig further into the details, you may find other properties that a simple account lacks.)

REMEMBER

An *abstract* class is one that exists only in subclasses. A *concrete* class is a class that is not abstract, but rather includes code that can be instantiated or executed.

To help clarify this distinction, let me use a second example. If I asked you to draw a circle, could you do it? If I asked you to draw a square, could you do that as well?

If I looked at both drawings, would they look similar to what I had envisioned when asking you to draw the items? I'm betting they would. The circle would be round, and the square would have four straight sides of equal length connected using 90-degree angles.

Now draw a shape. Yes, a shape. Will what you draw be similar to what I'm thinking? It would be amazing if that were the case, but odds are good that you simply don't have enough information to draw a shape similar to what I'm expecting, because the term *shape* on its own doesn't give enough information. (In case you're wondering, I'm picturing an octagon as the shape I wanted you to draw. Shape by itself is a bit . . . abstract.)

Describing the abstract class concept

An abstract class is a class with one or more pure virtual functions. Oh, great! That helps a lot.

Okay, a *pure virtual* function is a virtual member function that is marked as having no implementation. Most likely, it has no implementation because no implementation is possible with the information provided in the class, including any base classes. A conventional, run-of-the-mill non-pure virtual function is known as a *concrete* function. (Note that a concrete function may be virtual — unfortunately, C++ uses this term to mean *polymorphic*. See Chapter 22.)

The syntax for declaring a function a pure virtual function is demonstrated in the following class Account:

```
// Account - this class is an abstract class
class Account
{
  public:
    Account(unsigned accNo, double initialBalance = 0.0);

   // access functions
    unsigned int accountNo();
    double accountBalance();
    static int noAccounts();

    // transaction functions
    void deposit(double amount);

    // the following is a pure virtual function
    virtual void withdrawal(double amount) = 0;
```

```
protected:
  // keep accounts in a linked list so there's no
  // limit to the number of accounts
  static int count;     // number of accounts
  unsigned accountNumber;
  double balance;
};
```

The = 0 after the declaration of withdrawal() indicates that the programmer does not intend to define this function. The declaration is a placeholder for the subclasses. The subclasses of Account are expected to override this function with a concrete function. The programmer must provide an implementation for each member function not declared pure virtual.

I think this notation is silly, and I don't like it any more than you do. But it's here to stay, so you just have to live with it. There is a reason, if not exactly a justification, for this notation. Every virtual function must have an entry in a special table. This entry contains the address of the function. Presumably, at least at one time, the entry for a pure virtual function was 0. In any case, it's the syntax we're stuck with now.

An abstract class cannot be instanced with an object; that is, you can't make an object out of an abstract class. For example, the following declaration is not legal:

```
void fn( )
{
  // declare an account with 100 dollars
  Account myAccount(1234, 100.00);// this is not legal
  myAccount.withdrawal(50);       // what would you expect
                                  // this call to do?
}
```

If the declaration were allowed, the resulting object would be incomplete, lacking in some capability. For example, what do you actually expect the preceding call to do? Remember, there is no Account::withdrawal().

Abstract classes serve as base classes for other classes. An Account contains all properties associated with a generic bank account. You can create other types of bank accounts by inheriting from Account.

The technical term is to *instantiate*. Programmers say that the Account class cannot be instantiated with an object, or a given object instantiates the Savings class.

Making an honest class out of an abstract class

The subclass of an abstract class remains abstract until all pure virtual functions have been overridden. The class Savings is not abstract because it overrides the pure virtual function withdrawal() with a perfectly good definition. The class Savings knows how to perform withdrawal() when called on to do so. So does the class Checking, even if the answer is different. Neither class is virtual because the function withdrawal() overrides the pure virtual function in the base class.

Passing abstract classes

Because you can't instantiate an abstract class, it may sound odd that it's possible to declare a pointer or a reference to an abstract class. With polymorphism, however, this isn't as crazy as it sounds. Consider the following code snippet:

```
void fn(Account *pAccount);  // this is legal
void otherFn( )
{
   Savings s; Checking c;
   // this is legitimate because Savings IS_A Account
   fn(&s);
   // same here
   fn(&c);
}
```

Here, pAccount is declared as a pointer to an Account. However, it's understood that when the function is called, the address of some non-abstract subclass object such as Savings or Checking gets passed to it.

All objects received by fn() will be either class Savings or class Checking (or some future equally non-abstract subclass of Account). The function is assured that you will never pass an actual object of class Account because you could never create one to pass in the first place.

ON THE WEB

The online material at www.dummies.com/go/cplusplus8e includes a set of programs Budget1 through Budget5. Each program solves essentially the same problem: Both allow the user to create and collect the balance of a series of checking and savings accounts. However, each program in the sequence is a bit more object-oriented than its predecessors. Budget1 is a completely functional implementation with no concept of classes. Budget2 implements separate Savings and Checking classes. The Budget3 program factors the similarities in these two classes into a common, abstract `Account` class using the techniques presented in this chapter. `Budget4` and `Budget5` go on to use features presented in the following chapters.

Packing for Traveling (and Lunch)

Consider this section a bonus in your path to learning C++. Let's go on a little side trip, which means you will need to pack some things and then unpack them. On this trip, we won't go anywhere geographically, but rather on a learning adventure to take you to new heights!

When you take a trip, you tend to not just grab a shirt, some socks, and a few other belongings and head for the door. Rather, most people like to pack these items into a nice package — often a suitcase, although a duffle and even a trash bag can work if needed. Placing all items in the suitcase makes it easier to transport them. The only issue is that when you arrive at your destination, you then have to unpack everything.

In C++, there are a few things you can use to pack all of your various items together, but if you're unsure of what they will be, then there is one item that was introduced back in C++11 that has been improved with newer versions — the tuple.

A *tuple* is simply a container (like a suitcase) that holds a number of things. These things that are held, however, don't have to all be the same. Tuples are a part of the Standard Template Library, so you'll want to include the `<tuple>` header in order to take advantage of them. The following simple tuple holds values for a rectangle:

```
#include <tuple>
std::tuple<double, double > rect{4.0, 5.0};
```

A tuple is declared using `tuple` followed by an open (<) and closed (>) angle bracket surrounding the types of values (two doubles, in this case). This is followed by the name for the tuple you're declaring (`rect`, in this case) followed by the values being packed (`4.0` and `5.0`).

The following is a second example that declares a tuple called `info` that stores three values:

```
std::tuple<int, double, string> info(16, 17.99,
                                     "Large Pepperoni Pizza ");
```

With your tuple packed with values, the next thing to do is unpack it when you're ready to use it. This task is made simple by using structured binding, which was added in C++20. *Structure binding* is simply the process of unpacking a single object into multiple named variable in one step. Using the `auto` keyword and the variables to store your tuple items, the code is crispy clean. The following two lines unpack the two tuples you just created:

```
auto [ width, height] = rect;
auto [size, price, description] info
```

The following complete listing shows this in action and shows the power of using a tuple with structured binding. In this listing, a reference to a tuple as the parameter of the `displayPizzaInfo()` function is used to unpack the values:

```
#include <tuple>
#include <string>
#include <print>
using namespace std;

void displayPizzaInfo(const tuple<int, double, string>& info)
{
   auto [size, price, description] = info;
   println("Size:        {} inches", size);
   println("Price:       ${:.2f}", price);
   println("Description: {}", description);
}

int main()
{
   tuple<int, double, string> info(16, 17.99,
                         "Large Pepperoni Pizza");
   displayPizzaInfo(info);
   return 0;
}
```

All this talk of travel and pizzas is making me want to head to Chicago for some Gino's!

5

Object-Oriented Programming in Overdrive

IN THIS PART . . .

Introducing the assignment operator

Accessing the computer's file system and files

Handling program errors

Preventing coding problems before they happen

Introducing multiple inheritance

IN THIS CHAPTER

» Introducing the assignment operator

» Knowing why (and when) the assignment operator is necessary

» Exploring similarities between the assignment operator and the copy constructor

» Comparing copy semantics with move semantics

Chapter 24

Adopting a New Assignment Operator, Should You Decide to Accept It

Intrinsic data types are built into the language, such as `int`, `float`, and `double`, as well as the various pointer types. Chapters 3 and 5 describe the operators that C++ defines for the intrinsic data types.

The classes you create in C++ are also considered to be data types because a class can define the type of data it will hold, how that data is managed in memory, and what operations are allowed on that data. And, just as the intrinsic types can be used with operators, C++ enables you to define the operators that can be used with the class types you create. This is called *operator overloading.*

Normally, operator overloading is optional and not attempted by beginning C++ programmers. Many experienced C++ programmers (including me) don't think operator overloading is such a great idea, either. However, you will have to learn how to overload at least one operator: the assignment operator.

Comparing Operators with Functions

An operator is nothing more than a built-in function with a peculiar syntax. The following addition operation:

```
a + b
```

could be understood as though it were written as the following function:

```
operator+(a, b)
```

In fact, C++ gives each operator a function-style name. The functional name of an operator is the operator symbol preceded by the keyword `operator` and followed by the appropriate argument types. For example, the + operator that adds an `int` to an `int` generating an `int` is called `int operator+(int, int)`.

Any existing operator can be defined for a user-defined class. Thus, I could create `Complex operator*(const Complex&, const Complex&)`, which would allow me to multiply two objects of type `Complex`. The new operator may have the same semantics as the operator it overloads, but it doesn't have to. The following rules apply when overloading operators:

- You cannot overload the `.` (dot), `::` (scope resolution), `.*` (pointer-to-member access), `*->` (pointer-to-member access via pointer), `sizeof`, and `?:` (ternary) operators.
- You cannot invent a new operator. For example, you cannot invent the operation `x $ y`.
- The syntax of an operator cannot be changed. Thus, you cannot define an operation `%i` because `%` is already defined as a binary operator.
- The operator precedence cannot change. A program cannot force `operator+` to be evaluated before `operator*`.
- The operators cannot be redefined when applied to intrinsic types — you can't change the meaning of `1 + 2`. You can only overload existing operators when you're using newly defined types.

REMEMBER

Overloading operators is an idea that seems much smarter than it really is. Operator overloading can introduce more problems than it solves, with three notable exceptions that are the subject of this chapter.

Inserting a New Operator

The insertion and extraction operators `<<` and `>>` are nothing more than the left and right shift operators overloaded for a set of input/output classes. These definitions are found in the include file `iostream`. Thus, `cout << "some string"` becomes `operator<<(cout, "some string")`. Our old friends `cout` and `cin` are predefined objects that are tied to the console and keyboard, respectively. (I discuss the use of the extraction operators with `cout` and `cin` in more detail in Bonus Chapter 1 that can be downloaded.)

Creating Shallow Copies Is a Deep Problem

No matter what anyone may think of operator overloading, you need to overload the assignment operator for the classes you end up generating. It turns out that C++ provides a default definition for `operator=()` for all classes. This default definition performs a member-by-member copy. This works great for an intrinsic type, like an `int` where the only "member" is the integer itself:

```
int i;
i = 10;   // "member by member" copy
```

This same default definition is applied to user-defined classes. In the following example, each member of `source` is copied over the corresponding member in `destination`:

```
void fn()
{
   MyStruct source, destination;
   destination = source;
}
```

The default assignment operator works for most classes; however, it's not correct for classes that allocate resources, such as heap memory. The programmer must overload `operator=()` to handle the transfer of resources.

The assignment operator is much like the copy constructor (see Chapter 19). In use, the two look almost identical:

```
void fn(MyClass& mc)
{
   MyClass newMC(mc);     //of course, this uses the
                          //copy constructor
   MyClass newerMC = mc;//less obvious, this also invokes
                          //the copy constructor
   MyClass newestMC;      //this creates a default object
   newestMC = mc;         //and then overwrites it with
                          //the argument passed
}
```

The creation of newMC follows the standard pattern of creating a new object as a mirror image of the original using the copy constructor MyClass(const MyClass&). Not so obvious is the fact that newerMC is also created using the copy constructor. MyClass a = b is just another way of writing MyClass a(b) — in particular, this declaration does *not* involve the assignment operator despite its appearance. However, newestMC is created using the default constructor and then overwritten with mc using the assignment operator.

TIP

The rule is this: The copy constructor is used when a new object is being created. The assignment operator is used if the left-hand object already exists.

Like the copy constructor, an assignment operator should be provided whenever a shallow copy is not appropriate. (Chapter 19 discusses shallow-versus-deep copy constructors.) A simple rule is to provide an assignment operator for classes that have a user-defined copy constructor.

REMEMBER

The default copy constructor *does* work for classes that contain members that themselves have copy constructors, as in the following example:

```
class Student
{
  public:
    int nStudentID;
    string sName;
};
```

The C++ library class string allocates memory off the heap, so the authors of that class include a copy constructor and an assignment operator that (one hopes) perform all the operations necessary to create a successful copy of a string. The default copy constructor for Student invokes the string copy constructor to copy sName from one student to the next. Similarly, the default assignment operator for Student does the same.

Overloading the Assignment Operator

The DemoAssignmentOperator program demonstrates how to provide an assignment operator. The program also includes a copy constructor to provide a comparison:

```
//DemoAssignmentOperator - demonstrate the assignment
//                         operator on a user-defined class
#include <print>
#include <iostream>
using namespace std;

// DArray - a dynamically sized array class used to
//          demonstrate the assignment and copy constructor
//          operators
class DArray
{
  public:
   DArray(int nLengthOfArray = 0)
     : nLength(nLengthOfArray), pArray(nullptr)
   {
       println("Creating DArray of length = {}",
                nLength);
       if (nLength > 0)
       {
           pArray = new int[nLength];
       }
   }

   // DArray copy constructor
   DArray(DArray& da)
   {
       println("Copying DArray of length = {}",
               da.nLength);
       copyDArray(da);
   }
   ~DArray()
   {
       deleteDArray();
   }

   //assignment operator
   DArray& operator=(const DArray& s)
   {
```

```
        print("Assigning source of length = {}",
                  s.nLength);
        println(" to target of length = {}",
                  this->nLength);
        //delete existing stuff...
        deleteDArray();
        //...before replacing with new stuff
        copyDArray(s);
        //return reference to existing object
        return *this;
    }

    int& operator[](int index)
    {
         return pArray[index];
    }
    int size() { return nLength; }

    void display()
    {
        if (nLength > 0)
        {
            print("{}", pArray[0]);
            for(int i = 1; i < nLength; i++)
            {
                print(", {}", pArray[i]);
            }
        }
    }
  private:
    void copyDArray(const DArray& da);
    void deleteDArray();
    int  nLength;
    int* pArray;
};

//copyDArray() - create a copy of a dynamic array of ints
void DArray::copyDArray(const DArray& source)
{
    nLength = source.nLength;
    pArray = nullptr;
    if (nLength > 0)
    {
```

```
        pArray = new int[nLength];
        for(int i = 0; i < nLength; i++)
        {
            pArray[i] = source.pArray[i];
        }
    }
}

//deleteDArray() - return heap memory
void DArray::deleteDArray()
{
    nLength = 0;
    delete pArray;
    pArray = nullptr;
}
int main(int nNumberofArgs, char* pszArgs[])
{
    // a dynamic array and assign it values
    DArray da1(5);
    for (int i = 0; i < da1.size(); i++)
    {
        // uses user-defined index operator to access
        // members of the array
        da1[i] = i;
    }
    print("da1 = "); da1.display(); println("");

    // now create a copy of this dynamic array using
    // copy constructor; this is same as da2(da1)
    DArray da2 = da1;
    da2[2] = 20;    // change a value in the copy
    print("da2 = "); da2.display(); println("");

    // overwrite the existing da2 with the original da1
    da2 = da1;
    print("da2 = "); da2.display(); println("");

    return 0;
}
```

That's a lot of code, but you should be able to follow along with what's being done. To start, the class `DArray` defines an integer array of variable length: You tell the class how big an array to create when you construct the object. It does this by wrapping the class around two data members: nLength, which contains the length of the array, and pArray, a raw pointer to an appropriately sized block of memory allocated off the heap.

The default constructor initializes nLength to the indicated length and then pArray to nullptr. Within the constructor, if the length of the array is actually greater than 0, the constructor allocates an array of ints of the appropriate size off the heap.

The copy constructor creates an array of the same size as the source object and then copies the contents of the source array into the current array using the protected method copyDArray(). The destructor returns the memory allocated in the constructor to the heap using the deleteDArray() method. This method nulls out the pointer pArray after the memory has been deleted.

The assignment operator=() is a method of the class. It looks to all the world like a destructor immediately followed by a copy constructor. This is typical. Consider the assignment in the example da2 = da1. The object da2 already has data associated with it. In the assignment, the original dynamic array must be returned to the heap by calling deleteDArray(), just like the DArray destructor. The assignment operator then invokes copyDArray() to copy the new information into the object, much like the copy constructor.

I want to present two more details about the assignment operator. First, the return type of operator=() is DArray&, and the returned value is always *this. Expressions involving the assignment operator have a value and a type, both of which are taken from the final value of the left-hand argument. In the following example, the value of operator=() is 2.0, and the type is double:

```
double d1, d2;
void fn(double);
d1 = 2.0;         // type of this expression is double
                  // the value is 2.0
```

Setting the return type is what enables the programmer to write the following:

```
d2 = d1 = 2.0
fn(d2 = 3.0);     // performs the assignment and passes the
                  // resulting value to fn()
```

The value of the assignment d1 = 2.0 (2.0) and the type (double) are passed to the assignment to d2. In the second example, the value of the assignment d2 = 3.0 is passed to the function fn(), but the type of *operator=*() is matched to the declarations to find fn(double).

REMEMBER

A user-created assignment operator should support the same semantics as the intrinsic version:

```
fn(DArray&);     // given this declaration...
fn(da2 = da1);  // ...this should be legal
```

The second detail is that `operator=()` was written as a member function. The left-hand argument is taken to be the current object (`this`). Unlike other operators, the assignment operator cannot be overloaded with a non-member function.

TIP

If you don't want to type all the code in the `DemoAssignmentOperator` listing, you'll find it included with the downloadable files for this book. I recommend typing the code because it helps the learning process. Even if you enter mistakes, finding and fixing those mistakes is a learning moment. You will also find a second program called `DemoAssignmentOperatorSmart` included in the downloads. (It's the same name with *smart* added to the end.) The smart version of this program swaps the raw pointers for the more modern use of smart pointers.

By using raw pointers in the demo, you're able to see how the assignment operator is similar to a destructor and constructor, because it shows the need to clean up your pointer before creating your new `DArray`. Having said that, you'll find that the code in the smart listing is shorter and cleaner.

No Copying Allowed!

Just as there are times when you might want or need to create your own copy or assignment operator logic, there are also times when you might not want to allow your type to be copied or assigned. For example, if your type works with database connections, then allowing for a copy could cause errors such as two different objects trying to close the same connection. After the first object closes the connection, you'd risk undefined behavior as the second object tries to access the closed database. Another example is when you have an object that controls a large resource such as a large buffer or a large amount of system resources. By making this object non-sharable, you force the user to share access to the large resource instead of duplicating it.

Using the `delete` command, you can delete the default copy constructor and assignment operator if you don't want to define your own:

```
class NonCopyable
{
  public:
```

```
    NonCopyable(const NonCopyable&) = delete;
    NonCopyable& operator=(const NonCopyable&) = delete;
};
```

WARNING

An object of class NonCopyable cannot be copied via either construction or assignment. The following example generates an error:

```
void fn(NonCopyable& src)
{
   NonCopyable copy(src);    // not allowed
   copy = src;               // nor is this
}
```

An alternative way to prevent copying is declare the assignment operator as either private or protected:

```
class NonCopyable
{
  protected:
    NonCopyable(const NonCopyable&) {};
    NonCopyable& operator=(const NonCopyable&)
          {return *this};
};
```

TIP

If your class allocates resources such as memory off the heap, you *must* make the default assignment operator and copy constructors inaccessible — ideally, by replacing them with your own version.

Overloading the Subscript Operator

The earlier DemoAssignmentOperator sample program actually slipped in a third operator that's often overloaded for container classes: the subscript operator. The *subscript operator* ([]) allows you to access elements within an object such as an array or list.

The following definition allows an object of class DArray to be manipulated like an intrinsic array:

```
int& operator[](int index)
{
   return pArray[index];
}
```

This code is overloading the square subscript brackets [], which makes an assignment like the following legal:

```
int n = da[0]; // becomes n = da.operator[](0);
```

Notice, however, that rather than return an integer value, the subscript operator returns a reference to the value within pArray. This allows the calling function to modify the value as demonstrated within the DemoAssignmnentOperator program:

```
da2[2] = 20;
```

C++23 NEW

Starting with the C++23 standard, you overload subscripting so that you can create and access multidimensional arrays of your class types with simple syntax, like pArray[4,2]. Before C++23, you were forced to either use an array of arrays (for example, pArray[4][2]) to access multidimensional arrays or create an array of a type that itself contained multiple member items (such as a tuple). Starting with C++23, you can overload the operator[] to support multiple dimensions:

```
pArray& operator[](int row, int col);
```

With this style of overload, you'd then be able to access a multidimensional array of your item using the simple syntax of pArray[r,c]. Of course, adding dimensions to your arrays adds complexity, so you should use this only when necessary. (Digging further into this topic is beyond the scope of this book, but I wanted to make sure you're aware that this is now possible.)

The Move Constructor and Move Operator

In Chapter 19 I talk in detail about the copy constructor. Copy constructors and copy assignment operators are neat for retaining simple semantics for classes you create. However, since their inception, C++ programmers have not been happy with the inefficiencies they can create. Consider the following example:

```
MyContainer fn(int size)
{
   MyContainer localMC(size);
   return mc;
}

MyContainer mc(fn());
```

In this case, the function `fn()` creates a local `MyContainer` object `localMC` and then returns it to the caller by value. This simple call could result in the same `MyContainer` object being copied not once but twice:

1. As part of the return, C++ must make a temporary copy of the `localMC` object onto the return stack to return to the caller.
2. The subsequent call to the copy constructor copies the contents of this temporary object into the local `mc` object.

The second copy is unnecessary. Because the temporary object is about to be destructed anyway, the copy constructor could just "take" the assets away from the temporary object rather than endure the hassle of making a copy of something that's about to be put back on the heap anyway. This is the essence of the move constructor.

The move constructor looks like a copy constructor except for two factors:

- A move constructor takes the resources from the source and gives them to the target instead of copying.
- The argument of the move constructor is of type `MyContainer&&`, where the double ampersand means "use only for temporary values."

The following sample program shows both the move constructor and move assignment operator in action:

```
// DemoMoveOperator - demonstrate the move operator
#include <print>
#include <string>
using namespace std;

class Item
{
  public:
   Item(double nbr, const string str) : price(nbr),
   itemName(str)
   {
//       println("Constructing Item ({} - {})", nbr, str);
   }
   ~Item()
   {
//       println("Destructing Item ({} - {})", price, itemName);
   }
```

```
    //copy constructor
    Item(const Item& s)
    {
        println("Copying {}", s.itemName);
        price = s.price;
        itemName = s.itemName;
    }
    Item& operator=(Item& s)
    {
        println("Assigning {}", s.itemName);
        price = s.price;
        itemName = s.itemName;
        return *this;
    }

    // move constructor
    Item(Item&& s)
    {
        println("Moving {}", s.itemName);
        price = s.price;
        itemName = move(s.itemName);
    }
    Item& operator=(Item&& s)
    {
        println("Moving {}", s.itemName);
        price = s.price;
        itemName = move(s.itemName);
        return *this;
    }
  private:
    double price;
    string itemName;
};

Item fn(double n, string str)
{
    Item tmpItem(n, str);
    return tmpItem;
}
int main(int nNumberofArgs, char* pszArgs[])
{
    Item order1(7.99, "Original Nachos");
    // The following does a copy...
    Item order2 = order1;
```

```
    // The following does a move...
    order2 = fn(8.99, "Nachos created in fn()");
}
```

The output from this program appears as follows:

```
Copying Original Nachos
Moving Nachos created in fn()
```

Within main(), order1 is created and set to values of 7.99 and "Original Nachos" when constructed. This is followed by order2 being created and set equal to the values of order1. In this case, a copy for the Item object happens, as you can see by the output.

In the last line of main(), the function fn() is called and its return value is assigned to order2. Then fn() returns a temporary object that is then assigned to the order2 object using the move assignment operator, operator=(Item&&).

Within the move assignment, the code shifts items from a source object's data member to the new object. In the case of the itemName, which is a string, a call to the string's move() method is used to move the string instead of copying it. This is more efficient than the assignment that is performed within the copy operation because there's no need for an additional string to be created when you can simply shift from one to the other.

REMEMBER

If raw pointers were used instead of a string, the move logic would be more obvious because your code would assign the pointer address from the source object to the new object and would then assign the source object a nullptr to complete the move. This would leave the new object pointing to the itemName and the old object pointing to nothing

The end result of using move rather than copy is that the move code is almost always faster to execute than the copy code would have been. In the case of this short listing, the saved time is so minuscule that you wouldn't even have time to think about nachos, but with programs that are moving things such as large objects or doing a huge number of moves, the time would be significant. You might even be able to eat a nacho in the time difference.

ON THE WEB

Looking at the download for this chapter, you'll see that, in addition to the DemoMoveOperator listing just covered, I've also included a listing called DemoMoveOperatorPtr that uses a character pointer (char*) rather than a string. You can see within that listing how the move code addresses the moving of the pointer, along with setting the source pointer to nullptr. (I'm not including that particular listing in this book because you really should be using smart pointers instead of char* for such situations.)

TIP

THE RULE OF FIVE

The *rule of five* is a guideline you should apply when you're working with overloading or defining destructors, constructors, and the management of resources, Specifically, if you're going to define a destructor, a copy constructor, a copy assignment operator, a move constructor, or a move assignment operator (yeah, that's a list of five items), you should define all five. If you do one, do them all. This helps ensure that you're thinking (and applying) proper clean-up, copying, and moving so that you don't create shallow copies, cause double deletions, or leave pointers dangling in your code.

This rule replaces the older rule of three, which didn't include the move elements. Some developers will say that if you aren't doing any moving, you can get away with following only the rule of three — destructor, copy constructor, and copy assignment.

There is also a *rule of zero*, which is considered the best practice in modern programming. The rule of zero states that when possible, design your classes so that they don't need any of the five special functions.

IN THIS CHAPTER

» Accessing the computer's file system

» Finding files in a folder

» Answering the question of existence

» Determining how big it really is

Chapter 25

Playing with the Computer's File System

As they would say on *Monty Python's Flying Circus*, "And now, for something completely different . . ." You may know a great deal about the constructs of the C++ language, but there's still more to learn, and there's a library full of routines written in C++ that you can tap into.

In this chapter, I walk you through one of the areas of the C++ Standard Library that allows you to apply C++ to tap into information on your computer. Specifically, you'll find out how to work with computer paths, filenames, and folders. This information will be useful as you work with computer systems and programs that access files. This information is also applied within the first bonus chapter included with this book that you can download. Bonus Chapter 1 talks about reading (and writing to) files on your computer.

Working with Files Using Filesystem

Bonus Chapter 1 is all about reading and writing information to files. Before going there, however, we need to have a talk about files. You can't read a file if it doesn't exist. Similarly, you can't create a file if it already exists. If you're going to work with files, you must be able to navigate your computer's folders (also called directories) as well as be able to determine which files are on a computer.

To let you work with a computer's file system, the C++17 standard officially included a library namespace called `filesystem`, which is also part of the standard library (`std`). So, `filesystem` includes code to work with the file system! This code includes features for working with folders, files, and even file metadata such as file size, last update, and more. In newer versions, the `filesystem` code continues to be refined.

If you're working with filenames or file paths, you'll use `filesystem`. Uses for `filesystem` include:

- Creating and working with paths
- Seeing whether a file or folder exists
- Creating or deleting a folder
- Accessing a file's (or a folder's) metadata

Creating and Working with Paths

Having access to path and file information makes working with files easier, and `filesystem` gives you a safer way to work with path names and filenames using a type called `path`. Note that to use `path` (and the other code within `filesystem`), you need to include the `filesystem` library. The following example declares a variable that will hold a path:

```
#include <filesystem>
std::filesystem::path myPath = "myFile.txt";
```

This code snippet uses a path from `filesystem`, which (as mentioned earlier) is part of the `std` library. In this case, the path is simply the file named `myFile.txt`. What if you want to point to a file using a full path? The code snippet in the next listing creates a path that contains `myFile.txt`, which is stored in the `myFiles` folder off the root folder of a system. This includes preprocessor directives that set up the path correctly depending on whether the program is being compiled on a Windows, Apple, or Linux machine.

REMEMBER

Paths aren't the same across all computer platforms. On Windows, you use a backslash, and on Apple and Linux machines, forward slashes. Also remember that a backslash is a special character, so to use it within a string (double quotes), you must add two backslashes, which then translate to one:

```
#include <print>
#include <filesystem>

using namespace std;
using namespace std::filesystem;

int main()
{
    path filePath;

#ifdef _WIN32
    filePath = "C:\\myFiles\\data.txt";
#elif __APPLE__
    filePath = "/myFiles/data.txt";
#elif __linux__
    filePath = "/myFiles/data.txt";
#else
    filePath = "???";
#endif
    println("File path: {}", filePath.string());
}
```

REMEMBER

You can see in the code that two `using` statements have been included. A `using` statement allows you to access code from the various namespaces without having to include the full inheritance or hierarchical structure. If you didn't specify that you were using the `std::filesystem` namespace then, when you declared the path, you would have needed to fully qualify the code by including the namespaces with the files to be included:

```
std::filesystem::path filePath;
```

When you run this code, you should see the output based on the operating system you're using. For a Windows system, you would see:

```
File path: C:\myFiles\data.txt
```

On a Linux or Apple machine, you would see:

```
File path: /myFiles/data.txt
```

When you use preprocessor directives, the correct path structure is placed into the path variable called `filePath`. Once set, the path is simply printed to the console.

REMEMBER

A path isn't a string even though it looks like one. Rather, a path includes much more functionality related to paths. As such, if you try to simply print `filePath`, you might get a conversion error. Converting it to a string with the `string()` method avoids that problem. Table 25-1 presents just a few of the methods of the `path` class you might find of value.

TABLE 25-1 **filesystem::*path* Methods**

Method	Description	Output
`extension()`	The extension for the file	`.txt`
`filename()`	The last (rightmost) component of the path	`data.txt`
`parent_path()`	The path without the filename	`C:\myFiles\`
`stem()`	The filename without the extension	Data
`replace_extension(ext)`	Replaces the extension of the current filename with one passed to the function. If a new extension is not passed, then the file's current extension will be removed.	

The `replace_extension()` method makes it easy to create the path name for a backup copy of a file:

```
path myFile = "/home/bradley/config.xaml";
path myBackup = myFile;
myBackup.replace_extension(".bak");
```

Iterating over Folders

The filesystem makes your coding much easier when it comes to looking at which files are in a folder. Within `filesystem` is a method called `directory_iterator()` that lets you (no shocker here) iterate over a directory! Remember, directory is just another name for folder.

Using a `for` loop with range logic, iterating a directory or folder can be done with just a couple lines of code. Range logic is covered in Chapter 8. Using range logic makes it easier to loop through an object such as an array, or in this case files in a folder. Here's a complete listing that displays all files in the current folder:

```
#include <print>
#include <filesystem>

using namespace std;
using namespace std::filesystem;

int main()
{
    path dir = "./";
    path tmp;

    for (const auto& entry : directory_iterator(dir))
    {
        tmp = entry.path();
        println("{}", tmp.string() );
    }
}
```

Does That File Exist?

Have you ever tried to read a book you didn't have? Most people would consider that feat impossible. The same is true with files. If a file doesn't exist, you will have a problem trying to read it. As such, it would be nice if you had an easy way to determine if a file exists.

Your wish is `filesystem`'s command. In this case the command, or method, is simply `exists()`. Using the `exists()` method, you can test for the existence of a file. The following snippet fully qualifies the `exists()` method:

```
if( std::filesystem::exists(filePath))
{
   println("File exits");
}
```

If the file contained in `filePath` exists, the message affirming that fact is displayed.

Peeking at a File's Metadata

Exactly how big is that file? You can determine the answer to this question with a simple line of code:

```
file_size(myFilePath);
```

You can also determine whether it's a regular file or a folder. The following full listing provides files sizes as well as additional information on files within a folder:

```
#include <print>
#include <filesystem>
using namespace std;
using namespace std::filesystem;

void displayFileMetadata(const path& myFilePath)
{
   if (!exists(myFilePath))
   {
      println("Oops! This file does not exist: ",
          myFilePath.string());
   }
   else
   {
      println("Path: {}", myFilePath.string());
      println("Filename: {}", myFilePath.filename().string());
      println("Extension: {}", myFilePath.extension().string());
      println("Parent folder: {}",
                  myFilePath.parent_path().string());
      println("Is regular file? {}",
   is_regular_file(myFilePath));
      println("Is folder? {}", is_directory(myFilePath));
      println("File size: {} bytes", file_size(myFilePath));
   }
}

int main()
{
    path myFile = "/code/FileFacts.cpp"; //
    displayFileMetadata(myFile);
}
```

You should replace the file path and name with one on your system. One thing you might (or might not) notice is that if you enter a path formatted for the wrong operating system, the `path` object still works. In the listing just presented, the format of the path is set for Linux or Apple, yet this works on a Windows machine as well. The `path` object is aware of the platform and ensures the path is ported to the right format! The value stored in a path remains unchanged because of the porting behind the scenes.

The File System and Files

The functions in the `filesystem` namespace allow you to work with path names and filenames. As covered in this chapter, the code helps take care of portability across platforms and makes it easier to break apart the different elements of a path. This becomes important when you're reading and writing files, where you need to have a filename *and* you often need to specify the location of the file. `filesystem` helps you in this regard. Once you know the name and location of a file, the next step is to read and/or write to the file. That is the topic of Bonus Chapter 1, which you can download and read from the Wiley web site, `www.dummies.com/go/cplusplus8e`.

IN THIS CHAPTER

» **Introducing multiple inheritance**

» **Avoiding ambiguities with multiple inheritance**

» **Avoiding ambiguities with virtual inheritance**

» **Figuring out the ordering rules for multiple constructors**

» **Getting a handle on problems with multiple inheritance**

Chapter 26

Twice the Fun: Tapping into Multiple Inheritance

In the class hierarchies I discuss in other chapters, each class inherits from a single parent. Such single inheritance is sufficient to describe most real-world relationships. Some classes, however, represent the blending of multiple classes into one. (Sounds sort of romantic, doesn't it?)

An example of such a class is the sleeper sofa that creates the unbeatable combination of a harsh bed and an uncomfortable sofa. To adequately describe a sleeper sofa in C++, the sleeper sofa should be able to inherit both bed- and sofa-like properties. This is called *multiple inheritance.*

Describing the Multiple Inheritance Mechanism

Figure 26-1 shows the inheritance graph for class `SleeperSofa`, illustrating how it inherits from class `Sofa` as well as from class `Bed`.

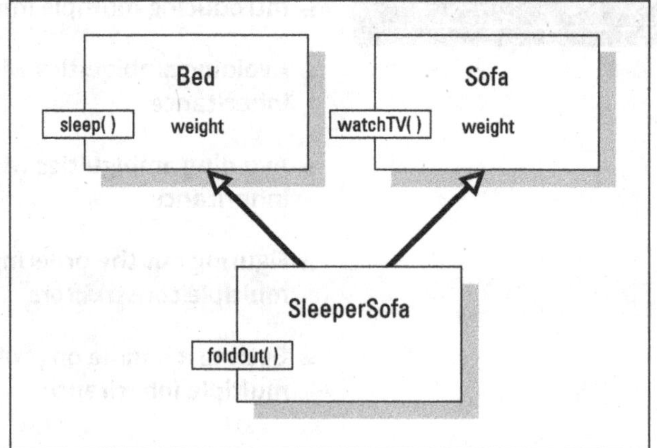

FIGURE 26-1: Class hierarchy of a sleeper sofa.

The code to implement class `SleeperSofa` looks like this:

```
// MultipleInheritance - a single class can inherit from
//                       more than one base class
//
#include <print>
using namespace std;

class Bed
{
  public:
    Bed(){}
    void sleep(){ println("Sleep"); }
    int weight;
};

class Sofa
{
  public:
    Sofa(){}
    void watchTV(){ println("Watch TV"); }
    int weight;
};

// SleeperSofa - is both a Bed and a Sofa
class SleeperSofa : public Bed, public Sofa
{
  public:
    SleeperSofa(){}
```

```
    void foldOut(){ println("Fold out"); }
};

int main(int nNumberofArgs, char* pszArgs[])
{
    SleeperSofa ss;

    // you can watch TV on a sleeper sofa like a sofa...
    ss.watchTV();          // calls Sofa::watchTV()

    // ...and then you can fold it out...
    ss.foldOut();          // calls SleeperSofa::foldOut()

    // ...and sleep on it
    ss.sleep();            // calls Bed::sleep()
}
```

Here, the classes `Bed` and `Sofa` appear as conventional classes. Unlike the examples in other chapters of this book, however, the class `SleeperSofa` inherits from both `Bed` and `Sofa`. This is apparent from the appearance of both classes in the class declaration — `SleeperSofa` inherits all members of both base classes. Thus, both of the calls `ss.sleep()` and `ss.watchTV()` are legal. You can use a `SleeperSofa` as a `Bed` or a `Sofa`. Plus, the class `SleeperSofa` can have members of its own, such as `foldOut()`. The output of this program appears as follows:

```
Watch TV
Fold out
Sleep
```

Is this a great country or what?

Straightening Out Inheritance Ambiguities

Although multiple inheritance is a powerful feature, it introduces several possible problems. One is apparent in the example in the preceding section. Notice that both `Bed` and `Sofa` contain a member `weight`. This is logical because both have a measurable weight. The question is, "Which `weight` does `SleeperSofa` inherit?"

The answer is "both." `SleeperSofa` inherits a member `Bed::weight` and a separate member `Sofa::weight`. Because they have the same name, unqualified references to weight are now ambiguous. This is demonstrated in the following snippet, which generates a compile-time error:

```
#include <print>

void fn()
{
    SleeperSofa ss;
    println("weight = {}", ss.weight); // illegal -
                                       // which weight?
}
```

The program must now indicate one of the two weights by specifying the desired base class. The following code snippet is correct:

```
#include <iostream>
void fn()
{
    SleeperSofa ss;
    println("sofa weight = {}", ss.Sofa::weight);
                                // specify which weight
}
```

Although this solution corrects the problem, specifying the base class in the application function isn't desirable because it forces class information to leak outside the class into application code. In this case, fn() has to know that SleeperSofa inherits from Sofa. These types of so-called name collisions weren't possible with single inheritance but are a constant danger with multiple inheritance.

Adding Virtual Inheritance

In the case of SleeperSofa, the name collision on weight was more than a mere accident. A SleeperSofa doesn't have a bed weight separate from its sofa weight. The collision occurred because this class hierarchy doesn't completely describe the real world. Specifically, the classes have not been completely factored. This means that they haven't been split up in an easy-to-understand manner that removes duplication.

Thinking about it a little more, it becomes clear that both beds and sofas are special cases of a more fundamental concept: furniture. (I suppose I could get even more fundamental and use something like "object with mass," but furniture is fundamental enough.) Weight is a property of all furniture. This relationship is shown in Figure 26-2.

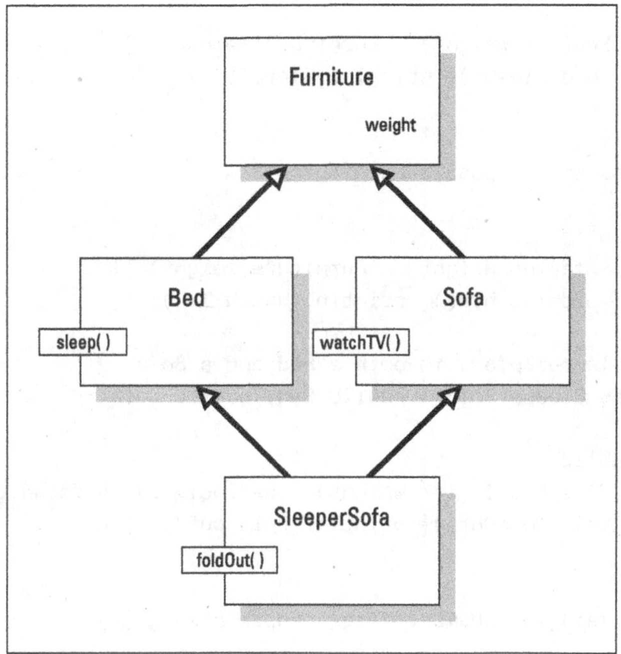

FIGURE 26-2: Further factoring of beds and sofas (by weight).

Factoring out the class `Furniture` should relieve the name collision. With much relief and great anticipation of success, I generate the C++ class hierarchy shown in the following program, `MultipleInheritanceFactoring`:

```
// MultipleInheritanceFactoring - a single class can
//                 inherit from more than one base class
//
#include <print>
#define TRYIT false
using namespace std;

// Furniture - more fundamental concept; this class
//               has "weight" as a property
class Furniture
{
  public:
     Furniture(int w) : weight(w) {}
     int weight;
};

class Bed : public Furniture
{
  public:
```

```
    Bed(int weight) : Furniture(weight) {}
    void sleep(){ println("Sleep"); }
};

class Sofa : public Furniture
{
  public:
    Sofa(int weight) : Furniture(weight) {}
    void watchTV(){ println("Watch TV"); }
};
// SleeperSofa - is both a Bed and a Sofa
class SleeperSofa : public Bed, public Sofa
{
  public:
    SleeperSofa(int weight) : Bed(weight), Sofa(weight) {}
    void foldOut(){ println("Fold out"); }
};

int main(int nNumberofArgs, char* pszArgs[])
{
   SleeperSofa ss(10);

   // Section 1 -
   // the following is ambiguous; is this a
   // Furniture::Sofa or a Furniture::Bed?
#if TRYIT
   println("Weight = {}", ss.weight);
#endif

   // Section 2 -
   // the following specifies the inheritance path
   // unambiguously but it sort of ruins the effect
   SleeperSofa* pSS = &ss;
   Sofa* pSofa = (Sofa*)pSS;
   Furniture* pFurniture = (Furniture*)pSofa;
   println("Weight = {}", pFurniture->weight);
}
```

Imagine my dismay when I find that this doesn't help at all — the reference to `weight` in **Section 1** of `main()` is still ambiguous. To prove this, change the line defining `TRYIT` to `true` and compile the code:

```
#define TRYIT true
```

"Okay," I say (not really understanding why `weight` is still ambiguous), "I'll try casting `ss` to a `Furniture`. "

```
#include <print>

void fn()
{
    SleeperSofa ss;
    Furniture* pF;
    pF = (Furniture*)&ss;  // use a Furniture pointer...
                           // ...to get at the weight
    println("weight = {}", pF->weight);
};
```

Casting `ss` to a `Furniture` doesn't work, either. Now, I see a strange message that the cast of `SleeperSofa*` to `Furniture*` is ambiguous. What's going on?

The explanation is straightforward. `SleeperSofa` doesn't inherit from `Furniture` directly. Both `Bed` and `Sofa` inherit from `Furniture`, and then `SleeperSofa` inherits from them. In memory, a `SleeperSofa` looks like Figure 26-3.

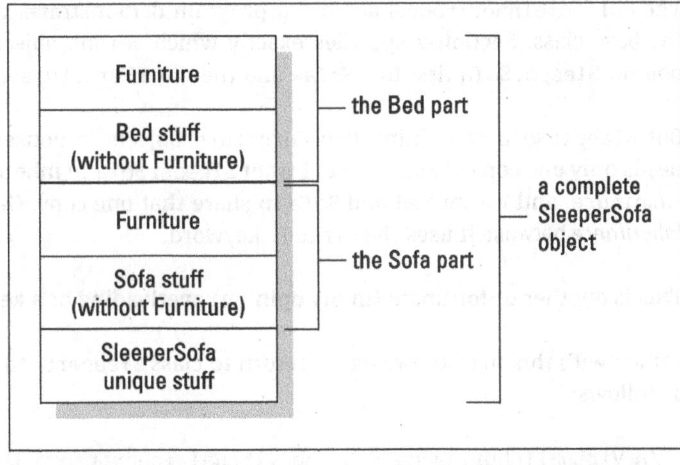

FIGURE 26-3: Memory layout of a SleeperSofa.

You can see that a `SleeperSofa` consists of a complete `Bed` followed by a complete `Sofa` followed by some unique `SleeperSofa` stuff. Each of these subobjects in `SleeperSofa` has its own `Furniture` part because each inherits from `Furniture`. Thus, a `SleeperSofa` contains two `Furniture` objects!

I haven't created the hierarchy shown back in Figure 26-2, after all. The inheritance hierarchy I've created is the one shown in Figure 26-4.

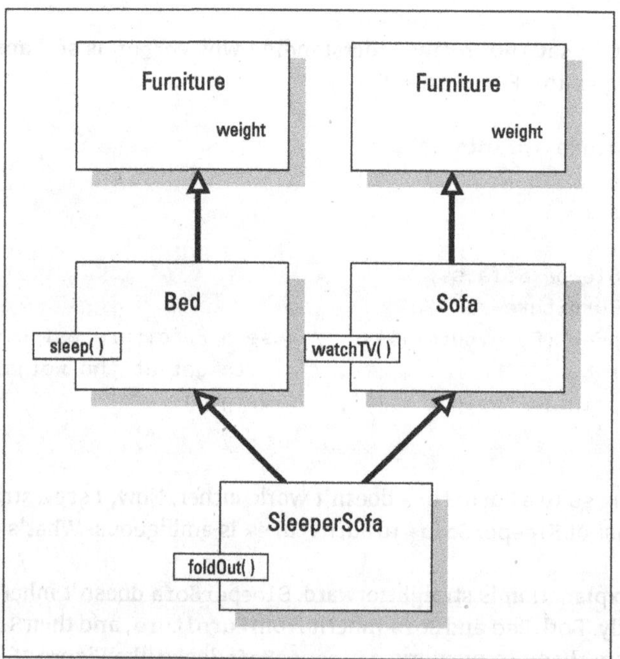

FIGURE 26-4: Actual result of my first attempt.

The `MultipleInheritanceFactoring` program demonstrates this duplication of the base class. **Section 2** specifies exactly which `weight` object by recasting the pointer `SleeperSofa` first to a *Sofa** and then to a `Furniture*`.

But `SleeperSofa` containing two `Furniture` objects is nonsense. `SleeperSofa` needs only one copy of `Furniture`. I want `SleeperSofa` to inherit only one copy of `Furniture`, and I want `Bed` and `Sofa` to share that one copy. C++ calls this *virtual inheritance* because it uses the `virtual` keyword.

TECHNICAL STUFF

This is another unfortunate (in my opinion) overloading of a keyword.

Armed with this new knowledge, I return to class `SleeperSofa` and implement it as follows:

```
// VirtualInheritance - using virtual inheritance the
//          Bed and Sofa classes can share a common base
//
#include <print>
using namespace std;

// Furniture - more fundamental concept; this class
//             has "weight" as a property
```

```
class Furniture
{
  public:
    Furniture(int w) : weight(w) {}
    int weight;
};

class Bed : virtual public Furniture
{
  public:
    Bed(int w = 0) : Furniture(w) {}
    void sleep(){ println("Sleep"); }
};

class Sofa : virtual public Furniture
{
  public:
    Sofa(int w = 0) : Furniture(w) {}
    void watchTV(){ println("Watch TV"); }
};
// SleeperSofa - is both a Bed and a Sofa
class SleeperSofa : public Bed, public Sofa
{
  public:
    SleeperSofa(int w) : Furniture(w) {}
    void foldOut(){ println("Fold out"); }
};

int main(int nNumberofArgs, char* pszArgs[])
{
   SleeperSofa ss(10);

   // the following is no longer ambiguous;
   // there's only one weight shared between Sofa and Bed
   // Furniture::Sofa or a Furniture::Bed?
   println("Weight = {}", ss.weight);
}
```

Notice the addition of the keyword `virtual` in the inheritance of `Furniture` in `Bed` and `Sofa`. This says, "Give me a copy of `Furniture` unless you already have one somehow, in which case we'll just use that one." A `SleeperSofa` ends up looking like Figure 26-5 in memory.

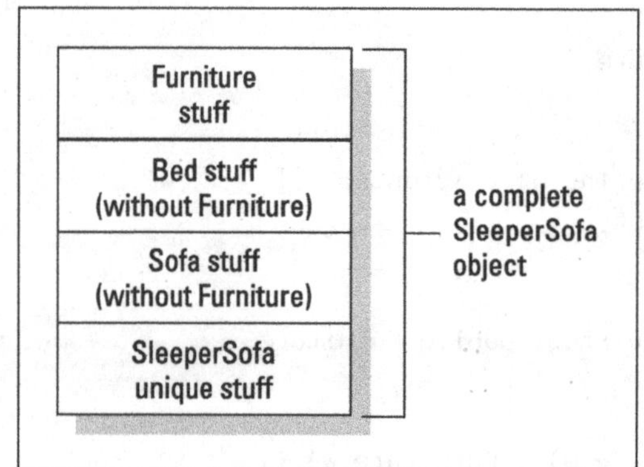

FIGURE 26-5: Memory layout of `SleeperSofa` with virtual inheritance.

Here, you can see that a `SleeperSofa` inherits `Furniture`, and then `Bed` minus the `Furniture` part, followed by `Sofa` minus the `Furniture` part. Bringing up the rear are the members unique to `SleeperSofa`. (Note that this may not be the order of the elements in memory, but that's not important for the purpose of this discussion.)

Now the reference in `fn()` to `weight` isn't ambiguous because a `SleeperSofa` contains only one copy of `Furniture`. By inheriting `Furniture` virtually, you get the desired inheritance relationship as expressed earlier, in Figure 26-2.

If virtual inheritance solves this problem nicely, why isn't it the norm? The first reason is that virtually inherited base classes are handled internally much differently from normally inherited base classes, and these differences involve extra overhead. The second reason is that sometimes you actually *want* two copies of the base class.

As an example of the latter, consider a `TeacherAssistant` who is both a `Student` and a `Teacher`, both of which are subclasses of `Academician`. If the university gives its teaching assistants two IDs — a student ID and a separate teacher ID — the class `TeacherAssistant` needs to contain two copies of class `Academician`.

Constructing the Objects of Multiple Inheritance

The rules for constructing objects need to be expanded to handle multiple inheritance. The necessary constructors are invoked in the following order:

1. First, any virtual base classes are constructed. They are called in the order in which the classes are inherited. Each virtual base class is inherited only once, even if inherited multiple times.

2. Then all nonvirtual base classes are constructed in the order in which the classes are listed in the derived class's inheritance list.
3. Next, the constructors for each member object in the derived class are called in the order in which the member object appears in the class definition (not the list in the initialization).
4. Finally, the constructor for the derived class itself is executed.

The base classes are constructed in the order in which they're inherited and not in the order in which they appear on the constructor line.

When it's time to call the destructors, the order is the reverse. It starts with the derived class, the member objects are destroyed, and then the nonvirtual base classes come next, followed by the virtual base classes.

Interfacing with C++

I want to clarify one topic so that you can respond in case it comes up in conversation at your local hangout. When talking about inheritance and object-oriented programming, consider the concept of an interface. An *interface* is simply a specification that defines a set of class methods and class properties that other classes must implement. An interface doesn't indicate how these are to be implemented. It says *what* needs to be done, not *how* it is to be done.

In C++, the concept of an interface is executed by using *pure abstract classes* — classes that have only pure virtual functions and no data members other than `static constexpr` members. An abstract class is basically a shell that cannot be instantiated on its own. Generally speaking, interfaces focus on completing a specific task. They often have names that starts with *I*, such as `IFurniture`, `IPrintable`, or `IShape`.

If you create a pure abstract class (interface), you should include a virtual destructor. This avoids situations where only a base class destructor is called.

Is It Better to Have or to Be? That Is the Question

In Chapter 21, I mention a rather important topic related to inheritance, which I'll bring up again now. Regarding modern C++ development, many proponents push the use of composition more than inheritance.

Composition is the use of a class or type within another class rather than inheriting a class. It's using classes as building blocks. For example, a `car` class can contain an `engine` class. The `car` class would not inherit the `engine` class. The car has an engine as a part of itself.

To be clear, you still create the classes individually. The `engine` class is a separate class from the `car` class. For composition, the `car` class simply includes the `engine` class.

There's a reason for clarifying that these are separate classes. This separation makes it easier for you to swap one component for another. You can pull out the `engine` class and replace it with a different `engine` class.

As I also mention in Chapter 21, this componentization used for composition is referred to as HAS_A. A car HAS_A engine. This is different from inheritance, where the relationship is described as IS_A. For example, a sleeper sofa IS_A bed. A sleeper sofa also IS_A sofa. A car is not an engine, but rather HAS_A engine.

The easiest way to determine whether you should use composition versus inheritance is to determine which is more accurate — using IS_A or using HAS_A:

- class A HAS_A class B = composition
- class A IS_A class B = inheritance

With multiple inheritance, any base classes that are used should align with IS_A. If a class doesn't align, it's more likely that it should be included within the class (composition) instead. In general, composition often makes more sense. Of course, it's also okay to have both inheritance and composition in the same class!

Reiterating a Contrary Opinion

You should now know that C++ supports multiple inheritance. However, many other object-oriented languages don't support it. It's important to know that not all object-oriented practitioners think that multiple inheritance is a good idea. Multiple inheritance isn't an easy thing for the language to implement; plus, it adds overhead to the code when compared to single inheritance, and this overhead can become the programmer's problem.

More importantly, multiple inheritance opens the door to additional errors. First, ambiguities such as those mentioned in the section "Straightening Out Inheritance Ambiguities," earlier in this chapter, pop up. Second, in the presence of multiple inheritance, casting a pointer from a subclass to a base class often involves changing the value of the pointer in sophisticated and mysterious ways. (Let's leave the details to the language lawyers and compiler writers.)

Third, the way in which constructors are invoked can be a little mysterious. Notice in the `VirtualInheritance` example that `SleeperSofa` must invoke the `Furniture` constructor directly. The `SleeperSofa` cannot initialize `weight` through either the `Bed` or the `Sofa` constructors.

I suggest that you avoid using multiple inheritance until you're comfortable with C++. Single inheritance provides enough expressive power to get used to.

IN THIS CHAPTER

- » Introducing an exceptional way of handling program errors
- » Finding what's wrong with good ol' error returns
- » Examining throwing and catching exceptions
- » Packing more heat into that throw
- » Setting expectations in your code
- » Making return values optional the right way
- » Being stringent with contracts in your code
- » Keeping the compiler going with `constexpr` exceptions

Chapter 27

Getting Ahead of Problems: Exception Handling, Contracts, and More

Though this chapter comes near the end of this book, the topic is one you should be thinking about from the beginning of your coding projects: Always consider what could go wrong with the programs you write and how your users might misuse your apps. More specifically, your code should take issues into consideration so that they provide the best possible experience for your users.

Making an Exception to What I Just Said

I know that it's hard to accept, but occasionally functions don't work properly — not even mine. The traditional means of reporting failure is to return some indication to the calling function. C++ includes a mechanism, called *exceptions*, for capturing and handling errors. The handling of error conditions with exceptions is the subject of the first half of this chapter. In the second half, I present solutions for helping your programs avoid crashing by doing things such as handling optional values, identifying what is expected, and even trying to prevent problems before they happen. But first, I'll make an exception. . . .

C++ includes a concept called exception handling for — you guessed it! — handling exceptions. *Exceptions* are simply an unexpected or erroneous condition that occurs when a program is running. For example, dividing by zero is undefined, so it can result in an exception. The exception mechanism is based on the keywords `try`, `catch`, and `throw`. (That's right — more variable names that you can't use.) In an outline, it works like this: A function `try`s to get through a piece of code. If the code detects a problem, it `throw`s an error indication that the calling function must `catch`.

The following code snippet demonstrates how that works in `1`s and `0`s:

```
// FactorialException - demonstrate exceptions using
//                        a factorial function
//
#include <print>
using namespace std;

// factorial - compute factorial
int factorial(int nbr)
{
   // you can't handle negative values of nbr;
   // better check for that condition first
   if (nbr < 0)
   {
      throw string("Argument for factorial negative");
   }
   // go ahead and calculate factorial
```

```
    int accum = 1;
    while(nbr > 0)
    {
        accum *= nbr;
        nbr--;
    }
    return accum;
}

int main(int nNumberofArgs, char* pszArgs[])
{
    try
    {
        // this will work
        println("Factorial of 3 is {}", factorial(3));

        // this will generate an exception
        println("Factorial of -1 is {}", factorial(-1));

        // control will never get here
        println("Factorial of 5 is {}", factorial(5));
    }
    // control passes here
    catch(const string& error)
    {
        println("Error occurred: {}", error );
    }
    catch(...)
    {
        println("Default catch ");
    }
}
```

Here, I have `main()` start out by creating a block outfitted with the `try` keyword. Within this block, it can proceed the way it would if the block were not present. In this case, `main()` attempts to calculate the factorial of a negative number. Not to be hoodwinked, the clever `factorial()` function detects the bogus request and throws an error indication using the `throw` keyword. Control passes to the `catch` phrase, which immediately follows the closing brace of the `try` block. The following is the output from this program. As you can see, the third call to `factorial()` isn't performed:

```
Factorial of 3 is 6
Error occurred: Argument for factorial negative
```

Justifying a New Error Mechanism?

What's wrong with error returns like FORTRAN used to make? Factorials cannot be negative, so I could simply have said something like this: "Okay, if `factorial()` detects an error, it returns a negative number. The actual value indicates the source of the problem." What's wrong with that? That's how it was done for ages. ("If it was good enough for my grandpa. . . .")

Unfortunately, several problems arise. First, although it's true that the result of a factorial can't be negative, other functions aren't so lucky. For example, you can't take the log of a negative number either, but logarithms can be either negative or positive. There's no value that a logarithm function can't return.

Second, there's just so much information you can store in an integer. Maybe you can have −1 for "argument is negative" and −2 for "argument is too large." But if the argument is too large, you want to know what the argument is because that information might help you debug the problem. There's no place to store that type of information. (Later in this very chapter, you can learn how to actually handle this situation by sending back an error value that's different from the function value.)

Third, the processing of error returns is optional. Suppose someone writes `factorial()` in such a way that it dutifully checks the argument and returns a negative number if the argument is out of range. If a function that calls `factorial()` doesn't check the error return, returning an error value doesn't do any good. (Later in this very chapter, you can also learn how to set up your function to prevent problems before they can happen rather than wait to see which error is tossed after the function is run.)

Even if you do check the error return from `factorial()` or any other function, what can the function do with the error? It can probably do nothing more than output an error message of its own and return another error indication to the caller, which probably does the same. Pretty soon, there's more error detection code than "real" code, and it's all mixed together.

Exception handling is what C++ programmers have used to handle these issues for decades. The exception mechanism addresses these problems by removing the error path from the normal code path. Furthermore, exceptions make error handling obligatory. If your function doesn't handle the thrown exception, control passes up the chain of called functions until C++ finds a function to handle the error. This also gives you the flexibility to ignore errors you can't do anything about anyway. Only the functions that can actually handle the problem need to catch the exception.

Examining the Exception Mechanism

Take a closer look at the steps the sample code undertakes to handle an exception. When the throw occurs, C++ first copies the thrown object to some neutral place. It then begins looking for the end of the current `try` block.

If a `try` block isn't found in the current function, control passes to the calling function. A search is then made of that function. If no `try` block is found there, control passes to the function that called it, and so on, up the stack of calling functions. This process is called *unwinding the stack.*

REMEMBER

An important feature of stack unwinding is that, as each stack is unwound, objects that go out of scope are destructed just as though the function had executed a `return` statement. This keeps the program from losing assets or leaving objects dangling.

When the enclosing `try` block is found, the code searches the first `catch` phrase immediately following the closing brace of the `catch` block. If the object thrown matches the type of argument specified in the `catch` statement, control passes to that `catch` phrase. If not, a check is made of the next `catch` phrase. Note that there can be more than one `catch` statement with different `catch` phrases based on the error type that is thrown. You can also have a generic `catch` (sort of a catch-all) using `catch(...)`.

If no matching `catch` phrases are found, the code searches for the next-higher level of `try` block in an ever-outward spiral until an appropriate `catch` can be found. If no `catch` phrase is found, the program is terminated.

Consider the following example:

```
// CascadingException - the following program
//           demonstrates an example of stack unwinding
#include <print>
using namespace std;

// prototypes of some functions that we will need later
void f1();
void f2();
void f3();

class Obj
{
  public:
    Obj(char c) : label(c)
```

```
      { println("Constructing object {}", label);}
    ~Obj()
      { println("Destructing object {}", label); }

  protected:
    char label;
};
int main()
{
    f1();
}

void f1()
{
    Obj a('a');
    try
    {
        Obj b('b');
        f2();
    }
    catch(float f)
    {
        println("Float catch");
    }
    catch(int i)
    {
        println("Int catch");
    }
    catch(...)
    {
        println("Generic catch");
    }
}
void f2()
{
    try
    {
        Obj c('c');
        f3();
    }
    catch(string msg)
    {
        println("String catch");
    }
}
```

```
void f3()
{
    Obj d('d');
    throw 10;
}
```

The output from executing this program appears as follows:

```
Constructing object a
Constructing object b
Constructing object c
Constructing object d
Destructing object d
Destructing object c
Destructing object b
Int catch
Destructing object a
```

First, you see the four objects a, b, c, and d being constructed as main() calls f1(), which calls f2(), which calls f3(). Rather than return, however, f3() throws the integer 10. Because no try block is defined in f3(), C++ unwinds f3()'s stack, causing object d to be destructed. The next function up the chain, f2(), defines a try block, but its only catch phrase is designed to handle a string, which doesn't match the int thrown. Therefore, C++ continues looking. This unwinds f2()'s stack, resulting in object c being destructed.

Back in f1(), C++ finds another try block. Exiting that block causes object b to go out of scope. C++ skips the first catch phrase for a float. The next catch phrase matches the int exactly, so C++ passes control to this phrase.

Control passes from the catch(int) phrase to the closing brace of the final catch phrase and from there back to main(). The final catch(...) phrase, which would catch any object thrown, is skipped because a matching catch phrase was already found.

TIP

Note that the catch phrases are using variables that are being passed by value. For example, the following is getting a float by value:

```
catch(float f)
```

This was done to keep the example simple for you to learn from. The program would be much better and more efficient, however, if it were using constant references to the error types being caught. This is because passing by value makes a copy, which takes time. Passing by reference does not. The `catch` would be better this way:

```
catch(const float& f)
```

The same change should be made to all the `catch` expressions if you want the best and speediest code!

What Kinds of Things Can You Throw?

The thing following the `throw` keyword is actually an expression that creates an object of some kind. In the examples so far in this chapter, I've thrown an `int` and a `string` object, but `throw` can handle any type of object. This means you can throw almost as much information as you want. Consider the following update to the factorial program, `CustomExceptionClass`:

```
// CustomExceptionClass - demonstrate the flexibility
//              of the exception mechanism by creating
//              a custom exception class
//
#include <format>
#include <string>
#include <print>
using namespace std;

// MyException - generic exception handling class
class MyException
{
  public:
    MyException(const string pMsg, int n,
                const string pFunc,
                const string pFile, int nLine)
      : msg(pMsg), errorValue(n),
        funcName(pFunc), file(pFile), lineNum(nLine){}

    string display() const noexcept
    {
        return format(
             "Error <{}> - value is {}\n"
             "in function {}()\n"
```

```
            "in file {} line #{}",
            msg, errorValue, funcName, file, lineNum);
    }
  protected:
    // error message
    string msg;
    int    errorValue;

    // function name, file name and line number
    // where error occurred
    string funcName;
    string file;
    int lineNum;
};

// factorial - compute factorial
int factorial(int nbr)
{
   // you can't handle negative values of nbr;
   // better check for that condition first
   if (nbr < 0)
   {
      throw MyException("Negative argument not allowed",
                  nbr, __func__, __FILE__, __LINE__);
   }
   // go ahead and calculate factorial
   int accum = 1;
   while(nbr > 0)
   {
       accum *= nbr;
       nbr--;
   }
   return accum;
}
int main(int nNumberofArgs, char* pszArgs[])
{
   try
   {
       // this will work
        println("Factorial of 3 is {}",factorial(3));

       // this will generate an exception
       println("Factorial of -1 is {}", factorial(-1));
```

```
        // control will never get here
        println("Factorial of 5 is {}", factorial(5));
    }
    // control passes here
    catch(const MyException& e)  // catch by reference is
                                 // better than by value
    {
        println("{}", e.display());
    }
    catch(...)
    {
        println("Default catch ");
    }
}
```

This program appears much the same as the factorial program at the beginning of this chapter. The difference is the use of a user-defined `MyException` class that contains more information concerning the nature of the error than a simple `string` contains. The factorial program is able to throw the error message, the illegal value, and the exact location where the error occurred.

REMEMBER

The values of `_FILE__`, `__LINE__`, and `_func__` are intrinsic `#define`s that are set to the name of the source file, the current line number in that file, and the name of the current function, respectively.

The first catch snags the `MyException` object and then uses the built-in `display()` member function to display the error message. The output from this program appears as follows:

```
Factorial of 3 is 6
Error <Negative argument not allowed> - value is -1
in function factorial()
in file C:\CPP_Programs_from_Book\Chap27\CustomExceptionClass\
  main.cpp line #51
```

Note that the output you see will have the folder name for where your listing is located. You might have also noticed the listing included second catch statement that has an ellipse (. . .) as its argument. This catch statement is a "catch all" that will handle any exceptions that might occur that have not already be caught by a more explicit catch.

Just Passing Through

A function that allocates resources locally may need to catch an exception, do some processing, and then throw it up the stack chain again. Consider the following example:

```
void fileFunc()
{
    ofstream* pOut = new ofstream("File.txt");
    otherFunction();
    delete pOut;
}
```

If you've read Chapter 9, you know that the memory allocated by `new` isn't returned to the heap automatically. If `otherFunction()` were to throw an exception, control would exit the program without invoking `delete`, and the memory allocated at the beginning of `fileFunc()` would be lost. (This is why smart pointers are a better option, but I'll go with the raw pointer for this example.)

To avoid this problem, `fileFunc()` can include a `catch(...)` to catch any exception thrown:

```
void fileFunc()
{
    ofstream* pOut = new ofstream("File.txt");
    try
    {
      otherFunction();

      delete pOut;
    }
    catch(...)
    {
        delete pOut;
        throw;
    }
}
```

Within this code snippet, `fileFunc()` returns the memory it allocated earlier to the heap. However, it isn't in a position to process the remainder of the exception because it has no idea what could have gone wrong. It doesn't even know what type of object it just caught.

The `throw` keyword without any arguments throws the current exception object back up the chain to some function that can properly process the error.

Scratching the Surface of Classy Exceptions

Up to this point within this chapter, I've explained the basics of exception handling in what I've shown. Entire books out there cover exception handling — including writing custom exceptions. There's also an `exception` class within the standard library. When writing custom exceptions (like the `MyException` class, earlier in this chapter), you can derive from the `std::exception` using inheritance as Chapter 21 explains and gain exception features in your class.

Though it's beyond the scope of this book to dig deeper into `try`, `catch`, and `throw` as well as to cover the classy `exception` class, that doesn't mean you should avoid exceptions. In fact, you should apply them to your code whenever you can. If not exceptions, then you should consider applying some other things that are `optional`, `expected`, and `contracts`, all covered in the remainer of this chapter.

Identifying What Is "Optional"

You'll find places in this book where a variable might not have had a value. It might be in these cases that you don't want to deal with returning an error but simply want to return the value. What many developers did in the old days of coding is make a dummy value to indicate that there is no value. As mentioned in the previous section, this might be done by setting a number to `-1` or returning a null value. This really isn't a good (or safe) manner in which to address the issue. Starting with C++17, programmers are able to declare variables in a manner that can represent that they might not have a value that exists. Programmers can make a variable "optional," by using the `optional` template:

```
optional<T>
```

This template is used to declare a variable of type `T` that might or might not be given a value. One prime use for this `optional` option is with functions that might fail but don't want to throw an error. For example, you might have a division function. If the function tries to divide by zero, the result is undefined. That isn't a standard value that can be returned, so an exception for dividing by zero would be thrown. By making the `return` type an `optional` value, you have a way of still running the function without causing the program to crash or without getting unexpected results. The following program compiles just fine, but is likely to crash or lock up when the second call to `simpleDivision()` is called. It's unlikely you will see the second `print` statement display:

```
#include <print>
using namespace std;

int simpleDivision(int numerator, int denominator)
{
   return (numerator / denominator);
}

int main()
{
   int goodTry = simpleDivision(10.0, 2.0);
   println("Good Try: {}", goodTry);
   // The following is division by zero, which is bad!
   int badTry = simpleDivision(10.0, 0.0);
   println("Bad Try: {}", badTry);
}
```

WARNING

This is a great example where using the `optional` template can help your program run better. The following is an update to the `simpleDivision()` function:

```
#include <iostream>
#include <optional>    // Needed if using optional
                       // template
#include <print>
using namespace std;

optional<int> simpleDivision(int numerator, int denominator)
{
   if (denominator == 0)
   {
      return nullopt;        // division by zero
   }
   return (numerator / denominator);
}
```

As you can see, the function now checks to make sure the division will work before doing the division and returning a value. If the division causes an error (such as dividing by zero), the function returns `nullopt` to indicate there is no value.

When you use the simpleDivision() function (or any function that uses an optional value), you need to determine whether you can use the returned value or whether that value isn't there. Fortunately, you can use a function called has_value()to see whether there's a valid result. This function returns true if there is, or false if not.

If there is a valid value, you can use a member function called value() to retrieve the value. *Note:* value() should be called only if you used has_value() and it returned true. To see this in action, check out the updated call to simpleDivision(), shown in the following new listing — one that can be combined with the previous snippet:

```
int main()
{
   optional<int> goodTry = simpleDivision(10, 2);
   if (goodTry.has_value())
   {
      println("Result: {}", goodTry.value());
   }
   else
   {
      println("Oops! Division by zero.");
   }

   optional<int> badTry = simpleDivision(10, 0);
   if (badTry.has_value())
   {
      println("Result: {}", badTry.value() );
   }
   else
   {
      println("Oops! Division by zero.");
   }
}
```

Notice that both goodTry and badTry each do a simple division. They then check to see whether the returned value was a value by using has_value(). If a value was returned, the number is printed using value(). If not, they a message is displayed. The output is:

```
Result: 5
Oops! Division by zero.
```

Note that you can skip using `has_value()` by simply checking to see whether the value is non-negative. For a variable that contains an `optional` value, you can use `*` to dereference the variable as an alternative to using the `value()` member function. This shortens the code a little, as you can see in the following updated `if` statement for checking `goodTry`:

```
if (goodTry)
{
    println("Result: {}", *goodTry);
}
else
{
    println("Oops! Division by zero.");
}
```

Were You Expected?

In C++23, expectations changed on what was expected to be returned from a function. Specifically, in C++23, a template was added to C++ to help make it easier to handle a function that might return an error rather than a value or an `optional` value. As you might expect, this template was called `expected`:

```
std::expected<T, E>
```

A function previously returned a type. Using this new template, a function can now return either a value of the type indicated by `T` when it's successful or a value of the type indicated by `E` if something happens unexpectedly. Consider a function that calculates the age of a person. It wouldn't be surprising for this function to return an integer from 0 to about 120. Suppose the function has an issue calculating the age of a person. In the past, the developer might simply return a value of `-1` or 999 because these are obviously bogus. But what if the program that calls the age function doesn't check for the bogus value and inadvertently uses 999 as an age? Crazy things could start happening. . . .

The `expected` template helps you avoid using an error value accidentally because it separates the error from the successful value. You can see this by noting that `expected` has two constructors:

» One is for when things go right (as expected):

```
expected(T)
```

» One is for when things go wrong (in an unexpected, bad way):

```
expected(unexpected<E>)
```

The second constructor works with an `unexpected` type. This `unexpected` type can be returned from your function to indicate there was an error. Here, `E` represents the data type of the error, which is normally something like a string or a custom error type.

REMEMBER

When your function encounters an error, you can use `unexpected` to indicate it's an error value.

You might feel like you've aged a few years after reading all this information. Let's see whether that's the case by creating a function that calculates age using the info just described. The following program also taps into a standard library function to work with time:

```
#include <expected>   // Needed to use expected
#include <format>
#include <chrono>     // Needed to use time/dates
#include <string>
#include <print>
using namespace std;

expected<int, string> calculateAge(int birthYear) {
   // Get the current year
   const auto now = std::chrono::system_clock::now();
   int currentYear = stoi(format("{:%Y}", now));

   // Validate input
   if (birthYear > currentYear)
   {
       return unexpected("The birth year is in the future");
   }
   if (birthYear < 1900)
   {
       return unexpected("The birth year is
  unrealistically old");
   }

   return currentYear - birthYear;
}
```

You can see that the calculateAge() function takes a year (birthYear) and uses it to determine how old a person is. The now() function is called to get the current date, and then using the format function you've seen before, the year is extracted from the current date (now), converted to an integer using stoi(), and then stored into the currentYear variable.

The code contains a couple of validation checks to make sure there isn't an error. If there is an error, unpexected() is called to wrap up a string into an error message that is returned. If everything looks good after validations are done, the calculated age is returned.

Using an Expected Value

After you have a function to calculate age, you'll want to use it. Because the result of the calculateAge() function could be either an int or an unexpected error, you can use the auto keyword on the variable that will get the return value and let C++ take care of which type it is:

```
auto result = calculateAge(1999);
```

If an integer value is returned (say, 27), you're free to use result just like you always would. But what if an unexpected returns an error value — in this case, a string?

You need to determine whether you can use the value that was returned. More specifically, you need to determine whether it has a value or an error. Fortunately, you can use one of three accessor functions to see what the expected value is holding:

- **has_value():** Checks to see whether there is a valid result. It returns true if there is, or false if not.
- **value():** Retrieves the successful result from an expected object. (This would be the valid age in your function.) This should be called only if you used has_value() and it returned true.
- **error():** Retrieves the error result from an expected object. It returns the error that was set. (In the case of the age function, that would be a string.) This should be called only if you used has_value() and it returned false.

The following main() function can be used with the calculateAge() function. You can see that it uses has_value() to determine what to print and whether to use value() or error() to obtain the value:

```
int main()
{
    auto age = calculateAge(2000);
    if (age.has_value())
    {
        println("Age is: {}", age.value() );
    }
    else
    {
        println("Error: {}", age.error());
    }
}
```

REMEMBER

This might seem like a little extra work versus just assuming things went correctly; however, that extra work helps to make your handling of errors cleaner. This is more type safe, which means the compiler will prevent you from accidentally using a type wrong. Because you can return strings and other error values that are different from the data type expected for a correct answer, you can also be more explicit.

Preventing Problems before They Can Happen: Contracts

C++26 NEW

In C++26, a new feature has been added to help you proactively avoid having errors in your functions. Though we often don't like to be held accountable for everything we do — like eating an extra plate full of nachos on game day — there are times when it can be good to be functionally correct. For instance, my doctor says I should cut back on nachos and limit my intake to one plate.

Contracts allow you to set up conditions for when your function can work. For example, some of the following conditions might be reasons to not run a function:

- A counter should be 0 or greater.
- When calculating age, the birth year should be greater than 1900.
- If dividing, the denominator should not be zero.

All these are conditions it would be nice to flag before you start running an associated function. A contract helps to define the behavior of a function by addressing conditions like these. It defines expected behavior in one of three ways using contextual keywords:

pre: Defines which preconditions should be true before the function is called

post: Defines which postconditions must be true after the function returns

contract_assert: Defines what must be true at a specific point when executing the function

Contract conditions are checked at runtime and, by default, generate an error if the condition fails. The value you gain, however, is that it's much clearer in your code what your functions expect for valid data. Consider the following function:

```
#include <iostream>
#include <print>
#include <contract>      // Needed to use contracts
using namespace std;

double averageScores(const int scores[], size_t count)
    pre(count > 0)
    post(r: r >= 0.0 && r <= 100.0)
{
    int total = 0;

    for (size_t ctr = 0; ctr < count; ++ctr)
    {
        contract_assert(scores[ctr] >= 0 && scores[ctr] <= 100);
        total += scores[ctr];
    }

    return static_cast<double>(total) / count;
}
```

In this listing, the `averageScores()` function takes an array of `int` values and the number of `int` values (`count`) that are in the array. This is used to calculate an average. Before the function will run, `count` must be greater than 0 based on the precondition defined with `pre()`. While running, a `contract_assert` checks each score to make sure it's from 0 to 100. If a score isn't in this range, the `contract` condition fails and a runtime error occurs. If the function is able to total the scores in the `for` loop, the total is divided by the count in order to calculate the average. The post contract condition indicates that the return value — represented by `r` in the `post()` clause in the function header — indicates that the value must be between `0.0` and `100.0`.

The following basic `main()` function calls `averageScores()`. Using this code, the function should run without issue in C++26:

```
int main()
{
    int scores[20] = { 95, 88, 76, 100, 67, 89, 92,
                       85, 73, 90, 81, 78, 84, 99,
                       65, 70, 93, 87, 80, 77 };

    double avg = averageScores(scores, 20);
    println("Average score: {}", avg);
}
```

The output would be:

```
Average score: 86.45
```

If you change one of the scores to be greater than 100, the `contract_assert()` fails. In this case, you'll likely get a runtime error saying there's a contract violation in `averageScores()`. If you change the count value being passed from 20 to 0 or a negative number, it too throws a runtime error, also indicating a contract violation based on the `pre()` condition.

WARNING

As stated, contracts are new in C++26. Many compilers disable contracts by default and thus require you to turn them on to be able to use them. Consult your compiler's documentation to see whether it supports contracts and to learn how to enable contracts.

KEEPING THE COMPILE GOING: CONSTEXPR EXCEPTIONS

We don't talk much about *constexpr* in this book, but it's sure to become a more important topic as you learn more about C++. The simple `constexpr` identifier tells the compiler to evaluate code at compile time. It can be used on variables, functions, or constructors that can run during the compilation process.

When you use `constexpr` with error handling, you can even catch problems at compile time and gain a better idea of what went wrong. Starting with C++26, you can keep your code executing if you catch an exception during compile time within a `constexpr` function. Previously, this would cause an error and thus prevent a full compile. It is beyond the scope of this book to cover exception handling at compile time, but I thought you should know that you have options if you find that you need such a solution.

6 The Part of Tens

IN THIS PART . . .

Avoiding bugs

Making your programs easier to share

IN THIS CHAPTER

» Enable all warnings and error messages

» Use a clear and consistent coding style

» Limit the visibility of your internals

» Add comments to your code while you write it

» Single-step every path at least once

» Avoid overloaded operators

» Manage the heap effectively

» Use exceptions to handle errors

» Declare destructors to be virtual

» Avoid multiple inheritance

Chapter 28

Ten Ways to Avoid Adding Bugs to Your Program

Nobody writes perfect code every time, all the time. As such, minimizing or eliminating errors is an obvious goal for developers. After all, no one wants errors in their code! In this chapter, you encounter several ways to minimize errors, as well as ways to make it easier to debug your code and remove the errors that might somehow get introduced.

Enable All Warnings and Error Messages

The syntax of C++ allows for lots of error checking. When the compiler encounters a construct it can't decipher, it has no choice but to generate an error message. Although the compiler attempts to sync back up with the next statement, it doesn't attempt to generate an executable program.

Disabling warning and error messages is a bit like unplugging the Check Engine light on your car dashboard because it bothers you: Ignoring the problem doesn't make it go away. If your compiler has a Syntax Check from Hell mode, enable it.

Don't start debugging your code until you remove or at least understand all warnings generated during compilation. Of course, enabling all warning messages and then deciding to ignore them does you no good. If you don't understand the warning, look it up. What you don't know *will* hurt you.

TIP

Some warnings and errors cause other warnings and errors. So, in many cases, fixing one issue can remove multiple errors and warnings.

Adopt a Clear and Consistent Coding Style

Coding in a clear and consistent style not only enhances the readability of your program but also results in fewer coding mistakes. A good coding style enables you to do the following with ease:

- » Differentiate class names, object names, and function names.
- » Know something about the object based on its name.
- » Differentiate preprocessor symbols from C++ symbols (that is, `#defined` objects should stand out).
- » Identify blocks of C++ code at the same level (this is the result of consistent indentation).

In addition, you need to establish a standard module header that provides information about the functions or classes in the module, the author (presumably, that's you), the date, the version of the compiler you're using, and a modification history.

Finally, all programmers involved in a single project should use the same style. Trying to decipher a program with a patchwork of different coding styles is confusing.

TIP

Most modern development environments will have a feature that automatically styles the formatting and indenting of your code. You just have to ask the development environment to do the clean-up! For example, if you use Code::Blocks, you can let it maintain your source code style for you. Choose Settings ⇨ Editor from the main menu, and then within the displayed dialog box select Source Formatter from the list of icons on the left. From the menu and tabs on the right of the source formatter dialog you can select your preferred source code style. Select OK to save your changes. Now from the main menu in Code::Blocks choose Plugins ⇨ Source Code Formatter to completely reformat your modules.

In Visual Studio Code, you can install an add-in to format code or use a built-in formatter by pressing a combination of keys. In Windows, press Shift+Alt+F. On a Mac, you can press Shift+Option+F. In Linux, you can press Ctrl+Shift+I.

REMEMBER

The less brain power you have to spend deciphering C++ syntax, the more you have left over for thinking about the logic of the program at hand.

Limit the Visibility

Limiting the visibility of class internals to the outside world is a cornerstone of object-oriented programming. The class is responsible for its own internals; the application is responsible for using the class to solve the problem at hand.

Specifically, limited visibility means that data members should not be accessible outside the class — that is, they should be marked as `protected` or `private`. In addition, member functions that the application software doesn't need to know about should also be marked `protected` or `private`. Don't expose any more of the class internals than necessary.

A related rule is that public member functions should trust application code as little as possible. Any argument passed to a public member function should be treated as though it might cause bugs until it has been proven safe. A function such as the following is an accident waiting to happen:

```
#include <memory>;
#include <iostream>;

class Array
```

```
{
  public:
    explicit Array(int s)
    {
       size = 0;
       // new throws exception if memory not available
       pData = std::make_unique<int[]>(s);
       size = s;
    }
    ~Array() = default;

    //either return or set the array data
    int data (int index)
    {
      return pData[index];
    }
    int data(int index, int newValue)
    {
     int oldValue = pData[index];
     pData[index] = newValue;
     return oldValue;
    }

  protected:
    int size;
    std::unique_ptr<int{}> pData;
};
```

The function `data(int)` allows the application software to read data out of `Array`. This function is too trusting; it assumes that the `index` provided is within the data range. What if the `index` is not?

What's needed is a check to make sure that the `index` is in range. In the following, only the `data(int)` function is shown, for brevity:

```
int data(unsigned int index)
{
  if (index >= size || index < 0)
  {
    throw Exception("Array index out of range");
  }
  return pData[index];
}
```

Now an out-of-range `index` will be caught by the check. (Making `index` unsigned precludes the necessity of adding a check for negative `index` values.)

C++23 NEW

This example illustrates the point of limiting visibility. The code would be better if you add the use of `std::expected`, as covered in Chapter 27. I've included the listing `LimitedVisibilty.cpp` in the downloadable files for this book; it allows your functions to verify that the index is valid before accessing any elements of the array. Of course, you could also use vectors rather than arrays to have even safer code.

Comment Your Code While You Write It

You can avoid errors if you comment your code while you write it rather than wait until everything works and then go back and add comments. I can understand not taking the time to write voluminous headers and function descriptions until later, but you always have time to add short comments while writing the code.

REMEMBER

Short comments should be enlightening. If they're not, they aren't worth much. You need all the enlightenment you can get while you're trying to make your program work. When you look at a piece of code you wrote a few days ago, comments that are short, descriptive, and to the point can make a dramatic contribution to helping you figure out exactly what it was you were trying to do.

In addition, consistent code indentation and naming conventions make the code easier to understand. It's all very nice when the code is easy to read after you're finished with it, but it's just as important that the code be easy to read while you're writing it. That's when you need the help.

Single-Step Every Path at Least Once

It may seem like an obvious statement, but I'll say it anyway: As a programmer, you *must* understand what your program is doing. Nothing gives you a better feel for what's going on under the hood than single-stepping the program with a good debugger. (Code::Blocks and Visual Studio Code both contain an integrated debugger.) By using the debugger to step through every single line of code (step), you can confirm exactly what your code is doing. Even without a debugger, you can read through each line of code in the order they would be executed.

Beyond that, as you write a program, you sometimes need raw material to figure out some bizarre behavior. Nothing gives you that material better than single-stepping new functions as they come into service.

Finally, when a function is finished and ready to be added to the program, every logical path needs to be traveled at least once. Bugs are much easier to find when the function is examined by itself rather than after it has been thrown into the pot with the rest of the functions — and your attention has moved on to new programming challenges.

Avoid Overloading Operators

Other than using the assignment operator `operator=()`, you should hold off on overloading operators until you feel comfortable with C++. Overloading operators other than assignment is almost never necessary and can significantly add to your debugging woes as a new programmer. You can achieve the same effect by defining and using the proper public member functions instead.

After you've been C-plus-plussing for a few months, feel free to return and start overloading operators to your heart's content.

Manage the Heap Systematically

As a general rule, programmers should allocate and release heap memory at the same "level." If a member function `MyClass::create()` allocates a block of heap memory and returns it to the caller, a member function `MyClass::release()` should return the memory to the heap. Specifically, `MyClass::create()` should not require the parent function to release the memory. This certainly doesn't avoid all memory problems — the parent function may forget to call `MyClass::release()` — but it does reduce the possibility somewhat.

Of course, it's even better to avoid using `new` and `delete` to allocate memory and instead use the safer `std::unique_ptr` and `std::shared_ptr`. Using `shared_ptr` means that the system will keep track of references to memory and free it when the last pointer using it goes out of scope. The `unique_ptr` function also handles memory resources for you and also deletes the allocation of memory when the pointer goes out of scope. Both of these functions help to manage the heap for you.

Use Exceptions to Handle Errors

The exception mechanism in C++ is designed to handle errors conveniently and efficiently. In general, you should throw an error indicator rather than return an error flag. The resulting code is easier to write, read, and maintain. Besides, other programmers have come to expect it — you wouldn't want to disappoint them, would you?

It isn't necessary to throw an exception from a function that returns a "didn't work" indicator if this is a part of everyday life for that function. Consider a function `lcd()` that returns the least common denominators of a number passed to it as an argument. That function doesn't return any values when presented with a prime number. (A *prime* number cannot be evenly divided by any other number.) This isn't an error — the `lcd()` function has nothing to say when given a prime.

C++26 NEW

The more recent versions of C++ have added features to exception handling to help you capture and respond to errors earlier. You should use `std::expected`, introduced in C++23, to handle errors that you can predict will happen. You can also work to catch exceptions earlier by using static exceptions as well as `constexpr` exceptions (added in C++26) that can be thrown during compile-time. Finally, you can also use `std::optional`, added in C++17, to help avoid using odd values such as `-1` or `nullptr` to represent missing data.

Out with the New and in with the Newer

In previous editions of this book, this section was called "Declare Destructors Virtual," and it recommended that you remember to create a destructor for your class if the constructor allocates resources (such as heap memory) that need to be returned when the object reaches its demise. Having created a destructor, don't forget to declare it `virtual` (almost) every time, especially if you know that your class is likely to be inherited and extended by subclasses. This was illustrated with a code listing that allocated memory using the `new` command.

But with modern C++, the better and correct way to avoid issues is to not use `new` and `delete`. Rather, you should use the smart pointers that were presented within this book. These were `unique_ptr` and `shared_ptr` that are part of the standard library. By using these, you don't need to use the manual process of `new` and `delete` because smart pointers manage everything for you! As a bonus, they provide better safety because they take care of calling destructors automatically to help prevent memory leaks.

Virtual destructors are still necessary if you choose to work with raw pointers (or if you need to manage someone's old code that uses them and you aren't allowed to update it). The use of `virtual` helps ensure that you're calling the destructor on the pointer's actual type versus a declared type (such as calling it on a `Student` object even if a pointer of a different type, such as a base class of `Person`, is being used).

Virtual destructors are also important to include if you're managing other types of resources, such as file handles, which would require explicit clean-up if you inherited them.

Why not simply add `virtual` to every destructor? What would it hurt?

Declaring any member in a class `virtual` means that C++ must add an extra pointer or two to each object of that class to keep track of its `virtual` members. For a small program, this might be okay, but if you expect your class to be used quite a bit, the overhead of extra pointers adds up.

TIP

As a general rule, if you expect someone to inherit your class, declare its destructor `virtual`. And if you're about to inherit from an existing base class, make sure its destructor is declared `virtual` as well.

Avoid Multiple Inheritance

Multiple inheritance, like operator overloading, adds another level of complexity that you don't need to deal with when you're just starting out. Fortunately, most real-world relationships can be described with single inheritance.

After you feel comfortable with your level of understanding of C++, experiment with setting up some multiple inheritance hierarchies. That way, you'll be ready when the unusual situation arises that requires multiple inheritance to describe it accurately.

IN THIS CHAPTER

» Pick your names wisely

» Use comments

» Write modular code

» Steer clear of reinventing the wheel

» Style your code

» Resist the temptation to leave problems for others

» Test, test, and then test again

» Use modern features

» Avoid hard-coded values

» Use version control

Chapter 29 Ten Ways to Make Your Programs Easier to Update and Understand

In this chapter, I recommend several ways to make your code easier to understand, share, and maintain over a longer period. It's easy to think that you know what your code does and that it's clear to understand, but after you move on to other tasks, you might forget what you did in the code you wrote. To make sure your code is clean, clear, and easy for you to not only understand but also update if needed, consider these ten suggestions.

Pick Names Wisely

If I tell you I named a variable `x`, can you tell me what `x` stores? What if I call it `z`? If I tell you it's an integer value, does that make it easier for you to tell what is being stored?

Did you guess that `x` stores the number of pets I own? If you didn't, I'm really not surprised because `x` is about as nondescript as you can get.

What if I say the variable is `nNumberOfPets`? Does that make it easier to know what's being stored? Of course it does! What if I say `ctr` rather than `x`? If `ctr` is being used in a loop, it's likely that `ctr` is a counter.

This might sound like a simple suggestion, but picking wise names for your variables is important. It's easy to default to simple letters; however, if you step away from the code for a few days or if you have someone else review the code, then what is being stored will likely be cryptic to them. Your program isn't impacted by longer variable names, so be wise and name your variables in a way that indicates what they're being used for.

Use Comments

The easiest way to remember what your code does is to write yourself a little note at the same time you're writing the code. Don't put off this task until later; rather, make it a part of writing your code. Writing comments should be considered as important as creating classes or writing loops.

Comments don't slow down your programs — they simply add information for you and anyone looking at your code to read. As such, there's no reason to avoid them. In fact, most organizations that have coding standards include standards for what comments should be included as a minimum. Many also include a structure for the comments, such as including the filename at the top of a listing as well as including information on any parameters and return values in comments preceding each function. You can use the following templates for commenting in key areas of your code:

Commenting at the beginning of a file:

```
/*
 * File: my_program_name.cpp
 * Author: {your name}
```

```
* Date: June 4, 2025 (The date you created the code)
* Version: 1.0 (You can update this with major changes)
*
* Description:
* This program does...{brief explanation of functionality)
*
* License: (If code could be shared or copied)
* (Specify license type, if applicable)
*/
```

Commenting before each class or template:

```
/*
 * Class: ClassName
 * Purpose: Description of what class or template does.
 * Attributes:
 *    - type AttributeName1: Description of attribute.
 *    - type AttributeName2: Description of attribute.
 * Methods:
 *    - methodName1(): Short description of method.
 *    - methodName2(): Short description of method.
 */
```

Shorter commented descriptions can be added to each method in the class or template. You can then include longer descriptions in the comments before each method:

Commenting before each method or function:

```
/*
 * Function: FunctionName
 * Purpose: Description of what function does.
 * Parameters:
 *    - type parameter1: Description of what parameter is.
 *    - type parameter2: Description of what parameter is.
 * Returns:
 *    - returnType: Description of what return value is.
 */
```

Write Modular Code

It can be easy to start writing code and adding more and more functionality as needed. It's like writing a book in that it would be easy to start writing and just keep going until everything is said. Of course, that would be a long read, and many topics would be repeated a few times. Rather, it becomes easier to read a book if you break it into chapters. Even better is to break each chapter into sections. The long sections become easier to read if you further refine the topics into smaller sections that are focused on a given topic. Just look at this chapter as a simple example.

Writing code benefits from the same strategy. Breaking code listings into focused sections and then further refining the sections can help modularize your code. These are the benefits:

- **The code is easier to understand.** Smaller, focused code is easier for others to understand and update (maintain) when looking at your code.
- **The code is easier to reuse.** Single-function or single-purpose code can be reused much more easily. For example, the `print()` function prints — that's all it does. Its singular focus of purpose means that it's easy to use in a variety of other programs.
- **Testing is improved.** By writing code in modules, you can test the code to see that it works. If it does, you don't need to test its internal details again unless something in the code changes.
- **Development happens faster.** Though it might be faster to write code for yourself as a single bulky listing, as your programs require more code, you can gain time by organizing and defining modules based on the previous items in this list. If you're working on a team, you can also gain development time by avoiding duplication of effort.

Steer Clear of Reinventing the Wheel

Why would you want to write code that someone else has already written? Okay, it may be to learn, as you do in this book, but outside of learning, most developers would prefer to focus on writing new stuff. The C++ Standard Library has lots of code that is already written that you can easily tap into. You use a few items from the Standard Library in this book, but it has lots of other classes, templates, functions, and more that you can tap into and use. If you want to learn, go ahead, but if your focus is on simply building a solution, take advantage of existing code. Search to see whether something exists in the Standard Library before writing it yourself!

Lots of third-party libraries are available. Some are free, but others have licensing fees in order for you to use them. If you use code from a third party, you should respect the licensing. Additionally, you should make sure any third-party code you use is from a reputable organization or that you have access to the source code to make sure nothing nefarious is happening in the code.

While I say you shouldn't reinvent the wheel, I'll also add that you should use caution when allowing artificial intelligence (AI) to write your code for you. AI can create C++ code as well as tell you what the code does. AI, however, is not perfect and can cause problems (called appropriately hallucinations). If you choose to use AI to create code, you should make sure you know what every line it generates does. Otherwise, you might end up with code doing things you don't like.

Style Your Code

Some people have messy rooms. Some people leave their dirty clothes in a pile in the corner. Some people leave dirty dishes on the table and in the sink for days. When it comes to your code, don't be one of those people. Organize and clean up your code. Give it some style!

What is style when it comes to coding? Simply put, it's making sure it's organized and presented in a clean, consistent manner. This can mean, for example, stating comments in a standardized manner, applying consistent naming standards, adding standardized indentation (such as three spaces), or using curly brackets uniformly either on the same line or on the next line.

How important is styling your code? It's important enough that I mention it not only here but also in the previous chapter!

Don't Leave Problems for Others

I'll get to that later.

It's easy to cut corners and do the bare minimum to get something working while telling yourself you'll fix the problem or fill out the details later in the correct manner. This statement is especially true for adding comments. Don't put off until later what you should do now. Though you might believe you'll fix the code later, later rarely comes. As such, take the time to do things right the first time.

Test, Test, and Then Test Again

Testing is more than simply running your program a few times to confirm that it gives the results you expect. Testing involves not only making sure your program works as expected but also making sure it works when the unexpected happens. Testing provides a number of benefits for making your programs better, including:

- **Eliminating issues:** It's better to find a problem (a *bug*) in your code or logic before a user does. If you find a bug at a hotel, you likely won't stay at that hotel in the future. Similarly, if a user finds a bug in your code, you risk them not using your code in the future.
- **Confirming reliability:** Testing your code over and over helps ensure reliability. You confirm that the code works as expected and works consistently time after time. By testing under a number of different conditions, you can confirm just how consistent and reliable your programs are.
- **Improving confidence:** If you've tested, tested again, and then tested even more, your confidence in knowing the code is less likely to have issues will increase.

A key to testing is not just making sure your code works as expected but also making sure it doesn't crash and burn when users do the unexpected. In listings presented early in this book, you prompt the user to enter numbers. If the user enters anything other than numbers, the programs crash because they have no error handling to deal with the non-numeric data. If you test the programs by simply entering a variety of numbers to make sure they work, the results look great. It's only when you enter a word or another character that the programs go crazy.

You might say, "I asked for a number, so why would the user enter anything else?" Um, they are *users*, so they are likely to enter something else simply because they can! That's why you have to test and then make sure you handle such situations.

Use Modern Features

I know people who are still using 20-year old versions of development languages. They learned the language and know how to write programs to solve problems with what that version of the language does, so they see no reason to switch to the more modern versions.

These developers, however, are taking big risks.

Tap into and use modern language features whenever you can. Sometimes you simply can't, because of backward compatibility issues, but if you can modernize, you should. Modern features tend to do a number of things, including improving performance, enhancing security, and often adding ease of use. For example, the `print()` command is easier for a new person to learn and understand than the `cout` command in C++. The `print()` command is an example that also can improve performance and security.

C++26 NEW

New features can also add new functionality. Many advanced features have been added to C++. For example, C++ has added modules for faster compilation, expanded the idea of concepts to add constraints on programming templates, improved resource management with coroutines and asynchronous programming, and increased the functionality of `constexpr` so that more code can be evaluated at compile time rather than runtime. It's not uncommon for modern features to help improve the more advanced uses of a programming language. The same is true for C++ because many of the items just listed are advanced topics.

Avoid Hard-Coded Values

It can initially seem much easier to use numbers than to use constants that you have to define first — until the number you're using needs to change. Though it might seem easy enough to use 3.14 instead of defining a constant for pi, what happens when you're told you need to increase precision and start using 3.14159 instead? You now have to search your code for all uses of 3.14 and make a change. If you had simply defined a constant, you would likely have to make only a single change.

You might think, "But wait — I rarely use pi!" This might be true, but pi is just one example — many other things can be a number. For example, a company might have 15 locations. This number of locations might be used in loops and other checks for store-related tasks. What happens when a location is closed or a new location is added? At that point, everywhere that number 15 was used would then become 14 or 16. A better option is to have simply set a constant to define `NumberOfStores`. Then you'd need to make only one change when the number changes.

REMEMBER

In most cases, you should avoid using hard-coded numbers. The constants don't add to the performance of your program, but they make maintenance and updates much easier.

Use Version Control

Version control isn't covered in this book, but it's an important topic for you as a programmer to know and understand. *Version control* is simply a process or system that keeps track of changes you make to your code. This allows you to roll back to an older version of your code if something goes wrong with a change you've made.

Version control also helps you back up your code. This means if you overwrite important information, you can pull up a previous version, which is especially important if you're working on a team where colleagues might change, overwrite, or accidentally (oh, no!) delete your code. In this manner, version control software can help developers collaborate without hurting each other's changes.

Some tools help you with version control. Git is the most popular one used by C++ programmers. It's often used with platforms such as GitHub, GitLab, and Bitbucket.

Version control can help you not only back up your code but also organize it, keep track of progress, and work better with others.

Index

Symbols and Numerics

A

B

C

F

G

H

I

J

L

M

N

O

R

S

T

U

W

X

Z

About the Author

Bradley L. Jones, the author of the 8th Edition, uses a variety of programming languages and helps others to learn them. These include languages such as C, C#, and C++, as well as ones that don't start with the letter *C*, such as Python, Java, and JavaScript. He has been recognized for a number of achievements, including eight times as a Microsoft MVP associated to C++. He is the proud husband of Melissa and the father of two daughters: Lilian and Aubrey. When Brad isn't enjoying time with family or working with the latest technologies, you can usually find him hanging out in virtual worlds, where he often joins others on crusades to rid dungeons of evil critters or be the first to cross a virtual goal line or achieve the highest score.

Stephen R. Davis (or just Randy), CISSP, was the author of the 7th Edition. He lived with his wife and two dogs in Corpus Christi, Texas. Randy was a proud father and grandfather. Randy developed browser-based applications for Agency Consulting Group.

Dedication

I'd like to dedicate this book to the person who shared his knowledge in its previous editions: the late Stephen R. Davis, better known as Randy.

Author's Acknowledgments

Though I might write many of the words that appear in this book, it is thanks to a multitude of other people that the words sound good by the time you get to read them. Additionally, though I write the words, it takes even more people to turn those words from a simple Word document into a full-fledged book. I'd like to thank the entire *For Dummies* team at Wiley for helping to make this book happen. This starts with Hanna Sytsma (along with Steve Hayes), who initially reached out and asked whether I'd be interested in tackling this project. After I said yes to them, it was Paul Levesque who helped with the scheduling and initial efforts of getting the book created. Becky Whitney deserves a big shout out for going through this book to makes sure my words were clear. Then there are Rev Mengle, Kristie Pyles, Athiyappan Lalith kumar, and many others on the editorial team who also guided the book through editing and production. (Of course, many others I didn't work with directly also helped.)

Though I've done everything I can to avoid making any errors in this book, I've programmed long enough to know that pesky bugs somehow make their way in. If you encounter any bugs, they are totally my fault. In fact, I thank William (Bill)

Steele and Ockert J. ("Hannes") du Preez for reviewing this book from a technical perspective. Like the input from the editors mentioned earlier, their views and suggestions also helped to make this a better book for you.

Thank you also to the guys who created *Gun Raiders*, *Dungeons of Eternity*, and *Walk Around Golf*. These are all virtual reality games I was able to escape to after hours of writing and coding samples for this book. Stepping into other worlds provided a nice break.

And finally, I'd like to acknowledge my wife, Melissa. She is the person who had to listen to me grumble when the support for a new C++26 feature wasn't working quite right or when the compiler just didn't like the code. Fortunately, the compilers continue to get better!

Publisher's Acknowledgments

Senior Editor: Jennifer Yee

Project Manager: Paul Levesque

Copy Editor: Becky Whitney

Technical Editors: William Steele and Ockert J. du Preez

Senior Managing Editor: Kristie Pyles

Content Development Manager: Carmen Krikorian

Senior Manager, Content Development: Chrissy Guthrie

Special Help: Rev Mengle

Managing Editor: Murari Mukundan

Production Editor: M. Athiyappan Lalith Kumar

Cover Image: © jbresco/Getty Images